The City of Blue and White

We think of blue and white porcelain as the ultimate global commodity: throughout East and Southeast Asia, the Indian Ocean including the African coasts, the Americas and Europe, consumers desired Chinese porcelains. Many of these were made in the kilns in and surrounding Jingdezhen. Found in almost every part of the world, Jingdezhen's porcelains had a far-reaching impact on global consumption, which in turn shaped the local manufacturing processes. The imperial kilns of Jingdezhen produced ceramics for the court, while nearby private kilns manufactured for the global market. In this beautifully illustrated study, Anne Gerritsen asks how this kiln complex could manufacture such quality, quantity and variety. She explores how objects tell the story of the past, connecting texts with objects, objects with natural resources, and skilled hands with the shapes and designs they produced. Through the manufacture and consumption of Jingdezhen's porcelains, she argues, China participated in the early modern world.

ANNE GERRITSEN is Professor of History and directs the Global History and Culture Centre at the University of Warwick. Since 2013, she has also held the Chair of Asian Art at the Universiteit Leiden where she teaches at the Leiden Institute for Area Studies (LIAS) and the Leiden University Centre for the Arts in Society (LUCAS).

The City of Blue and White

Chinese Porcelain and the Early Modern World

ANNE GERRITSEN

University of Warwick

CAMBRIDGE
UNIVERSITY PRESS

University Printing House, Cambridge CB2 8BS, United Kingdom

One Liberty Plaza, 20th Floor, New York, NY 10006, USA

477 Williamstown Road, Port Melbourne, VIC 3207, Australia

314–321, 3rd Floor, Plot 3, Splendor Forum, Jasola District Centre, New Delhi – 110025, India

79 Anson Road, #06-04/06, Singapore 079906

Cambridge University Press is part of the University of Cambridge.

It furthers the University's mission by disseminating knowledge in the pursuit of education, learning, and research at the highest international levels of excellence.

www.cambridge.org
Information on this title: www.cambridge.org/9781108499958
DOI: 10.1017/9781108753104

First published 2020
Reprinted 2021

Printed in Singapore by Markono Print Media Pte Ltd

A catalogue record for this publication is available from the British Library.

ISBN 978-1-108-49995-8 Hardback

....

This publication was made possible in part by a grant from the James P. Geiss and Margaret Y. Hsu Foundation.

GEISS HSU
FOUNDATION

This book is dedicated to Christopher, Matthijs and Bella, and to Christopher's donor

Contents

Figures

Maps

x

Table

Acknowledgements

My first trip to Jingdezhen was in 2005. If I had known then that it would take me this long to publish a book about its history, I might have thought twice about it. Over the past decade and a half, I have accumulated many debts. In my attempt to acknowledge and thank all those who have helped me along the way, I will inevitably not be able to name every individual; please know that I am deeply grateful for all the support, collegiality, guidance and help I have received throughout these years.

Some institutions and individuals, however, do need to be singled out, because without them, this book would never have been written. The Arts and Humanities Research Council granted me a two-year Early Career Fellowship, which allowed me to get the 'Global Jingdezhen' project started by appointing Stephen McDowall as the project's research fellow. 'Global Jingdezhen' was a memorable project; we held an international conference at the University of Warwick in 2010, organized an exhibition at the Bath Museum for East Asian Art with the help of the then curator, Michel Lee, and published some of the papers as a special issue in the *Journal of World History* in 2012. But it was also memorable because of the Icelandic volcano dust that grounded all airplanes in the days before our conference and the vagaries of taxi traffic in Nanchang that nearly prevented us from getting to Jingdezhen. It all turned out OK in the end, and Stephen contributed not only his superb research and writing skills, but his excellent companionship and good humour throughout, for which I am deeply grateful.

The Universities China Committee in London and the British Academy provided financial support for additional research trips to China, and several institutions granted me research fellowships during these years. I have benefited enormously from the generosity of the Asia Research Institute in Singapore, the Max Planck Institute for the History of Science in Berlin, the International Center for the Study of Chinese Civilization at Fudan in Shanghai, and the Netherlands Institute of Advanced Study, then in Wassenaar. They all offered the space and time to work, but even more importantly, the collegiality and friendship that makes such stays so stimulating and their impact so lasting. I am especially grateful to Anthony Reid and Geoff Wade at ARI, Dagmar Schäfer and Gina Grzimek at MPIWG,

Huang Chen and Zhang Ke at ICSCC, and the whole team at NIAS. The year in Wassenaar was especially memorable because of Liesbeth Koenen, Natalie Scholz, Kenda Mutongi, Sander Adelaar, Laura Fair and Florence Bernault.

These places all provided temporary respite from teaching and administration, but if the University of Warwick's Department of History had not been such an enjoyable and stimulating place to work, I would never have thought of porcelain as a subject of enquiry. I am grateful to all my Warwick colleagues, but especially to the wonderful women historians who served as Heads of Department during this project: Margot Finn, Maria Luddy and Rebecca Earle. Two people have been central to everything I have done at Warwick: Maxine Berg and Giorgio Riello. Maxine's work on ceramics and on global history formed the initial inspirations for this project, and her guidance and friendship has been phenomenal throughout its duration. Giorgio has been an awe-inspiring colleague and friend. We have run the Global History and Culture Centre, taught multiple courses on global history and on material culture, edited three books, organized numerous conferences, delivered papers and travelled the world together. Working with Giorgio has perhaps not sped up the process of writing, but it has profoundly shaped this book. I feel extremely fortunate to have had that chance. The commitment and enthusiasm of our students at Warwick have been superb reminders of why we do research in the first place.

Since 2013, I have been lucky enough to combine my appointment in Warwick with a secondment to Leiden University. Many people have been involved in making that possible; here I just want to mention the Kikkoman Foundation, the Royal Society of Friends of Asian Art (KVVAK), especially Rosalien van der Poel, Jan Maarten Boll, Pieter Ariëns Kappers, and Christiaan Jörg, as well as Kitty Zijlmans and Maghiel van Crevel in Leiden and Maria Luddy and Daniel Branch at Warwick. I continue to be grateful to be able to combine teaching history at Warwick, with teaching art history and Asian Studies at LUCAS and LIAS in Leiden.

In my travels to China, many people have extended their hospitality to me, for which I am extremely grateful. Dong Shaoxin, Deng Fei, Gao Xi, Liu Zhaohui, Huang Lu and their families made me feel at home everytime I was in Shanghai. Huang Lu and Maggie even travelled to Jingdezhen with me, helping me take some of the pictures that feature in this book. In Jingdezhen, Cao Jianwen, Huang Wei (May Huang) and Huang Qinghua shared their deep knowledge of ceramics with me.

Over the years, many colleagues and friends read chapters and offered invaluable comments that shaped this book. Some shared their specific knowledge with me: Saul Guerrero on colours and recipes; Karwin Cheung on

Korean ceramics; Ellen Huang on kiln transformations, Kenneth Hammond on maps and space, Christian de Pee on the tenth and eleventh centuries, and Masato Hasegawa on Korean ritual texts. Several others read chapters or parts when I wasn't sure how to proceed at all, including Kenda Mutongi, Stephen McDowall, Nir Avieli, Maxine Berg and Giorgio Riello. The advice and encouragement they all gave helped me enormously. Several people were good enough to plough through the entire manuscript: Kenneth Hammond, Alice de Jong, Victor Xu and Lin Fan. They, and the two wonderful anonymous readers for the Press, took valuable time out of their busy schedules to offer comments on almost every page of this book, preventing me from making many dreadful mistakes. (The many that undoubtedly remain cannot be blamed on anyone but me). In the final stages, the entire team at Cambridge University Press, but especially Lucy Rhymer and Lisa Carter, were both patient and encouraging. The search for illustrations benefited from the help of my students Heather Ashford and Tang Hui. A generous grant from the James P. Geiss and Margaret Y. Hsu Foundation made the colour illustrations possible.

As all those who combine teaching and administrative responsibilities with research and writing know, it takes time to write books. To those who have 'normal' jobs, it has probably seemed rather puzzling why it should have taken me so long to write this book. On many occasions, Dan and Anne Strauss in Cambridge provided a home from home, a very special place for us all (and not just because of the view of the UL from their house). My friends in Leamington have been (mostly) unquestioning and generous in their support, and none more so than my friend Joanna. Her regular quizzing about my progress punctuated our walks and conversations, and her encouragement was unfailing. It is a deep sadness to me that she is no longer here to see the final result. Vivien, Carol and Nina formed a strong support network during Joanna's final year, and I am pleased I can at last share this book with them.

My brothers and their families in Den Haag and Istanbul, my parents in Utrecht, and Christopher's siblings and their families in the UK have been constant in their support throughout these years, for which I am very grateful. My father passed away just before the book appeared. I will treasure the set of proofs he read, with his comments made even on the day he died. His approval meant the world to me. My deepest gratitude is reserved for the three people closest to my heart: Christopher, Matthijs and Bella. They have each faced profound challenges of their own during this time; my admiration and love for them is boundless. To them, and to the anonymous donor whose heart beats at the centre of our little family unit, I dedicate this book.

1 | The Shard Market of Jingdezhen

Most Monday mornings, an antiques market takes place in the southern Chinese city of Jingdezhen. There are antiques of all kinds for sale here, but pieces of ceramics are in the vast majority. Hundreds of sellers in this shard market display their goods on cloths and bags on the ground, and buyers lower themselves on their haunches to handle the pieces and negotiate a good price. On this seller's cloth (Figure 1.1), let's call him Mr Jia, one finds a green-glazed ceramic box decorated with a scaly dragon, a stack of blue and white tea bowls, small vases, stem cups, necklaces of glazed ceramic beads, snuff bottles, unglazed statuettes, and so on.

A first impression might suggest Mr Jia's goods are not particularly valuable: many of them are roughly made, dirty or damaged. Little effort has been made to display the objects individually, although similar items are broadly grouped together, such as the upside-down blue and white stem cups in the top right corner of the picture, and the small ornamental objects in the top left corner. If the goods offered for sale by Mr Jia and his colleagues in this antiques market do not immediately look appealing or valuable, why do visitors to the market get up at the crack of dawn to buy such items in this local market? The answer has to do with the price of Chinese ceramics in the global art market and with the pressures of time and money that obstruct extensive archaeological excavation, so that antiquities of mixed provenance can be sold off without any perceptible local or central governmental interference. This book examines the emergence of Jingdezhen as the early modern world's pre-eminent site of ceramics production, to connect the contemporary shard market to the past, the local to the global, and to show how this city of blue and white played a part in the mobility of things, people and ideas in the early modern world.

For many centuries, the ceramics produced in the Chinese empire were considered highly desirable, both within the empire's boundaries and far beyond. As early as the ninth century, Arab traders sailed through the Persian Gulf and the Arabian Sea, past the Bay of Bengal and through the Strait of Malacca, and into the South China Sea, to fill their dhows with goods from China: gold and silver wares, bronze mirrors, silver ingots, textiles, but above all ceramics. The shipwreck of an Arab dhow, discovered

Figure 1.1 Objects for sale at the shard market. Jingdezhen, May 2013. Photograph by the author.

in 1998 by fishermen at Belitung, between what are now the islands of Sumatra and Borneo, had 70,000 pieces of ceramics on board.[1] That ninth-century shipwreck not only testifies specifically to the vibrant trade between Bagdad in the Abbasid Caliphate (750–1258) and Tang-dynasty China (618–907), but also more generally to the enormous desire for ceramics made in China from consumers many thousands of miles away. Amongst those 70,000 pieces on the Belitung shipwreck were only a handful of white plates with blue designs.[2] It would take another 500 years or so before white vessels with blue designs were made in vast quantities in China, but from the early fourteenth century, demand for Chinese blue and white ceramics came from almost every corner of the earth, thereby significantly shaping the ceramics production in China until well into the nineteenth century. The pieces on Mr Jia's cloth, then, could easily have been intended for consumers in places well beyond the reach of this market.

Their manufacture, however, was probably local. Although we cannot be sure of the provenance of every object on Mr Jia's cloth, it is likely that many of these objects were made in Jingdezhen, the town known historically as the porcelain capital of China, and the place where this weekly shard market is held.

Located in the northeast of Jiangxi, a land-locked province in the southeast of China, the town is situated along the riverbed of the Chang (Map 1.1). To the north, east and south, mountains surround Jingdezhen; to the west are the marshy floodplains of Lake Poyang. The Chang provides important connections in all directions: upriver towards the mountains that in the past yielded clay, firewood and ferns for making glazes. In the same direction, across the provincial boundary, the Chang leads to the wealthy towns of the area known in the past as Huizhou now in Anhui province. Downstream, the Chang flows into Lake Poyang, connecting Jingdezhen to several small market towns situated on the banks of the lake, including Wuchengzhen. To the north, Lake Poyang provides access to the Yangzi, China's main east-west arterial river, connecting Jingdezhen to the main urban centres of eastern China and the ports on the East China Sea. In the past, the entrance of the Grand Canal, located further downstream on the Yangzi, facilitated access to the imperial capital in the north. Lake Poyang also connected Jingdezhen to the southern provinces by way of the Gan, the main north-south artery of southern China. Via the Gan, merchants could travel southwards to Guangdong province, reaching the merchant ships that gathered in the port of Guangzhou (Canton) from all over the world.

When exactly these goods were made is more difficult to say. Amongst Mr Jia's goods (Figure 1.1), we find a motley selection of objects in a variety of decorative patterns and styles, probably made during quite different periods. One or two of the upside-down stem cups with dark blue-grey decorations on a greyish background might well date back to the fourteenth and fifteenth centuries; the cream-coloured larger bowl may even be older. The upside-down bowl to the left, with the red square on the base and green and red flower decorations, more likely dates to the nineteenth century. Some of the small decorative bottles and vases probably date from the twentieth century, and the figurine of a reclining baby with beads around its head could even date from the twenty-first century. The state of the pile of blue and white bowls, quite dirty, damaged and simply decorated, suggests that these may have been buried and retrieved from a grave, but we will never know how exactly these objects found their way to this market; they are objects of unknown provenance. Even if we do not know the distances and routes along which these objects travelled from their place of manufacture to their arrival at the shard market, we do know that potters working

Map 1.1 Jiangxi Province. Map based on China Historical Geographic Information System (CHGIS), version 6.

over the centuries in the Jingdezhen area had the technology to produce all these: creamy-white monochromes during the eleventh and twelfth centuries, blue and white dishes in all shapes and sizes from the fourteenth century onwards, and brightly coloured pieces with enamel decorations from the eighteenth century. Jingdezhen's production of the finest porcelains lasted for many centuries.[3]

The pieces on the cloth represent only a small sample of the goods made in Jingdezhen, for consumers both within the Chinese empire and far beyond its boundaries. When the production of fine white wares started in the tenth century, Jingdezhen's ceramics appealed to local and regional consumers. Their reputation spread more widely in the eleventh century, when Zhenzong (r. 997–1022), the third emperor of the Song dynasty (960–1279), declared that he wanted porcelain from these kilns for his imperial court. Jingdezhen's ceramics circulated widely from then onwards, in part due to this association with the imperial court, and in part because of the translucent quality of Jingdezhen's white wares. From the late thirteenth, early fourteenth centuries onwards, when the potters in Jingdezhen started using cobalt blue systematically for the decorations of their white porcelains, Jingdezhen ceramics began to spread even more widely, well beyond the boundaries of the Chinese empire.[4] The world-wide appeal of this so-called 'blue and white' porcelain meant that the kilns of Jingdezhen grew to become the biggest and most significant site of ceramics production in the world. This exceptional position turned Jingdezhen into what we might call a 'global' ceramics production site: the potters based in Jingdezhen made porcelains that were desired and consumed everywhere. Until the early eighteenth century, Jingdezhen's combination of high-quality natural resources, accumulated technologies and the extensive manpower necessary for making porcelain was not matched anywhere else in the world.[5] Over the course of the eighteenth century, however, many other places in the world also discovered the required materials and technologies, and Jingdezhen gradually lost, first its unique position and eventually its ability to compete. Production in Jingdezhen continues until this day, but it no longer captures the desire of global consumers.

The goods for sale in this Jingdezhen market today are the traces of those centuries of porcelain production.[6] Those traces are worth selling today because of the site's long and illustrious history, and today's customers will buy the broken shards, fakes and reproductions for sale in the shard market because of the exorbitant prices that Jingdezhen's finest pieces fetch in today's global art market. For many of us who are out-priced in that market, owning a fragmentary piece of porcelain is as close as we will ever get to such pieces. But those same traces also point to deeper questions about the history of Jingdezhen. Jingdezhen emerged as the empire's premier site of ceramics production, but we do not yet fully understand what factors contributed to this and how it maintained this position over the course of at least seven centuries.

Unsurprisingly perhaps, Jingdezhen's production has attracted centuries of scholarly attention.[7] Art historians have focused on the porcelains themselves, their aesthetics, and evolving forms, styles and techniques; museum curators work with individual pieces as well as whole collections of porcelains, their taxonomies and identifications; archaeologists study porcelain finds in the ground and on the seabed.[8] Historians have tended to focus on Jingdezhen's wares as traded commodities, and examine their trade all over the world; anthropologists have focused on those who populated the city and worked in its kilns, while area specialists studied Jingdezhen within the context of the history of the Chinese empire.[9] Each of these scholars and scholarly traditions have contributed to this growing body of scholarship, asked questions that emerge from their own contexts, and sought to find answers on the basis of their own perspectives and disciplinary backgrounds. This study is no different, in that it draws heavily on earlier research, and that its questions are shaped by its current academic environment. Where it does forge a new path, however, is in its combination of approaches. In presenting a chronological overview of the porcelain production in Jingdezhen, this study draws on the work of art historians, curators and porcelain specialists, but offers a history of the town rather than of its products. It draws on the work of China specialists and examines Chinese primary sources but presents a work of global history rather than of sinology. It draws on the work of economic historians and considers the trade in porcelain that reached consumers all over the world, but it offers a cultural history of the meanings and representations that shaped the history of this extraordinary city. Most of all, this study situates Jingdezhen in a context that crosses cultural, linguistic and disciplinary boundaries.

Arguments

This study asks how and why Jingdezhen became the premier site of ceramics production in the world, and how it maintained this position from the eleventh to the late seventeenth centuries. To refer to this long timespan as early modern perhaps seems unusual. The term commonly, especially in the European or even British context, refers to the period 1500 to 1750, when certain characteristics marked the transition from the medieval to the modern world, including efflorescent economic growth, urbanization, conspicuous consumption, social mobility, overseas explorations and the emergence of challenges to orthodoxy and authority. In the context of this book, with its focus on both China and the wider world, these developments are not limited to the period 1500 to 1750; these characteristics are detectable in various forms throughout the period from the eleventh to the late seventeenth century, hence the use of the term 'early modern' to describe the period.

One way to answer questions about Jingdezhen's emergence and longevity in this early modern period is by considering global perspectives. Historians apply the term 'global' to a sheer endless range of phenomena, but I use it here to refer to factors that go beyond the boundaries of a single empire or nation state. For me, global history concerns the study of mobilities and the interactions that connect distinct parts of the world.[10] Global factors that had a bearing on Jingdezhen's development include, for example, the growth of consumer demand for Jingdezhen's porcelain in Japan and Korea, Central, South and Southeast Asia, the Middle East, Europe and the Americas. They also include the presence of Chinese junks that sailed to ports throughout Asia and into the Indian Ocean. Throughout the centuries under discussion here, the official policies about Chinese merchants participating in overseas trade veered between active encouragement and outright prohibition, but as the evidence from maritime shipwrecks shows, Chinese junks carrying ceramics continued to sail overseas throughout the period. Global factors also include the emergence of trading companies such as the Vereenigde Oostindische Companie (VOC) of the Dutch Republic and the English East India Company, whose merchants loaded vast quantities of porcelain into their ships' holds to supply consumers in Europe. Throughout the period, Jingdezhen was the only site of porcelain manufacture that produced goods to meet global consumer demand in terms of quality, quantity and diversity to suit the variety of tastes. Global factors, alone, however, cannot explain how Jingdezhen's potters accommodated these merchants' demands, and integrated them into their systems of production.

Another approach to the question of Jingdezhen's rise to a large-scale manufacturing site is the consideration of local factors. If we understand the term 'local' in its common-sense meaning, as having to do with the place itself and its immediate environs, then local factors include, amongst others, the natural environment of Jingdezhen. In principle, clay, water and fire are all that is required to produce bricks and earthenware implements, and most inhabited places in the world had access to such resources.[11]

Some places, however, especially places scattered throughout Asia, were able to produce far better ceramics than most other places, mainly because of the quality of the available natural ingredients: the local clay and stone, the water, and the vegetation on the surrounding hills. In the case of Jingdezhen, the natural resources, especially the superb quality of the clay, form a key local factor for explaining the prominence of Jingdezhen's ceramics throughout the early modern world. The site of the town, near not only high-quality resources but also efficient transportation routes in all directions, is another key local factor. Jingdezhen's location facilitated its growth as a site of production and sustained its gradual transformation from a series of scattered individual kilns to a complex and large-scale production site that exploited all the available resources in the region to manufacture millions of pieces of porcelain for consumers all over the world. Local factors undoubtedly played a part in Jingdezhen's historical trajectory, but like global factors, they alone cannot answer questions about who consumed Jingdezhen's ceramics, and how the goods reached their far-flung consumers.

I propose that the answer to such questions has to be found by considering the mobility of things, people and ideas. I argue that Jingdezhen became the early modern world's foremost site of ceramics production because of mobility, circulation and interaction. Circulation and mobility were key to Jingdezhen's development throughout the centuries between the eleventh and the early eighteenth centuries. Rather than separating local and global factors, I suggest that it is the interaction between local and global factors that explains Jingdezhen's growth. Rather than understanding the global as meaning 'encircling the globe as a whole', and the local as 'bounded space', I understand global and local as part of a spectrum of constructed spaces. In chronicling the historical path of development over more than seven centuries across that spectrum, I seek to demonstrate the significance of mobility, circulation and interaction between things, people and their ideas.

Using the idea of circulation and interaction in seeking to understand Jingdezhen's development over this long period poses somewhat of a challenge to current approaches in a number of fields, especially to fields where boundaries and differentiation are key. In many studies within the field of history, for example, boundaries have been drawn between those that take a global approach, seeking to answer questions about change over time by looking across cultural and political boundaries, and those that explore historical change from within the boundaries of a certain spatial or cultural context. The former suggests that in the past, as today, (almost) all parts of the world are connected in one way or another.[12] The latter suggests that separate units can be studied more or less in isolation. These might not always be positioned as 'local histories', after all, studies that confine themselves to (parts of) the Chinese empire remain within spatial and/or cultural boundaries, but often cover far too much geographical ground to be considered 'local'. The point is, however, that scholars who see themselves as working globally often pay little attention to the specifics of an individual place and focus on the perspectives that connect individual places with each other, while local historians tend to work on the assumption that spaces can be bounded and understood from the perspective of that place alone.

In terms of methodology, I argue that global and local history need to be integrated and should be seen as forming part of the same continuum. Such an argument is, of course, heavily indebted to the insight that all space, which includes scales such as the global and the local, is constructed rather than predetermined. The connections between the Chinese empire and the wider world are so numerous and intricate that we cannot but write the history of the Chinese empire *as* global history. To understand the history of the Chinese empire fully, we cannot merely look at patterns of change that occurred within its cultural and political boundaries.[13] Throughout this period Chinese ceramics manufactures used materials and designs that came from beyond the Chinese realm and produced goods that were desired by consumers all over the world. Only when we zoom out from the picture of China alone to view the wider picture, do we see the intricate patterns of connections and interactions that shape the early modern world, and China's place in it. By tracing the technological trajectories of ceramics production, the official policies and informal practices that governed the ceramics trade and domestic and global patterns of consumption, I aim to show not only these global connections, but also the ways in which the whole range of actors involved in ceramics production participated in these global processes. Jingdezhen's success can only be explained by understanding how global and local became part of the same network of interactions.

The manufacture of porcelain involved diverse groups of actors, from emperors and high officials at the capital to locally posted administrators, skilled potters and merchants. Their involvement changed over time, but ultimately, it was their choices and decisions that helped make China's ceramics global products, not just the demands of consumers in far-flung locations. Economic historians, similarly, used to focus mostly on Europe and discuss the global flows of Spanish-American silver into China as the direct outcome of a European desire for Asian consumer goods. This argument relegates Chinese production and the Chinese population to a passive role in the global flows of goods and currencies; Europeans desired Asian goods, the argument goes, and the fact that silver flowed into China was a mere side-effect, rather than a primary cause for global economic flows.[14] Scholars like Dennis Flynn, Arturo Giráldez and André Gunder Frank have shown the global impact of China's demand for silver, and have 're-oriented' the focus of economic history to Asia, and in particular to China.[15] My argument here follows along similar lines; to understand the global flows of porcelain, we need to focus on the active role the Chinese porcelain administrators, workers and merchants played in this. We need to see China's role in the global history of China. I argue that the administrators in charge of the production in Jingdezhen, appointees from the central state responsible for the selection of the finest porcelains for the use of the emperor, struggled to keep control over the production processes. Many of the sources they left behind, including the administrative records for sixteenth-century Jingdezhen, reveal the anxieties of these administrators over the flows of natural and human resources. Unfortunately, we will never know exactly what individual potters thought about the goods that went through their hands in pre-modern Jingdezhen, nor can we ever know the names of the many merchants who were involved in the transmission of Jingdezhen's goods to their consumers. The documentary records simply do not exist. But the agency of potters and merchants can be gleaned in other ways, and reading the sources, including not only texts but also the visual and material record for traces of their agency is one of the aims of this book.

Boundaries and differentiation are also key within the field of ceramics studies. Any first serious encounter with historical ceramics involves their identification: pieces of ceramics fit into a complex taxonomy that differentiates between production sites (or wares), types of decoration, shapes and functions. Crucial as such taxonomies are for the classification of pieces and the assignment of value and meaning, they also create boundaries and separations between technologies and designs that were closely connected. For the historian, the interactions between the different sites may be of more interest than their separation in distinct wares. This book highlights in particular the interactions between northern and southern kiln sites, and between different sites of production located around Jingdezhen, showing the crucial importance of those interactions for the development of Jingdezhen's manufactures.

Finally, this book considers ceramics as part of a wider cultural complex, instead of seeing ceramics as telling a separate and unique story in and of itself. Again, boundaries have often arisen between those who study texts and those who study things, or between those who study the history of art as opposed to the history of socio-economic change, or between those who study the history of China and those who focus on either Europe or the world as a whole. This book seeks to demonstrate that things and texts need to be studied together, as do art and society, and China and the world. Separations between those are meaningful in certain contexts, but in this particular study, texts and objects are all thought to be part of the same early modern cultural complex in which Jingdezhen's ceramics played a key role. To understand how it came to do so requires engagement with all of those aspects taken together. Economics and trade cannot be separated from the pleasures of aesthetics and consumer desire; the history of China cannot be isolated from the history of the early modern world as a whole.

Contexts

This study of Jingdezhen in a global and local context draws heavily on extensive scholarship in several fields, most notably of course in the history of porcelain. Much of the scholarship in this field is focused on identifying different materials, technologies, forms and styles of decoration that have shaped the history of this material. Exemplary books have been written about individual groups of porcelain, based on a specific period, such as *Porcelains of the Yuan Dynasty*, or a specific technology, such as *Underglaze Blue and Copper Red Decorated Porcelains*, or a specific kiln, such as *Gems of the Official Kilns*.[16] Other studies have attempted to integrate the different groupings into a single coherent story. He Li's book, simply entitled *Chinese Ceramics*, is a very good example of this, offering not only lucid essays that chronicle the main changes that took place over the longue durée from the Neolithic to the twentieth century, but also vivid colour images to illustrate those changes.[17] Together with the superbly detailed study of Chinese ceramics by Rose Kerr and Nigel Wood for the *Science and Civilisation in China* series published under the auspices of the Needham Research Institute, this research serves both as general catalogue of existing pieces and collections and as structuring device for our knowledge of porcelain.[18]

Building on that cumulative knowledge, this study tries to do something slightly different. When we identify separate sites of porcelain production, differentiate between the various styles such sites may each have produced, and distinguish between specific periods of production, the risk is that we only see differences, while losing sight of the more fluid flows of materials, fashions and designs that never stick to their allocated and predetermined boundaries. I am interested in the place of porcelain in the flows of knowledge and expertise between different sites of manufacture, interactions between consumers and producers, and connections between disparate parts of the world. Situating porcelain in the context of such flows, interactions and connections, is part of a broader material culture approach. Rather than seeing porcelain in isolation, and subdivided into further distinct types, I see porcelain as part of a larger complex of material goods, including, for example, the high-status decorative elements such as the silver lids, spouts or mounts that framed single pieces of porcelain, the straw and paper used for preparing the porcelain for long-distance transport and the assemblage of goods that accompanied porcelains as part of an order for the imperial household as much as the list of demands stipulated by the European trading companies. In this study, porcelain forms part of a continuum of interactions, connections and exchanges. Of course, that means the outcome is not really a history of porcelain; instead, it is an exploration of the place of Jingdezhen's porcelain in the global circulations of material culture.

Another way of approaching the history of porcelain is by way of its extensive and worldwide trade. A vast quantity of scholarship exists, exploring the trade in porcelain within China and beyond its borders in all directions. Some of it focuses on the place of porcelain manufacture and trade within the wider economic history of China; Richard von Glahn chose a visual representation of Jingdezhen's kilns for the cover of his *An Economic History of China*, suggesting its centrality, even if Jingdezhen only features on a small number of pages in the book.[19] Some of the studies on the porcelain trade focus on the routes by which it was traded, such as the Silk Roads, including the so-called maritime Silk Roads that delivered porcelains to Central, Southeast and South Asia, and the African coast, or the trans-Pacific route that brought porcelains first to the Americas.[20] Some of the histories of specific trade routes can only be recovered by studies of the shipwrecks that dot seashores and ocean floors around the world. Without maritime archaeology, we would not know where, how early and how extensively ships sailed with Chinese porcelain in their cargo. Without finding the Belitung wreck, now on display in the Asian Civilizations Museum in Singapore, we would have no idea about the extent of ninth-century shipments of Chinese porcelains aboard Arab dhows.[21] The cargoes of the Turiang and Royal Nanhai shipwrecks, both recovered from the east coast of the Malaysian peninsula, have helped reveal the level of interaction in the fourteenth century between ceramics producers in southern China and southeast Asia, including what is now Thailand, and consumers in what is now Indonesia.[22]

Many historians have written about the porcelain trade from the point of view of the destination of the traded goods. We now know that very few places in the world before 1800 were hermetically sealed off from Chinese porcelain. From small traces in archaeological records to vast quantities in domestic use, the legacy of the porcelain trade is visible throughout the world. Numerous books have been written chronicling the story of Chinese porcelain in a specific place, such as Christiaan Jörg's *Porcelain and the Dutch China Trade*, or George Kuwayama's *Chinese Ceramics in Colonial Mexico*, to name but two.[23] Of course the focus on destinations also means a focus on the commercial enterprises and the political structures that made that trade possible, in this case the Dutch East India Company and the Iberian empire in the Americas. Important as that focus undoubtedly is, especially where these institutions supply information on quantities, qualities and designs that no Chinese sources can provide, a focus on trade inevitably leads us away from the site of manufacture within China. The impression is created, in part by the sheer quantity of studies on the porcelains that left the Chinese empire that the Chinese were merely producing in response to demand from overseas.

It is my intention here to (re)insert the Chinese perspective into the discussion of the global circulations of Chinese porcelain. Rather than understanding that circulation as a series of vectors that point outwards from the site of production, with the agency all in the hands of the traders and overseas consumers, I focus on the ways in which the Chinese producers and merchants participated and played active roles in these processes. Of course, that means the outcome will not be a history of trade per se, but it will offer some thoughts on how the producers in Jingdezhen helped facilitate the global trade in porcelain.

The focus of this study, as will be clear from the above, will be the site of the manufacture of porcelain: the city of Jingdezhen. In that sense, it sets out with a similar mission to a recent study by Maris Gillette, entitled *China's Porcelain Capital*.[24] Gillette's sharp eye of the trained ethnographer and sympathetic approach to the difficult circumstances under which the artists, artisans and workers that made porcelain laboured in Jingdezhen make this a unique book in the English language.[25] Gillette situates the story of Jingdezhen in a long historical perspective, beginning with the prehistory of pottery in China, and covering, albeit briefly, thousands of years of history, highlighting the most significant changes in materials and production methods. She is especially interested in the history of state involvement in Jingdezhen that shaped so much of the backdrop for ceramics production in Jingdezhen, so this historical overview features some of the main changes in the organization of state involvement of the millennium from 1004 to the start of the second millennium. But understandably, it is a narrative told at speed; by page 29 we have reached 1780, and on page 43, the attention turns to the 'post-liberation era', i.e. from 1949. Like Gillette, I will situate my study in the longue durée, although my period will be slightly shorter, starting around 1000, with the first documented recognition of Jingdezhen as production centre for the imperial state, and ending in the eighteenth century, when Jingdezhen's central position in global porcelain manufactures gradually begins to wane.

Another highly regarded and widely read study on the global history of porcelain that allocated a central place to the city of Jingdezhen is Robert Finlay's 2010 book, *The Pilgrim Art: Cultures of Porcelain in World History*. Finlay's 1998 article in *Journal of World History* and the monograph that followed just over a decade later chronicle the history of porcelain, starting with the earliest history of porcelain creation between 2000 BCE and 1000 CE, and ending with what Finlay calls 'the decline and fall of Chinese porcelain' between 1500 and 1800.[26] It is true that Finlay's book is not solely about Jingdezhen, but about the porcelains that created and sustained a shared culture across the globe. Nonetheless, Jingdezhen features throughout the study. While Finlay draws extensively on the scholarship produced by scholars from China and Japan, primary sources in Chinese are not central to his book. In this study, without aiming for comprehensive coverage, I have attempted to integrate writings about Jingdezhen's porcelain in many languages from a variety of places and periods, including not just Chinese and Japanese, but French, German, Dutch and English. What my study adds to Finlay's global coverage are an engagement with the Chinese vision of Jingdezhen, and a more multi-centred perspective that challenges the dominance of the Anglo-centric version of the story.

Contents

Jingdezhen's story begins with the production of white wares in the tenth century. The first two chapters explore the early history of this ceramics production site. Chapter 2 focuses on the imperial recognition of the high quality of this region's white ceramics around the turn of the eleventh century, when the site gained its imperially bestowed name, Jingde. Chapter 3 considers the ways in which Jingdezhen's white ceramics began to circulate beyond the region's boundaries in the twelfth and thirteenth centuries. These two chapters show that the story of this site cannot be told by looking at it in isolation. In the eleventh and twelfth centuries, when Jingdezhen was producing high-quality white wares, it did so in competition with other sites of ceramics manufacture scattered throughout the Chinese empire. Their reputation rose within the empire and spread beyond the empire's boundaries, in part because of their popularity at the imperial court, but also because of their demand by overseas consumers in Southeast Asia. Jingdezhen's ceramics were made on the basis of knowledge of what kinds of ceramics were produced at other manufacturing sites and which goods were in demand by which consumers. Key to Jingdezhen's early growth was not only the quality of the local resources or the demands of overseas consumers, but the interaction between the two realms through the circulation of knowledge.

If Chapters 2 and 3 focus on white porcelains, Chapters 4, 5 and 6 chronicle the emergence and spread of blue decorations. In the thirteenth and fourteenth centuries, it was the introduction of cobalt, extracted both from mines within the Chinese empire and in Central Asia, that led to the appearance of what became Jingdezhen's most remarkable and recognizable product: white porcelain with blue decorations, simply known as blue and white. The interaction between global and local takes physical form here; destructive and non-destructive investigations into the composition of the cobalt used for such decorations has shown that frequently locally sourced cobalt was blended with cobalt that came from mines outside the empire's boundaries, especially from the Persian empire. The initial demand for blue and white decorated wares, and the early style of the decorations in geometrical patterns that cover the entire surface of the plate or vessel have been associated with Central Asia. In this period, Yuan-dynasty China (1279–1368) was connected to Central Asia and the Middle East through the Mongol empires founded by Genghis Khan's descendants. But I argue that the introduction of cobalt would have been far less significant without the southwards spread of the technology of underglaze line-drawn decorations. Such decorations were initially mostly used in kilns in northern China, but their popularity moved southwards in the twelfth and thirteenth centuries, first to the kilns in another Jiangxi kiln site known as Jizhou, and only from there to Jingdezhen. Arguably, cobalt became particularly effective as a tool for the decoration of ceramics, because it could be applied thinly in underglaze line-drawn decorations. I argue that the emergence of Jingdezhen's key commodity, blue and white porcelain, has to be understood, firstly, in the context of interactions between northern and southern kilns. Chapter 4 considers the connections between the Cizhou kilns in the north, and Jizhou

Figure 1.2 Blue and white shards in the Jingdezhen shard market. Photograph by the author, taken in May 2013.

in the south. Secondly, I argue that the spread of blue and white should be seen in the context of interactions between different Jiangxi sites of ceramics production, as we will see in Chapter 5. During the fifteenth and sixteenth centuries, we see again this inextricable combination of global and local factors. The appeal of Jingdezhen's wares continued to spread throughout the fifteenth- and sixteenth-century world, as Chapter 6 shows, when blue and white wares were introduced to and became embedded within entirely new cultural contexts.

Global consumer demand alone cannot explain Jingdezhen's development in this period; in fact, the response to global demand would not have been possible without the management of local resources and the organization of labour within the Jingdezhen manufactories. Chapters 7 to 10 focuse on Jingdezhen in the sixteenth century, beginning with an exploration of the place and its spatial environment. Chapter 7 seeks to redirect our gaze away from the production of ceramics for the imperial court towards the various constructed spaces within which ceramics were produced: the administrative space, the geo-physical space and the manufacturing space. Chapters 8 and 9 explore the local management of resources and zooms in on the organization of production and labour within the workshops of Jingdezhen. These two chapters demonstrate that local resources were the subject of intense competition between the local administrators and the workers in the kilns. The focus on the large-scale production of ceramics for distant markets and the increasingly large participation of the local and largely rural population in the labour tasks required for this production bring to mind the discussion about proto-industrialization. In the European context, where much of the proto-industrialization debates have been held, proto-industrialization is understood by some as the phase that preceded industrialization proper and created the conditions for the emergence of an industrialized society.[27] Not all agree about the value of the term, and several scholars have pointed out that proto-industrialization in Europe did not always lead to industrialization.[28] Whether the term is valuable for the case of Jingdezhen will be discussed in these chapters. Chapter 10 focuses on the objects themselves, showing that objects, too, connect local factors to global consumers. Chapter 11 argues that local and global should be seen not as separate contexts but as part of integrated, connected, interactive factors.

In the final chapter, I will return briefly to the present-day shard market, to consider how these historical discussions help us understand this place where buyers get up at the crack of dawn to buy a shard of porcelain, a cracked blue and white bowl or a fragment of a stem cup. One can buy almost anything here, from large brown stoneware pots for storing water to tiny snuff bottles decorated in radiant colours; from the remnants and waste products generated when shaped clay objects fail in the process of firing them (so-called kiln wasters) to goods excavated from graves; from cheap imitations to expensive fakes, and throughout, vast quantities of blue and white shards (Figure 1.2).

The goods for sale here raise important questions, about Jingdezhen's past, but also about contemporary China, where pressures of time and money obstruct extensive archaeological excavation; where antiquities of mixed provenance are sold off without any perceptible control of the local government or indeed the central state; and where the prices of ceramics in the international art market are so high that shards are worth selling and fakes are highly lucrative. The contemporary shard market connects the past and the present, highlighting the importance of understanding the historical contexts that contributed to the emergence of Jingdezhen as the early modern world's pre-eminent site of ceramics production. Hence it is the shard market that this book begins and ends with.

2 | City of Imperial Choice: Jingdezhen, 1000–1200

Where does the history of Jingdezhen's porcelain start? Perhaps surprisingly, this is not generally considered to be a vexed question; most narratives begin with the bestowal of the name of the Northern Song reign period (Jingde, 1004–1007) on the town (*zhen*). Choosing that date as starting point for the history of Jingdezhen's porcelain is, however, also misleading. It creates the teleological impression that from that point on, Jingdezhen travelled on a path that inevitably led to becoming the world's preeminent site of ceramics production, and it suggests exceptionality where there is none. In its account of the period between 1000 and 1200, this chapter shows that the goods produced in Raozhou prefecture (where Jingdezhen was located) were not unique but competed with goods from numerous other sites. Moreover, the history of Jingdezhen's porcelains is not the history of a single town, but the history of a web of connections that linked geographical spaces, natural resources and human skills. The history of Jingdezhen's porcelains should begin, I argue, with the emergence of that web of connections: a network that made the production of Jingdezhen's ceramics possible.

Lan Pu's Version of Jingdezhen's History

Of course, the history of Jingdezhen's ceramics has been told for centuries in many different ways. Here is one example from the late eighteenth century:

> Jingde wares were made during the Jingde reign period of the Song dynasty. The soil is white and clay-like, and [the wares have] a light and unctuous quality, and a smooth and glossy colour. Zhenzong [r. 997–1022] ordered that [these wares] be brought to the Palace as tribute, and that the four characters *Jing de nian zhi* 景德年製 ('made during the Jingde reign') be written on the base of the ceramic vessels. The vessels [made here] were particularly brilliant and delicate, and exuberantly beautiful. The manufacturers of the day imitated them, and they became known throughout the land. Thereupon everybody talked about ceramics from Jingde town, and thus the name of Changnan disappeared.[1]

This account was written by a man called Lan Pu (d. 1795), and included in 'The Record of Jingdezhen's Ceramics' (*Jingdezhen tao lu*). Jingdezhen was familiar territory for Lan Pu: he had grown up not too far from this area. Lan died before the work was completed, but by 1815 the final text that included this quote was produced with the help of his student Zheng Tinggui (dates unknown).[2]

Jingdezhen's ceramics, the topic of Lan Pu's book, were made in a town once known as Changnan, literally 'south of the Chang'. The Chang, in what is now northern Jiangxi province, flows in a south-westerly direction into Lake Poyang. As in so many places throughout the Song empire (960–1279), there were kilns in Changnan, but what made this area different, or so Lan Pu suggests, were the natural resources of the area, which made it possible to produce wares that were unusually white, thin and glossy. According to Lan Pu, it was Zhenzong who ordered these wares from Jingde to be brought to the imperial palace in Kaifeng, then the capital of the Song empire. Zhenzong, whose reign started in 997 and lasted until 1022, was the third emperor of the Song dynasty, successor to the first and founding emperor, Taizu (r. 960–976), and his brother, Taizong (976–997), who served as the second. Apparently, it was Zhenzong's decision, during the Jingde reign period, to demand that these tribute gifts or payments were inscribed with the name of his reign period.

In this version of events, then, 1004 was a momentous year: it marked the beginning of an exceptional relationship between the imperial court and this production site, a relationship that was not only to be enacted through the hands of the local craftsmen as they wrote the characters onto each individual piece, but also materialized in the ceramic bodies that would testify to that relationship thereafter. Ever after the early eleventh century, the town would be known by the name of Zhenzong's reign title.[3] Even if ceramics manufactures in other parts of the empire sought to imitate the beauty and brilliance of these wares, they would never legitimately bear the same physical testament to that exclusive relationship. For Lan Pu, then, the exceptional history of Jingdezhen not only begins in the year 1004, but from that moment onwards, Jingdezhen's unique and separate history should be understood as a story closely tied to the imperial court.

This late eighteenth-, early nineteenth-century version of the history of Jingdezhen was, of course, produced with the benefit of hindsight. When Lan Pu made these observations, he reflected on eight centuries of production, circulation and imitation that followed this initial imperial endorsement of wares from Jingde and wanted to suggest that the connection between Jingdezhen and the imperial court had been close, and more or

less constant during those centuries. It therefore made sense for him to
construct a history of Jingdezhen that began with the imperial endorsement of 1004. Lan Pu's version of Jingdezhen's history has found widespread acceptance, and since the early nineteenth century, most histories
of the porcelain of Jingdezhen start with this imperial endorsement dated
to the first year of the Jingde reign period.[4] The importance of this year was
made especially visible in the year 2004, when Jingdezhen celebrated one
thousand years of ceramic history. *Ceramics Today* pushed it even further,
claiming, more or less, that the ceramics history of the world began with the
events of 1004 in Jingdezhen:

> In 2004 the City of Jingdezhen will host the world to celebrate 1000 years
> as an imperial kiln production center, beginning with the Song Emperor
> Jing De in 1004. The story of Jingdezhen porcelain and its export
> throughout the world is an important chapter in the history of China and
> a foundation stone of world ceramic art. Jingdezhen porcelain captures
> the very heart of ceramic history, beginning with the spiritual beauty of
> Song, the natural essence of Yuan, the immeasurable blue of Ming, the
> multi-colored romanticism of Qing and the contemporary creations of
> modern China.[5]

For Lan Pu, 1004 was the year in which Jingdezhen's story became an
imperial story; *Ceramics Today* sees 1004 as 'a foundation stone of world
ceramic art'. Lan Pu never questions Jingdezhen's exceptionality; by
considering the period before that imperial endorsement and the wider
context of Jingdezhen's production between 1000 and 1200, we see a place
that is not so much exceptional or uniquely favoured by the imperial court,
but one that is part of a wider field of ceramics production, and thus competitive and market-driven.

Ceramics Manufactures in the Tenth Century

During the tenth century, the area that is now China was divided between
a number of empires that regularly waged war on each other. This period
of instability and division began in the 880s, and lasted until 979, when the
Song dynasty conquered the last of its rivals.[6] The first years of the Song
regime were therefore still chaotic, disruptive and characterized by military
conflict. Once scholar-officials were promoted to positions of political power
in the eleventh century, they began to play an active role in documenting
the history of the founding of the Song dynasty. In their accounts, which

largely came to be regarded as the standard version, the importance of war and the military in the first half a century of the Song regime was severely underestimated.[7] By the time the third emperor, Zhenzong, took over from his father Taizong in 997, the Song regime had begun to acquire legitimacy, and civil matters had started to gain the ear of the new emperor. It was in this context that depleted libraries began to get refilled, officials were appointed to document the activities of the emperors, imperial patronage of the arts re-emerged and storehouses (*ku*) for valuable goods like porcelain were re-established.[8]

In 990, the first year of the second Song emperor's Chunhua reign period, the emperor, Taizong, issued the first command that 'Porcelain of all regions should be contained in a porcelain storehouse (*ciqi ku*)'.[9] Dated 30 years after the founding of the Song, this reference to the existence of a porcelain storehouse and the selection of ceramics from various production sites throughout the empire underscores the shift away from military affairs towards the civilian realm, illustrated also by the investment in large-scale building projects of monasteries, pagodas and government buildings.[10] The imperial command also explains where these 'porcelains of all regions' were to come from: 'The porcelain storehouse at Jianlongfang shall be supplied with white porcelains and lacquerwares from Ming, Yue, Raozhou, Dingzhou and Qingzhou'.[11] The term Jianlongfang literally means 'Jianlong workshop', or the workshop named after the Jianlong reign period, which was the first reign period of the Song dynasty. The other terms are all familiar geographical references: Mingzhou, now the region where Ningbo is located on the eastern seaboard; Yue, the present Shaoxing, located in the area just to the west of Ningbo; Raozhou, or the central region of southern China where Jingdezhen was located; Dingzhou in northern China, and Qingzhou, to the northwest of the province of Shandong (Map 2.1).

All this suggests that during the reigns of the first emperors of the Song dynasty, the court was interested in collecting porcelain and lacquered goods for the personal use of the emperors, and that these were to come from specific sites scattered throughout the empire. Whether these specific sites were chosen because of their volume of production or because of the aesthetic preferences of the emperor, however, is not stated explicitly. We only know that the late tenth-century ceramics collected and stored at the imperial court by no means came from one single site.

This development continued under the reign of Taizong's son Zhenzong. According to the same source, in 1007, the fourth and final year of the Jingde reign period, Zhenzong issued a command that all the porcelains

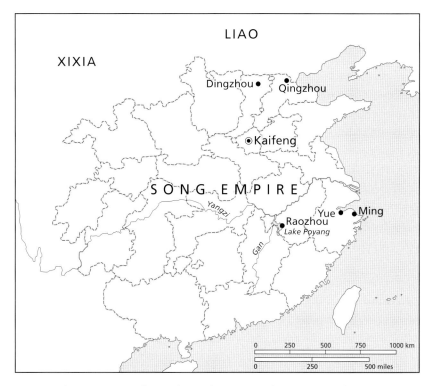

Map 2.1 The Song empire during the tenth century with ceramics production sites. Map based on China Historical Geographic Information System (CHGIS), version 6.

held in the storehouse be evaluated and sold, 'apart from those that have been received in the Fengzhuang [storehouse] as tribute'.[12] We know more about the Fengzhuang storehouse than about the porcelain storehouse at Jianlongfang: until the reforms of the mid-eleventh century, when this storehouse came under the control of the chancellor, the Fengzhuang storehouse contained treasure and precious goods for the personal use of the emperor.[13] It is interesting that the emperor made the decision to liquidate these assets and divest the court from the collections of porcelain goods that had entered the imperial storehouses, most likely by means of tribute and gifts from the various regions. More significant, however, is the explicit preference of the emperor to keep his personal collections. To some extent, the Song empire maintained a division between the financial resources of the empire on the one hand, and the Privy Purse (*Neicangku*), which contained coins, gold, silver and silk for the personal use of the emperor on the other.[14] The goods in the Fengzhuang storehouse fell in this latter category, as this imperial edict testifies, and may well suggest the emperor's personal liking for porcelain.

Of course, we have no way of knowing exactly which pieces of white por-celain and lacquerware from 'Ming, Yue, Raozhou, Dingzhou and Qingzhou' entered the tenth-century imperial storehouse, or what these looked like. We can only look at the archaeological record of the period, and at the imperfect legacy of goods from those sites held in museum collections, in other words, at goods that reflect the tastes of much later eras rather than the preferences of the early Song emperors.[15] On that basis, we can, however, make educated guesses. Ming and Yue refer, broadly speaking, to the eastern seaboard region now dominated by the port city of Ningbo and the urban conglomerations of Shaoxing on the southern banks of the Qiantang river and Hangzhou Bay. This area has a long history of production of high-fired stonewares with glazes in colours ranging from greyish green to olive green. The area around Shaoxing, previously known as Yue, gave its name to these wares, but they were produced at hundreds of kiln sites in the region. Generally, these tenth-century green-wares have been seen as the ancestor of celadon.[16] Some of these were extremely fine quality wares, especially those produced under the aegis of the Wu-Yue Kingdom, one of the polities of the tenth century. Established in 907 at the fall of the Tang, this political entity lasted until 978, well after the establishment of the Song dynasty. The Song initially conducted a tributary relationship with the Yue Kingdom; the documentary record for this period specifies that the Song court demanded ceramics as court tribute from the Wu-Yue regime. But fine ceramics production continued in this region, also after the demise of the Yue as a separate kingdom. Archaeological research in the Ningbo region (i.e. Mingzhou) has yielded large quantities of Yue wares dating to the ninth cen-tury, but large quantities of Yue shards have also been found in the Red Sea, the Persian Gulf, along the North African coast and in Indonesia.[17] It is not surprising, then, that the imperial command of 990 specified that Yue wares should be accumulated in the imperial porcelain storehouse.

While some of the Yue wares could be described as having a greyish white colour, green hues characterized the overwhelmingly majority. It was only the Raozhou kilns in the south and the Dingzhou kilns in the north that produced truly white porcelains. The Ding kilns were located in Quyang in Hebei Province, where as early as the eighth and ninth centuries, potters had access to clays that turned white in the firing process. These white-firing clays responded well to the high kiln temperatures required for creating thin but hard bodies, and on that basis, we could refer to these early Ding wares as 'porcelain' in the Western sense of the word, meaning that they were fired at a temperature above 1300 degrees Celsius and had a (near) translucent quality.[18] The Chinese term *ci*, conventionally translated as 'porcelain', refers to glazed, high-fired ceramics, though not necessarily fired above 1300 degrees Celsius. These appeared as early as the third century BCE, though the term did not come into use until the sixth century AD.[19] Ding porcelains consisted of simple shapes, often fired upside down (*fushao*), leaving an unglazed rim exposed, which was then covered with a metal ring. These refined, elegant and understated wares were in high demand, so much so that as early as the tenth century, a special office had already been established in the region of Dingware production to regulate issues of trade and taxation.[20] Archaeological evidence excavated from the tomb of an imperial consort suggests the high regard in which the early Song emperors personally held Ding wares. Consort of the second Song emperor, Taizong, and mother of the third, Emperor Zhenzong, Empress Li died in 977, and was buried in 1000 at Taizong's imperial tomb. Among the buried goods were 37 pieces of white Ding porcelain, 16 of which had the word *guan* ('official') engraved upon their base.[21] The presence of Ding wares in such an important imperial tomb, and their inscription with a term that directly connects the makers of the porcelain to the court confirms a close connection between Ding and the imperial household. We may well speculate, then, that the Ding wares found in this imperial tomb were similar to, or even examples of the wares from Dingzhou Taizong ordered to be collected for his storehouse.[22]

The kilns in Raozhou, too, were making fine white porcelain as early as the tenth century, as the archaeological record confirms. Until then, kilns in this region had been making what are known as Yue-type ceramics: high-fired stonewares with a green glaze. Excavations of several tenth-century sites in Raozhou demonstrate that it was in this period that white porcelains first made their appearance.[23] Initially made simultaneously with the green-glazed Yue-type ceramics, the region's brilliant white wares stood out, and the production of Yue-type ceramics declined.[24] The administrative record confirms that in Raozhou, a *zhen* was only established in the county of Fuliang in the first year of Jingde, i.e. in 1004.[25] It makes sense then, that Taizong's late tenth-century request for white wares 'from Raozhou' did not yet mention Jingdezhen.

In Taizong's request, 'The porcelain storehouse at Jianlongfang shall be supplied with white porcelains and lacquerwares from Ming, Yue, Raozhou, Dingzhou and Qingzhou,' the last geographical reference is more difficult to make sense of.[26] 'Qingzhou' refers to an area within present day Shandong province. While the region undoubtedly produced ceramics – almost every place in China had a kiln – there is absolutely no evidence to suggest that white porcelains were produced in Shandong during the tenth century.[27] It is possible that Qingzhou points to the location where the lacquerwares requested by the court were produced, as Hin-cheung Lovell suggested in

1973, but the evidence seems thin.[28] We know that Shandong was one of the regions where the Tung (or lacquer) tree used for the extraction of the sap used in lacquering grew, but it also grew in many other places, and archaeological finds of tenth-century lacquer are distributed over numerous sites.[29] There are relatively few lacquerware objects from the tenth century in museum collections, and it has proven difficult to point to specific production sites for those. However, unless new archaeological discoveries emerge that demonstrate white porcelain manufacture in this region, it seems marginally more likely that Qingzhou refers to a source of lacquerware.

What transpires from this overview is that of the sites mentioned in the imperial documentation, Ming, Yue, Raozhou and Dingzhou all produced fine white porcelains as early as the late tenth century. The imperial storehouses were filled both with goods collected through the tax system and referred to as local tribute (*tugong*), and with goods that were court tribute (*chaogong*), demanded from a specific production site or locality for the personal use of the emperor. These were specifically identified and selected, because it is by no means the case that ceramics from every production site were requisitioned through this system. The archaeological record shows that many other sites throughout the empire also produced ceramics during this period, but there is no reference to these in the extant sources associated with the imperial court dating to the tenth century. No mention is made, for example, of the brown and black ceramics made in Jizhou (i.e. Ji'an in present-day Jiangxi) and Jian (in present-day Fujian) during the Five Dynasties, nor the heavily potted wares made in the region of Cizhou in the north during the Tang and Five Dynasties period. All of these wares had somewhat thicker bodies, and were covered with green, grey or brown glazes. For whatever reason, these were considered less suitable for collection in the imperial storehouses or for the payment of imperial tribute from the region or did not match the personal preference of the emperor for 'white ceramics and lacquerware'.

So, should the history of Jingdezhen start in 1004? It is true that the material record for the period shows that the soils were 'white and clay-like' and that the fired wares from Raozhou were white and of a very fine quality, but their history dates from before 1004. Moreover, no Song-dynasty record has been preserved that states that 'Zhenzong ordered that they be brought to the Palace as tribute' and that 'the four characters *Jing de nian zhi* ("made during the Jingde reign") be written on the base of the porcelain vessels', as Lan Pu claims. The earliest preserved record for those claims is in fact a much later text: the seventeenth-century provincial gazetteer for Jiangxi (*Jiangxi tongzhi*), which contains a section about the management of porcelain production in Jingdezhen, entitled 'Governance of Ceramics' (*Taozheng*).[30] There we read that:

> The town (*zhen*) was established during Jingde of the Song. Officials were dispatched to organise the submission of tribute to the imperial capital in accordance with the needs of the administration, and they ordered the pottery workers to carve the year of establishment 'Jingde' in the [base of the] vessels. From then on, everyone referred to these as 'Jingdezhen porcelains'.[31]

Written hundreds of years after the event, we cannot take this account as authoritative. More significantly, perhaps, we also do not have any material evidence of ceramics that were not only made around the year 1000 in this region but also inscribed with the characters for the reign period (Jingde). Of course, the extant material and documentary record is only fragmentary, and the absence of evidence does not disprove their existence. But the evidence we do have – tenth-century documents that refer to a variety of production places of white ceramics that were all favoured at the imperial court – suggests Jingdezhen was not yet exceptional in the tenth and early eleventh centuries.

Why, then, Lan Pu's emphasis on Jingdezhen? Why did he choose to focus only on Jingdezhen on his book on ceramics (*Jingdezhen tao lu*), and what happened in Jingdezhen that, with hindsight, its story came to be told as an exceptional story? The answers to that question will transpire as the book unfolds; for now, we need to survey the scene more broadly, considering not only the immediate context of the year 1004, but also the developments throughout the empire over the course of the eleventh and twelfth centuries, to understand the ways in which Jingdezhen emerged. Only when we situate Jingdezhen in that wider story of the manufacture of ceramics throughout the empire, and of the circulation of those ceramics beyond the confines of the storehouses of the imperial court, can we begin to evaluate the relative importance of Jingdezhen.

Ceramics Production in Northern China, 1000–1200

The tenth century may have been characterized by consolidation for the Song imperial regime, the long eleventh century was a period of great economic and cultural flourishing, a period that arguably lasted into the twelfth century and beyond the end of the reign of Emperor Huizong in 1126.[32] The arts thrived, as testified by the paintings, poetry, literary writings and material culture of the period that remain today, and great strides were made in architecture and engineering, printing and education, commercial infrastructure and the development of the market economy.[33] Life in the city of Kaifeng was dominated to a certain extent by the powerful presence of the emperor and his household and the comings and goings of visitors and their entourages to the imperial court, but it was also punctuated by the regular rhythms of markets and religious festivals. Urbanization inevitably meant commercialization, with merchants delivering goods to urban residents, shops displaying wares for sale, and wine shops and restaurants supplying the residents with food and drink. The attractions of urban life were still relatively new in this period and generated a certain amount of anxiety among the residents.[34] One of the most highly regarded literary scholars of the eleventh century, Ouyang Xiu (1007–1072), recalled late in life an episode where he had to defend his enjoyment of such commercial establishments to the emperor. On that occasion, the emperor had once urgently summoned him, but when the servant knocked on his door, Ouyang was out, enjoying the delights of a nearby establishment that sold famous wine. The servant worried about telling the truth to the emperor about what had detained Ouyang, but Ouyang had reassured him, explaining that 'enjoying wine is but a regular human sentiment, and thus no crime, even for gentlemen and high court officials'. When the emperor later queried his wish to drink in a winehouse, Ouyang answered: 'My home is poor and without any utensils, while the wine shop is fully equipped with everything. So, when guests arrive, or relatives come from far, then we go there to drink'.[35] In Ouyang Xiu's case, the availability of fine wine and matching utensils in public places seems to have done away with the need to fully equip his own home.

Throughout the eleventh century, the Song regime was also beleaguered by external threats, especially the inhabitants of the steppe-lands to the north of the Song border known as Jürchen. The rule of Huizong ended when the northern capital Kaifeng in Henan province was invaded by Jürchen, Huizong and his successor Qinzong were captured, and what remained of the Song court was forced to find a temporary capital in the south. The Jürchen established their own dynasty in northern China known as the Jin (1115–1234) and continued to be at war both with what became the Southern Song dynasty in the south, and the Mongols in the north, whose threats and incursions became more persistent during the thirteenth century as they unified under a single ruler.

We know something of the wealth and sophistication of the Northern Song imperial capital Kaifeng during the eleventh century, because of its vivid description in a twelfth-century memoir by Meng Yuanlao, *A Dream of Splendour in the Eastern Capital.*[36] The descriptions of the author's memories bring the city to life, with its countless shops, temples, winebars and restaurants, the wealth of goods for sale, the varieties of foods and flavours sampled, and the rich material culture of the city that shaped behaviours and practices in the city. When one would drink wine in a winebar, the author recalled, 'one had to use a *zhuwan* [lit. pourer and bowl], a set made up of a basin and a bowl'.[37] Such sets, sometimes referred to as wine heaters, allowed the wine drinkers to pour warm water in the outer basin, thereby warming the wine inside the cup. These would be accompanied by a few more plates and bowls for the fruit and vegetable dishes that were enjoyed as accompaniment to the wine. If such fragmentary insights, veiled by the nostalgia of their author, into the experiences of urban consumers can tell us anything, it would be that the shapes of the objects, as well as the ways in which they were used in the social context of a conversation in a wine bar mattered. The type of ceramics used, the place where they were made, and their colour seemed to matter less. That may be because once the choice of an establishment was made, the consumer had no control over the crockery in which the drinks were served there. But that is true for the shape as much as the colour; and on this occasion, the shape mattered, because it helped to warm the wine, and thus determined how the drink was consumed. It may also be because the author's recollection of this style of socializing in the now inaccessible capital of Kaifeng, is implicitly contrasted with the ways in which wine is enjoyed in the south. Either way, the site of the vessel's manufacture was not mentioned. Yet the place where it was made, in a northern or southern kiln, for example, would have made a significant difference for the look and feel of the wine cup.

Ceramics made in the north of China were, and are, different because geological factors produced different kinds of clays in the north. The northern provinces are covered by vast coalfields, the result of millions of years of transformation of the vegetation that once grew upon a primary layer of clay. Over time, several more layers of soil were deposited upon that coal, mostly loess carried by the river systems that flow from the uplands in the far west and deposit that soil in the lower floodplains of the east. Depending on the thickness of these layers, different kinds of clays were dug up for making ceramics in the north. In some places, it was possible to reach the primary layers of clay, which could be described as kaolinitic, meaning they could be shaped and fired at high temperatures, and produced wares with a hard, white body. Technically, because of that high temperature, the potters in northern China who worked with that material as early as the seventh century were producing what is now referred to as porcelain. But by no means all the northern clays were like that; the majority contained more impurities, could not withstand such high temperatures, and fired to a greyish colour.[38]

Regardless of the type of clay used to form the bodies, kilns in the north produced stunning pieces during the eleventh and twelfth centuries. As museum collections with Song ceramics testify, some had fine, white bodies and simple transparent glazes; others had thicker, less attractive bodies, but covered with luscious glazes in spectacular colours.[39] A few of the northern kiln sites should be mentioned specifically, because in later centuries, these sites came to be associated with the imperial court of the Song dynasty.[40] Ceramics that came to be known as Ru wares are perhaps the most famous of these, although they are also the most rare and elusive of the Song kilns. Ru wares have a pale blue or 'sky blue' glaze, with a subtle crackle, and have been made in a variety of shapes and sizes. Extensive excavations in the province of Henan, where the Northern Song capital was located, suggest that most of the wares were made in Baofeng County, and that the majority of the wares were made between the middle of the eleventh and the early years of the twelfth centuries.[41] Today, only about 65 to 70 known examples exist, of which 23 are in the National Palace Museum in Taiwan, and several others form part of the collection of Sir Percival David (1892–1964), on loan to the British Museum in London.[42]

The recognition that Ru wares were special is evident in the historical record. See, for example, the following description by a man named Ye Zhi, about whom otherwise next to nothing is known, other than that he lived during the Southern Song dynasty, and that he wrote a short statement about northern ceramics that was integrated in a fourteenth-century collection of jottings (*biji*) by the eminent fourteenth-century scholar Tao Zongyi, who retired to the countryside when the Yuan dynasty government started to disintegrate:

> In this dynasty, the white ceramic vessels from Dingzhou are considered to have some flaws, making them less desirable for use, and thus the [court] ordered vessels from the kilns in Ruzhou that made green wares. The counties of Tang, Deng and Yao, all in Hebei province, all had [such kilns], but the Ru kilns were considered the most exceptional.[43]

We do not know what Ye Zhi meant with flaws (*mang* 芒), although it is conceivable that this refers to the above-mentioned Ding practice of placing the vessels upside down in the kilns, and covering the raw edge this created with a band of metal. The reference to Ding wares having flaws, and the subsequent preference for Ru wares is also mentioned in another contemporary source. The famous Southern Song poet and writer Lu You (1125–1210) wrote that 'At the old capital, Ding vessels did not enter the inner sanctum of the palace. They only used Ru vessels, because Ding wares had some flaws'.[44] The exclusive use of Ru vessels at the court reported by Lu You seems hard to confirm, although it is certainly conceivable that the court preferred the finest of the green wares that Ru wares exemplified.

The late Southern Song writer Zhou Mi (1232–1298) provides a much later example of the desirability of Ru wares, when he refers to Ru wares in his book of anecdotes entitled 'Wulin nostalgia' (*Wulin jiushi*). The book features nostalgic recollections of Hangzhou, the Southern Song capital, in the twelfth and thirteenth centuries, written after the city had been conquered by the Mongol troops in the 1280s. It included a story about the famous general Zhang Jun (1086–1154), who had been one of the key figures in the fight against the invading Jürchen. When Emperor Gaozong (1107–1187) visited the general in the middle of the twelfth century, not long before Zhang Jun's death, Zhang made a gift of Ru ceramics to the emperor. The gift included a pair of wine bottles, a wash basin for brushes, cups, dishes and several different shapes of vessels for burning incense. By the time of this gift, Ru wares were no longer being made, and their site of production in Henan, near the location of the Northern Song capital, had long become inaccessible to the Song emperors. The special quality of Ru wares clearly was embedded not only in their beautiful glazes and gentle shapes, but also in their association with a once-flourishing court that had been lost forever, especially once they were no longer made.

Several other types of northern ceramics deserve mention here. A group of porcelains referred to as Guan wares (*Guanyao*) includes elegant wares with a fine crackled glaze. The term Guanyao is used in the same way as Ruyao and Dingyao are used: named after a kiln site in a specific geographic location, where wares were made with an individual characteristic appearance. The historical documents make clear, however, that Guan is not a place name; the term *guanyao* referred to kilns established under the auspices of the imperial court, to supply the court with the wares it desired. Perhaps unsurprisingly in light of the above discussion, the wares the court desired were Ru wares, and thus the wares referred to as Guan wares look much like Ru wares. And like many other Song wares, Guan wares were not made at a single kiln site, but at several different sites, including two sites located within the city of Hangzhou and a third located beyond the boundaries of the capital but still in its vicinity.[45] A third member of the elite group of fine Song porcelains is referred to as Ge wares. Like Guan,

Figure 2.1 Dish with lavender-coloured glaze. Jun-ware, ca. 960–ca. 1279. Inv. no. AK-MAK-1273. Collection KVVAK, Rijksmuseum, Amsterdam.

Ge is not a geographical reference, but literally means 'elder brother'. Our understanding of the exact location of these kilns and of the relationships between these different sites continues to change, especially in light of ongoing excavations and technological innovations in the available research tools.[46]

In the eleventh and early twelfth centuries, fine ceramics were also produced at several other northern kiln sites, including the Jun kilns in Henan, and at the Yaozhou kilns in Shaanxi. Jun wares (Figure 2.1) had glazes that range in a colour from blue to purple, sometimes with splashes of copper-red.

At Yaozhou, potters made fine stonewares with green glazes ranging in hue from bluish-green to bright green and olive-green, which later came to be known as celadon (Figure 2.2).[47] This term, celadon, refers to stonewares glazed with a coating that contains traces of iron, which turns into a greyish-to bluish-green hue when fired in an oxygen-poor environment. We know about this from the official history of the Song dynasty. Such official histories were always prepared for publication by the successor dynasty, so this record was produced during the Yuan dynasty. It listed 'ceramics tribute' as one of the attributes of Yaozhou in monographs on geography, but recent evidence has brought to light that there was even an official bureau for dealing with the trade and tax payments of ceramics in this region as early

Figure 2.2 Shallow dish, decorated with a band of flowers and leaves. Yaozhou, twelfth century. Collection KVVAK, Rijksmuseum, Amsterdam, inv. no. AK-MAK-1696.

as 1008.[48] All this underscores the significance of the many different kiln sites distributed throughout the northern provinces for the economy and administration of the empire.

Moreover, most of the kiln sites distributed throughout the northern provinces made wares that imitated those made in other places, especially where these enjoyed a great reputation. Many sites surrounding the county of Cizhou, now in southern Hebei, produced ceramics known as Cizhou or Cizhou-style wares. This group of wares is highly varied in style and design, but they included wares that closely resembled Ding wares. While the white clays found near the Ding kilns could be fired at very high temperatures (and hence Ding wares are technically speaking porcelain), the Cizhou clay was rougher, and did not respond well to firing at high temperatures, so these wares are known as stoneware. This part of southern Hebei was, and is, a coal-mining region, and kilns fired with coal were in operation here from the late Tang through to the Ming and Qing dynasties, although the vast majority of Cizhou wares dates from the Song and Jin dynasties.[49] The clay found here was faintly reddish in colour, so the bodies were generally covered with a white base colour known as slip. Of course, stonewares covered with a white or cream-coloured layer of slip could never be confused with the thin bodies and translucent glazes of high-fired Ding wares, but the Cizhou potters could create something that was not unlike Ding ware.[50]

From the late eleventh century, the potters working at the Cizhou kilns often decorated the white slip using a brush and dark brown or black pigment, creating a wide range of lively patterns and designs. Wares with these decorative patterns included bottles, bowls and jars wares that were widely used for the brewing, storing, and drinking of wine, and have been found throughout the northern provinces. Archaeological finds are now beginning to clarify just how widespread these wares were, also in the southern provinces.[51] What all this shows, is that during the Northern Song, and in the northern provinces after the loss of the north to the Jin dynasty, a wide variety of ceramics were produced, both with very individual styles and singular, characteristic associations and use practices, and with designs or styles that were shared between different production sites. The practice of referring to types of porcelain by the name of the place where they were produced has had the effect of turning place-names into short-hand references to individual types of ceramics, such as Ding, Ru and Jizhou. Names of places became metonyms for the ceramic wares produced in the region, which suggests they were distinct and separate. Seen in combination, this overview of ceramics made in the northern provinces between 1000 and 1200 illustrates the efflorescence of the economy, the sophistication of the consumers, the differentiations of the market, but especially the circulation of technologies, designs and styles of the Song dynasty.

Ceramics Production in Southern China, 1000–1200

After 1126, when the Song regime lost the north to the Jürchen and was forced to move its capital to the southern city of Hangzhou, political factors created the most obvious division between the north and the south in what was until then a unified Song empire. Before 1126, however, it was environmental factors, and specifically geological factors, that gave rise to one of the main differences between north and south. This geological distinction between north and south had a significant impact on the ceramics production of the empire. In the northern provinces, the potters had access to clays made up from loess, or from weathered igneous rock located underneath the coal strata. In the south, potters also had access to igneous rock, but instead of being located underneath coal, it was relatively close to the surface, and had been weathered in such a way that the clay often still contained some elements of quartz and mica. Secondly, and more importantly, in the south one could find rock made up from volcanic ash, which also contained high levels of quartz and mica. This material needed several processes of pulverization and purification by means of submerging it in water to separate the lighter material from the heavier particles before it could be used. But the result was a clay that had high plasticity and could withstand extremely high temperatures, and thus produced porcelain. Such quartz and mica-rich volcanic clays could only be found in southern China. At the same time, of course there were also many kiln sites distributed throughout the south that produced stonewares made from clays from weathered rock.[52] Their bodies ranged in colour from white and grey to darker browns and reds, and their fineness depended on the extent to which the potters could refine or purify that material before shaping the bodies.

Nigel Wood has pointed out the simple technology of the methods in use at the southern kilns: the potters shaped bodies from a single material, then glazed them with a mixture consisting of the same material used for the bodies and limestone (calcium carbonate), and finally fired these to a temperature of around 1250°C.[53] The clay they used had been formed through the decomposition of feldspathic minerals, and as we saw in the north, that specific attribute meant that the material could withstand firing at high temperatures. The high quartz content of this clay also meant it had a crystal-like or 'sugary' quality when fired, and the high levels of potassium gave them a certain translucency.[54] The use of limestone in the glaze, prepared by first burning it with wood and ferns and then washing it to remove the fern ash, would become a 'defining feature' of southern porcelains.[55]

In Yuezhou, the area where in the tenth century the Wu-Yue empire had flourished, a type of greenware was produced from the ninth to the eleventh century.[56] Potters working in Yaozhou had sought to imitate this early form of celadon. It was in high demand at the imperial court, as we see in an imperial edict requisitioning these ceramics together with other goods dating to 1068: 'Ten bolts of thin satin (*ling*), ten bolts of red gauze (*sha*), and 50 pieces of 'secret colour' porcelain (*mise ciqi*)'.[57] Only the most refined of the Yue wares were referred to as 'secret' or 'mysterious' colour, but it was not clear what these pieces looked like until fourteen pieces of Yue ware were unearthed from a tomb at a Buddhist monastery in Shaanxi together with an inventory detailing that 13 of these were the so-called 'secret colour' porcelains.[58]

At Longquan county in Zhejiang, potters also made celadons, using a mixture of white and reddish clay that was soft and easy to work, leading to a vast production of initially thickly potted wares, with grey bodies typically covered with an olive-green glaze. Archaeological excavations have identified hundreds of kilns in this region, some dating to as early as the tenth century, but after the political upheavals and the relocation of the Song capital to nearby Hangzhou in the early to mid-twelfth century, Longquan production gradually increased both in quantity and in quality.[59] The Longquan potters did this by adopting a technique from the Guan kilns. These kilns, as we already saw, had been established within and near Hangzhou to manufacture wares that resembled the highly desirable but no longer manufactured Ru wares.[60] To create the necessary unctuous, jade-like quality of a Ru glaze, and possibly to disguise that the clays used were somewhat rougher than those used in the north, the potters of the Guan kilns used a layering technique when applying the glaze.[61] This technique was also applied at other kiln sites, including at Longquan, and eventually led to the production of pieces of greenware porcelain with ultra-thin clay bodies, covered with thick layers of glaze.

In that way, the southern celadons may have had bodies that fired to a reddish or even dark brown colour, but their thickly applied glazes hid the colour of the bodies from sight. At other sites, the colour of the bodies was hidden from view by using dark brown glazes. This was especially the case for the production of bowls used for drinking tea. Tea had been consumed in the deep south of China long before the Song dynasty, but the culture of tea drinking spread rapidly to other regions during the Song. The cultivation of new and more refined teas, especially in Fujian, the growth of commercial structures that facilitated the distribution of goods throughout the empire, the spread of urbanization, the increasing significance of Buddhist monks and the use of tea in Buddhist rituals all contributed to this spread.[62] The circulation of ceramics throughout the empire neatly fits into this same set of changes, and contributed actively to the growing popularity of the culture of tea. Connoisseurs determined the kinds of ceramics that were particularly suited to the enjoyment of specific teas, for example, by enhancing the colour contrast between the tea and the bowl.

The tea leaves that were ground to a fine powder and whisked with hot water to make a frothy green drink looked particularly stunning against a dark background. Two Song-dynasty kiln sites in the south of China produced just such dark-glazed bowls for drinking tea: Jian and Jizhou. The Jian kilns, located in Jianyang in coastal Fujian, produced the widest range of what became known as 'tea wares'. The shapes were simple: bowls that fill two hands folded together, some more rounded, others sharply conical, often standing on a small round foot. It was the glazes that were varied and most striking: ranging from reddish brown to blueish black, they covered most of the stoneware bodies, leaving the foot exposed, to reveal the thickness of the glaze. The different patterns of the glaze have evocative names such as hare's fur (with tiny silver-grey lines in the glaze), oil-spot (with little round dots like drops of oil on water) or partridge feather (dark glaze mottled with splashes of lighter colour).

Further inland from Jianyang, in Jizhou prefecture in southern Jiangxi, potters also made dark-glazed tea bowls, not unlike the wares made in Jianyang. There is evidence at both of these sites of production from as early as the tenth and eleventh centuries. In the world of porcelain collectors and museum curators, such brown- and black-glazed ceramics have come to be known as Tianmu in Chinese, a name that refers to the Buddhist monasteries on Mount Tianmu, 80 km west of Hangzhou, where such brown bowls were used in Chan-Buddhist ceremonies. During the Song dynasty, Japanese monks came to southern China to study with famous Buddhist teachers, and brought back not only sacred texts and new insights, but also brown and black tea bowls to use in what became Japanese Zen rituals.[63] Because of this affiliation with Japanese collections of teabowls from China, these brownwares are also known as *temmoku*, which is the Japanese translation of the name of the mountain, Tianmu. Finally, tea bowls and teapots were made further to the north in Yixing county in Jiangsu province. The characteristic red clay known as purple clay (*zisha*), fired but usually left unglazed, and therefore slightly absorbent, was considered to have outstanding qualities for retaining and enhancing the fragrance of tea.[64]

All of these wares circulated in the marketplace where they vied for the attention of consumers, and all of these wares had characteristics that set them apart from each other. In that extremely busy market-place, it was only during the course of the eleventh century that the white porcelains of Jingdezhen began to attract particular attention.[65] The slow growth of Jingdezhen's production is visible in the, admittedly patchy, tax record for the region. Prior to 1077, the prefecture of Raozhou submitted tax payments that were based on six units: the prefectural capital of Raozhou itself, together with five other county-sized units: Dexing, Fuliang, Yugan, Anren and Shitou. No separate entry for Jingdezhen is listed, and the figures are not broken down per county; only a total payment is given of 25,470 strings of cash (*guan*).[66] For 1077, the record lists Jingdezhen, and breaks down the amount for each of the counties. The tax raised in Jingdezhen alone amounted to 3,337 strings of cash, an amount that is only slightly lower than the total amount raised in Fuliang county as a whole.[67] Of course the officials compiling these records were based within the central administration and could only ever have a partial view of what was happening locally. Moreover, the records transmitted are patchy and provide at best fragmentary evidence. The fact that we have the tax records from Jingdezhen for 1077 is more unusual than their absence for other years, and it is difficult to draw conclusions from this imperfect evidence. At the very least, however, it shows that in the late eleventh century, ceramics production in Jingdezhen played a significant role in the regional economy.

Less than a decade later, the central government established a local bureau for the management of the finances of the porcelain production. Both the exact date of that establishment and the wider context within which this occurred require some explanation. During this time, there was a wider movement to manage the finances of the empire by establishing offices that exerted control over all commercially produced commodities. As in previous dynasties, the Song state asserted a monopoly over certain common commodities, such as wine, salt, iron and tea. These commodities generated a very substantial income stream for the government. In 1077, 32 per cent of the revenues collected by the Song government came from land taxes, of which the vast majority were payments in kind (i.e. grain), but 35 per cent came from excise payments, in other words, indirect taxes levied over commercial interactions.[68] In some cases, the state held a monopoly over the production of goods, as in the case of liquor; in other cases, the state sold licences to merchant houses to trade in certain commodities, such as salt; and in the case of iron, it was a combination of both.[69] Luxury commodities that did not form part of the Song monopoly structure were all liable to taxation by the imperial government. In 1072, the controversial Northern Song reformer Wang Anshi (1021–1086) had established a State Trade Bureau (*shiyi wu*, also known as the 'Market Exchange Office') as part of his widespread overhaul of the imperial financial organization.[70] Wang Anshi's aim was to do away with the monopolies held by certain merchant associations, so that instead of the merchant houses, the State Trade Bureau could regulate the prices of certain commodities and retain all the profits. When Wang Anshi fell out of favour in 1077, the State Trade Bureau and many of its associated offices were abolished, but in the decades that followed, offices were established that similarly created a local arm of the imperial state that regulated commodity prices.

There is some debate over when exactly the bureau in Jingdezhen was established. In the *History of the Song*, we find the claim that the office was established in 1082: 'In the eighth month (of the fifth year of Yuanfeng), the 'Office for the Exchange of Many Goods' (*boyiwu*) for the Jingdezhen kilns in Raozhou was established'.[71] The term 'Exchange of Many Goods' is explained elsewhere in the *History of the Song* as including various luxury goods, such as satins and brocades, lacquerware and porcelain. The *History of the Song* was edited and published during the Yuan dynasty, at least two hundred years after the establishment of this office. A later date of 1085 (the eight years of the Yuanfeng reign period of Emperor Shenzong) appears in a different source, namely Li Tao's (1115–1184) *Continuation of the Comprehensive Mirror for Aid in Government, Expanded Version* (*Xu Zizhi tongjian changbian*). Here we find the statement that in the ninth month (of the eighth year of Yuanfeng), Jingdezhen in Raozhou established an 'Office for the Exchange of Many Goods' (*boyiwu*).[72] Li Tao compiled the *Continuation of the Comprehensive Mirror* during the Southern Song, using the court records he had available to him, so his information should be more reliable than the information given in the *History of the Song*, but the collection as a whole does not survive, and in the Qing dynasty (1636–1912), the remaining texts were extensively edited. We have no other specific details on the establishment of this office, but from the late eleventh century onwards, the production of ceramic goods in Jingdezhen was substantial enough to generate significant revenues for the imperial court, through the payment of direct taxes levied on Jingdezhen, and through the taxation of the porcelain trade by means of the 'Office for the Exchange of Many Goods'.

The increasing prevalence of local, regional and empire-wide trade during the Song dynasty as a whole, and the movement of people from the north to the south, first during the final decades of the Tang dynasty, and again during the conquest by the Jin dynasty, meant a great circulation of people, goods and technologies throughout the empire. Excavations of urban areas and graves, palaces and hoards, have all uncovered vast quantities of Song-dynasty ceramics. The variety of ceramics in each individual location underscores this circulation of goods. Even when there was a prevalence of certain wares in specific areas, no ceramics were limited to a single place, and no place only had one kind of ceramics. Throughout the period from 1000 to 1200, a wide variety of wares were available commercially, to suit consumers ranging from the emperor and his household to urban residents, monks and merchants. In that light, the idea that Jingdezhen's wares somehow tell an individual and separate story that begins as early as 1004 makes little sense. White ceramics were valued, but not exclusively so; similarly, the court accumulated ceramics, but not exclusively from Jingdezhen. The story of Jingdezhen's white wares, then, is not a unique story of exclusivity, but one of circulation, competition and interaction.

3 | Circulations of White

> The ceramics [site] of Jingde in the past was made up of more than 300 kilns. Its vessels of clay were pure white and without blemish; of old they have been sold in different places, and they have always had the epithet 'Rao jades'.[1]

This is how a man named Jiang Qi opened his 'Notes on Ceramics' (*Taoji*). The text describes a large-scale production site known as Jingde, most likely during the long thirteenth century, which produced pure white and blemish-free porcelains. These porcelains were sold widely, were reminiscent of jades, and were associated with a place referred to as Rao. Rao was a prefecture in Eastern Jiangnan circuit, which encompassed the county of Fuliang where the town of Jingdezhen was located.[2]

The text by Jiang Qi contains the oldest extant description of the porcelain manufactures at Jingdezhen, and for that reason alone, the text itself, its various editions and its author have all received remarkable scrutiny. The date of the text, however, remains hotly contested.[3] Some place the text in the thirteenth century, between 1214 and 1234 to be precise. Rose Kerr and Nigel Wood, for example, authors of the volume on ceramics in Joseph Needham's *Science and Civilisation in China*, use this early thirteenth-century date, relying on the evidence presented by the famous ceramics expert Liu Xinyuan (1937–2013) and his colleague Bai Kun.[4] The French archaeologist and ceramics scholar Zhao Bing offers a slightly later date than Liu Xinyuan and Bai Kun, arguing the text should be seen as a product of the mid-thirteenth century.[5] Others have always considered this a Yuan era text (i.e. dating between 1279 and 1368); for example, the scholar Ma Wenkuan argued for a fourteenth-century date, suggesting that Jiang Qi wrote 'Notes on Ceramics' between 1323 and 1325, under the Yuan regime.[6]

This chapter considers the spread of ceramics produced in the Chinese empire to destinations within Eurasia, East- and Southeast Asia, and throughout the Indian Ocean during the thirteenth and early fourteenth centuries. It charts the circulation of Raozhou ceramics as they were traded through the region and far beyond, beginning to show the intricate ways in which local knowledge about making and selling things feeds into and is fed by global patterns of consumption. Moreover, it shows how the look and feel of Raozhou's porcelain, or the materiality of these goods, changed during this period. To understand these changes, this chapter suggests, one has to consider both local factors, such as the availability of raw materials in the immediate vicinity of the kilns, and global factors, such as the desire for large vessels amongst consumers of porcelain in nomadic communities and in the Islamic worlds of Central Asia. The combination of both local and global factors is key in understanding the changes that occurred during this period.

The majority of the wares produced in Jingdezhen during the thirteenth and early fourteenth centuries were what have become known as *qingbai* wares, a term that literally means blueish-white and refers to the colour of the glaze. As we already saw in the previous chapter, the clays used in Raozhou turned white when fired at high temperatures. For the glaze, the potters used the same material, but mixed with limestone, which in turn had been burnt with ferns and then washed to remove the fern ash. When fired, this kind of glaze became a translucent white, with a blueish tinge especially where the glaze pooled.

The image in Figure 3.1, a fragment of the base and side of what was probably a round box with a lid, shows all these elements: a relatively fine clay that has fired to a white body, covered in a glaze that is mostly translucent, so that the whiteness of the body is visible where the glaze is thin, but gaining a blueish tinge where the glaze has pooled in the undulations on the side of the box.

Although there were some entirely undecorated wares, most of the wares from this period have some kind of decorative element. Patterns made by pressing a mould into the clay are the most common, with floral sprays or simple leaves appearing in slight relief under the glaze.[7] More delicate incisions, or even intricate carved patterns in the inside and the outside of vessels created more visible patterns, including dragons and fiery pearls on a particularly striking late example included in Nigel Wood's study of *qingbai* glazes.[8] Many of the bowls and dishes have a slightly lobed rim, just enough to reveal the bluish quality of the glazes. A small number of Jingdezhen *qingbai* examples from the Southern Song have an unglazed edge. The British Museum has a bowl with a *qingbai* glaze and an edge covered with a thin band of copper.[9]

Even as early as the twelfth century, Jingdezhen's ceramics had a reputation.[10] The opening lines of a twelfth-century poem reflect this: 'In Fuliang they are highly skilled in firing ceramics/colours that have been likened to exquisite jade'.[11] The poem was written to mark the departure

Figure 3.1 *Qingbai* shard from the Freer-Sackler Gallery. Southern Song dynasty. The piece was made in Jingdezhen but found at the Ban Kruat kiln complex in Thailand. Freer Gallery of Art and Arthur M. Sackler Gallery, Smithsonian Institution, Washington, DC: Gift of Mr and Mrs Roy Galloway, FSC-P-4761.

from the region of the poem's recipient, a Mr Xu, who had served as capable magistrate in the county of Fuliang and had therefore never allowed himself to indulge his desire to acquire local products. Such impartiality was unheard of, the elders of the locality had exclaimed, or so Hong Mai, the twelfth-century author of a commentary to this poem, wrote when he included the poem in his collection of jottings (*biji*). If this poem is evidence of anything, it is of the author's recognition of the particular skills present in this region and the noteworthy quality of that local product: a jade-like porcelain. Another Southern Song author, Wu Zimu, listed white porcelain amongst the many pleasures of the southern capital (i.e. Hangzhou), together with such varied delights as lacquerwares from Wenzhou, shopping and small pavilions under the trees.[12] This latter example of the popularity of white ceramics points to their circulation. The southern capital was quite a distance from Raozhou, but goods from all over the empire were available for sale in the very urban streets of Hangzhou. The point is that the potters working in Raozhou catered not only for their local clientele and made products that the local magistrate would know about, but they also made their goods to please consumers and markets well beyond their locality.

How far beyond the locality these products were sold in the thirteenth century is one of the topics of discussion in Jiang Qi's 'Notes on Ceramics'. 'Now, in Zhe East and Zhe West, the vessels they admire are the yellow-ish black wares that come from the kilns at Hutian'.[13] Zhe refers to the two circuits to the east of Jiangnan East, under which Raozhou resorted during the Southern Song dynasty (Map 3.1). This preference for blackware, thus, is ascribed to consumers located in the coastal provinces.

These consumers, Jiang Qi tells us, prefer the stoneware bowls with dark glazes that range from a dark yellow-ish brown to dark black that were popular for the consumption of tea. Hutian, where these wares were made, are the kilns located a few kilometres southeast of Jingdezhen.[14] This pref-erence is in contrast to consumers in the central provinces: 'In Jiang, Hu, Chuan and Guang, they appreciate the *qingbai* wares from the kilns in town'.[15] This last 'town' is not specified, but since the text opens with the ref-erence to Jingde, we can assume this refers to kilns within Jingdezhen. The *qingbai* wares, the text suggests, were made at the kilns within the city, while the blackwares were made at Hutian. The geographical references Jiang Qi uses are interesting; they do not map precisely onto either the Southern Song or the Yuan situation. Between the Song and the Yuan, the admin-istrative units changed quite significantly, so probably terms he used were commonly used terms for certain regions rather than references to specific administrative units. However, whether it is the Southern Song circuits he refers to or the Yuan provinces, the region identified as 'Jiang, Hu, Chuan and Guang' refers broadly speaking to the south-central regions of the empire.

More valuable detail for merchants follows: 'In the category of bowls: fish in water [designs] with high stem; for small dishes: dizzying [patterns], cir-cular waves [lit. 'sea eyes'], and snowflakes; these are [goods] that make a profit in Chuan, Guang, Jing and Xiang'.[16] In other words, he identi-fies more specific tastes that match certain geographical references, this time describing the region that encompasses the central western area of Sichuan, the southern coastal region of Guangdong and Guangxi, and the

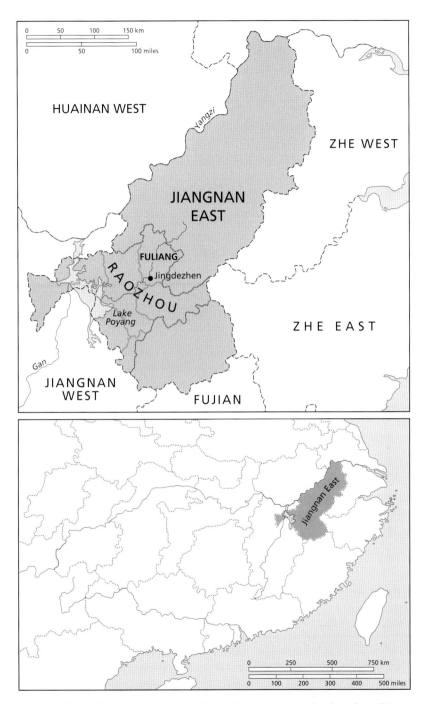

Map 3.1 Map of the southern circuits during Southern Song. Map based on China Historical Geographic Information System (CHGIS), version 6.

central regions of Jinghu and Xiang [today's Hunan and Hubei]. A further set of items is identified as profitable in the region of the central and coastal provinces of what are now Jiangxi, Zhejiang and Fujian. Again, the descriptions are extremely specific, providing details on which shapes (bowls, dishes, platters or jars), what kind of base (high stem, or in the shape of the hooves of a horse), which designs (betelpalm, lotus leaf etc) and appearances ('embroidered flowers', or 'silver embroidery') are considered desirable where. 'It is always the case that per location specific items must be selected'.[17] Undoubtedly, the advice on how to please customers and turn a profit was valuable information, as was the knowledge of what to do with rejects, such as the items where 'the colour was unattractive and of the kind that can only be thrown away'.[18] Known as 'yellow rejects' (*huang zhuo*), they could still be sold to residents of Jiangsu and Anhui, even if the consumers of Guangdong, Fujian and Zhejiang would not buy these. This sums up his overview of the different kinds of vessels: 'The various grades of vessels that are made by and large are like this'.[19]

The Global Movement of White Porcelain in the Long Thirteenth Century

Jiang Qi's recommendations on how best to select the right products for one's customers is delightful, and perhaps not surprising in light of what we know about the flourishing economic climate of the period. The history of the Song dynasty is not only a story of the flourishing of art, material culture and philosophical pursuits, but also of population growth, urbanization, technological innovation and commercial prowess. Between 1127 and 1279, the merchants of the Southern Song empire engaged actively in trade throughout the empire, as well as beyond its land-based and maritime borders. Ceramics were an extremely successful commodity for trade. The white ceramics made in Jingdezhen as well as a variety of ceramics from other kiln sites throughout the empire, together with a wide range of commodities produced within the empire were exported in vast quantities, in exchange for raw materials and luxury goods from Japan, Southeast Asia and the Indian Ocean regions.

One way of visualizing the commercial networks within which the Southern Song merchants operated is by seeing them in a wider perspective, as Janet Abu-Lughod's famous map makes possible (Map 3.2). In *Before European Hegemony: The World System A.D. 250–350*, Janet Abu-Lughod offers a way of conceptualizing the connections of the thirteenth-century world that cut

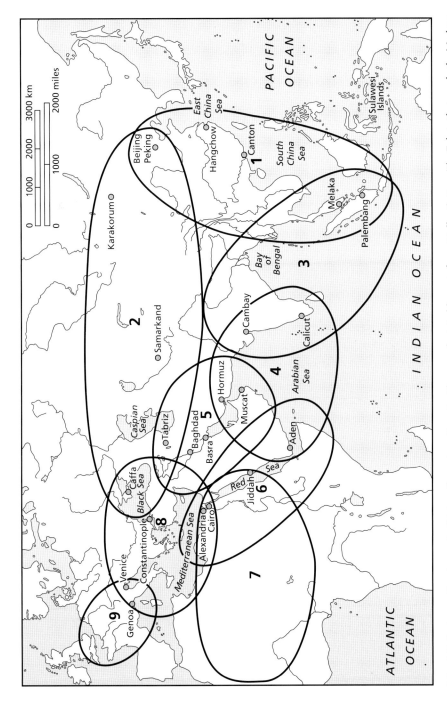

Map 3.2 Systems of exchange in thirteenth-century Eurasia. The map depicted here, is from Riello, *Cotton: The Fabric that made the Modern World*, p. 26. Riello's map is based on the map by Abu-Lughod, with some adjustments.

through its geographical and cultural distinctions and its political boundaries. She argues that there were eight distinct yet overlapping regions in the world of the late thirteenth- and early fourteenth-centuries.[20] According to her, there was a 'European subsystem', which included the southern Netherlandish early industrial centres of Bruges and Ghent, the cities of the Champagne fairs in northern France, and the commercial hubs of Genoa and Venice; a second sub-system in the heartland of Eurasia, which combines the Mongol steppe zone, Baghdad and the Persian Gulf, and Cairo and the Red Sea; and a third, Asian sub-system, which incorporates the Indian Ocean and the region stretching from the Malacca Straits to the Chinese empire. Abu-Lughod's eight distinct regions are thus subdivided into three sub-systems, each with their own centres of gravity.

The key to her argument is not so much the separation into regions and sub-systems, but the overlap between them. Each of the separate regions formed a distinct unit, within which merchants could move reasonably freely, and expect familiar trade practices and a coherent assemblage of goods considered desirable. In the case of the Southern Song empire, for example, the merchants could easily trade their goods throughout the empire, but also with the merchants of the Jin empire in the north, and southwards in Southeast Asia. At the same time, the northern parts of China, which first formed part of the Song empire, then fell into the hands of the invading Jin forces and eventually became part of the Mongol empire, were also connected to the steppe lands of Central Asia. Genghis Khan's (1162–1227) rise to power in the Mongol steppe in the late twelfth century and his early thirteenth-century conquests in Central Asia had begun the creation of a single political entity that stretched across Central Asia.[21] Eventually, by the mid-fourteenth century, the Mongol empire that was Genghis' legacy stretched from the coast of China in the east all the way to the Adriatic Sea in the far west. The key nodes that connected the trading worlds of southern China and Southeast Asia with the Silk Roads and the Mongol steppe were the cities located where the circles overlap: the capital of the Yuan regime in Dadu (today's Beijing) and the central Mongolian city of Karakorum, the capital of the Mongol Empire between 1235 and 1260. Similarly, the Southeast-Asian port cities along the Malacca Straits formed the nodes that connected the trading networks of the South China Sea with the Indian Ocean networks.[22] All kinds of Central Asian, South and Southeast Asian goods considered desirable by consumers in Southern Song China entered the markets in China through these networks. Similarly, China's white porcelains travelled vast distances through the same networks and nodes.

Abu-Lughod's visualization of these overlapping networks, and her analysis of the ways in which these regions formed their own trade systems made a significant contribution to our understanding of the global picture in the late thirteenth- and early fourteenth centuries. The thirteenth- and fourteenth-century worlds consisted of separate cultural realms, divided for example by linguistic and religious divisions, but at the same time, there were significant connections between these separate cultural realms, forged by the mobility of people, animals, ideas and things. The writings of Marco Polo are a useful illustration of the ways in which such connections came into being during this period. The account of the thirteenth-century Venetian who travelled along the Silk Routes was what made the distant lands of the previously unimaginable east imaginable for the first time for late-medieval Europeans. Polo's *The Description of the World* brought places like Samarkand, Baghdad and Zaitun to the attention of his European readers, and conjured up images of material goods such as silk, porcelain and cloth of gold.[23] Very few Europeans outside the highest religious and secular elites would have personally owned goods that had come from the Far East, and even fewer would have followed in Marco Polo's footsteps and travelled along the Silk Roads, but his stories were widely read and his readers could form an image of 'the East', including the lands referred to as Cathay (China).[24] The famous white porcelain vase, now amongst the most treasured possessions of the San Marco in Venice and known as the Polo vase, exemplifies the material goods that reached Europe from China.[25] It is not really relevant whether the man we know as Marco Polo actually served at the court of Khubilai Khan, and whether he carried back this vase with his own hands. What matters is the existence of a series of connections that stretched across Central Asia, between the trade networks of Northern Europe and East Asia and between the merchants in Venice and the potters in Jingdezhen.

The Appearance of a Different Kind of White

At some point over the course of the thirteenth century, the goods manufactured in the kilns of Jingdezhen started to look different. Figure 3.2 illustrates the point. Instead of the nearly transparent glaze covering the fine white clay, we see a white clay that is covered more thickly with a less transparent, blue-toned glaze. There is a lotus scroll moulded on the interior, and a flower medallion in the centre of the interior. While such moulded decorations pressed into the body before the glaze is applied are not new,

Figure 3.2 Bowl with an egg-white glaze (*luanbai*), also known as *shufu*. There is a lotus scroll moulded on the interior, and a flower medallion in the centre of the interior. There is a mark on the interior wall. Jingdezhen, Yuan dynasty. Sir Percival David Collection, PDF.452; ©The Trustees of the British Museum.

the thickness and opacity of the glaze are. The term for this glaze is *luanbai*, literally, the white of eggshells or egg-white. Technically speaking, this glaze contains a lower quantity of plant ash, leaving a higher proportion of the silica and quartz elements that do not dissolve in firing, which in turn had the effect of reducing the transparency.[26] Recent research has also suggested that the methods used for firing the porcelains, including a slower cooling process, were changed so as to enhance the opacity of the wares.[27]

The *qingbai* pieces manufactured in Jingdezhen were made in elegant shapes that showed off the bluish tinge of the glaze: bowls with pinched shapes to create the impression of flower petals, or boxes and vases impressed with a mould to create decorations in relief. The thicker and matter *luanbai* glaze did not lend itself as well to the use of shaping to show off the variety in the tinge of the glaze, and thus relied more heavily on carving and moulding to add decorative patterns in the shape of flowers and dragons. When the mould was incised with a pattern, then the ceramic body of the vessel was flattened by the mould, except where the incised pattern was, leaving the decorations to appear proud on the surface. Using this method, moulds could also be used to place characters under the glaze on the surface of the bowl. A significant number of *luanbai* pieces have been marked in this way with the characters *shu* and *fu*, which has given the name 'shufu wares' to this group. They are not exclusively marked with *shu* and *fu*; we also have pieces with *tai* and *xi*, and with *zhong* and *he*, terms that could variously be read as abbreviated terms for high offices of the imperial administration and felicitous expressions meaning long life, or peace and justice.[28] The significance of these inscriptions has been debated at length, to date without much consensus.[29] The inscriptions could well refer to specific high offices within the Yuan imperial court, but more likely, they suggest the use of these vessels for ritual purposes within a variety of imperial offices. While the court may have wished to imprint its exclusive ownership over these wares, and thereby over the symbolic value of the rituals in which these vessels were used, imperial control over this type of vessel was far from complete, as the appearance of so-called *shufu*-type wares throughout Southeast Asia suggests.

New scientific methods of testing available to archaeologists have confirmed the difference between *qingbai* and *luanbai*, especially in the case of the excavations of the Hutian kilns, located to the south of the town of Jingdezhen. They covered an area of 40,000 square metres, and were in constant use from the tenth to the seventeenth centuries.[30] This kiln site yielded hundreds of broken pieces of ceramics, the vast majority of which were white-glazed ceramics, including *qingbai* and *luanbai* shards from the Song and Yuan dynasties.[31] Extensive research has confirmed that both the glaze recipe and the firing methods changed during this period.[32] What has been more difficult to confirm are the reasons for these changes. Some have suggested that the Mongols preferred the white of *luanbai* wares, more solid and matte than the high gloss of the transparent *qingbai* glazes because of their preference for the colour white.[33] Indeed, for the Mongols, the colour white had strong associations with blessings and good fortune, and was used to underscore political power by means of a white banner or standard.[34] As we saw, however, white porcelain had already gained imperial favour during the Northern Song dynasty, and cannot really be regarded as an innovation under Mongol rule.[35]

Others have pointed to differences in the bodies: slightly different compositions of the clay used for the bodies may have required a thicker, more matte glaze to cover the impurities of the body. This last suggestion raises the question of why the change in clay. Most common is the suggestion that local supplies of kaolinized clay had been exhausted and were replaced with a combination of two ingredients: a locally found porcelain stone, and a clay found in the Gaoling mountain range referred to as kaolin. The latter substance is usually described as refractory, meaning it only melts at very high temperatures, and is described in Chinese as providing the bone structure of the porcelain body, while the more fusible porcelain stone provides the bulk or the flesh of the body.[36] The combination of the two ingredients for making porcelain had other advantages, too: the relative proportion of the two ingredients could be adjusted depending on the firing temperature of the kiln to create the best results.[37]

We have, thus far, observed two transformations that set the porcelain manufactures of Jingdezhen apart from other places that also manufactured white-glazed ceramics during the Southern Song and Yuan dynasties. Firstly, the discovery of a nearby supply of kaolin, which could be added to white clay, to create a substance that was flexible enough to create thin, delicate and detailed forms, strong enough to hold its shape when it had been formed into large vessels, and refractable enough so that it could be fired at high temperatures, thereby creating an extremely hard material. White clay could be found throughout southern China and in parts of northern China, but by itself, especially in its non-kaolinitic form, could not be fired at very high temperatures. While kaolin occurs in many parts of the world, usable deposits of kaolin were and are rare, not only in China but throughout the world, especially a supply so easily reachable by river transportation, and found as close to the surface as they are in the Gaoling mountains.[38] And secondly, the lowering of the proportion of plant ash in the glaze, which meant that the glaze became less thin and liquid in the firing, and left more trace elements unmelted, leading to a thicker and less translucent glaze. And while it may well be possible to point to specific factors present in the context that suggest intentionality behind these developments, it is equally possible that environmental factors, i.e. the increasing scarcity of certain resources and their replacement with others, explain these transformations, or indeed, that these developments are the result of a combination of a variety of factors. The product that emerged from these changes, the matte, egg-white porcelains that have been referred to as *shufu* wares after the characters imprinted upon the wares, or as *luanbai* after the colour of the glaze, were clearly popular within China and beyond, as they have been found in excavations throughout the trading world of the Chinese.

In 1127, the northern provinces that had been part of the Song empire (Map 2.1) came under the control of the Jin empire (1125–1234), which stretched into the northern steppe lands inhabited mostly by nomadic groups. Throughout the thirteenth and early fourteenth centuries, under the regime of the Southern Song (1127–1279), the most immediate markets for white porcelains from the southern provinces were located just north of the Jin-Song border. Further to the west, the Western Xia dynasty had already been established by Tangut peoples in 1038, and from its key location in what are today's provinces of Gansu and Ningxia, this regime positioned itself as a kind of middleman in all negotiations with the traders of the Silk Road territories. Excavations in Western Xia and Jin territories have all yielded substantial amounts of white porcelains, many of which had been manufactured in the southern provinces and were brought there by trade.[39] Less visible in the archaeological record are the quantities of silver, tea and silk that were also traded regularly from the provinces under Southern Song control, although these were regarded as tribute payments, and therefore show up in the historical records of the period.

After the unification of Central Asia under the Mongol regime of Genghis Khan's descendants and the establishment of the Yuan dynasty in 1279, traders on the overland trade routes into Central Asia carried even larger quantities of goods between China and its Inner Asian trade partners. In earlier centuries, these routes into Central Asia had been far less travelled. Only intrepid individuals ventured out there, such as the seventh-century monk Xuanzang, who travelled to Inner Asia and northern India in search of Buddhist knowledge and texts.[40] Xuanzang's journey continued to fire the imagination about this region for many centuries; his story featured in numerous tales, novels, plays and paintings.[41] But the associations were with the endless dangers and supernatural adventures Xuanzang encountered along the Silk Roads, with his trusted helpers, including Sun Wukong the monkey king, and with the Western Paradise and (Buddhist) Enlightenment his journey came to represent. The territories to the West of the boundaries of the empire largely remained part of a spiritual and/or fictional realm. Moreover, nomadic peoples with very different cultural practices and religious beliefs from the Han-Chinese population inhabited these infertile lands.[42] In the past, the relationship between groups that lead a nomadic existence in Central Asia and the sedentary Han-Chinese population had frequently been tense; the Han perceived the nomadic groups as posing a threat to their lifestyle and built defences to keep them out. More recently, it has become clear to what extent the two groups were in fact mutually dependent on each other: the nomadic groups provided animals, animal products and know-how of and access to the rich resources of Central Asia and its trade routes, while the sedentary agriculturalists traded their grains and manufactured goods.[43] Undoubtedly, the geographical area of the Silk Roads was of great significance for the Chinese empire, because it was from here that large supplies of goods unavailable within the empire were sourced, such as horses, jade and other precious stones, pigments, metals, aromatics and drugs, to name but a few.[44] Regions now known as Gansu and Xinjiang, the Mongol capital of Karakorum and Central Asian cities like Samarkand, Nishapur and Tabriz formed part of very different cultural realms. With climates and landscapes inhospitable to sedentary agriculture, Gansu, Xinjiang and the regions further to the West were largely inhabited by mobile or nomadic populations, who spoke a variety of Central Asian languages, and had social, cultural and political systems that differed from the regions predominantly inhabited by Han-Chinese populations. Yet the movement of people, goods and ideas along these trade routes also created and enhanced the connections that brought the sites of ceramics manufacture in China within the reach of remote peoples.

The Overseas Trade in White Wares

Between the early twelfth century and the mid-fourteenth century, white wares made in Jingdezhen were distributed not only along overland trade routes but also beyond the maritime boundaries of the Chinese empire. Song and Yuan China's immediate neighbours, Korea and Japan, were important consumers of Chinese porcelains: large quantities of Song dynasty ceramics have been found in Japan, both in museum collections and in archaeological excavations, and fine pieces of *qingbai* porcelain from Jingdezhen have been found in tombs dated to the Goryeo dynasty in Korea (918–1392).[45] Perhaps the best example of the volume of the export of high-fired wares from China comes from the fourteenth-century Sinan shipwreck. In 1977, the National Museum of Korea (Kungnip chungang pangmulgwan) in Seoul published a catalogue to accompany the exhibition entitled 'Sinan haejŏ munmu' or 'Relics from the seabed near Sinan'.[46] It featured several hundred items that had been recovered from the seabed only a year earlier, after a fisherman had found a piece of celadon in his nets, leading to their discovery. The location of the wreck of this fully loaded Chinese vessel near the coast of Bangchuk-ri on the island of Jeungdo-myeon, which forms part of the island region Sinan-gun in South Jeolla Province, suggests the ship was hugging the Korean coast on its way to Japan (Map 3.3).

The wooden ship must have drifted off course and hit rough waters before sinking between the numerous small islands off the south-western tip of the South Korean peninsula. The wooden hull measured 28 metres long

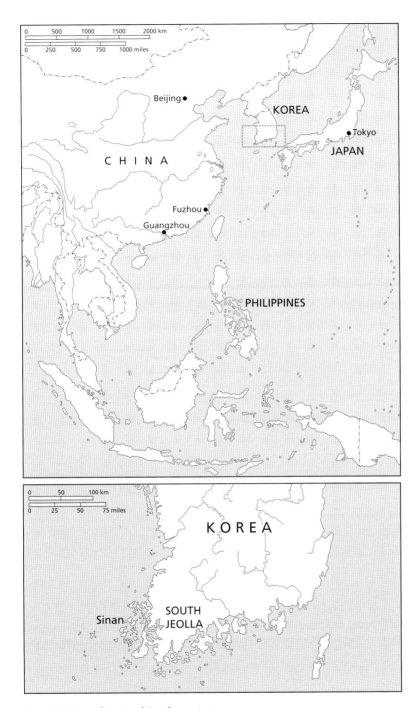

Map 3.3 Map of East and Southeast Asia.

and 9 metres wide, and had been embedded in the seabed for 600 years; most of the hull had been eaten away by shipworm, leaving behind the part submerged in mud out of reach of the worms.[47] The catalogue was published in English and Korean, so the team of maritime archaeologists, historians and museum curators must have had some inkling of the international importance of this find. It would take some time, however, for the significance of the fisherman's find to become fully clear.

The following year, volume 24 of the 1978 issue of *Oriental Art* featured a short piece on the discovery by John Ayers, who had established the Far Eastern Department at the Victoria and Albert Museum only a few years earlier.[48] It was not until the next year that the first proper analysis of the wreck's cargo appeared. Li Dejin, Jiang Zhongyi and Guan Jiakun of the Chinese Academy of Social Sciences published their report in *Kaogu*, China's foremost journal of archaeology.[49] Their opening sentences reveal what they were most impressed by: 'According to the report, 7,168 historical relics were retrieved from the shipwreck. Amongst them, there are 6,457 pieces of porcelain, including 3,466 pieces of celadon, 2,281 pieces of white porcelain, 117 pieces of black glazed wares (Tianmu glaze), 79 pieces of Jun-style ware, and 574 other ceramic pieces. Furthermore, there are 230 metalware objects: 130 bronze pieces, such as candle holders, incense burners and weights, and brass cymbals and cooking pots. There are 33 bags of copper cash, altogether 106,000 pieces'.[50] The coins were strung into bundles and tagged to indicate their owners.[51] The list continues and ends with the observation that this probably amounts to about a third of the cargo, with the rest still lingering on the seabed.

Over the following years, further research was carried out, especially on the seabed, retrieving many more items as well as the hull of the ship itself. An international symposium was devoted to the Sinan wreck in 1982, with an exhibition in Tokyo and a full set of proceedings published in Nagoya; the American maritime archaeologist D. H. Keith published an article in the journal *Archaeology*, several studies appeared in *International Journal of Nautical Archaeology*, and further research was carried out in China.[52] We now know that the figures Li, Jiang and Guan reported were indeed underestimates. The mixed coin assemblage in the cargo, for example, is now said to amount to 28 tons of copper cash, i.e. 8,000,000 coins. The ceramic pieces come to a total of 16,800 pieces, 10,000 of which are high quality porcelains, and 6,000 of which have survived whole.[53] Perhaps more importantly, researchers have been able to use the packing slips in the cargo to date the wreck more precisely than before.[54] It now seems the ship was loaded in Fujian in 1323, was bound for the Japanese port town of Hakata (present day Fukuoka), and specifically to the Higashiyama Temple in Kyoto, one of the five great *zen* monasteries of Kyoto.

The size and value of the cargo of the Sinan wreck made this an exceptional find, but this ship was by no means the only ship that travelled between the eastern seaboard in China past the Korean coast to Japan. Charlotte von Verschuer's analysis of mostly documentary evidence has shown both the quantity and the importance of these trade connections.[55] She suggests that ships with a tonnage of 150–200 metric tons regularly sailed between China and Japan, and that a wide range of commodities from China were in demand in Japan: copper coins, ceramics, silks, aromatic plants and scholarly writings (books and tracts). For their part, the Japanese sent ships on an almost yearly basis to China, to export gold, silver and pearls, prestigious craft objects like weapons and lacquered goods, timber, and mercury and sulphur.[56] New discoveries in nautical archaeology have already made and continue to make a significant difference: over 200 shipwreck sites have been identified along the coastline of the Korean peninsula, of which thus far only a fraction have been systematically investigated.[57] Clearly, throughout the Goryeo period (918–1392 CE), and especially during the latter half, there were active trade connections between China, Korea and Japan, in which white porcelain played a key role. Janet Abu-Lughod's map (Map 3.2) does not include Korea and Japan within any of its encircled regions, but the porcelain records show that the circle enclosing the Chinese empire should also include Korea and Japan.

Chinese ceramics were also in high demand in Southeast Asia. When a scholar-official named Zhao Rugua served as the Quanzhou Inspector of Maritime Trade (*Shibosi*) in the early thirteenth century, he made the comment that merchants from all over Southeast Asia were trading in porcelain.[58] Porcelain was by no means traded exclusively; Zhao Rugua listed it merely as one product amongst a vast variety of traded goods, including precious metals, textiles, especially silk, incense and different kinds of woods, medicinal substances like rhubarb root, dyestuffs, wine, sugar, glass, tin, and so forth. But he was specific about the place names and the products for each country, and ceramics goods are not mentioned for every country. Merchants from places like Zhenla (now Cambodia), Sanfoqi (the Samboja Kingdom, which scholars have generally equated to Srivijaya) and Shepo (now the island of Java) were all said to be trading ceramics. Most of the references to ceramics provide no details on shapes or designs, except for one instance, in the list of goods exchanged with Java, where Zhao Rugua specifically describes the ceramics as *qingbai*, bluish-green and white.[59] By the time the diplomat Zhou Daguan visited Cambodia at the very end of the thirteenth century, trade with China was very well established. 'Land and people of Cambodia' (*Zhenla fengtu ji*), Zhou Daguan's description of a year-long journey to what is now Angkor (Cambodia) in 1296–1297, states that green wares (celadon) from Quanzhou and Chuzhou were amongst the most sought-after Chinese goods.[60] Finally, Wang Dayuan, a fourteenth-century imperial official based in Quanzhou and author of 'Brief History of Island-dwelling Peoples' (*Daoyi zhilüe*), told of two voyages in which he covered Southeast Asia and the Indian Ocean, and made mention of the use of Chinese ceramics in roughly half of the 100 countries he visited.[61] Wang also listed the various products exported during the Yuan dynasty, including various (precious) metals such as tin, iron, copper, gold and silver; textiles including brocades and satins, but also blue and red cottons; porcelains and earthenware; and manufactured items such as gold and silver ornaments, lacquerwares and beads.[62] These thirteenth- and fourteenth-century records were written with different audiences in mind, but they all seemed to wish to suggest that manufactured commodities flowed from the Chinese empire into Southeast Asia, and that a wide range of goods from Java, Sumatra, Borneo and the numerous smaller islands in the South China Sea were exported to the Chinese empire.

The archaeological record bears the accounts of these authors out, confirming the widespread presence of porcelain in the trade goods exchanged between the Song empire and its nearby neighbours throughout Southeast Asia. Excavations carried out in the Philippines, for example carried out in the late nineteenth century when this part of the world came under American control, yielded large quantities of *qingbai* ceramics.[63] The vast quantities of ceramics that have been excavated, many of which are now in the collections of the University of Michigan Museum in Ann Arbor, illustrate that the trade and exchange between China and the Philippines was especially vibrant and diverse during the Yuan dynasty, continuing into the Ming dynasty (1368–1644). During this time both finely potted white wares and sturdy, more heavily potted, objects for use in ritual and ceremony, were exported to the Philippines by the Chinese.[64] Ongoing excavations at Satingpra on the eastern coast of southern Thailand also continue to reveal the sizable trade in *qingbai* ceramics carried out here.[65] A fourteenth-century shipwreck provides further evidence of the extent of these connections. This mid-fourteenth-century Chinese ship, now known as the Turiang wreck, was heading to Borneo with a cargo that included large quantities of not only Chinese ceramics, but also Thai and Vietnamese ceramics. Her journey came to an end in the South China Sea, off the coast of Malaysia. Many of the Thai and Vietnamese ceramics have underglaze decorations painted in slip including stylized fish and floral designs and calligraphic scrolls.⁶⁶ The 'multinational ceramic cargo' of the Turiang, as Sten Sjostrand and Claire Barnes have called it, shows not only that the Chinese were actively trading throughout Southeast Asia, but also that the Chinese potters were not alone: they were in direct competition with the Thai and Vietnamese potters.

Sites excavated in Sri Lanka show that the Chinese traders did not limit themselves to the territories that could be reached via the East and South China Seas. They also sailed regularly into the Indian Ocean.⁶⁷ Until the late twelfth century, the connections between the Coromandel Coast, the Malacca Straits and the entrance into the South China Sea were to some extent controlled by the kingdom of Srivijaya.⁶⁸ This maritime state was based on a mixture of Buddhist and Hindu beliefs and had its capital on the island of Sumatra. From there it extended its power across Southeast Asia, into the Indian Ocean to the West and into the South China Sea in the east. Between the seventh and twelfth centuries, Srivijaya was a wealthy and powerful force in the Southeast Asian maritime world by serving as entrepot for all trade with China. Together with its coastal counterpart, the Khmer polity of Funan, Srivijaya paid regular tribute to the Song state, where Srivijaya was known as Sanfoqi.⁶⁹ The decline of Srivijaya in the twelfth and thirteenth centuries opened up the trade routes to the island kingdom of Java, but perhaps more significantly for the trajectory of this region: it opened up a pathway for conversion to Islam. Historical evidence shows that Islam's spread was gradual and driven predominantly by Muslim merchants, whose trade created connections between China, the Malabar Coast, the Malay Peninsula, Sumatra, Brunei, Java, the Southern Philippines and Malacca.⁷⁰

The spread of Islam connected what Prange has called 'Monsoon Islam' with the Chinese empire.⁷¹ To visualize these connections, it may be useful to look at the routes the famous fourteenth-century Moroccan traveller Ibn Battuta (1304–1369) chose for his journey. He started in 1325 with a journey to Mecca via the North African coast and Cairo, Tabriz and Basra, Jeddah and Aden on the Arab peninsula and south along the East African coast to cities like Mogadishu, Mombasa, Zanzibar and Kilwa. Between 1332 and 1347 he travelled eastwards via a more northerly route, reaching Samarkand after passing to the north of the Black Sea and the Caspian Sea. Delhi, Uttar Pradesh, the Malabar Coast and the Maldives, Sri Lanka, Malaysia, Quanzhou on the South China Coast, and eventually home via Shiraz and Damascus – Ibn Battuta left very few places untouched. Over his lifetime, Ibn Battuta traversed numerous seas – the Mediterranean, the Red Sea, the Black Sea, the Persian Gulf, the Arabian Sea and the Bay of Bengal (in other words, the Indian Ocean), the Malacca Straits, the South China Sea and the East China Sea – and at no stage did he leave the *Dar al-Islam* (lit. the House of Peace), the realm within which Islam could be practiced peacefully.

Wherever Ibn Battuta arrived, he found communities of believers with whom he shared the main outlines of belief and practice, even if he felt compelled to comment on the minutiae of difference in religious observation, and was able to gain status and employment as judge (*qadi*), ruling in accordance with Islamic religious law on the basis of his legal training in Fez.[72] Ibn Battuta was certainly not the first Islamic commentator on China, but like Marco Polo's text, Ibn Battuta's travel account was widely read, and helped circulate knowledge throughout the extended world of Islam.[73] Here is his description, for example, of making porcelain:

> The Chinese pottery (porcelain) is manufactured only in the towns of Zaytun and Sin-kalan. It is made of the soil of some mountains in that district, which takes fire like charcoal, as we shall relate subsequently. They mix this with some stones which they have, burn the whole for three days, then pour water over it. This gives a kind of clay which they cause to ferment. The best quality of (porcelain is made from) clay that has fermented for ten days. The price of this porcelain there is the same as, or even less than, that of ordinary pottery in our country. It is exported to India and other countries, even reaching as far as our own lands in the West, and it is the finest of all makes of pottery.[74]

What surprises Ibn Battuta most, is that these 'finest of all makes of pottery' are exported to India, even reaching 'our lands in the West', where they are clearly highly valued, but that in Zaytun, where they are manufactured, they cost no more than 'ordinary pottery' does in his own country. For many readers, however, it was probably the description of the manufacturing method that stood out most: soil that takes fire like charcoal, clay that ferments for ten days; it must have seemed an unlikely story. Marco Polo had also written about the manufacture of porcelain, and similarly emphasized the unusually long duration of the clay preparation processes.[75] Even if their fourteenth-century readers had never seen this magical material called porcelain or doubted the veracity of this story of patient waiting for clay, Polo and Battuta contributed to a circulation of knowledge and ideas about porcelain that reached far beyond the trajectories of individual pieces of porcelain.

Throughout the Islamic world and going back to as early as the eighth century, we find ample evidence of the export of Chinese *qingbai*.[76] A twelfth-century Chinese record of Persia (*Bosiguo*) describes people with dark skin, who wear their hair in tight curls, and decorate themselves with gold jewelry and blue patterned cloth. Kings are described as seated on tiger skins, riding on elephants, followed by hundreds of attendants with swords, and the author also notes a variety of foods served on porcelain platters.[77] Of course, there was a long tradition of making ceramics throughout the Islamic world, but porcelains from China were held in high regard throughout the region and sometimes used as inspiration for creating new shapes, glazes and designs in Islamic ceramics.[78] Chinese porcelains have turned up in varying quantities in excavations all over the Islamic world, including the Red Sea region. The eleventh and twelfth-century arrival of *qingbai* in Fustat from Aden, Elizabeth Lambourn and Phillip Ackerman-Lieberman have shown, led to discussions, preserved among the Geniza documents in Cairo, about how this hithertofore unknown material should be classified, so that it could be purified and used appropriately.[79] Sometimes the quantities of excavated *qingbai* ware are small: one single *qingbai* shard in an excavation in Karak (Jordan) dated to the thirteenth century.[80] The port of Sharma in Yemen, on the other hand, excavated in 2001 and 2002 by the archaeologist Axelle Rougeulle, has 'the richest corpus of Chinese imports ever found on an Islamic site of this period', with a wide variety of Song porcelains from many of the kilns we discussed in the previous chapter: Jingdezhen, Jizhou, Yue in Zhejiang, the Jian kilns in Fujian, Yaozhou in Shaanxi and Changsha in Hunan.[81] By the fourteenth and fifteenth centuries, Chinese porcelains had become well integrated in the exchange and gift economies around the Red Sea, as Éric Vallet has shown.[82]

The western Indian Ocean of course included the African continent; porcelains manufactured in China also entered into the African trade networks in large quantities. The archaeologist and ceramics expert Zhao Bing has been part of several archaeological excavations along the Swahili Coast, which reaches from Somalia in the north southward to Mozambique and the northern parts of the island of Madagascar. Excavations in the coastal regions of what is now Kenya, most notably in Kilwa Bay, have shown the extent of this trade: vast quantities of *qingbai* shards were found throughout the region.[83] There is also a significant continuity over time, with the earliest pieces of Chinese ceramics reaching the African coast as early as the ninth century, and variation between the periods in terms of the types of wares imported and their provenance in China.[84] But Chinese porcelains were not just offloaded from ships in the ports and used in the immediate vicinity of the coast; they were carried across the African continent, as a single Song-dynasty *qingbai* shard found in Mali testifies.[85]

The traders in the Indian Ocean would have made use of the monsoon winds, just like Ibn Battuta did when he visited the Indian subcontinent.

The various directions of Battuta's travels in the Indian Ocean, westwards to the southern tip of the Arab peninsula and along the African coast and eastward towards Bengal, and to Banda Aceh and the coast of Sumatra, were all driven by the monsoon winds. The entire Indian Ocean that stretched from Madagaskar and the east coast of Africa to the numerous islands of what is now Indonesia, and northwards into the Red Sea and the Persian Gulf was crisscrossed by extensive trade routes that depended on the seasonal pattern of the monsoon. In the winter, the prevailing winds blow from the northeast, sending ships from the Indian subcontinent westwards towards the Arab peninsula, into the Red Sea and southwards along the East African coast. In summer, winds drive ships in the opposite direction, allowing ships to sail from Swahili lands in central East Africa across the Indian Ocean to reach Calicut in south India, Sri Lanka and from there northwards towards Calcutta and Bengal. Long distance trade was certainly possible, and the archaeological evidence of thirteenth-century Chinese porcelains along the coast of Africa demonstrates that goods made in China reached these destinations, but much of the trade and interactions also occurred on a much smaller scale and over shorter distances.

Throughout the thirteenth century, white ceramics manufactured at a variety of sites in southern China, including Jingdezhen, were shipped by traders all over the eastern Afro-Eurasian continent and throughout the Indian Ocean and the China Seas. From a bird's eye perspective, the differences between land and water, between mountains and lowlands, between dry steppe and green fields would be visible and striking. Urban formations might take different shapes, with the spires of cathedrals very distinct from the domed shapes of mosques or the upward-turning eaves of Buddhist temples, as would styles of dress or shapes of sail. Socio-political boundaries would be much harder to perceive than geo-physical separations like mountain ranges, deserts and bodies of water. For a traveller by land or sea, the environmental differences and natural boundaries and barriers mattered, of course, as did the cultural distinctions manifest in the diverse linguistic, religious and legal systems he would have encountered. But beyond those differences, visible from a distant perspective, the traveller on the ground would be able to observe numerous similarities, connections and comparabilities throughout the fourteenth-century world, as indeed Marco Polo, Ibn Battuta and Zhou Daguan did. If one had to represent these connections metaphorically, one would have to turn to a spider's web rather than a series of arrows, a network rather than a linked chain, with multiple nodes rather than a single centre. And throughout all those nodes and networks the presence of white ceramics.

4 | From Cizhou to Jizhou: The Long History of the Emergence of Blue and White Porcelain

This chapter explores the emergence of blue and white porcelain in Jingdezhen. This has often been told as a global story. Cobalt was sourced from Central Asia, and arrived in China by means of Islamic merchants, who moved freely throughout the Mongol empire that extended across the Eurasian landmass. Not only merchants and cobalt circulated throughout Eurasia, but also consumer demands from Central Asia. The emergence of cobalt blue decorations on the type of large white dishes that were popular in the eating practices of the steppe and in Central Asian societies, then, is seen as a story of regional adaptation to global tastes. This chapter adds a distinctly local dimension to this story. It argues that the production of blue and white ceramics benefited not only from the introduction of Central Asian cobalt and consumer demands from outside the Chinese empire, but also from the circulation of local technologies, especially the application of metal-based pigments onto the unglazed surfaces of ceramics to create line-drawings and brush-painted decorations. As we will see, that technology was popular initially in the northern provinces, and moved southwards around the time of the loss of the north to the invading Jin dynasty in the twelfth century. Over the course of the twelfth and thirteenth centuries, southern kilns changed the ways in which ceramics were decorated. No longer were they producing monochromes: wares decorated with a single-coloured glaze; they started to manufacture pieces with patterns and line-drawings under the transparent glaze, first in the nearby Jiangxi kiln site of Jizhou, and only then in Jingdezhen. The introduction of cobalt may well be a global story, but it cannot be understood without adding this local dimension as well.

In 1935, when Sir Percival Victor David (1892–1964) acquired one of the two vases that now carry his name at Sotheby's for £360 (Figure 4.1), he may not have known how influential this piece and its companion vase would go on to become.[1] Known together as the 'David vases', they were made in the by then well-established centre for porcelain manufacture, Jingdezhen in Jiangxi province, during the Yuan dynasty, and in 1351 donated together with an incense burner to a temple in Yushan county, not far from Jingdezhen by a man named Zhang Wenjin.

Figure 4.1 The 'David vases'. Blue and white porcelain vases, Jingdezhen, 1351. H 63.6 cm × W 20.7 cm. Sir Percival David Collection, PDF B613 and B614; ©The Trustees of the British Museum.

Our precise knowledge about the man who presented them and the temple that received them comes from the inscription under the glaze on the side of the vases.[2] 'In Xinzhou circuit, Yushan county, Shuncheng township, Dejiao village in the Thorn-stick Pool Brotherhood, the disciple of the revered supreme master Zhang Wenjin with pleasure donates an incense burner and flower vases – a pair - to pray for and to protect the propriety and prosperity of the whole family and the peace and accord of its sons and daughters'.[3] The vases are a prime example of the advanced skills of the Yuan-dynasty ceramicists in Jingdezhen; the shape of the vases, which had been modelled on bronze examples, the quality of the glaze, but above all the use of the cobalt blue pigment all point to an exceptional piece made by superb craftsmen.

Although we have instances of the use of cobalt to decorate ceramics long before this moment, notably during the Tang dynasty, we have no pieces made in Jingdezhen, decorated with cobalt, that can be given a definite date earlier than these pieces. As a result, the David vases have come to play a key role in the dating of all blue and white ceramics. Because of the precision by which this object can be dated, 1351 has been used as the latest possible date before which (*ante quem*) blue decorations on white ceramics made their appearance. The Sinan shipwreck, dated so precisely to 1323, has also come to play a prominent role in dating the appearance of blue decorations. Ceramics scholars have often taken the complete absence of objects decorated with cobalt blue under the glaze in this substantial shipment of a wide variety of wares as categorical evidence that China did *not* produce any blue and white wares before 1323. There is little doubt about the date of the Sinan shipwreck itself; the packing slips inside the crates on the shipwreck speak for themselves. But those who loaded the ship in 1323 for their assumed customers in Japan simply may have chosen not to include any blue and white wares. Their absence in one place at one specific moment in time cannot serve as conclusive evidence for their absence in all other places at that time. In fact, it has proven extremely difficult to establish when exactly the potters in Jingdezhen first started to incorporate cobalt blue into their decorative schemes. Nonetheless, scholars have often taken the absence of blue and white on the Sinan shipwreck as indicating a date after which (*post quem*) production of blue and white porcelain began in earnest in Jingdezhen. Between 1321 and 1351, the general argument goes, blue pigment made its very first appearance in the ceramic industries of Jingdezhen, and within no more than a few decades, led to the appearance of items of the most extraordinary quality, as represented by the David vases.

The appearance of Adam T. Kessler's book in 2012, provocatively entitled *Song Blue and White Porcelain on the Silk Road*, raises a challenge to the conventional dating of the appearance of blue and white ceramics.[4] Kessler's voluminous study (of a total of 678 pages) is far too complex to do it justice here, but ultimately, his point is simple: blue and white was already in production well before the appearance of the David vases, in fact, already before the Yuan dynasty, hence the title of his book. This overall argument rests on several pillars of evidence. Firstly, archaeological finds (blue and white shards) from northern territories that formed part of the Western Xia (Xi Xia) state (1038–1227) and the Jin dynasty (1115–1234) that have conventionally been cross-dated to the David vases, and thus assumed to date from after 1323. If we do not cross-date these shards with the David vases, but date them instead on the basis of their local context, then it suddenly seems far more likely that they should be dated to the period before 1323. In fact, Kessler uses circumstantial and contextual evidence to suggest that these finds are more likely to date to the Southern Song dynasty, in other words, from before 1279. Secondly, he argues for a reinterpretation of the nomenclature of blue and white porcelain. Kessler posits that textual records of the Song and Yuan dynasties have been misunderstood because of the translation of the term *qingbai* (literally, *qing* means 'blue' and *bai* means 'white') as 'bluish-white' instead of as 'blue and white', as Kessler would have it.[5] If we were to translate *qingbai* as 'blue and white', then suddenly we see a whole range of textual evidence of the presence of this *qingbai* before 1323. Both of these are highly controversial interventions in what is an extremely well-established field of porcelain studies. The use of the David vases for the purpose of dating shards is standard practice; the translation of *qingbai* as 'blue and white' is almost unheard of, as Kessler himself admits.

Kessler has a third string to his bow: the date of the introduction of cobalt into the imperial kilns of Jingdezhen. In his book, he explores the exact nature and impact of the introduction of 'cobalt' into the ceramics manufactures of Jingdezhen, arguing that cobalt already arrived in the Jingdezhen kilns before 1323. In the context of contemporary science as we understand it in the West, the meaning of cobalt might seem uncontroversial. Cobalt (Co, to name it by its chemical name) is one of the metals listed on the periodic table. 'Discovered' in 1735 by George Brandt in Stockholm, the word cobalt comes from the German 'Kobold', which means goblin or evil spirit. The association between evil spirits and this chemical element comes from the difficulties in mining cobalt. Often, cobalt is found in the earth together with arsenic, which was harmful for the miners' health. The physical properties of cobalt are described as follows: 'Cobalt is a sturdy, gray metal, which resembles iron and nickel. Although cobalt is ductile it is also somewhat malleable. […] Next to nickel and iron, cobalt is one of the three naturally occurring magnetic metals. […] Cobalt's melting point is 1495 degrees C with a boiling point of 2870 degrees C. The density is 8.9 grams per cubic centimetre'.[6]

Within Western scientific discourse, this factual, detailed information about atomic mass, magnetic quality, boiling point and density defines what cobalt 'is'. Cobalt fits into a system of classification: it resorts under the transition metals, which in turn are part of inorganic chemistry. If one excavates the history of knowledge about cobalt from this perspective, then indeed it makes some sense to claim that George Brandt 'discovered' cobalt in Stockholm in 1735. Unfortunately, that perspective gets us no closer to an understanding of the history of cobalt in a wider, global context. In the context of the history of China, cobalt is a more complex subject with a history that long predates 1735. The controversies in the literature centre around four separate though related disputed areas: what is the Chinese term for the pigment referred to in Western terminology as cobalt, or to put it another way, what exactly do the various terms in circulation relating to the blue pigment used for ceramics decorations refer to; where is, or are, the places of origin of the blue pigment used in the manufacture of porcelain; how is the pigment created, or, more precisely, what is the chemical composition of the pigment; and when did such pigment come into usage in the manufacture of Chinese porcelain?

Numerous answers have emerged in the very extensive literature that all address one or more of these 'what, where, how, and when' questions, but to date no consensus has been reached. The main sticking point in resolving this issue is that it is difficult to determine whether the different terms in usage in historical documents refer to discrete substances, or whether there is overlap, confusion and imprecision in the application of the different terms. It is conceivable that the various terms refer to distinct source locations, although to date it has not been possible to prove this. There are at least three different possibilities. It could be that the Mongols sourced their cobalt from Central Europe, from the rich mines in the Schneeberg fault in the massif of the Erzgebirge in Saxony to be exact. It could also be that the mines in the Persian Kashan Mountains had yielded the cobalt. But there is also little doubt that from the fifteenth century onwards, the potters used cobalt mined within Chinese territory, and specifically in the mines of Yunnan.[7] One way of distinguishing between the different sources of cobalt (and possibly thereby resolving the issue of the nomenclature in Chinese) is to consider the chemical composition of the pigment. The iron content of cobalt varies significantly, as does the amount of arsenic, depending on where and how it was mined. To date, this research has mostly been done by means of destructive techniques, although new possibilities are becoming available all the time. More problematically, the composition of the cobalt found at the same place could change significantly over time. Finally, the different names applied to cobalt, as well as the source and chemical composition varied significantly over time. There can be little doubt that the blue pigment applied to the few Tang dynasty wares we have is quite different from the blue pigment applied to the single blue and white object identified in the Jizhou kilns, and that these differed again from the fourteenth-century Jingdezhen blue and whites.

Despite ongoing research in these areas, it remains impossible to match the numerous Chinese terms for cobalt with specific chemical substances or to determine the exact source of the pigment used in all the different kilns and at different times. Kessler's painstaking work shows that it is a distinct possibility that cobalt came into use in the porcelain manufactures of southern China *before* 1323. It is clear from Kessler's tone that he has met with (and continues to expect) some resistance in the course of his research.[8] For various reasons, colleagues in China, Taiwan and the West have insisted that the David vases be seen as the extraordinarily successful implementation of a very new technology, dating not only the first introduction and experimentation but also the development and refinement of the use of cobalt decorations to a window of not more than 22 years. For Kessler, what is most innovative, and thus most important about blue and white porcelain is the use of cobalt for the decorations under the glaze. It is undoubtedly true that the colour blue, in combination with the very white surfaces created by the specific type of clays used in Jingdezhen made for a splendid combination that became a sensational commercial success. That success makes some sense if we compare the subtle and understated elegance of the fine monochrome ceramics produced before the Yuan dynasty with the lively patterns and striking colour combination of Yuan-dynasty blue and white. It is the difference between on the one hand, the less accessible imperial taste that was intended to be exclusive, and on the other hand, the easy-access, mass appeal of blue and whites. As fourteenth-century antiques collector Cao Zhao put it in his manual of taste, *Essential criteria for appreciating antiques (Gegu yaolun)*, produced in the late Yuan or early Ming dynasty: when blue and whites were just appearing in the market place, they had a hint of vulgarity.[9] If we see Song monochromes next to Yuan blue and whites, it is indeed almost impossible to believe this development happened in a mere 22 years.

It seems to me, however, that the contrast between Song monochromes and Yuan blue and whites is too stark and leaves out a crucial transitional step. That step is the re-invention and subsequent innovation of the use of underglaze painting. The main argument I would like to make is this: the Jingdezhen innovation of underglaze cobalt-blue decoration on a white ceramic surface relied not only on the introduction of cobalt, but also on the adoption in Jingdezhen of the technique of underglaze painting. When cobalt-blue decorations on white surfaces started to appear, these relied not only on the availability of cobalt-blue pigment, but also on the skill of the Jingdezhen potters to apply this pigment with a small brush on the shaped but unbaked surface of the bodies *before* glazing and firing the object. The ability to do this successfully hinged on skills closely related to the work of painters and calligraphers. Before the 'invention' of blue and white ceramics, the Jingdezhen potters did not use this technology; their skills were located in their work with white and transparent glazes.

This part of my argument centres on a local factor: the introduction of the technology of underglaze painting and calligraphy, which I argue came into Jingdezhen via the nearby ceramics centre of Jizhou. The Jizhou potters, in turn, adopted this technology of underglaze painted decorations from the ceramics centres in the north, collectively known as the Cizhou kilns. My argument can be separated in several sub-arguments as follows: During the Northern Song dynasty, the Cizhou potters used the technique of underglaze painting on ceramics. The technology was not exclusive to Cizhou, but during this time it was hardly used in the sites of ceramic production in the south.[10] The technology of underglaze painting was exported from Cizhou to several places, including to the south, and specifically to Jizhou (Jiangxi province) during the course of the twelfth century. During the thirteenth century, it was the Jizhou potters who experimented with a variety of styles, including underglaze painting on a white surface. By the end of the thirteenth century, and into the early fourteenth century, the Jizhou kilns started to decline, and potters and the technology moved to Jingdezhen, where it made possible the transition from monochrome ceramics to wares decorated in blue and white. Below, I will trace the connections between ceramics production sites located in the north and those in the south through the movement of people and objects in light of the southward migrations of the twelfth and thirteenth centuries, making the case for the importance of a connection between the Cizhou kilns, and the southern production centres of Jizhou and Jingdezhen.

This argument shows that the history of the emergence of blue and white porcelain in Jingdezhen cannot be told as a Jingdezhen story alone. Instead, it has to be seen as part of a bigger story that starts with the production of ceramics decorated with underglaze, brush-painted decorations. That story begins not in Jingdezhen, but in the northern provinces with the production of Cizhou and Cizhou-style wares, and from there moves first to Jizhou in Jiangxi, and only then to Jingdezhen. It is true that in Jingdezhen, that production relied on the use of cobalt as a pigment for the brush-painted decorations, which led to the striking combination of blue decorations on a white surface. The use of cobalt for the creation of pigment was in itself undoubtedly a significant innovation, but the use of metal-based pigments for underglaze, brush-painted decorations was not. In the northern provinces, potters had applied underglaze, metal-based pigments on light-coloured surfaces since the tenth century, especially in the production of Cizhou-type ceramics. Without the development of this technology in the north, and its move to the southern provinces, Jingdezhen's innovative use of cobalt may not have been possible.

Cizhou and Cizhou-type Ceramics

The history of the group of wares broadly referred to as Cizhou wares goes back to archaeological finds from tombs dating to the sixth century, but more generally, production in this region is assumed to have started during the Five Dynasties period in the tenth century.[11] During the Song, Jin and Yuan dynasties, two main centres in present-day Hebei province were manufacturing Cizhou ceramics, each encompassing a cluster of separate kilns: at Pengcheng near the city of Handan, and at Guantai in Ci county, the county that gave the wares their name.[12] But as recent and ongoing archaeological investigations reveal, similar wares were produced far beyond the confines of the prefecture of Cizhou in the Song Dynasty. Production stretched from southern Hebei province to northern and central Henan Province, including Tangyin in the Central Plains, and Shanxi and Shandong provinces.[13] By Ming times, Ci county in southern Hebei was the only remaining site of any significance, and production has continued here on a small scale until today.[14] The appearance of Cizhou wares varies widely, but many have a cream or brown-coloured base layer (or slip) that was applied to mask the colour of the baked clay itself, which was often a rather unattractive greyish colour. This base layer then formed the background for further decorations in a range of techniques: the application of a

Figure 4.2 Glazed stoneware vessel for wine storage, decorated in sgraffito technique. Cizhou, fourteenth century. Collection KVVAK, Rijksmuseum, Amsterdam. Inv. no. AK-MAK-108.

coloured glaze to this surface, brown or black decorations in an iron-based pigment painted on the cream-coloured base layer or patterns created by carving or incising the layer of slip, revealing the contrasting colour underneath the slip. The vessel in Figure 4.2 has this effect of a darker glaze into which a flower pattern has been carved, revealing the lighter-brown colour of the body itself.

The shapes varied quite widely, but so-called *guan* or wine-jars, large vessels for the storage of alcohol (also produced in large volume in this region), and oblong ceramic pillows are most common.[15] Although the

Figure 4.3 Gray stoneware pillow with underglaze painted decoration. Cizhou ware, Song-Yuan dynasty. 13.4 × 22.9 cm. Cleveland Museum of Art. Gift of Mrs Langdon Warner 1915.506.

wares from this region, now commonly referred to as Cizhou-type wares (*Cizhou yao xi*) were never considered to be imperial ware, they have long had a collector's value, and can be found in all major museums with a Chinese ceramics collection, including the Shanghai Museum and the National Museum of China. The Handan Museum probably has the largest collection, but the British Museum, the Metropolitan Museum of Art in New York, the Victoria and Albert Museum in London, the Asian Art Museum in San Francisco, and the Chicago Art Institute also have substantial collections of Cizhou ware.[16]

Broadly speaking, if we look at the history of Chinese ceramics, then we see that from the Han dynasty until the late eighth or early ninth century, Chinese ceramic wares were glazed. Only rarely were any decorations applied to the body before it was glazed, with the only exception perhaps the iron-brown spots that appear on certain greenwares (celadons).[17] Then, in the late Tang dynasty, painted ornamentation under the glaze suddenly began to appear, not in one but in two assumingly unrelated locations: in Hunan province at the Tongguan kilns near Changsha, and in Sichuan province at the Qionglai kilns.[18] The underglaze decorations we see on these Tang dynasty wares are sketchily painted designs, sometimes described as 'blurred', in bird, flower and splashed patterns.[19] They were popular while these wares were produced, but they were not continued in style or technology when the production in Sichuan and Hunan came to an end.[20] To date no one has been able to identify a direct link between the ninth and early tenth-century wares of the southern kilns of Changsha and Qionglai, and the emergence of painted decorations on Cizhou wares in the north of China from the tenth century onwards.[21] It is clear, however, that the practice of painting decorative patterns under the glaze was one of the many styles of decorations in use by the potters in the Cizhou region, and emerged as early as the late tenth century. And instead of blurred and splashed patterns, we find finely painted flowers, plants and animals, detailed patterns and geometric shapes that cover the surface in a systematic fashion (Figure 4.3).

The black painted decorations in the black-and-white ceramics from Cizhou were created by the use of a mineral (magnetite, or magnetic iron oxide), commonly found in the iron ore reserves of northern China. Magnetite was used by mixing this mineral with a small quantity of clear slip or glaze and applying it with a thin brush. The style of painting on Cizhou ceramics is closely related to painting on paper and silk and covers a similarly wide range of subject matter: themes from nature, human figures, animal subjects and calligraphic texts. In comparison to the high aesthetics of the imperial wares of the Northern Song, the appeal of these painted wares is their simplicity and directness. As Li and Kwan put it, they 'cannot be said to be masterpieces, but they were true to life, the life of the lowest levels of society; they were simple and unadorned, genuine and true'.[22] Not only the subject matter but also the style of painting ranged widely, from broad-stroke decorative patterns to small-scale, fine-brush calligraphic paintings and highly detailed narrative designs.

It appears, then, that in the northern provinces, from the tenth century, there was a wide-ranging production of ceramic objects with decorations applied by brush to the ceramic bodies. In the southern provinces during this same period, vessels tended to be monochrome: white clays covered with transparent glazes in the case of *qingbai*, various clays covered with greenish glazes in the case of Yue wares and celadons, and grey and brown clays covered with dark glazes in the case of blackwares. Clearly production varied, depending on the quality of the local clay and its colour after firing, the availability of minerals and other ingredients for pigments and glazes, and, presumably,

consumer preferences, which were more or less defined regionally, as stated
in Jiang Qi's 'Notes on Ceramics'. But as we saw in the same text, consumer
demand also transcended regional boundaries, and locally produced goods
were transported across vast distances to meet that consumer demand.
Ceramic goods from northern and southern kilns circulated throughout the
realm. A recent survey of archaeological materials found in hoards dating to
the late tenth, eleventh and early twelfth centuries by Song Donglin confirms
this circulation of goods. He looked at the distribution of ceramic wares in
hoards found in four different regions that cover mostly the northern territory
of the Chinese empire, and a small number of hoards from the southwest. Of
course, it was the northern territories where most of the fighting took place,
and where people were forced to leave their possessions behind if and when
they decided to flee the invading Jürchen, so it is unsurprising that the majority
of the hoards is found in the north. A total of 38 hoards yielded 1,800 pieces of
ceramics, including 86 pieces of Cizhou ware found in seven separate hoards.
The results clearly show the distribution of wares made at the northern Ding
kilns and the southern Rao (Jingdezhen) wares throughout all four regions.[23]
Interestingly, it was only those two types, Ding and Rao, that were found in all
regions; most of the other wares, including Cizhou wares, were found closer to
the site of their production.

 This pattern changed, however, during the thirteenth century. Urban
areas were prime sites for circulation of goods from all over the empire.
In the great city of Yangzhou in Jiangsu, for example, archaeological
excavations at North Gate have yielded Yuan-dynasty ceramics from
Cizhou kilns in the north as well as the great southern kilns in Longquan,
Jingdezhen and Jizhou, suggesting a wide-ranging mixing of objects and
designs in Yangzhou.[24] One splendid example of Cizhou pieces finding
their way to Jiangxi consumers is a pair of vases, with a brown floral-
pattern design painted on a cream-coloured slip under a clear glaze, placed
inside a grave in the mid-thirteenth century.[25] The pattern is known as an
interlocking waterweed design, and covers the entire surface of the vase
apart from a series of continuous dark bands around the base of the vases.[26]
The two vases stand over 52 cm tall, and were excavated in 1986 from a
tomb in Ruichang city in Jiangxi, where they are now on display in the
local museum. Scholars have some disagreements over where exactly these
vases were manufactured; either in Cizhou in Hebei, or at the Bacun kilns
in Yuzhou prefecture in Henan.[27] Either way, these vases are the product of
northern kilns, but buried in a southern tomb in 1257.[28]

 Jiangxi tombs often contained northern ceramics, including Ding wares,
Jun wares and Cizhou wares. Ding wares were particularly popular in the

south, it seems. A pair of vases with carved peony patterns made at the kilns in Dingzhou in southern Hebei was excavated in 1968 from a grave in Yongxin county in Jizhou. The vases were dated to the first year of the Yuanyou reign period (1086). A tomb excavated in 1972 in Poyang county, part of the same prefecture that Jingdezhen belonged to, contained several Ding vases, bowls and plates that were dated to the early twelfth century.[29] The British Museum collection also includes a shard of white-glazed porcelain, carved with a phoenix. It was made in the north at the Ding kilns but found in the south: in Yonghe county in Ji'an in south-central Jiangxi.[30] Finally, a late Song-dynasty Ding vase was excavated in Wuyuan county (now in Jiangxi, but then part of the region known as Huizhou). The tomb belonged to the magistrate of Leping county (bordering Jingdezhen), Wang Chengyi and his wife.[31]

More evidence of the circulation of northern goods in the south came to light with the 1980 discovery of a large Yuan-dynasty hoard in Gao'an county in Jiangxi. This spectacular find yielded not only a large quantity of wares from southern kilns such as Jingdezhen and Longquan, but also three very precious pieces from the Jun kilns and one piece of Yuan-dynasty Cizhou ware.[32] A hoard found in the same year, in Yongxin county (Jizhou) also yielded a Cizhou covered winejar.[33] The Yongxin hoard contained a wide variety of southern wares, including *qingbai* plates from Jingdezhen, Longquan bowls and jars, and a tall Jizhou vase, as well as over one thousand copper coins, mostly dating to the Song dynasty. There were also coins from earlier dynasties such as the Tang, Liao, Jin and Yuan, suggesting a mid-Yuan dynasty date for the hoard, but to date nothing further is known about the hoard.[34] An excavation at the port of Quanzhou in Fujian also yielded several Cizhou wares, suggesting a possible location for the export of northern ceramics to overseas locations in Southeast Asia.[35]

Goods clearly moved from the northern manufacturing sites to consumers in the south, but not exclusively: in the thirteenth century, southern-made ceramics were also in demand by northern consumers. The excavation of a tomb in Hebei demonstrates this.[36] The tomb belonged to Zhang Honglüe (d. 1296), scion of a prominent northern military family and eighth son of Zhang Rou (1190–1268), who first served the Jin dynasty as an official, but surrendered to the Mongols in 1218. Zhang Rou's grave was excavated first; the tomb for Zhang Honglüe and his wife was found in the same tomb complex, but only excavated at a later stage. In the front chamber of Zhang Honglüe's tomb, ceramics of a wide variety of kilns were found, including wares from kilns in Jingdezhen, Longquan, Jun, Cizhou and Jizhou. The quality and range of the wares clearly points to the high value attributed to ceramics during the Yuan dynasty.[37] For our purposes, however, the significance of these finds is that they testify to the circulation of northern and southern wares throughout the realm.

The Importance of Jizhou

We already came across references to Jizhou: several excavations carried out in one or other of the counties of Jizhou prefecture in south-central Jiangxi yielded wares from northern kilns, and we have seen references to wares made at the Jizhou kilns. The prefecture of Ji, referred to as Jizhou during the Song and Yuan dynasties, and known as Ji'an during the Ming dynasty, is located along a river, the Gan, which indirectly connects Lake Poyang in the north of Jiangxi to the provinces along the south coast, including Guangdong and Guangxi.

The source of the Gan lies in the mountainous south of Jiangxi province. The Gan flows northwards for about 885 km, emptying into the southern part of Lake Poyang near the provincial capital Nanchang. To the north, the lake narrows near the strategically located town of Jiujiang, where it connects to the main east-west connecting river, the Yangzi, or Changjiang, and forms one of the main floodplains for this extensive river system. To the south, the Gan connects to Ganzhou, and from there, via the Meiling Pass, to Guangdong and the South China Sea. The Gan is a significant river precisely because of the connections it provides between the economically advanced region of the lower Yangzi delta and the southern provinces along the coast. From the Tang dynasty onwards, it was also one of the main river systems along which the Han-Chinese population migrated southwards.[38] Especially the middle reaches of the Gan, the fertile floodplains of Jizhou (Ji'an), reached a high level of cultural and economic development during the Song dynasty. The towns located along the riverbanks of the Gan developed first, but the fertile hinterland in the Gan valley followed soon after. Riverside towns like Luling, Jishui and Taihe grew into economically stable and culturally sophisticated localities during this period.[39] The flat and hilly lowlands lent themselves to the cultivation of a variety of crops including rice and other grains and produced a surplus to sustain the populations in urban settlements, while the mountains yielded wood and other crops. Numerous smaller tributary rivers connected the main towns in the surrounding counties, creating an easily navigable river system throughout the region. By the end of the Song dynasty, the region could

Map 4.1 Ming Jiangxi. Map based on China Historical Geographic Information System (CHGIS), version 6.

boast a formidable literati presence, built on outstanding success in the civil service examination system.[40] Jizhou's scholars made their mark in the region by writing about the associations, academies and sites of worship that featured in the local landscape.

Famous scholars from the region include such eminent figures as the poet Yang Wanli (1127–1206), the Southern Song statesman and poet Zhou Bida (1126–1204), the scholar Ouyang Shoudao (b. 1209) and the Song chancellor and loyalist Wen Tianxiang (1236–1283). Such figures not only left an extensive literary heritage, they also created scholarly networks that enhanced the reputation of Jizhou well beyond the region. Yang Wanli, one of the four masters of Song poetry, was widely known for his political achievements and particularly for his poetry. Within striking distance of Luling, the main cultural centre of the region, there was Bailuzhou Academy, where Ouyang Shoudao taught and Wen Tianxiang studied. Long after having left the region, Wen Tianxiang still reflected on his time at Bailuzhou. The Buddhist complex of Jingju Temple, within walking distance of Luling, in the Qingyuan mountains, also attracted visitors from all over the realm and beyond. It has, in fact, been described as 'an endless stream of visitors'.[41] There were numerous Buddhist temples in and around the towns, but also in secluded spots in the mountains, and there were also several Daoist temples in the region.[42] Undoubtedly, the fertility of the land and the strategic importance of the river connections helped the economic prosperity of the region. Scholars converged in Jizhou, and their examination successes, local academies and temples enhanced the empire-wide reputation of the region, which in turn attracted other scholars, religious leaders and artisans.

Historians of Song China may well know about the flourishing economic and scholarly prowess of Jizhou without ever having heard of its kilns, while ceramics specialists might well be able to identify what Jizhou wares look like without much awareness of Jizhou's flourishing schools, academies and temples.[43] The Jizhou kilns are located on the outskirts of the main town of Luling, across the river from Jingju Temple. The nearest town to the kilns, Yonghe, is located on the banks of the Gan. These kilns, known variably as the Yonghe kilns or the Jizhou kilns, began producing ceramics in the late Tang dynasty, and lasted until the end of the Yuan dynasty. Today, the outlines of some of the kilns still shape the landscape (Figure 4.4).

Documentation of the kilns is scarce, but by combining historical and literary references with archaeological finds and the material heritage found in private and museum collections we can form a general impression of the ceramic production in this region. Among the wares produced here, dark-glazed *temmoku* tea bowls are probably the best-known. Over the course of the twelfth century, the Jizhou potters began to experiment more with their production methods, which led to a greater variety of colours, patterns and designs in the dark glazes. Among the best-known are the fine stripes in the brown glaze that resemble hare's fur, the round shapes in the dark glaze known as oil spot, or the streaks known as tiger skin.[44] Compared to the Jian tea bowls, the Southern Song Jizhou tea bowls appear in a striking variety of designs and a range of intensities of dark glazes.

Not only the glazes, but also Jizhou shapes are more varied than what was produced at most other kilns during this time, including pillows, statuettes,

Figure 4.4 Overgrown kiln remains in the town of Yonghe, near Ji'an, Jiangxi province. Photo by the author.

water-pourers, long-necked bottles and censers. And these shapes, again, display varied glazes and methods of decorations, including green celadon-style glazes, underglaze painted patterns and decorative patterns made with papercuts and leaves. The impression is of a rich and varied centre for ceramic production, where creativity and variation were held in greater esteem than the perfection of a single style. When the British ceramics scholar A.D. Brankston visited the Yonghe kilns in Jizhou in 1937, he acquired a large number of shards, precisely for this purpose of illustrating the wide variety of wares produced here.[45] The proximity to the Buddhist temples of the Qingyuan mountains raises an interesting question about the relationship between the monks and the kilns. Recent research carried out by scholars based at the Shenzhen Museum has sought to flesh out this relationship. The Yonghe kiln site is about 2–3 square km in size, and encompasses several temples, monasteries and nunneries. Benjue Temple, for example, of which not only archaeological traces remain but also the Song dynasty pagoda, is probably the most famous of these, but there are numerous others. This pagoda, constructed of eight floors of brick and wood, stands at 36 metres high, and was established during the Tang dynasty. When the construction was restored in 1984, they excavated copper coins and a statue of the Buddha from the top floor, confirming the Tang dynasty date of the building. It stands as a striking monument in the landscape now but will have done so even more when it was built, and in the many centuries that it stood there, marking the landscape and signalling the main Yonghe kiln site to visitors from afar. The flourishing of these religious sites coincides more or less with the height of production at the kilns. It seems more than likely that the production at the Yonghe kiln site and the flourishing of the temples in the area all thrived on the basis of the same economic growth that characterized this region in the twelfth and thirteenth centuries.[46]

The kiln site at Jizhou, then, is noteworthy for several reasons. It was located in an extremely rich area, in the sense of economic wealth and natural resources as well as the cultural prominence of the area's academies, temples and teachers. It also catered for a wide range of consumer tastes by making goods that looked remarkably like the best wares produced in other regions. Often, what the Jizhou potters produced were wares that matched closely wares from other sites, even if they did not quite attain the same standards of quality. Like the Jian-ware inspired brown-glazed wares, there were cream-glazed monochromes that looked like wares made at the Ding kilns in the north, a process Zhao Bing simply called imitation.[47] The British Museum also has a dish that was made in Jizhou, but closely resembles a white-glazed dish made at the Ding kilns. While Ding wares are made of white clay that can be fired at high temperatures, the Jizhou wares have slightly rougher bodies, were fired at lower temperatures, and resulted in a slightly darker greyish colour body. But like the Ding potters did, the Jizhou potters impressed a floral pattern on the clay that helped produce a product that resembled a Ding-ware dish (Figure 4.5).[48]

But perhaps the most striking similarity is between wares from Cizhou and Jizhou. The Cizhou patterns include flowers and plants, insects and landscapes, dragons and phoenixes, and although the Jizhou designs are distinguishable, there can be little doubt of communication of some kind.[49] As John Guy put it: 'The influence of Cizhou ware was spread in South China largely through the wares of Jizhou in Jiangxi Province, an area renowned for its white-and-brown coloured wares'.[50] In the 2002 *Dictionary of Chinese Ceramics*, authors Wang Qingzheng and Chen Kelun state, quite matter of factly, that 'the [Jizhou] wares with brown designs on a white ground were created under the influence of Cizhou ware'.[51] Quite apart from the somewhat problematic use of the term 'influence', the statement is rather

Figure 4.5 Glazed stoneware bowl with impressed designs. D 12.6 × H 3.9 cm. Jizhou, Song dynasty. Inv. no. 1973,0726.230. © The Trustees of the British Museum.

vague: 'brown designs on a white ground' is a very broad characterization that could refer to numerous different Jizhou wares, and the description of creation 'under the influence' is not very helpful either.[52] So what exactly was the nature of the relationship between the Cizhou kilns in the north and the Jizhou kilns in the south? How did it come about, and how is it significant for understanding the emergence of blue and white ceramics?

Visually, the similarities between wares made in the far north at the Cizhou kilns and in the southern prefecture of Jizhou are striking. For example, Cizhou wares are known for their use of decorative elements

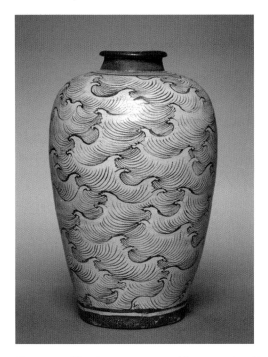

Figure 4.6 Glazed stoneware vase with waves painted in slip. Jizhou ware, twelfth–thirteenth centuries. H 26.3 × D 16.70 cm. Gifts of J. H. Wade and Mr and Mrs J. H. Wade; and purchase from the J. H. Wade Fund by exchange. Cleveland Museum of Art, 1980.186.

that fill the spaces of the surface, such as hatching patterns carved into the surface under a cream-coloured glaze.[53] The famous Cizhou pillows often also have regular patterns that fill the entire surface.[54] Vases made in Jizhou may be covered with a very different pattern, but here, too, regular patterns can fill the entire surface of the decorated object.[55] See, for example, this Jizhou vase from the Cleveland museum collection, which has a stylized wave pattern that covers the entire surface of the object (Figure 4.6).

What is striking is the decorative style of a repeated shape that covers the entire surface in a rather free and dynamic pattern. In contrast to the monochrome glazes of the Song dynasty, these busy decorative patterns convey a completely different approach to the decoration of ceramics, and one that the Cizhou and Jizhou potters clearly shared.[56]

In the following figures, we see two vases with flower patterns, made in Cizhou (Figure 4.7a) and Jizhou (Figure 4.7b) respectively.[57] The flower decoration on the Cizhou vase is simpler, and on the Jizhou vase more elaborate, with peony, lotus and hibiscus flowers, and small butterflies moving

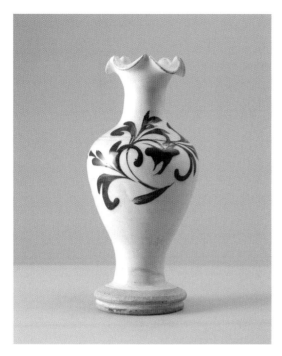

Figure 4.7a Cizhou ware vase with floral decoration and foliated rim, Cizhou kiln-sites, twelfth–thirteenth centuries. H 20.3 × D 9.4 cm, D at base 7.4 cm. Lent by the Sir Alan Barlow Collection Trust. Image © Ashmolean Museum, University of Oxford, LI1301.187.

Figure 4.7b Stoneware vase, with painted flower and insect design. Jizhou, twelfth–thirteenth centuries. Collection of The Museum of East Asian Art. Heritage images.

Figure 4.8 A small painted Jizhou vase, Southern Song-Yuan dynasty. © Christie's
Images / Bridgeman Images.

in between. But the impact of the stylized flowers in near black on the
cream-coloured background, with quite a lot of the background left white
(as opposed to the infill method discussed above) is exactly the same. It was
a highly popular design that appears in several other examples from both
kilns.[58]

Both kilns also used the device of a frame, medallion or cartouche to set
apart the most striking part of the decoration.[59] And both frames feature
the lively depiction of an animal. In Figure 4.3, we saw a Cizhou pillow,
dated to the Song dynasty, with a cartouche, featuring a deer-like animal
moving through the landscape. In Figure 4.8, the cartouche frames a small
animal with thin legs moving at speed through a landscape rendered only
in the thinnest of lines.

In both Cizhou and Jizhou, lively animal shapes are a fairly common
occurrence.[60] In an example of a Cizhou-type jar in the collection of
the Rijksmuseum, we see how this same decorative motif features again
(Figure 4.9). It has a painted decoration on a cream slip, featuring a
galloping horse running through grassland. There are several similar
objects in European collections, sometimes described as 'coarse jars' used
for the storage of foodstuff.[61] It is also most likely a product of the sixteenth century, as Wang Ching-Ling has shown, and thus problematic for

Figure 4.9 Cizhou-type stoneware jar with galloping horse and sprig of flowers. Ca. 1500–1600. Collection of the KVVAK, Rijksmuseum, Amsterdam, AK-MAK-536.

our argument, but as Jessica Harrison-Hall points out, such objects were very common and circulated widely over a long period of time, without being considered by ceramics collectors.[62] Several Jizhou pieces remain, dated to the thirteenth century, that feature decorations in black on a cream-coloured slip base. Several feature a medallion, inside which a deer (*lu*, homophone with the word for blessing) leaps forward amongst sparse grasses. Often, patterns of stylized leaves and flowers fill the space around the medallion.[63] It was a standard pattern, which appears repeatedly on pieces made in Jizhou, including on a damaged pot found in archaeological excavation in Jizhou, which features a very similar deer design, but here with circular swirls between the medallion.[64] Of course there are differences between these two specifically, and between Cizhou wares and Jizhou wares more generally. But the similarities in the overall effect, especially in the group of wares with a lace slip base and dark decorations on the surface, are striking enough to assume some kind of contact between the two.[65]

One of the ways of making sense of the connection between the designs produced in Cizhou and Jizhou is to situate it in the context of Song dynasty patterns of migration. Throughout the Song dynasty, office holders moved around the empire on a regular basis to take up their posts in or near the capital in the north, or in one of the provinces throughout the realm. Liu Jin (*zi* Yuanzhong, son of Liu Hang), whose 1086 Yongxin tomb in Jizhou (Jiangxi) included a pair of (northern) Ding vases, had served for some time in high posts in the capital in the north and in Yingzhou in Hebei, but also in the eastern and northern circuits of Jiangnan, where he was eventually buried. Liu Jin moved in the highest circles and corresponded with famous Song dynasty literary figures like Huang Tingjian (1045–1105) and Su Shi (1037–1101), as well as with the Song political reformer Wang Anshi, so it is impossible to be sure when he acquired the pair of Ding vases. Such objects already had a collector's value in the Northern Song, although the ceramics scholar Fan Fengmei speculates that Liu acquired them when he served with the Chengde army in Baoding in Hebei, very near the production site of Ding wares.[66]

After the loss of the north to the invading Jin dynasty, large numbers of people migrated from the northern provinces to the south, where a new (temporary) capital was established. The migration was driven in part by the disruption caused by the invasion of the Jürchen troops, but also by the natural disasters of the period, not least of which was the dramatic change of the course of Yellow River bed after it breached its banks in 1048.[67] This 'southward migration' has been widely discussed, especially in terms of its impact on the scholarly elites, for whom this traumatic experience of exile and loss featured for many years in literary forms. Figures are notoriously unreliable, but Valerie Hansen and Ken Curtis claim that: '20,000 officials, 100,000 clerks, and 400,000 army soldiers and their families' crossed the Yangzi in 1126–1127 alone.[68] According to Wu Songdi, the population of Jiangxi swelled during the Southern Song. In part, he explains, this was because of the garrisons established in Jiangxi after the loss of the north. The stationing of large numbers of soldiers created opportunities for migrants servicing the garrisons in a variety of roles, but officials also fled south, again with their extended retinues, as did those of lower socio-economic status who were in search of economic stability. Wu Songdi's figures demonstrate that Jizhou had the highest number of migrants of all the Jiangxi prefectures, and served as a centre for migration.[69]

Amongst those who moved south and settled in Jizhou after the crisis of 1126 were even members of the imperial clan, as John Chaffee has shown. Zhao Bolu (1135–1202) settled in Jishui county in Jizhou.[70] The famous Jizhou scholar and teacher Zhou Bida wrote an epitaph for Zhao Bolu. In fact, the Zhou family, very prominent in Jizhou after the collapse of the Northern Song, had themselves migrated to Jizhou from Guancheng in Zhengzhou in the north. Another imperial clansman settled in Luling after serving as an official there, and yet another, Zhao Gongheng (1138–1196) moved to Luling where he never participated in the examinations but 'devoted himself to local pursuits', which included Daoism, astronomy, medicine and divination', while his four sons all passed the *jinshi* examination.[71] Zhou Bida also wrote an epitaph for a clansman named Zhao Gongyu (1136–1203), who moved to Jizhou because his father had served there, and married into a local Jizhou family.[72] Several other members of the imperial family did not settle in Jizhou, but served in Jizhou, and created a connection with the region in that way.[73] People gravitated towards Jizhou, because of its cultural institutions and economic opportunities. Together with their cultural belongings (books, but also ideas and knowledge), they brought material culture in the form of tangible (objects) and intangible (skill-sets for making things, preferences and tastes in design) possessions. The production of material goods in Jizhou, it seems to me, reflects this influx of northern people and objects.

The evidence we have for a connection between Cizhou in the north and Jizhou in the south is undoubtedly patchy: it has long been established that people migrated from the northern provinces to the south when the Jin was established in the north, and Hangzhou became the temporary capital of the Southern Song, but we do not know the exact numbers of people who migrated, nor do we know exactly where they went. We know that the population of Jizhou grew during this time, and we know the names of a small number of individuals who migrated from the north specifically to Jizhou. In other words, in the wider pattern of migration, it seems entirely plausible that not just the small number of individuals for whom we have records, but a larger group of people from the northern provinces did indeed end up in Jizhou. We also have evidence that specific objects moved from the north to the south: people in the south were buried with objects that had been made in the north. Did they bring the objects south themselves, or were they brought south by traders? Again, we do not have specific numbers of objects, but we have a plausible scenario that northern objects were brought in substantial numbers in the south. We even have evidence that objects from the north were in existence in Jiangxi province, and in Jizhou prefecture to be exact, even if their existence in burial chambers does not prove their circulation amongst the living. However, their presence amongst burial goods provides a plausible explanation for the fact that there are significant similarities between the objects from the north, Cizhou specifically, and those made in Jizhou.

From a technological perspective, however, this requires further consideration. How exactly would the potters based in Jizhou deal with objects made under entirely different circumstances and with significantly different materials? The most significant difference between the kilns in Jizhou and those in the Hebei region (i.e. Cizhou) is the firing method. While the southern kilns, including Jizhou, used wood to fire the kilns, the northern kilns all used coal. This also meant a difference in the firing temperature inside the kilns, and a difference in the level of oxygen inside. The shape of the kilns was also different: northern kilns are all shaped like a steamed bun (*mantou*): rounded domes with chimneys next to them, while the remaining kiln in Jizhou shows a rectangular shape climbing up the side of a hill.

Undoubtedly, very different technical skills are in operation at these two sites, and I am not suggesting that the manufacture of Cizhou-style wares in Jizhou included the wholesale appropriation of the northern manufactures. In fact, I am arguing the opposite: I am suggesting that the Jizhou potters were already making a wide variety of objects, shapes, designs and glazes within their own manufacturing context, and added Cizhou-style wares to their repertoire. The integration of Cizhou-style wares would not have been more difficult than the adoption of Ding-style wares or Longquan-style celadon glazes. More importantly, it was the idea of working with a brush to apply the pigment to the surface of the clay body that was most significant, and this was not a technology that depended on clays or kilns. Far more important for the success of this technology was the preparation of the pigment, which was then applied to the layer of slip by brush. As we already saw, in Cizhou, the potters used an iron-oxide pigment, as did the potters in Jizhou.

Of course, specific technologies and knowledge are often mobile. They do not exist as reified entities, but are embedded in people, ideas and things. None of those are tied to one place, and none of those can be entirely controlled. As people move, things and ideas are moved both with intention and purpose, and unintentionally and imperceptibly. We have seen a small fraction of the spectrum of the mobility of people and things here: migratory patterns, political shifts, travel and trade, but also burial and the passing of time mean that people, objects and their associated ideas move from one context into another. Calling this entire complex of patterns 'circulation' suggests a regular, knowable pattern, while in fact the movement is more like water flowing, crawling and seeping into unexpected spaces, and forming unpredictable vein-like patterns: connected but not always flowing back and forth, some flows broader and others only brief or sporadic. But one thing is clear: gradually, the kilns in the south started to move away from the light-green or white monochrome glazes and started to apply painted decorations with brushes under the application of the glaze. Starting in the north, the practice spread southwards, along with people, objects and design ideas, and gradually, the southern kilns began to adopt this practice. Jizhou first, but as we will see in the next chapters, gradually also the potters working in Jingdezhen.

5 | From Jizhou to Jingdezhen in the Fourteenth Century: The Emergence of Blue and White and the Circulations of People and Things

The previous chapter has argued that the history of the emergence of blue and white porcelain in Jingdezhen cannot be told as a Jingdezhen story alone. Instead, it has to be seen as part of a bigger story that starts with the production of ceramics decorated with underglaze, brush-painted decorations. That story begins not in Jingdezhen, but in the northern provinces with the production of Cizhou and Cizhou-style wares, and from there moves first to Jizhou in Jiangxi, and only then to Jingdezhen. It is true that in Jingdezhen, that production relied on the use of cobalt as a pigment for the brush-painted decorations, which led to the striking combination of blue decorations on a white surface. The use of cobalt for the creation of pigment was in itself a significant innovation, but the use of metal-based pigments for underglaze, brush-painted decorations was not. In the northern provinces, potters had applied underglaze, metal-based pigments on light-coloured surfaces since the tenth century, especially in the production of Cizhou-type ceramics. Without the development of this technology in the north, and its move to the southern provinces, Jingdezhen's innovative use of cobalt may not have been possible.

Chapter 4 also showed the key role that Jizhou played in the transmission and circulation of materials and technologies. After the invasion of the Jürchen and the establishment of the Jin dynasty in the north in the early twelfth century, when the northern kiln sites became less accessible, southern kiln sites started to produce wares that looked much like northern wares. The Jizhou kilns in Jiangxi were especially key, I have suggested, because Jizhou not only had the right kind of resources (clay, wood and fern), but also a useful infrastructure (such as river transportation routes in close proximity to the kilns) and a diverse body of consumers. Jizhou attracted scholars and teachers, merchants, monks and students, including visitors and migrants from the north, meaning that there was a ready market in the region with financial resources and a circulation of ideas about taste and fashion. And yet, while the production of ceramics flourished in Jizhou during the twelfth and thirteenth centuries, Jizhou ultimately did not go on to become the porcelain capital of the empire; Jingdezhen did. Jizhou did not become the site where blue and white ceramics, the most successful commodity of the early modern world, were produced; Jingdezhen did. This chapter asks when and why Jizhou's production came to an end, and how Jingdezhen could emerge from this period as the most successful production site of the premodern world.

The Song-Yuan Transition and the Jizhou Kilns

Wen Tianxiang, also known simply as Wenshan, is amongst the most illustrious men in Chinese history. Scholar, minister-of-state, poet and general, he famously resisted the invading forces of the Mongol leader, Khubilai Khan. In the face of defeat at the hands of the powerful invaders, he attempted several times to raise an army and resist but was outnumbered and overpowered. He was captured, tortured and sent to jail in Beijing, where he spent three years. He was eventually executed in prison, after refusing the repeated attempts by Khubilai Khan to persuade him to join the new Yuan regime. His alleged bravery in battle, his ongoing refusals to bend to the invader and serve two masters (i.e. the Song emperor he had sworn allegiance to and the new Yuan ruler) and the memorable poems about loyalty and steadfastness he composed in jail have made him an enduring icon of patriotism and loyalty.[1] There are memorials to Wen Tianxiang throughout the world, including in the New Territories in Hong Kong, Taiwan, Singapore and the United States, but none of these memorials are as big as the memorial site in Ji'an in Jiangxi Province, near the place where Wen Tianxiang was born.[2]

Perhaps somewhat surprisingly, Wen also features in an anecdote in a fifteenth-century expanded edition of one of the classical texts of ceramics appreciation, the *Essential Criteria for Appreciating Antiques*:

> The story goes that Chancellor Wen of the Song [dynasty] [i.e. Wen Tianxiang] walked past the kilns [in Jizhou]. A transformation occurred in the kiln (*yaobian*), and [the ceramics objects] turned to jade. Henceforth they did not fire [ceramics] here anymore. Today there are still traces of these kilns among the dwellings. During the Yongle reign period, some jade bowls and small cups were excavated, so perhaps this is true. It has been like this from the Yuan [dynasty] until today.[3]

As this story would have it, the presence of this powerful figure near the kilns caused a transformative process within the kilns, sometimes referred to as transmutation. As a result, instead of porcelain vessels, jade ones emerged. This story, for which there is no historical corroboration, would go on to be repeated in many other writings. The early Qing scholar Fang Yizhi (1611–1671) wrote:

> The Yonghe kilns in Jizhou produced [ceramics] from the Song dynasty onwards. Even today one can find vessels made by [the famous potters] Shu Weng and Shu Jiao. [But] the locals say that during the time of Wenshan [i.e. Wen Tianxiang], kiln transmutation occurred, and the kilns declined.[4]

In Fang Yizhi's version, the transmutation of the kilns and their subsequent decline is merely co-temporaneous with Wen Tianxiang's lifetime, without there necessarily being a causal relationship between the two. 'The Record of Jingdezhen's Ceramics' author Lan Pu included a slightly different version again:

> It is said that the potters were making pots at the kilns when Chancellor Wen of the Song walked by, and this led to the [vessels] turning into jade. The potters feared that this would become known by the emperor, so they sealed up the openings and stopped firing [the kilns] and fled to Rao[zhou]. Therefore, to start with, Jingdezhen had many potters from Yonghe.[5]

Lan Pu leaves out the element of *yaobian* – transmutation of the kilns; we will return below to the significance of this kiln transmutation process. What is fascinating is that the story of the decline of the kilns in Jizhou somehow became attached to the figure of Wen Tianxiang as early as the fourteenth century, and subsequently was told and retold, especially during the Ming and Qing dynasties.

Even if the fact that the Jizhou kilns eventually declined is not disputed, the question of when exactly this happened is more difficult to establish. There can be no doubt that during the thirteenth century, i.e. during Wen Tianxiang's lifetime, and into the fourteenth century, Jizhou was still a flourishing site of ceramics production. As we saw in the previous chapter, Jizhou ceramics were characterized by variety. Jizhou's potters continued to manufacture shapes, styles and designs known from other sites distributed throughout the empire, integrating these techniques and designs into their local practices. A good example is this simple ceramic cosmetics box, made in Jizhou during the fourteenth century (Figure 5.1).

The box has been decorated with the motif of the flowering plum with a crescent moon. The theme of the flowering plum was popular amongst the scholarly elite across various genres, including the so-called ink-plum paintings.[6] As Hou-mei Sung Ishida has shown, the genre was practiced amongst a refined group of Jiangxi-based painters and scholars.[7] The appearance of the same theme on ink painting and ceramic surfaces illustrates the close proximity in which Jizhou's scholars, painters,

Figure 5.1 Stoneware box with prunus and crescent moon design. Jizhou, fourteenth century. Museum of East Asian Art. Heritage Images/Getty Images.

religious leaders and ceramics makers operated.[8] This theme had grown enormously in popularity in the Southern Song dynasty, as is testified by numerous depictions in paintings, poetry and on ceramics. The scholarly elite embraced its associated ideas of beauty, hope and renewal (through the early appearance of the prunus after winter), and transitory beauty (because of the rapid fall of the blossoms in early spring storms and rain).[9] The Jizhou potters were responsive to this demand, as several examples of Jizhou bowls decorated with this design show.[10] But the stoneware box is made from a white or cream-coloured body, so that it looks a bit like the type of cream-coloured and white ceramics manufactured in the Fujian kiln site of Dehua around this same time. This kind of combination of styles and designs suggests the continued creativity and vibrancy of Jizhou's ceramics during the fourteenth century.

While production continued in Jizhou, the Southern Song empire as a whole did undergo a very significant transformation in the late thirteenth century. Despite Wen Tianxiang's heroic efforts at resistance, the Southern Song dynasty, already weakened by the move southwards and the establishment of the Jin dynasty in the northern provinces, capitulated in 1279 to Mongol forces that had posed a significant threat ever since their unification under Genghis Khan and his successors. The Song regime came to an end, and for the next hundred years or so, a Mongol-led regime presided over a Chinese-style dynasty known as the Yuan. Militarily and politically speaking, the transition from the Southern Song to the Mongol-Yuan regime that occurred around 1279 was a major upheaval. Non-Han rulers established their capital in Dadu (present-day Beijing), appointed new administrators, and issued their own laws. The structure of command at the top changed radically, as did the role of the military, the place of religion and the importance of trade. Even the population of the small southern region of Jizhou, far from the imperial capital, undoubtedly felt some impact of these political transformations.[11]

One of the consequences of the establishment of this new regime was that the official vision of the economy changed. Previously, the Song regime had officially sought to restrict the role of foreign merchants, limiting their access to Song territory. Of course, there was a vibrant interregional trade and active mercantile culture, but the official regulations of the Song dynasty aimed at asserting imperial control over the amount of overseas trade. As numerous studies have shown, the efficacy of that control was limited, to say the least, and especially the ports along the eastern seaboard were actively engaged in private overseas trade.[12] Nonetheless, the presence of overseas merchants in inland centres of commercial significance had been significantly restricted during the Song dynasty. During the Yuan dynasty, however, the official regulations recognized the significance of merchants and encouraged their activities. This opened the interior to the presence of merchants not only from nearby communities within Asia, but also overland from (Islamic) Inner Asia.

This openness to the influx of merchants and connections to consumers from far afield is, arguably, visible in the material culture of the Yuan dynasty; certainly, the production and management of high-value manufactured commodities changed during this period.[13] The high valuation of gold, for example, is a Mongol characteristic, visible not only in the circulation of gold objects (vases, flasks, bowls), but also in textiles and even in decorations on glazed ceramics. The importance of silk textiles (with or without gold weave) in the Mongol cultural context also cannot be overestimated. The extensive administrative structure of the Yuan dynasty dealing with all processes associated with the production of textiles is some indication of the importance of textiles during this time. Diplomatic exchanges, the confirmation of rank and status, the accumulation and storage of wealth, the ties of loyalty and support, none of these would have been possible without the steady and closely controlled production of high-quality textiles.

While significant transformations took place at the empire-wide level which reverberated locally, at the local level, many aspects of life also remained the same. For the majority of the population in Jizhou, the patterns of agricultural activity continued to provide the structures and rhythms of daily life. For the elites, too, ownership of land continued to provide regular income, they enjoyed continued access to literacy and, perhaps to a lesser extent, social and cultural status in public life.[14] Political status gained from civil service examinations and official appointment did become more difficult to achieve for Han-Chinese elites, especially during the period when no examinations took place.[15] Instead, elites explored other roles in literary writing circles, secretarial and tutorial positions, academies, schools and learned societies.

The material record – Jizhou wares collected in museums and excavated by archaeologists throughout the empire – shows that production at the Jizhou kilns did not end with the Southern Song, as the Wen Tianxiang anecdote suggested, but continued during the Yuan dynasty.[16] Moreover, during the Yuan dynasty, Jizhou's potters continued to innovate their styles and designs, so that what James Watt has termed a 'Yuan style' of ceramics began to emerge in Jizhou. According to Watt, this was 'the result of the amalgamation of artistic traditions current in North and South China before the conquest of the Southern Song by the Mongols in the late 1270s'.[17] It is characterized by 'an emphasis on three-dimensional modelling and by the complexity of surface decoration'.[18] The censers, vases, bottles and pillows made in Jizhou during the Yuan dynasty could certainly be seen to fit with this 'Yuan style'. While Song-dynasty pieces from Jizhou have softly rounded shapes and designs that are produced by experimenting with monochrome glazes, the Yuan pieces, in contrast, often have broken lines and underglaze decorations, applied by brush. The understated and refined elegance of the Song wares makes place for decorations with bold lines and lively designs. This fourteenth-century vase (Figure 5.2), made to hold flowers on an altar, was decorated with a design of lotus on the neck with two dragon- or fish-shaped handles; on each side of the vase is a 14-lobed medallion filled with a design of breaking waves. The neck of the vase has a basket weave pattern, and around the foot we see a zig-zag pattern.

Aside from the waves and geometric patterns in many varieties we see in Yuan Jizhou pieces, we find depictions of loosely painted animals (phoenix,

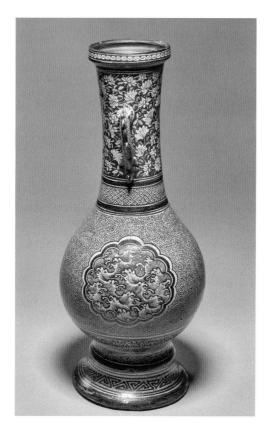

Figure 5.2 Altar vase made in Jizhou. 1300–1368. Inv. no. 1936,1012.85.
© The Trustees of the British Museum.

deer, birds, butterflies and ducks) and plants, such as bamboo, cherry blossoms, water lilies and plums. There is often a fluidity and liveliness to these designs, and such a broad variety that it suggests experimentation and dynamic development. This vase combines many of these elements (Figure 5.3). The phoenix is a common design element on objects made in Jizhou, full of dramatic movement inside the panel that only just contains the pair.[19] Around the panel we see an interlocking wave pattern that covers the surface, like in the medallion in Figure 5.2. The bands around the top and bottom of the vase, around the neck, and on the protruding shape, are all covered with geometrical patterns.

Two dated pieces of Jizhou ware confirm continued production during the Yuan dynasty.[20] The first of these is a damaged vessel excavated in 1983 in Jizhou, and now in the collection of the Ji'an County Cultural Heritage Office (Figure 5.4). The inscription around the mouth of the vessel refers

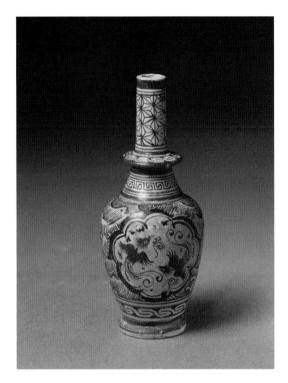

Figure 5.3 Painted stoneware vase with a pair of phoenixes within panel. H 15 cm. Jizhou, 1300–1368. Inv. no. FE.161–1983. © Victoria and Albert Museum, London.

to the cyclical date of *dingwei*. Cyclical dates come around every 60 years, so it is not always easy to determine which of the options is correct. In this case, the options include two Southern Song dates (1187 and 1247), and two Yuan dates (1307 and 1367).

The first of these four dates can be discounted because we have no other example of this kind of underglaze painted decoration using an iron oxide from the twelfth century. One of the earliest examples of the use of iron oxide in underglaze decorations manufactured in a southern kiln is dated to the thirteenth century (1209).[21] The last of the four, 1367, can also be discounted, because of the local disruptions in the region of Lake Poyang around the Yuan-Ming transition. No other Jizhou-kiln objects dated to the last year of the Yuan dynasty survive. That leaves two possible dates: 1247 and 1307. Both of these are possible, and both dates would serve to confirm that during the Yuan dynasty, production in Jizhou continued.

The second of the two dated objects was originally in a private collection, and only came to light as part of the preparatory research for the extensive Jizhou exhibition held in Shenzhen in 2012 (Figure 5.5).

Figure 5.4 Jizhou vessel (wine jar or *guan*), dated *dingwei*. Guo Xuelei, ed. *Chanfeng yu Ruyun*, p. 159.

This bowl has a reign period: Zhiyuan, and a cyclical year (*jimao*), which could refer to 1279 or 1339. On the basis of historical documentation, Geng Sheng suggests the 1279 date is accurate here, but both dates serve to confirm the Yuan dynasty as the time of production.[22] Both objects have the kind of wave patterns that James Watt has connected to the Yuan production at Jizhou. It seems likely, then, that both the thirteenth and the fourteenth centuries were still periods of flourishing and dynamic development in Jizhou. Clearly, Fang Yizhi's statement that production had already ended during Wen Tianxiang's time has to be discounted. The transition from Southern Song to Yuan rule in Jizhou was in the political transformations it brought about, but it was even more visible in the shift in taste and decorative designs it initiated. Jizhou continued to produce and even experiment with new styles and decorative schemes during the Yuan.

However, after the end of the Yuan dynasty, we see no further developments in style that allow us to date Jizhou wares to the early Ming dynasty. The British Museum collection contains a black-glazed stoneware vase with a rustic white pattern of flowers and animals from the collection of George Eumorfopoulos, allegedly made in Jizhou. Unusually, the vase

Figure 5.5 Dated Jizhou bowl, Yuan dynasty. After Guo Xuelei, ed., *Chanfeng yu Ruyun*, plate 107, page 160.

has been dated to the Ming dynasty, although there is no explanation or justification for this dating, and it perhaps seems unlikely that this is in fact a Ming object.[23] If this were a Ming-dynasty object, then it would be one of the very few Jizhou wares in museum collections dated to the Ming dynasty. Most comprehensive in his documentation of the end of Jizhou production is the contemporary scholar Gao Liren, who argues for a late Yuan–early Ming end date. The material evidence confirms his point. Most museum collections of Jizhou wares are made up of Song, and especially Southern Song wares. Some also have Yuan Jizhou pieces, but generally far fewer than Song Jizhou ware.[24] From what is contained in museum collections alone, it seems relatively little of high quality was produced in Jizhou after the end of the Yuan dynasty.

Archaeological excavations have thus far not led to a dramatically different perspective. An overview of several recent excavations in Jizhou confirms the kilns were most active during the Southern Song.[25] Excavations of tombs and hoards throughout Jiangxi have also yielded numerous wares from the Jizhou kilns, but almost all dated to the Southern Song.[26] One Yuan dynasty black-glazed vase was excavated in 1980, now held in the Jiangxi provincial museum.[27] Beyond Jiangxi, the picture is more or less the same. There have been extensive finds of Jizhou wares that can be dated to the Southern Song in tombs and hoards in Sichuan, Anhui and Jiangsu, to name but a few, and only one or two objects datable to the Yuan have been identified.[28] The material record thus confirms the decline of Jizhou's ceramics industry, dating it broadly speaking to the middle of the fourteenth century, nearing the end of Yuan rule. Small-scale production may well have continued – almost all areas with clay produce ceramics of one kind or another – but not to such an extent that they were preserved. Jizhou wares dated to the Ming dynasty rarely make an appearance in collections and excavations. Clearly, then, we can use the material record to date the decline of the Jizhou kilns to the middle of the fourteenth century, around the time of the collapse of the Yuan regime and the establishment of the Ming dynasty.

Explaining Decline in Jizhou

Even if we can make a strong case for the decline of the kilns, it is more difficult to find evidence that provides a clear-cut explanation for the decline of ceramics production in Jizhou. As usual, the most likely explanation draws on a number of factors occurring simultaneously. It is entirely conceivable that the mid-century political disruptions took a heavy toll on the region. During the middle decades of the fourteenth century, the Gan River valley was the scene of very heavy fighting.[29] Some of the most devastating clashes between the troops of the Mongol rulers and two different rebel armies took place around Lake Poyang in 1363.[30] The unrest that followed will undoubtedly have had an impact on the economy of the region in general, and perhaps even on the kilns specifically. On the other hand, it does not seem to be the case that the region suffered in the long term. Economically and culturally speaking, Jizhou recovered remarkably quickly. In fact, significant changes took place in Jizhou soon after the fighting came to an end and peace had been re-established. The region was renamed: from the establishment of the Ming dynasty onwards, the prefecture was named Ji'an. More importantly, Ji'an came to play an important part in the establishment of Confucian leadership at the Ming imperial court. After Ming rule had been founded in the new capital Nanjing, the first emperor of the Ming dynasty came to rely heavily on a small group of key figures from this part of Jiangxi. They included men like Chen Mo (1305–ca. 1389) and Liu Song (1321–1381), who had grown up and served as tutors in Taihe under the Yuan regime but were selected to serve in high office at the capital after the establishment of Ming rule. They were joined later by Xie Jin (1369–1415), who was the top candidate in the provincial examinations of 1387, and passed the imperial examinations in 1388.[31] These figures were only the first instance of what became a substantial outflow of talent from the entire prefecture of Ji'an. It seems unlikely that this emergence of highly successful scholar-officials would have been possible if the region was still experiencing disruptions and unrest.

Many more Ji'an men were selected for high office by the Yongle emperor in the early decades of the fifteenth century, of whom Grand Secretary Yang

Shiqi (1364–1444) was probably the most famous. What is relevant here is not only the fact that many Ji'an men were selected for the highest offices during the first part of the Ming dynasty, but also that so many men were successful in the imperial examinations during the late fourteenth and early fifteenth centuries. The Ji'an success rate during the fifteenth century is amongst the highest for the entire Ming empire.[32] The examination success of men from Ji'an can partially be attributed to the old adage that success breeds success; it is likely that the experiences and connections of the early generations helped those who came later. There can be no doubt, however, that the social, cultural and economic environment from which these men emerged was extremely conducive to examination success. Clearly, Ji'an prefecture as a whole recovered well from the chaos and upheavals of the mid-fourteenth century when the Yuan came to an end, and the Ming was established. And yet, the ceramics manufactures did not recover. Local battles, and warfare more generally, may well have led to the disruption of kiln production during the civil wars at the end of the Yuan and during the disruptive early stages of the establishment of rule under Zhu Yuanzhang, who would become the first emperor of the Ming dynasty in 1368. But if examination success could be re-established so quickly in this region, then why could the ceramics works not be re-established?

The local gazetteer from Ji'an gives us a clue that could help explain the decline in Jizhou when it claims that 'at the end of the Song dynasty, the clay was exhausted and the kilns changed, and thus they [i.e. the potters] moved [their enterprise] to Fuliang'.[33] In other words, the gazetteer claims that the decline of the Jizhou kilns was caused by a depletion of resources, and so the potters moved to Fuliang. It is worthwhile, however, looking more closely at this claim, which consists of several separate elements: the dating (i.e. late Song, *Song mo*); the exhaustion of the clay (*tu jin*); the transformation of the kilns (*yao bian*); and finally, the move to Fuliang (*yi zhi Fuliang* 移之浮梁). Leaving aside, for the moment, the reference to the late Song date, the first claim, the depletion of the clay, is in itself a likely scenario. The clay used in Jizhou for the manufacture of ceramics came from the nearby mountains, most notably the Qingyuan mountains. But these are neither very high nor very extensive, so it is quite possible that potters eventually needed to go further afield to acquire clay. Moreover, for the glazes, a mixture of ferns and clay was required, and it is not unthinkable that not only clay, but also fern and firewood became scarce during this time. The second claim is more difficult to explain; what exactly does 'a transformation of the kiln' mean? The term *yaobian*, sometimes rendered as kiln transmutation, usually refers to the chemical transformation process that occurs inside the kiln as the goods are fired at high temperature. The high temperatures cause a transformative process that affects not only the clay body but also the glaze and brings about a particular colour or colour pattern. In modern usage, the term refers to the unintentional as well as the intentional effects of the high heat. In other words, *yaobian* can mean a misfired piece with discolouration, which may have surprising aesthetic qualities, but it can also refer to the deliberate manipulation of glaze ingredients, temperature and oxygen in the kiln to bring about a particular and desirable colouration.[34] The earliest references to *yaobian*, however, refer to the unintentional effect of a transformation occurring inside the kiln. A Song author, Zhou Hui (b. 1126), discussed the occurrence of such a kiln transformation in Jingdezhen. He dated the anecdote to the Daguan reign period of Song Huizong (1107–1110), in other words, before his own birth. He described the kiln transformation as producing something that was red like cinnabar (*zhusha*), and *yinghuo*, a term that means bewildering and perplexing, suggesting some of the awe and fear these transformations inspired. Such things were considered *fanchang*, lit. unnatural, i.e. not in line with what is regular, and thus *yao*, a term that has associations not only with enchantment, but also with demonic aspects of bewitching appeal. 'The kiln workers immediately destroyed these'.[35]

In that sense, then, kiln transmutation occurring in Jizhou can be understood as a reason for leaving this production site. If we return briefly to the anecdotes told about Wen Tianxiang and the decline of the kilns that opened this chapter, we see that there, too, transformative processes were linked to a sense of fear and foreboding, and thus leading to the abandonment of the kilns in Jizhou. In the fourteenth century, Cao Zhao wrote: 'A transmutation took place in the kilns and [the ceramics objects] turned to jade. Henceforth they did not fire [ceramics] here anymore'.[36] In connection with the gazetteer's claim that the clay was exhausted here, we might well wish to explain these kiln transmutations as referring to firing processes that had been unsuccessful due to the use of a different kind of clay brought in to replace the supplies that had been used up. Perhaps the make-up of this different kind of clay led to the unpredictable kiln processes that are described as 'kiln transformations', but are really just failures. However, rather than drawing on our contemporary understanding of chemistry to 'explain' what occurred here, it makes more sense to use the contemporary mind-set that explained the departure from Jizhou. Of course, the inconvenience of a failed kiln load and the possibility of financial loss mattered, but there was more at stake. Unpredictable firing processes somehow suggested a greater danger, to which a departure from the area seemed the appropriate response.

The final part of the claim in the gazetteer offers a simple suggestion about what the potters did next. 'They moved it to Fuliang'. The word I have rendered here as 'it' and above as '[their enterprise]' is *zhi* 之, a noun that means 'it' or 'him' or 'them'; grammatically speaking it refers to the object of the verb 'to move'.[37] The implications of this claim are more momentous than their matter-of-fact delivery suggests. The idea that potters left their kilns in Jizhou behind, and moved *en masse* to Fuliang (i.e. Jingdezhen) is frequently repeated, but can we find any historical documentation for the claim? One author wrote a short description of Song dynasty ceramics 'from the town of Yonghe in Luling county in Jiangxi'.[38] After a reference to famous Jizhou potters Shu Weng and his daughter Shu Jiao, and ranking some of the Jizhou wares on a par with wares from the Ge kilns, the author continues with a personal anecdote:

> I once obtained a wash-basin (*pan*) and a round-bellied jar (*ang*) of greenish white and glossy black material. When one pours water into these, the water remains unchanged (i.e. fresh) even after a whole month. Looking at them, one knows these are antiquities.[39]

Vessels whose antiquity can be proven by their ability to store and preserve water serve to confirm not only the quality of the ceramics production here, but the connoisseurship of their owner. A further anecdote follows:

> The story goes that a kiln worker entered the kiln while making vessels. A transmutation led to the vessels turning to jade. The workers feared this matter would become known by the authorities, so they sealed the openings and fled. They went to Rao[zhou] to work. Hence in today's Jingdezhen there are many men from Yonghe amongst the kiln workers.[40]

We know little about the author of this text, a late Ming man from Yixing in Jiangsu named Wu Bing, beyond that he gained his *jinshi* degree in late Wanli (1619), and served as magistrate in Ji'an prefecture from 1640.[41] This same story about Jizhou wares was also included in the 'Assorted Jottings of Shi Yushan' (*Shi Yushan bieji*), authored by the early Qing poet, scholar and official Shi Runzhang (1619–1683).[42] Yushan was the courtesy name (*hao*) of Shi Runzhang.[43] Repetition of the claim that Jizhou's workers went to Jingdezhen does not turn claim to fact, although for some scholars the evidence is persuasive enough.[44]

So far, we have not addressed the first part of the claim: the statement that this occurred in the late Song. We have already established that production at Jizhou continued beyond the end of the Song dynasty in 1279, to at least the middle of the fourteenth century. We might explain the statement simply as an error of fact, perhaps the result of a lack of precise information available when *Gegu yaolun* came into being. It is worth pointing out that the 1387 edition of *Gegu yaolun* does not mention this transformative process. The original description of Jizhou wares merely states: 'Their colour is like that of red (or purple) Dingware. They have thick bodies, and their form is coarse (*cu* 麁), they were fired in Jizhou, and they are not worth very much money'.[45] It is only the mid-fifteenth-century expanded edition by Wang Zuo and Shu Min that makes reference to Wen Tianxiang and the late Song disappearance of production in Jizhou.[46]

But other than historical inaccuracy, there is another possible explanation. Recent scholarship has started to explore the kiln site of Linjiang, 20 km north of the town of Yonghe, where the majority of the archaeological research has been carried out, and the current remains of the Jizhou kiln site are located. This site, further downstream along the Gan River is in many ways similar to Yonghe, and thus both are unquestionably part of the same production group. However, the dating is significantly different. Production at Linjiang seems to have continued into the Ming, during which time, the potters based at Linjiang continued to produce. Interestingly, what the Linjiang potters specialized in during the Ming dynasty were celadons to look like Longquan wares, blue-grey wares (*qinghui*), white-glazed wares and *qinghua*, in other words: blue and white wares.[47] The ways in which the history of ceramics is told has been profoundly affected by what has been found and continues to be found in the soil and on the seabed. Ever since the late 1970s, when the number of archaeological excavations started to increase, and reports of extensive finds of ceramic shards became more readily available, ceramics specialists have drawn on those finds to challenge or substantiate stories about the emergence, development and decline of certain styles, shapes, technologies and designs. The appearance in excavation records in Jizhou of three white shards with blue decorations, for example, posed a significant challenge to the narrative that identified Jingdezhen as the place of the 'discovery' of blue and white ceramics.[48] The fact that it concerns only a small number of pieces – a small saucer, a fragment of a larger bowl and a *yuhuchun* wine bottle – is probably less significant than the evidence it provides of the technical capabilities of the potters working at Jizhou during the Southern Song and Yuan dynasties.[49] The object itself does not tell us anything about the context from which this emerged. Was it part of a wider move to innovate through experimentation, or was it copying something that was already in place somewhere else? Was it considered a successful and replicable experiment, and have other examples simply never been found, or was it a one-off? Most likely, the production of blue and white in Linjiang occurred on a small scale, and it was concentrated on the kiln site of Linjiang, which continued to produce even after the Yonghe site had been largely abandoned. Undoubtedly, this is a significant finding, but unless many more pieces are located, it remains somewhat experimental and small-scale.

Finally, it is also conceivable that the reason for the decline of the Jizhou kilns is not to be found exclusively within Jizhou itself, but shaped by factors external to Jizhou. Perhaps Jizhou's kilns were no longer financially viable, its manufactures less desirable, as its competition became stronger? Perhaps we have to look at Jiangxi as a whole to get the full picture of Jizhou's decline. After all, the gazetteer already told us that the potters who fled the transformations in the Jizhou kilns escaped to the manufactures in Fuliang, i.e. to Jingdezhen. To explore this matter further, we need to return to Jingdezhen. We left Jingdezhen in the previous chapter as the site where ceramics with underglaze, brush-painted decorations using cobalt as pigment first emerged during the early fourteenth century.

Fourteenth-Century Jingdezhen

Thus far, we have emphasized the creativity and diversity of production in Jizhou. By comparison, Jingdezhen was perhaps less wide-ranging in its variation, but in Jingdezhen, too, there is evidence of experimentation with different styles. Potters made wares that looked like Longquan-style celadons, white wares that looked like products from the Ding kilns, and blackwares that looked like Jizhou and Jian wares.[50] In fact, this small number of blackwares provide important evidence for the exchange of technologies between Jizhou, Jian and Jingdezhen. A team of scholars based at the Institute of Ceramics affiliated with the Chinese Academy of Sciences in Shanghai was able to examine closely the shards of blackwares excavated near Jingdezhen. The pieces were found in the Southern Song/Yuan strata of the excavation, which allowed them to confirm their dating. Subsequent analysis of the chemical composition of their bodies enabled scholars to determine where the pieces came from, identifying some as made in Jizhou, some at the Jian kilns in Fujian, and some in Jingdezhen. Moreover, and perhaps most interestingly, the quality of the items made in Jingdezhen was clearly lower than the Jizhou and Jian pieces, suggesting a process of experimentation and learning in Jingdezhen, to try and absorb the technology that was already at a further stage of development in Jizhou and Jian. In other words, these pieces of black ceramics from dispersed locations but found in close proximity in Jingdezhen prove the circulation of materials and technologies between Jizhou, Jian and Jingdezhen.

Despite that demonstrable experimentation, in the thirteenth century all of the wares Jingdezhen potters made were monochromes, and the vast majority of the wares made in Jingdezhen were the blueish white *qingbai* wares for which the site was famous.[51] These ceramics produced for thirteenth-century consumers circulated well beyond Jiangxi, as finds in hoards dated to the Southern Song make clear. Goods considered worthy of being stashed away and buried in such a way that invaders or looters cannot find them, tell a story of value. Of course, not all the goods included in a hoard would have been considered exactly equal in value, but in comparison to the absent goods, the goods not stashed and therefore lost, the hoarded goods gain at least comparable value. Noteworthy, then, to see Jizhou and Jingdezhen wares buried together, as they were, for example, in a hoard in Sichuan.[52] Similarly Southern Song blackwares from Jizhou were excavated together with wares from Jingdezhen at a site outside the city gates of Baoyou City in Yangzhou (Jiangsu).[53] The authors of the excavation report use the evidence to make a point about the extensive trade in ceramics, and the centrality of Yangzhou in the circulation of commercial goods, including porcelain, from the Song dynasty onwards. But it is worth noting that in terms of the quality and quantity of the goods found here, ceramics from Jizhou and Jingdezhen circulated together, and both in areas well beyond their sites of manufacturing.

Over the course of the fourteenth century, the Jingdezhen repertoire was extended with a significant innovation: the use of a brush to apply iron-based pigment to the white surface before glazing and firing the object. There is no evidence in Jingdezhen itself to prove conclusively that potters did this before the fourteenth century, and it is clear that when the experimentation with blue and white decorations began, *qingbai* wares also continued to be produced. We see this, for example, in what has been excavated at the Hutian kilns. These kilns are located slightly outside of Jingdezhen, and we have known for more than 80 years that this is where Jingdezhen's blue and white wares were first made. The site gained initial status as 'major cultural heritage site' in 1959, and warranted further protection in 1979 and 1982.[54] After an initial report on the archaeology of the site was published by Liu Xinyuan and Bai Kun in 1980, extensive state-funded excavations took place here between 1985 and 2004. They have shown that the kiln site spreads out to the southeast of the town centre of Jingdezhen, along the Changhe tributary known as the Nanhe (South River). The earliest production here was

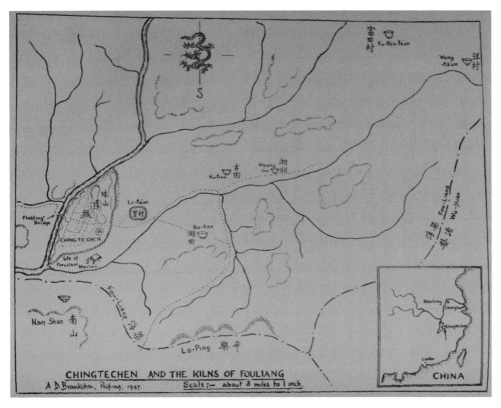

Map 5.1 Map of Jingdezhen, drawn by A. D. Brankston, and included in his *Early Ming Wares of Chingtechen* (Beijing, 1937): 54.

probably as early as the tenth century, and lasted into the Ming dynasty, although sites closer to Jingdezhen's town centre gradually took over during the growth of production in the sixteenth century. In June 1937, a young civil engineer from Britain visited Hutian, marked as Hu-tien in the centre of the map he drew (Map 5.1).

Archibald Brankston had been born in China, was fluent in Chinese, and had been involved in the preparations for the exhibition of Chinese art at the Royal Academy in London in 1935–1936. The following year, the Universities China Committee in London sponsored him on a visit to the kiln sites of Jingdezhen and Jizhou.[55] Brankston observed that there were 'hundreds of kilns' outside the town of Jingdezhen, of which he thought Hutian was the most important kiln site. When he was there in 1937, the 'paths, streambeds and fields [were] strewn with fragments and the mounds consist of nothing else but broken porcelain and seggars' (sic).[56] Brankston only looked at the shards that were visible on the surface and that he could see by looking 'into anything like a hole in the ground', but on that basis, he was able to observe a difference between wares on the east of the site, which he described as 'the finest *ying-ch'ing* with engraved designs', and wares decorated with blue on the western edge of the site.[57] Over time, he established, more and more wares with cobalt blue decorations started to appear at the Hutian site, although Brankston was not able to investigate everything, as 'bandits, who wander in groups among the hills' prevented him from visiting these sites.[58]

The first arrival of brush-painted underglaze decorations in Jingdezhen coincides with the beginnings of decline of the Jizhou kilns. I propose that it was the Jizhou potters who came to Jingdezhen and introduced this technology in the fourteenth century, drawing heavily on what they themselves had learned from the Cizhou potters and from the actual examples of ceramics from Cizhou that had found their way to Jiangxi. Is it possible to prove this? The ceramics specialist Feng Xianming (1921–1992) already hinted at this when he claimed there was 'a quite intimate relation between the blue and white of Jingdezhen and the color underglaze painting of the Jizhou kilns' and thought that the geographical proximity between Jizhou and Jingdezhen was enough to 'prove' the connection.[59] Unfortunately, that confident claim alone is not enough; Feng offers no substantiation. In so far as I know, there is no detailed, written documentation of this connection between Jizhou and Jingdezhen. Nor have I been able to find a so-called 'smoking gun' in the form of a piece of ceramics made in Jizhou but excavated in or near the kilns in Jingdezhen. If Jizhou's goods circulated throughout the empire, and if its potters travelled from Jizhou to Jingdezhen, bringing their craftsmanship and technologies from Jizhou to Jingdezhen, then arguably, we could expect to see material traces of this interaction in Jingdezhen. Would potters travelling from one site to another bring pots with them? Would the archaeological records show that there was a demand for Jizhou's ceramics in Jingdezhen? The archaeological records of excavations in the greater Jingdezhen region to date do not confirm the presence of Jizhou wares in Jingdezhen.

There are, of course, circumstantial explanations for the absence of Jizhou ceramics in Jingdezhen. In Jizhou, the potters worked in close proximity to the scholarly and religious elites of that region. They were not only physically close, with the kilns located precisely between Luling, the very cultured home of a large scholarly community, and the famous meeting point for scholars and monks at Jingsi monastery in the Qingyuan mountains. But Jingdezhen was a place more or less devoid of scholars. There was very little reason for scholars to be in Jingdezhen; the only members of the elite who lived in Jingdezhen were probably there for the few academies, schools and temples in the area. Perhaps that is why we find Jizhou wares in hoards in Yangzhou (Jiangsu) and throughout northern Jiangxi (Yichun, Gao'an and Nanchang), all places with significant literati populations, but not in and around the workshops in Jingdezhen themselves. One Yuan scholar, Hong Yanzu (1267–1329), who was appointed to the position of headmaster at an academy in Jingdezhen, wrote a poem expressing his despair at being stationed in Jingdezhen, fearing he would go grey early in a place so filthy and noisy.[60]

In the absence of direct textual and archaeological evidence for the presence of Jizhou examples in Jingdezhen, one might consider the visual similarities between Jizhou and Jingdezhen decorative elements at least suggestive of the possibility of exchange between the two sites. As we saw in Chapter 4, the two blue and white temple vases now known as the David vases are famous not only for their stunning beauty but also for the firm date they provide for the manufacture in Jingdezhen of blue and white porcelain (Figure 4.1). The date of 1351, written in the underglaze inscription on the neck of the vase, provides incontrovertible evidence of the superb quality of blue and white decorations in the middle of the fourteenth century. We have good reason to believe some of the potters who worked in Jingdezhen in the waning decades of the Yuan dynasty, i.e. in the middle of the fourteenth century, had previously worked in Jizhou. A close look at the decorative elements on the David vases reveals a similarity to the decorative schemes in use in Yuan Jizhou, even if the pigment in use in Jizhou was an iron-based mineral, not cobalt.

Starting from the top of the David vase, we see a division in separate bands, something done in similar fashion on vases and bottles from Jizhou. The David vase has a band around the top featuring a chrysanthemum, and a branch that winds its way round, with sculpted leaves coming off the main branch encircling the vase (Figure 5.6). Jizhou wares, too, show winding patterns of flowers and leaves that encircle the vessel (Figure 5.7).[61]

The next band of the David vase contains a series of pointed plantain leaves (Figure 5.8) surrounding the inscription on the neck. A pattern of leaves around the neck also appears in several Jizhou (and Cizhou) examples, including Figure 5.7.[62] The shading effect achieved by adding thin parallel lines is also visible on both examples.

The string of flowers that encircles the David vase (Figure 5.9), again, can be found in a similar form as decorative element in Jizhou examples (Figure 5.10).

Figure 5.6 Chrysanthemum with strings of leaves. Decoration in band around the David vase. Detail of Figure 4.1.

Figure 5.7 Jizhou vase decorated with chrysanthemum and string of leaves. After Guo Xuelei, ed., *Chanfeng yu Ruyun*, Plate 114, page 172.

The band around the base of the David vases, finally, also has a very similar characteristic: small niche-shaped borders around a Buddhist decorative symbol in the middle, which we see in both the David vases (Figure 5.11) and around the neck of the Jizhou vase in Figure 5.7.

The phoenix that spreads its multi-feathered wings on the David vases (Figure 5.12) is also a recurrent theme in other kiln sites, including Jizhou. See, for example, the phoenix on the Song-dynasty Jizhou vase, painted with brown pigment on white slip (Figure 5.3), but also on brown tea bowls, and in reserved slip on brown vases.[63]

Figure 5.8 Plantain leaves. Detail of Figure 4.1.

Figure 5.9 String of flowers. Detail of Figure 4.1.

The sharp-clawed dragon that encircles the centre of the David vase is undoubtedly the focal point of many underglaze painted decorations.[64] Jingdezhen ceramics of the fourteenth century often feature a dragon, sometimes encircling a vase as we see in the David vases, sometimes curling from left to right on the surface of a large plate, sometimes curling round the plate so that the head meets the tail, and sometimes in pairs chasing pearls.[65] The blue dragon appears in strong contrast with the white background, especially in the way the slightly darker bands above and below it frame the dragon. By the mid-fourteenth century, dragons had already appeared on ceramics for several centuries, as is testified by the dragons imprinted on Ding wares made in the early eleventh century (Figure 5.13).[66] Because of the white clay covered in clear glaze, the imprinted image does not always come through clearly in photographs, but this line drawing based on a dragon-incised Ding-ware plate in the National Palace Museum shows the motif in a clearer way (Figure 5.14).[67]

Figure 5.10 Detail of censer, made in Jizhou, Southern Song dynasty. Jiangxi provincial museum. Published in Guo Xuelei, ed., *Chanfeng yu Ruyun*, Plate 086, page 134–5.

Figure 5.11 Niche-shaped decorative detail of Figure 4.1

The dragons in brown slip on a cream background such as they were made in Cizhou are more clearly visible than the imprinted dragons on white wares.[68] The dragons that featured on the David vases, then, had many ancestors, some from within Jingdezhen, and some from beyond Jingdezhen, including Cizhou.[69]

Conclusion

The Jizhou kilns were influenced directly by the Cizhou kilns and there is a great likelihood that after the fall of the Northern Song, many Cizhou artisans fled to Jiangxi province and spread the technique of color under-glaze ceramics to Yonghezhen. Yonghezhen is nearby Jingdezhen; hence there is a quite intimate relation between the blue and white of Jingdezhen and the color underglaze painting of the Jizhou kilns.[70]

Figure 5.12 Phoenix detail of Figure 4.1

Figure 5.13 Creamy white Ding porcelain dish with copper-bound mouth rim and a three-clawed dragon carved on interior. Sir Percival David Collection PDF.159; ©The Trustees of the British Museum.

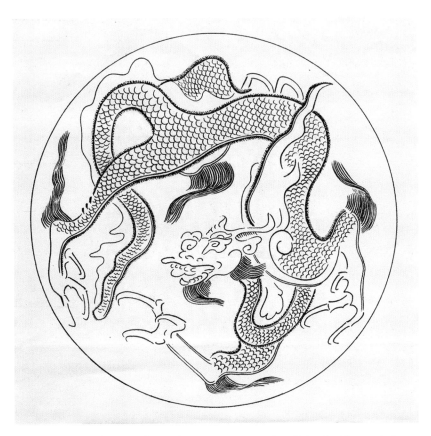

Figure 5.14 Line drawing of a Jin-dynasty Ding-ware plate. Printed with permission from the National Palace Museum, Taiwan.

For Feng Xianming, author of this quote, the relationship between the various sites is unproblematic: Cizhou 'influenced' Jizhou, and Jizhou and Jingdezhen are 'nearby', hence a 'quite intimate relation' between these two kiln sites. If one wants to avoid the problematic concept of influence to explain the relationship between two artists or styles, and if one considers mere physical proximity as insufficient proof for the existence of such a relationship, then it becomes more difficult to identify the connections that existed between Jingdezhen and the various other sites that shaped Jingdezhen's modes of manufacture and styles of production. This chapter has sought to explain these connections in a different way, without using the idea of 'influence'. I have argued that we have to recognize the importance of the movement of people, technologies and objects to explain the emergence of Jingdezhen's blue and white porcelain. We cannot tell the story of Jingdezhen as an exclusively local history, as the story of a single, bounded, exceptional place. We have to recognize the importance of the movement of people, technologies and objects throughout the region, the empire, and throughout Eurasia. Equally, we cannot tell the story of Jingdezhen as one exclusively shaped by global products and global consumer demands. It is the combination of global and local that shapes Jingdezhen's history; it is the multi-facetted and unpredictable flow of interactions at the local, regional, empire-wide and global level that allow us to make sense of the emergence of the blue and white wares that became such a prominent feature of the material world of the fifteenth century.

6 | Blue and White Porcelain and the Fifteenth-Century World

Having discussed the emergence of blue and white porcelains in the previous two chapters, and the global and local circulations that made that emergence possible, I turn in this chapter to the objects themselves. This chapter explores the ways in which blue and white porcelains travelled away from their site of production in Jingdezhen, into new cultural contexts, where they acquired new meanings and values. In that process, I argue, the blue and white porcelains retained a certain distinctiveness: their attraction and high value were in part to do with the fact that they were associated with a remote site of production, and a cultural context that was different from their new environment. In other words, their value was in some ways determined by the fact that they were exotic and different. On the other hand, their difference did not prevent them from becoming part of a new cultural context. They became embedded into new localities, where they acquired specifically local meaning and significance.

Mapping the Fifteenth-Century World

The image in Map 6.1 depicts a fifteenth-century vision of the world.[1] On the right-hand side of the map we see the Korean peninsula; the vast landmass in the centre of the map represents the Chinese empire, and on the left-hand side we see the outlines of the Arab Peninsula and Africa (with a large lake in the centre). Toponyms in Chinese characters on the map confirm locations like Iran and Mesopotamia, Egypt, the Mediterranean, France, Spain and Germany. Known as the 'Map of the Integrated Lands and Regions of Historical Countries and Capitals' (*Honil Gangni Yeokdae Gukdo Jido*), or 'Map of the Integrated Lands' for short, offers extraordinarily detailed insight into the geographical knowledge of its Korean cartographers. The size of the Korean peninsula and the accuracy of the coastline suggests that the part of the world they were most familiar with was Korea.[2] The maker of the 1402 map on which this copy was modelled, a man named Yi Hoe, had earlier completed a map of Korea, which contains much of the same detail as this 'Map of the Integrated Lands'.[3] Japan appears to the south of Korea,

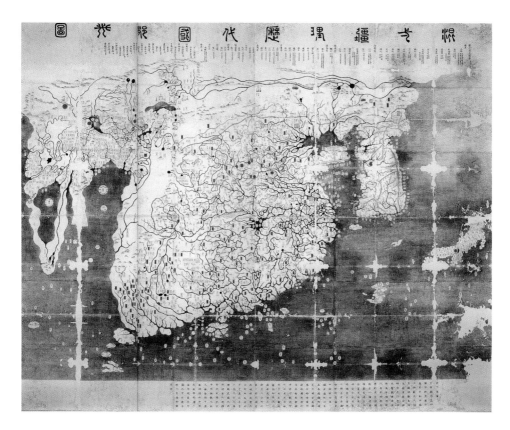

Map 6.1 *Honil Gangni Yeokdae Gukdo Jido* (Map of the Integrated Lands and Regions of Historical Countries and Capitals). Painted on silk, 164 × 171.8 cm. Undated. Held at Omiya Library, Ryûkoku University.

and is depicted as significantly smaller than Korea, while Kyushu appears to the north of Japan, a mistake made in exactly the same way in a map of Japan brought to Korea in 1401. Most likely, it was this map that provided the cartographers of the 'Map of the Integrated Lands' with information about Japan.[4] The discrepancy in size between Korea and Japan perhaps illustrates the sense of cultural superiority the Korean scholarly elite felt over Japanese culture in the fourteenth and fifteenth centuries.[5]

The central part of the 'Map of the Integrated Lands' represents the Chinese empire, by far the largest unit on the map. The text in Chinese characters that appears along the bottom edge of the map provides a detailed description of two earlier Chinese maps that formed the source of the map's information on China.[6] Both of these earlier maps are now lost, although there is an extant late fourteenth-century map, the 'Amalgamated Map of the Great Ming Empire' (*Da Ming hunyi tu*), which is thought to have been based on one of these.[7] So, for the depiction of Korea and Japan, the makers of the 'Map of the Integrated Lands and Regions' relied on Korean and Japanese sources, and for the depiction of China, the map used Chinese sources.[8] For the representation of the Middle East and the Arab Peninsula, Africa, the Mediterranean and Europe, the 'Map of the Integrated Lands' relied on knowledge that was available in China, but had originated from Islamic geographers with access to the Chinese empire during the Mongol period.[9] The 'Map of the Integrated Lands' was made by combining and integrating diverse bodies of knowledge in several languages, thereby creating a material object that was at once embedded in its local space and meaningful beyond that locality. The map illustrates that the fifteenth century was a period in which knowledge about the Eurasian landmass and its surrounding oceans spread across religious and linguistic boundaries. It also shows the potential of objects to move along the same land-based and maritime routes that facilitated the circulation of knowledge. This chapter will seek to demonstrate that some of the porcelain objects that were traded and gifted within these networks similarly conveyed meanings that were at once associated with distant worlds and locally embedded. They were powerful objects precisely because they communicated knowledge about the wider world and at the same time contained values relevant within the immediate context. Arguably, they played an active role in both: it was the movement of objects that gave material form to a beholder's awareness of distant and unfamiliar worlds, and it was the value of the object that created meaning within the object's local environment.

The Indian Ocean

For many centuries, the Silk Roads that stretched across Central Asia had provided access eastwards to central parts of China, and westwards into Europe. But with the decline of the Mongol empire and the development of navigational and ship-building technologies, maritime trade networks gradually increased in importance. This included the Indian Ocean networks, which extended from eastern Africa to the islands of Southeast Asia. Within this region, the monsoon winds led to the creation of rhythmic patterns of trade. Seasonal winds facilitated movements towards certain ports at specific times of the year, but also necessitated extended stays, while ships and their crews waited for the winds to turn. Networks of merchants bound by similar patterns of movement and rest emerged within the monsoon world.

Geographically remote regions, thus, were drawn together in the beginning of an integrated economic system, with a shared mercantile culture.[10] Merchants from the Indian kingdoms were most centrally located within this maritime realm, with their bases along the Coromandel and Malabar coasts. Merchants from the land-based Islamic states and empires entered this region from the numerous ports in the Gulf, on the Arab peninsula, and along the Red Sea, while Chinese merchants entered via the Malaccan Straits in the eastern Indian Ocean. Swahili coast-based traders from Africa accessed the western regions of the Indian Ocean. Islamic traders who had the benefit of advances in Arab seafaring technology (shipbuilding as well as navigation) were the first to draw the region together by creating a trading zone that was strengthened by their shared membership in the House of Islam (Dar al-Islam) as early as the ninth century. Merchants traded a wide range of goods: gold from Africa was sold in India, nutmeg from the Moluccas in Southeast Asia was for sale in East Africa, and coffee from Yemen in Malacca, to name but a few examples. Cotton was one of the few commodities that flowed in all directions, as Giorgio Riello's masterly book illustrates. Cotton's main sites of production were in India, but similar designs have been found in the far extremities of the Indian Ocean. One pattern, the so-called goose (*hamsa*) pattern, has been found on textiles found in Sulawesi, now in Indonesia, but also in old Fustat, now Cairo in Egypt.[11] While Islam created a religious structure within which people and ideas could freely move, cotton serves as a concrete example of the cultural integration that comes from a shared lived experience. It is a moving thought that bodies were clothed in a material with the same look and feel at distances of thousands of miles, and that the physical remnants of these materials still exist to testify to this.

The transitory existence of cotton and other textiles, which rarely last across the centuries, means that we cannot use textiles to tell historical narratives as easily as we can with more durable materials. Porcelain, on the other hand, was shared across distances of thousands of miles, but generates almost the opposite problem: its longevity distorts the ways in which the stories get told. There is a risk that we overestimate the significance of porcelain, because so much of it has been found across such vast distances and over such extended periods of time. Archaeological assemblages yield far more porcelain than anything else, yet the coffee and tea, cottons, silks and other textiles, spices and staple foods that vanished without a trace long ago all circulated along with porcelain, quite possible in larger quantities. That said, porcelain's distribution throughout the Indian Ocean region tells an important story.

It was during this time, in the early decades of the fifteenth century, that the Ming empire extended its maritime power and ventured into new territories.[12] In the service of first the Yongle emperor (r. 1402–1424) and then the Xuande emperor (r. 1425–1435), the eunuch Zheng He (1371–1435) led seven expeditions, taking place between 1405 and 1433.[13] Each expedition brought a fleet of hundreds of ships, laden with goods made in China, into the ports of the South China Sea and the Indian Ocean and along the African coast. Though their exact size continues to be debated, each of these so-called 'treasure-ships' that set sail as part of Zheng He's fleets was large enough to carry crews of thousands of men and their provisions, as well as cargos full of metals and coins, silks and porcelains.[14] In 1433, for example, the cargo prepared for Zheng He's seventh voyage included 443,500 pieces of ceramics made in Jingdezhen.[15] Orders of that magnitude inevitably had a major impact on the production site. When the imperial workshops were not able to fulfil the demands of the Ming court, officials used harsh measures to extract the required goods from local production sites.[16] But undoubtedly, the experience of the previous six voyages had made clear how much porcelains were in demand. Together with metals, coins and textiles, porcelains were considered to be effective tools in the establishment of overseas diplomatic and commercial relations in the places where Zheng He's ships docked: Hormuz, Aden, Dhofar and ports along the Arab peninsula and the east coast of Africa.[17] The fleets of treasure ships returned to Ming China with raw materials, gems, pearls, manufactured goods, incense, spices, even exotic animals. Moreover, the ships returned with knowledge about the wider world. Zheng He's voyages illustrate both the accumulation of geographical knowledge of the world, and its application to overseas travel and trade in early fifteenth-century China.[18]

Much has been written about these journeys.[19] My point in mentioning Zheng He here is not to discuss the man or the voyages, but to highlight their importance for the creation of trade and distribution networks for Chinese-made goods, especially along the East African Coast and in the Persian Gulf. The Zheng He voyages stand out in world history for several reasons: the size of the ships, the number of men involved, the geographical reach of the voyages, and perhaps most of all, their abrupt ending. Many narratives of world history refer somewhere to the voyages of Zheng He as a last flourish of maritime China, after which the shutters suddenly came down and Ming China began its long and self-imposed period of isolation.[20] In the context of world historical overviews, Zheng He's voyages are not usually referred to as voyages of discovery.[21] Chinese ships already sailed these routes during the fourteenth century, before Zheng He, and large quantities of goods from China already reached these places long before Zheng He arrived there.[22] Yet, Zheng He's voyages were crucial: they served to develop and strengthen these existing interactions between the Ming empire and locations throughout the South China Sea, the Indian Ocean, the Middle East and the African coast. The fifteenth century, thus, was a period of Eurasian circulations and movements: of people, of goods and of knowledge.

It is, of course, true that Zheng He's imperially sponsored journeys of the early fifteenth century did not continue; they were followed by a period in which the Ming empire turned away from the sea and rejected official engagement with trade. In the era after Zheng He, the Ming state imposed restrictions on all overseas interaction.[23] Perhaps unsurprisingly, this had a significant impact on the global circulation of Jingdezhen's porcelain. For a short time in the early fifteenth century, during the time of the so-called trade ban, porcelain made at kilns outside China, in Vietnam and Thailand, for example, was far more visible than goods from Chinese kilns.[24] The 'Ming-gap', as Roxanna Brown has styled it, has become ever more visible in light of recent maritime archaeological discoveries.[25] The temptation has been to see this Ming gap as evidence of the long-term isolation of the Chinese empire, and to characterize China more generically by a lack of interest in the overseas world. However, the patterns of porcelain production and trade during the fifteenth and sixteenth centuries, as this chapter seeks to demonstrate, show that this characterization is wrong. Apart from a short period in the fifteenth century, Ming China responded actively to the global desire for porcelain. That trade may not have been imperially sanctioned or state sponsored, but the Chinese traders nonetheless continued to play an active role in the fifteenth-century circulations.

The question this chapter focuses on concerns the ways in which porcelain became part of new cultural contexts. We know that Chinese porcelain was in demand throughout the fifteenth-century world: blue and white porcelain made in Jingdezhen during the fifteenth century has been found throughout the Mongol heartland, in the main Middle Eastern cities, including those around the Red Sea, throughout the Indian Ocean, including the East African coast, India, and in large quantities in Southeast Asia. We also know that it arrived at these destinations by way of various means of transport and way stations: porcelains were often transported from their place of manufacture to their final destinations via a series of collection points, entrepots, markets and shops. Many if not most pieces of porcelain would have been transported by more than one means of transport: shipped, then carried by carrying pole, and then shipped again, or shipped and then loaded onto camels. Material, textual and archaeological evidence testifies to the success of that transport across the globe, reaching consumers almost everywhere on the early modern planet, although some evidence, most notably shipwrecks, also shows its hazards and failures.

We know much less about what happened to these pieces of porcelain as they gradually became part of new cultural contexts between the late fourteenth and the end of the fifteenth century. Below, I will discuss several examples of pieces of Chinese porcelain, or close imitations of it, that became integrated into new cultural contexts: pieces of porcelain depicted in a late fourteenth-century manuscript from Baghdad; pieces of blue and white that formed part of early fifteenth-century Korean ritual instructions; Chinese porcelain in a shipwreck found in the Philippines; and finally, the depiction of a single piece of blue and white porcelain in a painting of the Italian Renaissance. These diverse examples serve to underscore the point that Chinese blue and white porcelain had a distinctiveness that marked these pieces out as different in all of these fifteenth-century contexts. At the same time, each of these distinct pieces had become integrated into a new context, where it acquired local significance. It is precisely this combination that I argue makes these fifteenth-century pieces of porcelain significant. The pieces I discuss in this chapter are both distinct, because they originated from elsewhere, and unremarkable because they had become part of the self: imbued with meanings that were assigned to them in a specifically local context. They retained their otherness while speaking to the self; they were connected to the global yet part of the local. Just like the map at the start of the chapter, they were powerful objects precisely because they communicated knowledge about the wider world while retaining values relevant within the immediate context.

A Late Fourteenth-Century Manuscript from Baghdad

In 1396 in Baghdad, a calligrapher completed a copy of the poetic works of the Persian poet Khwaju Kirmani (1290–1349?), including a poem about Humay and Humayun, written in 1331.[26] The poem narrates the adventures of Prince Humay, son of the King of Syria, who falls in love with Humayun, a woman he only sees portrayed in a painting. Humay sets out to find Humayun, daughter of the Emperor of China. He eventually finds her, after many adventures that include capture by pirates and shipwreck, and becomes the emperor of China himself.[27] One of the illustrations

Figure 6.1a Humay and Humayun in the garden. British Library Manuscript Add. 18113 folio 40v.

included in the 1396 manuscript depicts Humay and Humayun in a garden surrounded by musicians (Figure 6.1a).[28]

The illustrations were added to the manuscript by an artist identified as 'Junayd' (*fl.* Baghdad, c. 1396). Junayd signed one of the illustrations depicting the Humay and Humayun story and is also presumed to be the artist of all the others accompanying the 1396 manuscript.[29] In fact, it is these illustrations that the manuscript is mostly known for; they are the earliest known examples of what came to be known as 'the classical style of Persian book painting'.[30]

Seated in the centre of the image, Humay and Humayun face each other while holding hands and offering gifts: Humayun a flower, and Humay a small, metal receptacle. Those who surround them all match the central pair in their gazes and gestures; looking at each other or at the couple, the 'audience' is represented in various modes of presenting the pair with gifts,

Figure 6.1b Detail of Figure 6.1a

flowers, food and music. In the foreground, offerings are prepared on a small table, including a small round metal bottle with a narrow central spout, and three pear-shaped bottles with elongated necks. Two of the bottles have blue line drawings on a white ground.[31] Most striking amongst the three bottles is the central one: a large blue vase with a white dragon (Figure 6.1b).

We do not know if, and if so, when or where the painter saw an object like this blue vase with the white dragon. The Musée Guimet in Paris owns a contemporary piece of a different shape, but with a decorative design that is reminiscent of the depicted object (Figure 6.2),[32] and the National Museum of Iran also has a plate that has been decorated similarly with a striking white dragon, painted in white slip on top of a blue surface.[33] The depiction of a blue and white vase in this 1396 Persian painting raises an interesting question. Should it surprise us that a pear-shaped vase with blue glaze and white decorations in the shape of a dragon – in shape and decorative design so characteristic of Chinese objects – features here in an illustration made in Baghdad, in the fourteenth century, to accompany a Persian poem?[34]

Of course, the answer is no. The exchange of art and material culture between Iran and China first flourished when Iran formed part of the Mongol empire, i.e. in the late thirteenth and early fourteenth centuries. Large quantities of blue and white porcelain were imported into Iran, both overland by way of the Silk Road, and by sea. The exchange of goods and

Figure 6.2 Meiping vase decorated with a white dragon on cobalt blue porcelain, China. Yuan dynasty, thirteenth and fourteenth centuries. Musée Guimet.

people led to significant cultural and artistic exchanges visible specifically in ceramic production.[35] So-called 'Chinese elements' came to play a key role in the flourishing of Iranian painting and decorative arts such as ceramics, metalwork and glassware.[36] Moreover, a significant number of Persian manuscripts of the late fourteenth and early fifteenth centuries depict blue and white ceramics.[37] Basil Gray's classic study on the subject looked at the leading six manuscripts of this period and noted '31 miniatures in which 56 ceramic vessels are represented'.[38] While he acknowledges that some of these may have represented Persian ceramics made in imitation of Chinese wares, he argues on the whole that 'the blue and white of the miniatures is really Chinese'.[39]

It is not surprising, then, that a tray table with Chinese ceramic bottles stands in front of Humay and Humayun, but it is worth reflecting on the significance of their depiction here. On the one hand, the position of the tray table in the middle foreground marks the objects as significant. The positioning of the human figures surrounding the object underscores this: to the left a standing figure carrying a further object to add to the objects on the tray, to the right kneeling figures inclined towards the tray table, and further individuals above the objects gazing down upon them. The couple is the focal point of the upper half of the painting, but the tray table matches their centrality in the lower half. Moreover, the blueness of the bottle with its contrasting patterning suggests the significance of the item. Amongst the rich patterns that cover every bit of the surface of this painting, the shape and colour of the curling, swirling dragon stand out. And yet, the objects also blend into the painting. Their elongated shapes and the floral and curved patterns on their surface echo the shapes and surfaces that surround them. Moreover, the objects seem to form a seamless part of the richly patterned material context. There are patterned surfaces everywhere: the clothing, the textiles covering the furniture, the metalwork of the trays and urns, even the grass and flowering plants in the background all look like patterned surfaces of varying materials. The three bottles, positioned to underscore their value and highlight the striking shape of the dragon, have become such an integrated part of the painting that at first glance one hardly notices them. It is precisely this combination of striking difference and seamless fit into an existing decorative pattern that makes this blue and white piece of porcelain an easy object to integrate into new context.

A Fifteenth-Century Ritual Manual from Joseon Korea

A second example of this combination of blue and white porcelains' distinctive otherness and local integration and meaning comes from Joseon Korea (1392–1897). We already discussed the superb skills of Joseon cartographers at the start of this chapter. They formed part of a political and cultural entity that drew on the strength of the previous Goryeo regime, which had been in existence since 918. But that regime was also revitalized by a new rulership that had taken the throne in the late fourteenth century. Over the course of the fifteenth century, Joseon Korea formed a lasting diplomatic and economic relationship with Ming China, developed a strong Confucian base for its social and political organization, invested in the growth of science and technology, and, with the help of Ming troops, fought off the Japanese invasions of 1592–1598. The relationship with Ming China was important in all these endeavours: officially

Figure 6.3 Drawing of a ritual jar with rosettes and a three-clawed dragon. From *Annals of Sejong* 世宗實錄, *juan* 132, 'Ritual vessels', 19a.

a tributary state of the Ming, Joseon Korea paid regular tribute to the Ming court, and in exchange, could expect military protection as well as cultural patronage.[40] This patronage took many forms. Korean scholars collected and studied the writings of Chinese Confucians and provided commentaries on and editions of these writings. They participated in the annual tributary mission to Ming China to purchase books, paintings and items to grace the Confucian scholar's desk such as ink-stones, water droppers and porcelain brush-rests. They even created their own landscape paintings that combined their longing for famous sites of the Chinese landscape with new interpretations of their Korean environment. The scholarship and the visual and material culture produced in Korea during this period was distinctly Korean, yet clearly indebted to Ming China.[41]

Porcelain played a very particular role in this nuanced relationship between Ming China and Joseon Korea. To illustrate that role, Figures 6.3 and 6.4 present examples of blue and white porcelain integrated into a distinctly Korean context.

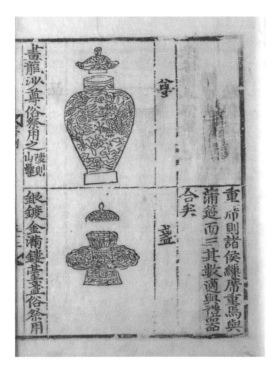

Figure 6.4 Drawing of a ritual jar with five-clawed dragon. From *Gukjo oryeui* 國朝五禮儀, *juan* 1, 'Images of ritual implements', 52a.

In Figure 6.3, we see a drawing of a ceramic jar with wide shoulders and tapering sides, a lid suspended above the mouth of the jar, with a wide base standing on a multi-layered mount, presumably made of carved wood. The design of the jar reveals a line around the mouth of the jar, a cloud pattern with rosettes around the shoulder, and a large three-clawed dragon encircling the jar as a whole. Kwon Sohyun, who has studied the representation of blue and white porcelains in ritual texts, has identified a very close match to this drawn object: a Chinese blue and white jar dated to the Xuande period by means of an underglaze inscription. The Xuande emperor had donated several such jars to the Korean royal court in 1430. The drawing of a jar in Figure 6.4 is much less recognizable as Chinese: the rosettes have gone, and the dragon and cloud pattern covers the entire surface of the jar. Both of these drawings served as guidance for the Korean manufacture of blue and white porcelain. The Korean potters had the raw materials, the technology and the skills to make pieces that reflected the close connection with China. Few Korean examples of blue and white jars of the fifteenth century remain, although a small number of splendid jars can be found in Korean collections.[42] These examples show that the Korean potters adapted the Chinese models, and created new, Korean versions of these shapes and designs.

These drawings come from ritual handbooks dated to the early fifteenth century. The first drawing is from a ritual text (known as *Orye* 五禮) that was appended to the annals of Sejong, which had been completed in 1451. During the reigns of the third king, Taejong (r. 1400–1418), and the fourth king, Sejong (r. 1418–1450), several modifications were made to state rituals. In 1444 Sejong gave the order to compile the prescriptions of state rituals. According to the preface of the text, the section on auspicious rites is taken from a 1415 document produced during the reign of Taejong. The second drawing is from the *Gukjo oryeui* 國朝五禮儀, a further revision of the *Orye*. Initially developed under the reign of Seongjong (1457–1494), it was completed in 1474.

A regime built on the principles of Neo-Confucianism, Joseon Korea held ritual in high regard. Under the rule of King Sejong, several texts were promulgated that stipulated in detail how the rituals and ceremonies of the state were to be performed. These included the rites for honouring ancestors, ceremonies to mark important occasions in the agricultural calendar or to welcome embassies from overseas, and the ritual performances to celebrate a royal birth or mourn a death. Illustrated versions of these texts detailed the appropriate shapes and materials to be used in such ritual performances. Blue and white porcelain was not used exclusively: metalware and lacquer objects were also used in court rituals. The general shortage of precious metal, however, meant that the use of porcelain was encouraged for ritual use.[43] As a consequence of this suitability of blue and white porcelain, the Korean production of such ceramics flourished. In times of economic hardship, however, such as during and immediately after the Japanese invasions of the late sixteenth century, it was difficult to produce enough of these items for ritual use. In such cases, as Kwon Sohyun writes, 'blue and white porcelain jars with the dragon design were even imported from the Ming Dynasty'.[44] Blue and white porcelain of both Korean and Chinese manufacture, thus, came to perform a crucial role in the ceremonial performances of the Korean court.

The blue and white porcelains depicted in these illustrations of ritual texts have a distinctiveness that marks them as Chinese. It is precisely that distinctive association that makes these objects valuable. A vessel decorated with a five-clawed dragon marked such an object out for imperial use in Ming China; the distinctiveness of the five-clawed dragon design made it exclusive. This also worked within the Korean context, because of the close connection between Ming China and Joseon Korea, forged through their diplomatic bonds, ongoing trade and scholarly exchange. Materials and technologies could be shared between the two polities, and blue and white porcelain could be distinct enough to serve as marker of kings and emperors yet shared to the point that it could be adopted and integrated within a new context of the Joseon dynasty: distinctively Chinese, yet meaningful within the Korean ritual context; strikingly different yet seamlessly integrated.

A Fifteenth-Century Shipwreck in the Philippines

In 1996, a shipwreck was discovered in the northern part of the Palawan Strait in the South China Sea. Palawan is one of the over seven thousand islands of the Philippines, and this elongated island stretches out from the northern tip of Borneo in the south, towards Luzon, one of the main islands in the north of the Philippines. Several shipwrecks, dating from the eleventh to the sixteenth centuries and loaded with Chinese goods have been found along the island of Palawan, suggesting that the Palawan Strait was one of the main shipping routes between China and the islands in the South China Sea.[45]

This fifteenth-century shipwreck would become known as the Lena Shoal junk. It had been found first by fishermen, who plundered the site significantly before the archaeological excavations could be started. Figure 6.5 shows stacked rows of porcelain lying directly on the wooden remains of the hull, embedded in the sands of the seabed. The excavations that followed its discovery revealed that the Lena Shoal junk carried a cargo consisting of not only blue and white porcelain, but Chinese ceramics of many other types (stonewares and earthenware), as well as ceramics from Thailand, Vietnam and Burma, various metal objects such as tin ingots and bronze bracelets, musical instruments, and a large quantity of elephant tusks.[46] The variety of goods on board and the range of places of origin represented in the cargo underscore the diversity, mobility and interactions that characterized fifteenth-century maritime trading patterns.

The islands of the Philippines, especially the main landmasses of Luzon and Mindanao, had long been known to the sailors and merchants who travelled between there and the coast of China. One of the main trading routes took the Chinese ships via the island of Taiwan to Luzon and Mindanao, and from there via Palawan to the Moluccas, Borneo and Java.[47] The Lena Shoal junk and the multitude of other shipwrecks found in the South China Sea testify to Chinese participation in a flourishing maritime trade network that connected the Mediterranean and the Red Sea via the Indian Ocean

Figure 6.5 Cargo from the Lena Shoal junk on the seabed. Photo credit: Franck Goddio. From *Lost at Sea*, Photo 9, page 18.

with the South China Sea and the islands and ports of Southeast Asia. Port cities like Hormuz, Angkor (now in Cambodia) and Melaka (now in Malaysia) served as 'crucial pivots' for the movement of raw materials and manufactured commodities throughout this maritime network and were 'vital for the dissemination of religious ideas, representations, and institutions'.[48]

The islands were named the Philippines by Spanish colonialists, who settled here in the sixteenth century and established Manila as the capital in 1571.[49] Soon after 1571, Manila came to hold a key position in the development of trans-Pacific trade between China and the Americas. Before the sixteenth century, however, these islands were considered peripheral to the flourishing maritime networks of trade and interaction. Scholars identified two key areas in this network: one located around Hormuz and Aden in the Arabian Sea and the western parts of the Indian Ocean, including Gujarat and the northern coast of India; the other from the Coromandel Coast through the Malaccan Straits to the ports of mainland Southeast Asia and the South China Coast.[50] Seen from the perspective of those key areas, the pre-colonial societies of the Philippine islands were thought to be remote. Moreover, they were considered to be somewhat passive and static societies, where it was only the influx of luxury foreign goods that initiated processes of change and led to an increased social and cultural complexity.[51]

Chinese porcelain, imported into the Philippines, was considered one of the key luxury foreign goods. As Robert B. Fox put it in 1967, 'influences from China loom large in the culture history of the Philippines', which meant that 'the porcelain trade from China, later from Annam and Siam, eclipsed the ceramic art of the Philippines'.[52] The sheer quantities of Chinese porcelain findings in the Philippines seemed to confirm these islands as mere recipients of traded goods.

Archaeological discoveries of the last decades, however, have led to new interpretations. The Pandanan shipwreck, discovered in 1993 and dated to the middle of the fifteenth century, turned out to have very few Chinese ceramics in its cargo. The overwhelming majority of the goods on board had been manufactured and loaded on board in Vietnam, including not only ceramics but also metals, coins and glass beads.[53] The significance of the Pandanan shipwreck was to confirm Roxana Brown's 'Ming gap' argument: in the middle of the fifteenth century, the ships were loaded with ceramic goods from outside China, most likely because of the efficacy of the Ming trade bans during this period.[54] The shipwreck of the Santa Cruz, excavated in 2001, and dated to the late fifteenth century, had a far wider range of goods on board than the Pandanan shipwreck, with ceramics from China, Thailand, Vietnam and Burma, as well as glass beads, ingots, wooden utensils and stone implements.[55] It showed not only the ongoing internationality of the goods in circulation, but the return of Chinese ceramics in circulation.[56] Clearly, the trade ban, which had prevented Chinese ceramics from entering into the Southeast-Asian market for some time, had lost its efficacy by this time. More importantly, as the scholarship of Bobby C. Orillaneda shows, on the basis of these shipwrecks and various other land-based excavations, these foreign goods interacted in very specific ways with local communities. On the one hand, the exotic quality of these imported goods conveyed socio-political authority and economic power to the elites who had access to such goods. On the other hand, these ceramics came to play integral roles within 'entirely local strategies of power'.[57] Similarly, more recent excavations of burial sites reveal the presence of not only Chinese bowls but also locally made earthenwares, showing that local production continued to exist despite the influx of foreign goods.[58] Overall, then, Orillaneda presents a convincing case that the Philippines were more than peripheral in fifteenth-century maritime trade, and that the imported goods were integrated in nuanced ways into complex and dynamic local societies. Here, too, it seems to me that Chinese porcelain succeeds at performing two roles simultaneously: to convey its value through its distinctiveness and otherness, and to take on locally constructed meaning. The distinctiveness of the pieces is preserved, yet also allows it to form an integral part of an entirely different cultural complex.

A Bowl with Fruit in Renaissance Italy

In the late 1460s, the Veronese painter Francesco Benaglio (1432–1492) painted a Madonna and child figure (Figure 6.6). The Madonna, dressed in rich, gilded textiles, gazes serenely down onto the child, who wears only a red coral necklace and a coral bracelet on each wrist. The child rests on a green cushion with an embroidered gold edge, placed on a dark drapery, which in turn covers a marble parapet. In the background is a 'stylized' landscape:[59] we see travellers on a road, a castle on top of a mound, and, to the left of the Madonna, cultivated fields behind which ships are sailing on a river or sea. Most strikingly, for our purposes, on the ledge next to the infant stands a single bowl containing several pieces of fruit. One of these is adorned with a large fly or beetle, and one single cherry dangles from the side of the bowl. The bowl has a white body, a latticed band around the upper edge and around the foot of the bowl, and a base decorated with overlapping, elongated ellipse shapes.

Of course, the painting is full of symbolic references: the apple in the bowl represents original sin, while the cherry can refer both to the sweetness of the baby and to the blood of his sacrifice. The fly on the apple might refer to the imminent transformation from food into rotten matter, but like all the other objects also serves to underscore the painterly skills of the artist. In that context, then, how should we understand the significance of the porcelain bowl by the side of the infant Christ?

In the 1460s, Chinese porcelain was extremely rare in Europe, in contrast to the Middle Eastern rulers, who owned substantial collections of porcelain.[60] One of the few exceptions was the famous Fonthill vase, now in the National Museum of Ireland, that had been made in Jingdezhen in the first decades of the fourteenth century, and first entered Europe in 1338 as part of a Chinese diplomatic mission to Pope Benedict XII. It was given silver mounts and gifted to Charles III of Naples in 1381 and continued to be gifted and exchanged amongst members of the highest elite in medieval and early modern Europe.[61] Very few ordinary men and women would ever have seen this exceptional piece or other pieces of Chinese porcelain.[62] The wealthy patrons and collectors of art in Florence, the Medici family, were amongst the few who owned pieces of blue and white porcelain from China, in fact, Lorenzo de Medici owned more than 50 pieces by the end

Figure 6.6 Francesco Benaglio, 'Madonna and Child'. Tempera on panel transferred to canvas. Late 1460s. Courtesy National Gallery of Art.

of the fifteenth century.[63] There are fifteenth-century records of orders for porcelain bowls decorated with blue leaves, which suggests that it may well be possible that Benaglio had seen just such a blue and white piece of porcelain from China.

So why did he choose a piece of porcelain to depict next to the baby child? Dr A. I. Spriggs, who wrote one of the first systematic studies of porcelain as it appeared in Western paintings, called this painting the first example of 'unmounted fifteenth-century blue and white introduced into Italian paintings'.[64] He described the bowl as a 'lotus-pod' shape, and identified two fifteenth-century bowls in the British Museum that closely resembled the one that Benaglio depicted. Jessica Harrison-Hall, who discussed this painting more recently, identified an even closer match.[65] Spriggs has little to say about why this single piece of porcelain appeared in Benaglio's painting, although Harrison-Hall refers to Spriggs when she states that porcelain was so rare at this time that it 'was considered a material suitable for presentation to God, representing perhaps a zenith of material wealth'.[66] She is undoubtedly right: all the other attributes in the painting – the coloured textiles, the gold stitching, the coral beads – are there to echo the importance of the Christ child. The single piece of porcelain, such a rare and precious material, signals exceptional value. At the same time, the piece fits, or is made to fit, seamlessly into its Renaissance surroundings. The elongated ellipses that encircle the round base of the bowl echo the circles with elongated ellipses on the cloth that Mary wears; the edging that frames the lip of the bowl matches the beaded edge of Mary's dress. Perhaps the ellipses on the bowl even match the coral beads around the infant's neck and the edgings around the cushion and the cloth on which he rests. Like we saw in the previous examples, the piece of porcelain in the painting is distinct and valuable precisely because it is an exceptional piece, made of an unfamiliar material that few of those gazing at the painting would ever have seen. And yet, in the context of the painting, it does not merely suggest otherness. By way of its association with the baby Jesus, and by the ways in which its patterns match the other valuable materials in the painting, the bowl has become part of this new context, fully embedded into the world of this painting. It speaks to the beholder both as part of the other and as part of the self.

These four fifteenth-century examples can only point to the possibility of this interpretation, yet it seems to me at least possible to argue that blue and white porcelain had these two characteristics. On the one hand, it had a distinctiveness that made it immediately recognizable as Chinese and valuable. On the other hand, it had a certain adaptability in its shapes and decorative patterns that allowed it to be appropriated and embedded into new contexts. In those contexts, it could acquire new meanings, and communicate those values not only from the outside but from within that context. In the next chapters, we return to Jingdezhen itself, and the inner workings of this production site during the sixteenth century, when demand for Jingdezhen's blue and white rose, not only in all these remote locations, but within the Ming empire itself, for which the sixteenth century represents a period of steady development and growth.

7 | The City of Blue and White: Visualizing Space in Ming Jingdezhen, 1500–1600

Until now, our focus has been on the material legacy of production in Jingdezhen, and the global and local circulations of objects and designs. In this chapter, we shift our focus away from things and towards space, especially the space of Jingdezhen and the physical environment in which these goods were produced. Where exactly was Jingdezhen? What kind of place was Jingdezhen in the sixteenth century? How should we visualize this city of blue and white ceramics production? Ostensibly simple, these questions take us from identifying a location by placing a marker on a map, to questioning the meaning of the place, and exploring the different ways in which this city has been imagined and visualized. Historians have learnt a great deal from geographers and have sought to integrate more nuanced and complex understandings of space into their historical work. Most importantly, we share the insight that space should not be understood as a given set of unchanging geo-physical factors, but as a dynamic construction. The implication of that insight is that it behooves us as historians to ask questions about what kind of representations of historical space have come down to us, and whose constructions these represent. In other words, we may well wish to know where Jingdezhen was located, but we should also unpack that location, by asking how, when and by whom that location of Jingdezhen was established. We should question the ways and forms in which that location, and knowledge about that location was transmitted, taking into consideration the multiple shapes and meanings the place accrued over time, established by different actors and for varied audiences.

In what follows, I begin with an exploration of the geo-physical environment that shaped Jingdezhen's past, followed by a discussion of Jingdezhen's place within the administrative structures of the Ming empire. Gradually, the unit of analysis becomes smaller; from Jingdezhen's place in the administrative organization of the empire, the regional environment and the kiln locations that make up the Jingdezhen kiln site complex, we move to the spatial lay-out and organization of the imperial kilns within that complex, and end with the space of a single workshop within the imperial kiln. Of course, these are overlapping units that share many features, but at the same time, each of these represent distinct conceptions of Jingdezhen's space.

Physical Space

The most significant mountain range in the region was Huangshan. The peaks of this mountain site feature extensively throughout Ming cultural formations; paintings, poems and travel writings of the Ming frequently feature Huangshan, and in religious terms, too, Huangshan was a significant site.[1] As the crow flies, the peaks of Huangshan are about 135 km to the northeast of Jingdezhen (186 km on foot through the mountains, and closer to 200 km via Wuyuan by road). In administrative terms, Huangshan was part of an entirely separate political entity, as it fell under the administrative control of a separate province. Geographically speaking, however, the peaks of Huangshan formed part of the same mountain range that spread out across a wide region and reached the vicinity of Jingdezhen. It was the Huangshan foothills that provided many of the natural resources on which Jingdezhen's production depended, such as the wood that burnt the fires and the ferns that melted the glazes. The part of this mountain range closest to Jingdezhen, the Gaoling mountains, yielded an even more crucial resource: these foothills provided the white clay that was named after these mountains, known in English as *kaolin*.[2] The small town of Yaoli, located circa 56 km to the northeast of Jingdezhen, roughly halfway between Jingdezhen and Huangshan, and near the source of a direct river connection with Jingdezhen, served as a distribution point for these crucial resources. The Chang had its source to the north of Jingdezhen, in the Huizhou county of Qimen, and flowed through Fuliang county in a more north-south direction before it arrived in Jingdezhen.[3] Qimen also supplied high quality clay to Jingdezhen.[4] Mountains and rivers were key to Jingdezhen's survival, and provided a regular transport of key resources that travelled from high in the mountains in the northeast downriver through the valleys to the lower plains of Jingdezhen. For a large part, these resources arrived from beyond the provincial boundaries, which serves to underscore the irrelevance of the provincial administrative structures and boundaries for the productivity and commercial activities of Jingdezhen.

The same river, the Chang, flowed out of Jingdezhen towards the west for another 90 km before reaching the lake. This part of the river was equally significant, as this was the waterway by which the merchants carried the finished goods to most of their consumers.[5] By river, it was a distance of over 80 km to the county seat of Poyang, and just 20 plus km beyond Poyang, the ships carrying the finished porcelains arrived on the lake. The key distribution node lay on the opposite side of the lake, where the town of Wucheng was located. Surrounded by water on three sides on a spit of land, Wucheng was the site from where the porcelain was distributed in all directions. Some were transported in a northerly direction, to the Changjiang (Yangzi), and from there to the lower Yangzi delta and via the Grand Canal to the imperial capital. Others were shipped in a southerly direction via the Gan, the main north-south arterial river in the region, to the provincial capital Nanchang and eventually even reaching the south coast. It was because of these key river connections that the inland location of Jingdezhen could become the porcelain production site that serviced the entire world. Map 7.1 illustrates the geography of the region. Surrounded by mountains, Jingdezhen sits in the valley formed by various riverbeds, giving access to both mountains to the northeast, and the flatlands surrounding Lake Poyang to the west of Jingdezhen. These natural features formed the basis for all other socio-political and cultural-historical developments in Jingdezhen.

Jingdezhen in the Administrative Space of the Sixteenth Century

The difference between physical space and administrative space hardly requires an explanation. The founding of the Ming dynasty in 1368 had seen the establishment of 13 core provinces that for the first time resemble the outlines of their contemporary equivalents. Most relevant for us is Jiangxi, the landlocked province in the southeast of the Ming empire in which Jingdezhen was located. The provincial capital in the north of Jiangxi was Nanchang. Long understudied, in part because of paucity of histor-ical records, Nanchang has recently begun to emerge from the shadows of history. Built on the banks of the Gan river, surrounded by marshland and lakes and under constant threat of flooding, the city benefited from the early Ming fortification of its walls and the gradual improvement of water man-agement infrastructure, allowing the city to expand in area and population.[6] Tengwang Pavilion is one of Nanchang's most famous landmarks; towering over the Gan and visible from a long distance, it was and is a beloved subject of poems, paintings and ceramics decorations.[7] But the city had little else to enhance its reputation as a rather out of the way provincial capital.

Ming Jiangxi shared a border with five other provinces (Map 4.1). Immediately to the north, but separated by the Yangzi river, was Nanzhili, or Zhongdu province (the province of the capital) as it was known before the Yongle emperor moved the capital from Nanjing to the north, near the Great Wall. This region encompassed the fertile agricultural lands of the

Map 7.1 Raozhou prefecture. Map based on China Historical Geographic Information System (CHGIS), version 6.

lower Yangzi delta, and prosperous commercial centres like Suzhou and Yangzhou. The southern part of Nanzhili province, Huizhou, shared a border with the region where Jingdezhen was located. To Jiangxi's north-east was the coastal province of Zhejiang, with Hangzhou and several other significant port cities, from where goods from Jingdezhen were transported overseas, for example to Japan. Along Jiangxi's eastern border was a mountainous zone that separated Jiangxi from Fujian. The southern part of Jiangxi province, Ganzhou, was and is inhabited by a population that speaks quite a different dialect from the central and northern part of the province. In linguistic, but also in many other ways, this southern part of Jiangxi is more closely aligned with Guangdong, Jiangxi's southern neighbour. Finally, Huguang (nowadays divided into Hubei and Hunan) shares a border with Jiangxi all along the western and north-western edges of the province.

The river Gan flows from the southern parts of the province northwards, where it meets the region of marshes and lakes known as Lake Poyang, which serves as an overflow for the Yangzi river. Transport of goods and the movement of people all follow this flow of the river in a north-south direction; far less movement occurred across the mountains in the east towards Fujian. More migration of people occurred in a westerly direction – a popular saying has it that Huguang was filled with people from Jiangxi (*Jiangxi tian Huguang*) – most likely in a bid to avoid the exorbitant tax demands made on Jiangxi, which served as one of the main suppliers of grain for the imperial capital.[8]

All Ming provinces were further subdivided into prefectures; Jiangxi had 13 prefectures of varying size, from small but densely populated prefectures like Jiujiang and Nankang in the north, crisscrossed by rivers, lakes and waterways, to the much larger prefectures in the south, such as Ji'an with its fertile flatlands, and mountainous Ganzhou. Raozhou, the prefecture in Jiangxi's northeast in which Jingdezhen was located, had some of all these characteristics, encompassing the eastern edges of Lake Poyang; the mountainous region suitable for tea production in the north, where Raozhou borders Huizhou; fertile agricultural lands in the south; and inaccessible mountains in the far east of the prefecture where it meets the provincial borders of Fujian (Map 7.1). The prefecture was administered from the prefectural capital, located near the edge of Lake Poyang. The prefectural government in turn supervised the affairs of the six counties that made up Raozhou prefecture: Fuliang, Poyang, Leping, Dexing, Yugan and Anren. Each of these counties had a county seat, with imposing offices for the county administrators, including the county magistrate. From Jingdezhen to the county seat of Fuliang was a distance of just over 10 km, or a couple of hours walking distance. The prefectural capital was further: the more than 80 km from Jingdezhen to the prefectural capital of Raozhou would have meant a two-day walk. But regardless of those distances, for those who lived and worked in Jingdezhen, both the county seat and the prefectural seat probably seemed the equivalent of the imperial court: imposing and undoubtedly associated with power, but remote and hardly relevant in daily life.

Fuliang, the county in the northeast of Raozhou prefecture that encompassed Jingdezhen, has a surface area of around 2,800 km², making it roughly the same size as Luxemburg, and smaller than Rhode Island. It was largely mountainous, with a relatively small proportion of arable land, though the climate was very suitable for agriculture and forestry.[9] Reliable population figures for premodern China are notoriously difficult to obtain, but at least they can be used for their indicative quality. Throughout the Ming dynasty, the Fuliang population figure remained constant at roughly 100,000, with only minor fluctuations.[10] Today, the population figure for rural Fuliang has more than doubled, and that is without including the urban population of Jingdezhen, which now forms a *shi*, a separate administrative unit for large conurbations. In terms of administering this sizable population in the sixteenth century, this was handled by only a small group of centrally appointed civil servants, which included one magistrate, assisted by a deputy and an assistant magistrate charged with documentation and record keeping; two officials charged with education and examination matters; and two officials in charge of public security: the district jailor and the police chief.[11] Of course, this small group of imperial officials had staff members drawn from the local elite to support their administrative duties, but on the whole, during the Ming dynasty, the layer of officialdom was thin, and the ratio of officials to members of the population high.

Fuliang county was to some extent an exceptional county, in that the town or *zhen* of Jingde fell under its jurisdiction and formed part of the county tax obligation. As the county was the smallest administrative unit, such *zhen*, as we already saw in earlier chapters, held an unusual position within the administration of the empire. The term applied to places where the population accumulated for a specific reason such as trade, but also manufacturing sites such as the kiln sites of this region. The application of the term implied a tax responsibility, but the administration of the town fell entirely under the umbrella of the county governance. In administrative terms, then, the town of Jingdezhen was hardly noteworthy. From the perspective of the imperial administration, such *zhen* mattered only for what they could yield; asserting control, it was assumed, could be done via the officials based in the county offices.

Describing the location of Jingdezhen and its surroundings in this way follows closely the administrative structure. Starting from the largest unit (the whole empire), we worked our way down the administrative levels: from province (Jiangxi) to prefecture (Raozhou) to county (Fuliang), and finally, to the town (*zhen*) of Jingdezhen. This is the way in which the administration of the empire visualized this space, but equally, it is how the state delegated the power of the imperial framework to the local level. For the workers in Jingdezhen, the administrative officials who were based roughly 10 km to the north, at the yamen in the capital of Fuliang, represented the emperor, both symbolically and in practical terms through the execution of the law. The administrative structure of the empire was designed to claim ownership of, and extend imperial control over, the entirety of the territory of Great Ming, down to the smallest unit. That administrative vision of the space yields a map that seeks to organize the space for its own purpose; it places markers on that map to highlight sites of administrative activity and uses lines to create an impression of strict boundaries that separate administrative territories and units of taxation.

Manufacturing Space

Administratively speaking, a market town or *zhen* held a position of low import-ance; in geo-physical terms, the town sat in a strategic location, surrounded by mountains that provided resources and alongside rivers that were valuable for maintaining connections with other locations and the transportation of resources and goods. But the manufacturing space was yet again a different kind of space and a different way of drawing the map. While the name Jingdezhen suggests a single town, in discussions of ceramics production in this region, Jingdezhen referred not to a single site but to a network of locations and sites distributed throughout the region. Archaeological excavations are only slowly uncovering the extent of these sites, and the likelihood of a reliable and com-plete picture is not high. More than 30 different sites were active throughout the period of production in this region, which started probably as early as the Tang dynasty (eighth century) and continues to this day.

For the Ming dynasty, we know that some of the ceramics production sites were indeed located within the boundaries of the *zhen*, most notably of course the imperial kiln complex, about which more below. But there were others: on the west bank of the Chang, 1 km from the town centre, in the northwest of the area known as Zhushan (Pearl Mountain), is Shibadu kiln site, and in the eastern suburbs of the town Shuinichang kiln site, both of which are known to have been active in the fourteenth and fifteenth cen-turies. In the northern suburbs, 3 km from the town centre of Jingdezhen on the eastern banks of the Chang was the kiln site of Guanyinge (Guanyin pavilion).[12] Undoubtedly, there were numerous other, smaller sites within the boundaries of the town, some of which may still appear in archaeo-logical excavations, but most of these will now lie forever buried under the vastly expanded urban development of multi-story buildings and roads that make up today's Jingdezhen.

Several other Ming sites of porcelain manufacture were located within Fuliang county, in the vicinity of, but outside of, the town of Jingdezhen. The following description comes from the 1525 gazetteer for Jiangxi, the oldest province-wide document we have for Jiangxi.[13] 'Porcelain comes from Fuliang. Most beautiful is the porcelain from Jingdezhen. Next (in quality) are porcelains from Hutian market (*shi*), and the lowest (quality) are those from Macangdong'.[14] The description appears in the section on local products (*wuchan*), where the compiler lists porcelain in a matter of fact manner between the *fuling* fungus (used for its medical properties), the white peony (also used as a medicinal plant), *wuyao* (a medicinal root), copper and bran.[15] Listing the production of porcelain on a par with wild herbs and roots harvested from the hills and the small-scale mining of copper in one of the counties of the prefecture, all of which even taken together can only have yielded a fraction of the size and scale of the production of porcelain in the region is striking. Either the compiler had very little knowledge of the extent of porcelain production in this region, or, more likely, the size and scope of the production was not relevant in this context; the aim was merely to provide a complete list of each separate product produced here.

Nonetheless, the reference to these three ceramics production sites in a document dated 1525 is important, confirming not only manufacturing at these sites, but also their official recognition *as kiln sites* by the administrative officials in the region who compiled the gazetteer. Hutian is situated about 4 km to the east of the town centre of Jingdezhen. We have encountered Hutian before; it has long been known that the area to the east of the town centre, which encompasses not only Hutian but also a kiln site known as Yinkangweng further to the east, hosted multiple kiln complexes. Yinkangweng, in the far east of this region, was mostly active during the Song dynasty, and over time, new kiln sites were developed in a westerly direction, gradually moving closer to the town centre.[16] The place identified as Macangdong in this sixteenth-century document, nowadays known as Yaoli, mentioned above, is about 60 km to the northeast from Jingdezhen. Recent archaeological research has revealed a third Ming-dynasty site, located at 21 km to the southwest of Jingdezhen, in Pengjia Village, near the town of Liyang.[17] Established in the Yuan, but further developed during the early Ming, the site had several gourd-shaped kilns, and produced a range of wares, including blue and white wares, white-glazed wares, wares glazed with a purple (*zijin*) or mocca (*jiang*) glaze, and a celadon-type ware.[18] Its location further downstream along the Chang suggests this site probably had access by river to some of the same resources that from Liyang's perspective lay further east, on the other side of Jingdezhen, but may well also have drawn on resources from Leping, the county to the south of Fuliang.

What this shows is that the landscape can be ordered not only by means of the administration that was imposed from above, or by means of the geo-physical characteristics that shaped the landscape 'from below', but by means of a third layer that sits between these two. The various manufacturing sites that fall under the broader heading of Jingdezhen form a fine-mazed web across the landscape. Of course, their location was shaped by the natural environment: always by the side of a river for transportation purposes, and usually in a flat area for the ease of building the various structural spaces for manufacturing porcelain. The goods these kilns produced were not part of the official manufactures that occurred at the imperial kilns; they were privately owned kilns (*minyao*). But as we will see below, their production was in many ways also tied in with the official administration, and shared technological know-how, and even the labour force. Jingdezhen, then, can also be understood as a manufacturing space, denoting the independent but connected network of production sites scattered across this region.[19] These visions of space are not entirely independent entities; there are connections, interactions and negotiations between them all, but it is useful to tease them apart, to see their dimensions more clearly.

Imperial Space

Within this network of kiln sites within Jingdezhen and scattered across the region around Jingdezhen, one ceramics production site (*chang*) stood out above all other kilns: the imperial kiln, known as *guanyao* during the Ming dynasty. This single kiln has come to dominate our understanding of Jingdezhen. The term 'Jingdezhen' is often used as shorthand, meaning just the imperial kiln, ignoring the different spatial dimensions that the term Jingdezhen also encompasses: the administrative unit to which this *zhen* belongs, the intricate relationship between the town and its natural surroundings, and the various manufacturing sites that together make up Jingdezhen. It is not surprising that the term Jingdezhen has come to be regarded as synonymous with the imperial kiln, such is its dominance in documentary and visual records of the place. But as will become abundantly clear in the following chapters, the imperial kilns could not have existed in Jingdezhen had it not been for the local administrative structure, the representatives of the imperial administration who were posted to the region to oversee production, the regional geographical features and the privately owned kiln sites scattered around the immediate surroundings of the imperial kiln.

In what follows we will apply a fourth lens to the region and zoom in on the imperial manufactures to show how the state imposed the imperial agenda on this space. Throughout the sixteenth century, the imperial court had need for a large supply of ceramics, ranging from vessels used in the emperor's rituals and sacrifices and the rituals held throughout the court including all the offices of the imperial administration, to the ceramics for imperial banquets and entertainments, and for daily use throughout the imperial household. The size of the imperial household was substantial: it included not only the emperor and his consorts and their children, but also the palace attendants and a large eunuch staff. It also extended beyond the main base of the court in Beijing to the 'secondary court' in Nanjing and to the palaces for the members of the imperial clan in the provinces.[20] If we keep in mind that there were 100,000 eunuchs in the Ming imperial household, each of which maintained a household of one or two servants and often an adopted son, then we get some sense of the numbers of ceramics required. In 1433, for example, the court issued a demand to Jingdezhen for 443,500 pieces of ceramics, and in 1577, the demand was for 174,700 pieces. Such large demands were not issued every year, and it often took the imperial kilns many years to fulfil the demand, but inevitably, the imperial demand absorbed a substantial part of Jingdezhen's production.

As had been the case under the previous dynasties, the Ming imperial administration established a porcelain office to manage the procurement of porcelain from Jingdezhen. This office oversaw production at the imperial kilns, and managed all the aspects this entailed, from acquiring the raw resources and hiring the labour to make the goods, to packing and transporting the goods to the imperial court. The sixteenth-century handbook that details these administrative and supervisory processes has been preserved in the form of a work called *Taoshu* [Book of Ceramics], which has been transmitted in *juan* 7 of the Wanli edition of the Jiangxi provincial gazetteer.[21] This gazetteer was originally compiled by Wang Zongmu during the Jiajing reign period, in 1556, an edition that does not survive separately, and subsequently expanded by Lu Wan'gai, who published the work in 1597. This work, I argue below, not only describes the various administrative processes that formed part of imperial production but exerts its power over them.[22] We do not have a visual depiction of Jingdezhen dating to the Ming dynasty, but this text does the same thing: it creates an image of the imperial space in Jingdezhen. The text serves as 'point of intersection between the central government and local society' and forms one of the 'building blocks in the imagined empire', as Joseph Dennis puts it. The space that is conjured up before our eyes in this text, then, is the vision of the imperial kilns that the imperial state wishes its audience to see; Jingdezhen thereby becomes a vision of imperial space.[23]

See, for example, this description of the lay-out of the kilns. 'Inside [the imperial kiln complex], one finds the main hall, divided into three separate spaces, behind which there are smaller workspaces, connected by a hallway … on each side, there is a wing with three spaces inside; there are three gates on the south and east side', and so on.[24] All the different buildings are identified: various gates, a drumtower, storehouses on the east and west side (with on each side six inner and eight outer storehouses), a hut for the overseer (later extended to a three-pillar shed), a place for locking people up, and 23 separate workshops or work divisions. These 23 workshops are each named individually, detailing the number of workspaces the workshop has or the volume of the space. The workshop where the saggars are made is the biggest, with 33 workspaces. Saggars are the clay dividers used to ensure the vessels do not fuse when they are being fired in the kiln; larger and rougher than the pieces of porcelain placed inside them, they had to be strong enough to withstand the extremely high temperatures inside the kiln. Any functioning kiln always needs a vast amount of this so-called kiln furniture; hence a workshop consisting of 33 separate spaces allocated to their production. The workshops for making the different kinds of porcelain vessels all have around seven or eight workspaces, while specialized tasks, like writing characters on the vessels, only require one workspace.

One could simply read this as a list of buildings, large and small, used for a variety of purposes. But the text does more than merely list the buildings; it asserts control over the buildings and assigns them their place within the spatial hierarchy. The power of the authorities is represented within the space in the form of the shed for the overseer and the room for imprisoning people. The lay-out of the buildings shows which buildings are more important than others. The lay-out follows the basic rules of Chinese architecture: the main series of halls facing the front of the complex, situated along the central axle of the space are the most important buildings; they host the offices of the official administration and thereby represent imperial space. The smaller workstations behind these buildings, and those facing sideways are less important than these front-facing official spaces, but still highlight their proximity to the main business of organizing the manufacture through the connecting corridor. The spaces where the actual work tasks are carried out, the 23 workshops, are placed further away from the central axis, facing in various directions, and are not connected to the main administrative offices. In other words, this lay-out of the buildings as it is accounted for here prioritized imperial control and administrative tasks, while delegating the labour tasks of the manufacturing processes to a lesser place.

The space surrounding the ceramics manufactory is also narrated in full detail. There are several shrines inside and outside the site, two large wells, several storehouses for different types of firewood, and dormitories for the workers. To the west lies the old magistrate's office, to the east, along the road towards Jiujiang, six different types of kiln are located. There are 16 kilns just for firing the large fishbowl vats, 20 altogether for firing coloured pieces, large items and small-sized vessels, and a total of 44 kilns for firing saggars. We already saw that a very large amount of space was allocated to the workshop where saggars were made, and now we see that the largest group of kilns was devoted to firing them. The saggar kilns themselves also came in different sizes, depending on the size of the porcelain objects the saggars were intended to hold, and used about the same quantity of fire-wood for each firing as the colour kilns (both saggar kilns and kilns for firing coloured ceramics were heated to a lower temperature than single fired porcelains). In each single firing, a saggar kiln produced about 70 or 80 saggars, some of which could be used repeatedly, but most only served once or twice.[25] So the principles of architecture assigned the greatest importance to the tasks of administration and governance, foregrounding that aspect and highlighting its significance. The principles of space, how-ever, underscore a different kind of significance: that which is assigned more space than anything else and demands more resources than anything else clearly has a material significance, forming the material basis on which the other production rests, and without which the other tasks cannot be completed.

It is worth dwelling briefly on the impact of this production of saggars when we visualize the space: to produce enough saggars, these kilns must have been firing on a continuous basis, and there must have been more workers allocated to producing saggars than any other task. Yet these workers were involved in the production of a roughly made, disposable object that was never intended to be seen again. In terms of the quantities of clay, firewood, labour and waste product the manufacture of saggars took up in Jingdezhen, saggar production was huge, and yet saggars remain entirely overlooked in most visual representations of ceramics production. Only when we visualize the space based on its discursive representation does this manifest itself, and we see that the division of the space is not only intended to assert ownership over the final products – the porcelains intended for the imperial court – but a claim over the bodies of the workers and the labour they perform.

As we have seen, the text orders the space by placing the buildings within the hierarchical structures of Chinese architecture, but also by means of creating separations and divisions. The division between saggar-making and porcelain vessel production is one example; the separation between the imperial kilns and the privately owned kilns is another: wares fired for supplying the imperial court are referred to as 'imperial wares' (without any guarantee, of course, that these wares would actually make the journey to the court), in contrast to the privately owned kilns, where wares are fired for commercial purposes by private enterprises. The text creates the difference by prescribing separate actions; for example, when firing a kiln filled with imperial-quality porcelain, the process of placing the pieces inside the kiln is different from the process for firing non-official wares. To protect the imperial wares from the flames, they are separated from the fire by rows of empty saggars, and to protect the contents of the kiln from the atmosphere (technically speaking to maintain a reducing atmosphere) and to prevent the emergence of cracks and air vents, the kiln is completely covered with a layer of mud. At the private kilns, where the load of the kiln was not as precious, and productivity and profit mattered more, that protective layer is omitted, and more goods are placed inside the kiln, separated from the fire simply by a row of coarser wares.[26] That separation between imperial and private is created throughout the text, and highlights that what mattered to the authors was a material differentiation between the two.

To achieve that, clays are sourced from different places, are treasured for their individual characteristics, and are combined in specific proportions according to separate recipes. The weight of clay used for each type of pot is meticulously specified.[27] Similarly, the cobalt comes in different qualities and is allocated depending on the size of the object that is to be decorated.[28] Each created object has come through a process that is separated out from the processes designated for other kinds of objects, creating the impression repeatedly that we are dealing with material separations. Even the fuel that fires the kiln is separated into categories: boat fuel is different from water fuel. For the first variety, the wood was felled and brought to the rivers in the surrounding area, loaded onto boats delivered to the town by boat. This fuel was drier, but more expensive. The other kind of fuel consisted of wood felled in the hilly region along the Chang, upriver from Jingdezhen, pushed into the river and brought downriver on rafts. These rafts were made up from large pinewood split into two or four pieces, which were simply floated downriver from higher up in the mountains. This fuel was known as 'river-fuel'.[29] This type of fuel was cheaper, but wetter, and produced more smoke, which could have an impact on the quality of the porcelain. The cost of firewood amounted to about a third of the overall cost of a kiln-load of ceramics, so of course these distinctions mattered a great deal. The temptation was always there to swap the two kinds and sell wet fuel for the price of dry fuel, or to stockpile and dry out wet fuel in the spring and summer, and sell it at a premium in the late summer and autumn when the rivers were running dry and less fuel floated directly to the town.[30] So, it is entirely unsurprising that the gazetteer seeks to classify these material differences, and impose systems that keep those material separations in place.

The separation is also visible in the recipes for the different colours, and the allocation of specific tools for each of the workshops. The tools for preparing pigments and mixing colours are quite different from the tools required for preparing the clay or for packing the finished goods for transport. Again, in the narrative of the gazetteer, each of the spaces is provided with its own, separate list of material objects that make that space tailored specifically for the required task. None of the spaces are interchangeable or multi-functional. The tools are even categorized by the material they are made from. Within a specific workshop, there would be the tools made of wood – the upright part of the pestle, the buckets, the planks for making boxes, the frames for drying bodies – there were tools made of metal – the bowl for rinsing the clay, the hammer for beating the clay – there were bamboo tools, items made from stone, and of course items made of fired clay: the bricks, the washing vats, and the pestle and mortars used for mixing the pigments. Grouping the materials together creates a separate category for them; describing the spaces listing the individual items within them enhances the separation of the spaces. Separations and divisions clearly matter; or perhaps put more precisely: clearly matter to the authors of the gazetteer. Writing about separate spaces is not so much an act of description as an active intervention in the organization of space. The text, written by administrators and local powerholders, actively organizes the space. The text created distinctions, and by writing about these materials in these spatially divided ways, the administrators seek to extend their power over the materials. For those in charge of allocating resources, for example, whether that concerns quantities of clay per worker, or weight of cobalt issued per vessel, categorizations and classifications are key. Jingdezhen's famous division of labour, equally, is part of the structure of power in Jingdezhen. If we read the gazetteer as an extension or tool of the powerholders in Jingdezhen, then the text seems to serve effectively in that capacity and shapes the imperial space in accordance with their vision of Jingdezhen.

The units of space may be getting smaller in our discussion here, but the point remains the same: Jingdezhen means different things to different people, and these can be understood as different visions of space. Those visions of what Jingdezhen signifies, or why Jingdezhen matters, in turn, shape the representations of space in Jingdezhen. For some, Jingdezhen means a commercially productive town, situated at the lowest rung of the administrative ladder, for others a region with a specific set of physical conditions that facilitate the production and trade of ceramics, or indeed a network of ceramics sites that share resources, technologies and skills to create a unified set of ceramics production sites. As we have seen, the maps that represent these different visions share some of the physical features of the landscape but highlight different aspects that fit that vision. If we see the landscape through the eyes of the imperial kiln administrators, as we have done in this section, we see yet another view of Jingdezhen, one that emphasizes the nodes of imperial control, and the modes of manufacturing that suggest the separation of imperial wares from other modes of manufacturing in the region. Jingdezhen's space is imagined in such a way that it not only allows for such separation but also facilitates the imposition of order over the production process, including not only the manufactured goods but also the labour of the workers and their bodies. The imperial vision of Jingdezhen is about control and ownership.

Workspace in the Cobalt-Painting Division

The final example is the vision of Jingdezhen as seen through the eyes of the worker, who performs his task within the confines of a single workshop that forms part of the complex of the imperial kiln. As we already saw, the imperial kiln was organized based on a division of labour. No workshop made a single piece of porcelain from start to finish; the workshops were the institutional subdivisions of the imperial kiln responsible for a specific part of the manufacturing process. Workshop, then, is a slightly misleading name; work division is perhaps a more accurate rendering of the term, but I will use both terms below. In the sixteenth century, the process within the imperial kilns was divided up into 23 such subdivisions or workshops. Some of these workshops were responsible for the production of a specific shape, such as large bowls or wine goblets or plates; some supervised a specific production process, such as creating designs using a mould, or painting decorations or writing characters; others were divided by the raw material they worked with, such as clay, different kinds of wood, metal and bamboo. These organizational units were then further subdivided into rooms or workspaces. The work division in charge of painting, for example, had the use of seven workspaces.[31] Here, four supervisors and 19 painters devoted themselves to the task of applying cobalt blue decorations to the leather-hard bodies.[32]

The cobalt they worked with was an extremely precious commodity, and jealously guarded by the authorities as it was known to disappear into the pockets of those who had access to it. The painters were not trusted with their own supply of cobalt; they were allocated a fixed amount twice a day, once at the start of the day, and once at noon, so that they never had access to more than half a day's worth of cobalt.[33] For applying the cobalt to the vessels, the workshop was equipped with tables, on which the leather-dry pieces were placed, and small stools for the painters to sit on while they painted.[34] This workshop, however, also supervised the preparatory processes required to produce the cobalt-based pigment. This involved pounding the cobalt with hammers or pestles so that it was pulverized and washing the cobalt in small containers with water to separate the pure cobalt from its surrounding material, which was pulled out of the water by means of a magnet. This purified cobalt was then pounded in mortars for three whole days, after which it was carefully placed in sealed boxes and guarded carefully, until it was allocated for the painters to use. The space, therefore, was filled with all kinds of equipment: tables and stools, pestles and mortars, washbasins, buckets, boxes, brushes and paintings. All these pieces had to be stored, put away when not in use, and arranged in a suitable manner for the workers when the relevant task had to be performed.

The example of the paintings might illustrate this. 'On the day of painting with cobalt, they hang up the painting scrolls in advance, creating separate sections for "heaven and earth, dark and yellow,"[35] and the painters sit down in accordance with their seat number'.[36] The painters are not free to choose their own seat or to decorate according to their own inspiration; they are ordered, as the paintings are organized, in separate groups according to very basic divisions such as heaven and earth, dark and bright. As we have seen before, the underlying reason was not productivity or simplicity, but order and control. The cobalt was so precious, and the risk of stealing so great that the supervisors even had to worry about the painters making weaker mixtures, with less pure cobalt and more cheaper additives mixed in. To avoid this, the painters had to sit in their allocated seat, so that afterwards they could be reunited with the vessels they had painted. If a different mixture had been used, then this would be visible in the finished product. A much darker blue was evidence of too much cheaper material mixed in with the more expensive cobalt. So even at the workshop level, the organization of the space, and the allocation of bodies into that space, was ordered from above.

And yet, at this level of the organization of space, it was by no means possible to order every aspect of the workshop space, because the use of the workshop space was also determined by the labour tasks. The illustration in Figure 7.1 is instructive here. The image comes from one of the most famous late Ming books about the natural world and the tools available to

Figure 7.1 Song Yingxing, 'The works of heaven and the inception of things'
(*Tiangong kaiwu*), middle *juan*, 15b-16a.

human beings to create and maintain order in that natural world.[37] Song
Yingxing's text, entitled 'The works of heaven and the inception of things'
(*Tiangong kaiwu*) reflects on the many materials, processes, tools and
methods that were available for the creation of that order in the natural
world. The illustrated version of the text, which dates from the early seventeenth century, affords us small glimpses of yet another vision of the workshop space. There is no emphasis on built enclosures here or on the framing
structures that were so clear in the text of *Taoshu*. Instead, the black lines
that form the frame of the picture perform the same function and separate
the image on the right from the one on the left.

The images provide momentary glimpses, rather than visual narratives
of one step followed by another. The image on the right shows two workers
dipping the dried pieces into a large porcelain vat filled with water; the
image on the left shows two separate processes simultaneously, but both
involve the application of cobalt to the surface of the leather-hard bodies.
The higher vignette within the image on the left shows a round table, with
a worker seated on a ceramic stool. His right hand holds the brush, while
his right elbow rests on the edge of the round table; the left hand holds the
round tabletop, and swivels the table round, hence the single central leg,

which forms the turning point for the table. This way, the table turns while the right hand stays steady, and the brush paints a straight line all along the upper edge of the vessel (*da quan*: applying a circle). On the table, next to the circle-maker stand the vessels awaiting this process.

The lower image has a square table, with a more comfortable high-backed chair, where a single painter applies '*huiqing*' (cobalt) to the small vessels. Both are highly skilled tasks, one of which requires a steady hand, regular pressure and complete control, while the other relies on the creativity and free-flowing brush of the painter. The frame of the picture combines the two cobalt-based tasks into a single image, with the tools, pieces of equipment and body shapes of the men indicating the difference between the two tasks. At this lowest administrative division or workshop level, then, it is the coherence of the tasks related to cobalt that organizes the space. Because the cobalt-related tasks are quite varied, ranging from pounding the raw material and preparing the pigment for use, to using a fine brush to paint the pieces, this workshop was subdivided into seven separate workspaces. Instead of the organization and administration taking centre stage, however, it was the labour tasks that drove the organization of the space. The various loose pieces of equipment such as stools and tables could be moved and arranged in accordance with the requirements of the task, making use of the flexibility of the workspace.

Of course, these accounts, which highlight different aspects, reveal close interdependencies. The mountains and rivers, the offices of the county administration, the office buildings of the imperial kiln, and the numerous workspaces all coexisted in this sixteenth-century moment that we have highlighted here. They were not located in physically different spaces, but I have sought to argue that each of these accounts asserts its own order over the space, thereby representing different visions of the space. This city that produced blue and white porcelain, eventually to serve almost the entire world, was known for the work that one labourer sitting in a chair with a brush in his hand carried out. But that application of cobalt blue on a white ceramic surface could not have happened without other workers in that same space preparing the cobalt, washing it, pulverizing it and mixing it to the right proportion. In turn, the workers in this workshop were dependent on the production processes in the other workshops, and overall, their work formed part of the way in which the imperial state organized its procurement of porcelain. The imperial kiln formed one small part of the administration of the whole empire. Because porcelain production was dependent on a set of resources that was only available in this specific location, the entire operation of imperial production happened here, in Jingdezhen. In turn, this meant that the knowledge about production, the required skills, and the design ideas also all circulated within this region, informing the various private kilns, of which we only see a fraction in the archaeological evidence today. Space, in this sense of the word, is not about physical space alone, but about the assertion of meaning upon that space.

8 | Anxieties over Resources in Sixteenth-Century Jingdezhen

The previous chapter explored Jingdezhen's ceramics manufactures from the perspective of space. Different maps and other representations of the region revealed that there are many ways of seeing Jingdezhen. Different views of Jingdezhen emerge, depending on whether we see Jingdezhen in its natural environment or as part of the imperial administration, as an isolated kiln complex or part of a connected network of sites associated with ceramics production. These different views do not represent independent spatial units, but interdependent realms or nested layers. Of course, there are independent factors or agents that shape such realms, but it is their interconnectedness that matters. As we saw in the previous chapters, it is precisely the fluidity and circulation between them that explains the emergence of Jingdezhen as foremost site of ceramics manufacture in the fifteenth century. The manufacture of high-quality goods and their production in large quantities were possible because of the fluid circulation of raw materials and technological know-how, and the connected modes of transportation available throughout the wider region.

This chapter and the next focus on the sixteenth century, when cracks start to appear in this interconnected system of production. As we will see, the fluidity of the system also caused significant anxiety over resources, including both supplies of material goods and access to a skilled labour force. While the anxieties over labour and skill form the subject of the next chapter, this chapter focuses on the question of resources. Who owned the wood required for firing the kilns, and who could set the price of that wood? Who had access to the equipment and tools that furnished the various workshops, and who controlled the expensive pigments required in the production of fine ceramics? As we will see, questions over ownership and price, access and control arose in all of the stages of the production process. For the representatives of the imperial administration, i.e. the officials who were posted in the local county capital, Fuliang, and had supervisory responsibilities over the production of the porcelains that would go on to make up the imperial tribute, there was most at stake. For these administrators, the fluidity that characterized the movement of resources amounted to a loss of control over the costs of production and thereby over the goods they needed to supply. In the Europe-focused discussions of proto-industrialization, this phase of economic development is thought to include the involvement of the rural workforce in manufacture through the so-called 'putting-out system', the growth of manufacturing for distant markets, and a 'dynamic build up of capital, entrepreneurial and manufacturing skills, mercantile contacts and markets, and a growing wage-labour force'.[1] Rather than arguing for a set of precise parallels, I point to some meaningful similarities, including one of the consequences of proto-industrialization as described by Pat Hudson:

> As businesses increased in size, activities were spread over a wider geographical area and marginal costs tended to rise. Also lack of control over the often unspecialised work-force made production deadlines and uniform quality difficult to achieve, and embezzlement of materials became an increasing problem. Centralised production was seen to result because it solved these difficulties.[2]

In Jingdezhen, one of the consequences of the flows of resources and the circulations of knowledge into the realms of private producers was a gradual but persistent leaking away of control and power for the imperial administration. As we will see below, it was the anxiety over this circulation and fluidity that led the imperial kiln administrators to seek, almost desperately, to stem the flow and maintain control, ultimately without much success. The text that forms our main source for this discussion should be understood as one of the tools of the administrators to assert not only meaning over the space, as we saw in the previous chapter, but also control over what happened within that space.

Fuel for Firing the Kilns

Amongst all the resources required for porcelain production in Jingdezhen, fuel undoubtedly accounted for the largest in terms of quantity.[3] In contrast to kilns in the north of the Chinese empire, which used coal, the southern kilns were all fired with wood. In principle, supplies of firewood were available in ample quantities in the surrounding mountains. The size of the kilns varied, and the levels of humidity in the environment fluctuated, which meant that the requirement for fuel also changed accordingly. One firing of a single kiln could use as much as 180 *gang* (shoulder-loads) of firewood. The term *gang* refers to the weight measure one human labourer could carry by means of carrying poles on their shoulder, generally assumed to amount to roughly 100 catty (*jin*) or 50 kg. This means that the total weight of firewood for a single kiln firing could amount to 9,000 kg of wood.[4] The stated quantity of 180 *gang* was an upper limit; a more typical kiln firing took 160 *gang*, which still amounted to 8 tonnes of firewood. The sheer volume of fuel required for a single firing of a full-size kiln made the cost of fuel crucial for the sustainability of production.

As we saw in the previous chapter, fuel was distinguished on the basis of its method of delivery to Jingdezhen. Private wood merchants, who were not employed by the imperial kilns, took care of these fuel deliveries, and these men were paid for their firewood by weight. Wood delivered by boat was more expensive than the wood delivered by floating large pieces downriver, but from the point of view of the kiln firing more importantly, these two types of fuel differed in terms of their moisture levels. Levels of humidity in the kiln always had an immediate impact on the atmosphere within the kiln. Generally speaking, the authors of *Taoshu* tell us, the kilns should use 60 per cent fuel delivered by boat, and 40 per cent fuel that had floated downriver. The drier boat-fuel was to be used for getting the fire started, but once the fire was established and the flames had spread, then the switch to the damper 'river fuel' could be made.[5]

So long as the mountains provided ample quantities of wood for fuel, and the rivers provided convenient transportation routes, the supply of fuel to fire the kilns was unproblematic, and fuel circulated freely between the various production sites. The imperial kiln administrators were alarmed to find, however, that the wood merchants succeeded in passing off river fuel that had simply floated downriver, as the more expensive boat-fuel.[6] The firewood traders would lean on the minor clerks who oversaw the process of weighing the goods and determining the price, forcing these minor clerks to accept one kind of fuel for the other kind. The implications could be serious; they supplied either damp wood or a mixed load, containing both the drier and damper variety, both of which would be enough to spoil the fired goods. Moreover, the required quantities of wood per kiln firing eventually had an impact on the environment, making fuel an increasingly scarce commodity. In turn, that scarcity not only led to an increase in the price of fuel and jeopardized the regularity of its delivery to the imperial kiln, but also opened up opportunities for competition over that supply.

The scarcity of the wood supply, of course, created opportunities for financial gain for the traders who depended on the same fuel for their livelihood. As the administrators found, when the value of firewood was 0.03 tael per shoulder-load (*gang*), the merchants would keep behind a large quantity, thereby increasing the scarcity of the supply. They would lay the moist firewood in the sun to dry out near where it was felled, so that they had to pay little or no transportation costs, and then bide their time until the increase in demand drove the prices up.

> In the autumn and winter, when the rivers dry up, far fewer boats arrive [to deliver fuel in Jingdezhen]. Meanwhile, the porcelain merchant boats come and go (*tengyong*), [increasing the demand for fuel], so that the price of fuel rises, and the price they can get for their fuel goes up to four *fen* (0.04 tael).[7]

The word chosen to describe the arrival and departure of the merchant boats, *tengyong*, is usually reserved for galloping horses rushing about, for rushing water or rocketing prices. The sense of urgency and the frantic nature of the movements of the merchants' ships are clearly conveyed. Worryingly, the administrators observed, the price hike had an immediate impact on the workshop managers responsible for sourcing the firewood for the kilns: 'They borrow and buy on credit, but then are not able to repay their debts'.

In the first instance, the imperial kiln administrators responded to this alarming situation by seeking to control the price of fuel. 'Firewood is to be bought in set quantities, and at a price that is set in advance'. The administrators determined that the price should be fixed at 0.04 tael per one hundred catty (i.e. 50 kg).[8] The official in charge would get out his steel-yard, weigh 100 catty and pay 0.04 tael for that, regardless of fluctuations in the actual price.[9] Moreover, the officials set a maximum amount of fuel that should be used per firing. On the basis of close inspections, the officials determined that 160 shoulder-loads should suffice, with ten further loads permitted if required. The total amount of firewood allocated per firing of a kiln, then, was set at 170 loads, and any individual who was able to econo-mize within that amount was to be rewarded for that.[10] By setting a single price for the two kinds of fuel, the administrators were clearly hoping to eliminate the practice of hoarding fuel to sell it for the higher price, and by establishing a maximum quantity of wood to be bought per firing, they sought to limit the power held by the traders of fuel.

To combat the problems with the fuel supply, including the theft of wood supplies, the officials who were there to safeguard the interests of the imperial administration proposed a system of round the clock surveillance and record keeping.[11] Officials and their representatives were required to keep watch over the firewood from the moment it left the storehouse until it arrived at the kilns: 'We also inspect the period of time between issuing the firewood and its arrival at the kiln. The craftsmen keeping watch over the stoking of the kiln also watch over the fire. Their leaders keep watch without

Figure 8.1 Fuel loaded on board a ship. Frank B. Lenz, *National Geographic* magazine November 1920.

distinguishing day and night, so that it becomes hard to allow thieves in'.[12] Moreover, officials at the provincial secretariat (*buzhengsi*) were ordered to enter all the relevant details in financial record books.[13] These could then be presented for inspection, so that the price paid for firewood and the quantities used in firing the kilns could be checked against these new regulations. 'Only when there are no surpluses or shortfalls should any money be handed over'.[14]

Without a steady supply of fuel in the form of firewood, none of the kilns in the region could function. The hills and mountains of Jiangxi were all covered by ferns, brushwood and pine trees, so in principle, this resource was readily available. The network of rivers and the downstream location of Jingdezhen made it relatively simple to distribute firewood to the kilns scattered throughout the region (Figure 8.1). The increase in production to meet growing demand and the growing scarcity that ensued all caused anxiety amongst the imperial kiln administrators. The various measures proposed all testify to this anxiety, including setting a fixed price, imposing limitations on the total quantity of firewood to be used per firing, extensive record keeping of all interactions, and ongoing inspection and surveillance. But, of course, precisely because the imperial kilns needed to manufacture in such vast quantities and fire such large kilns, they could only do so by extracting the necessary resources from a wide region and depending on the circulation of supplies and networks of merchants that operated well beyond their reach. It seems unlikely that their proposed measures had the desired effect. The kilns surely could only be fired if the imperial administrators accepted a certain amount of fluidity in the system of supply and demand.

Tools for Equipping the Workshops

When firewood arrived in its various forms at the kiln complex, it required no further processing before it could be put into the kiln fires. Other basic materials, such as stone, wood and iron required several manufacturing processes before they could be turned into the numerous tools and pieces of equipment that furnished the workshops. The required materials and the manufacture of tools and equipment added a not insignificant cost to the overall production cost of a piece of porcelain, which had to be accounted for. 'In the production of vessels and porcelains, the cost of the equipment that the craftsmen use has often been estimated in the price of the individual pieces of porcelain'.[15] The problem was, according to the administrators of the imperial kiln, that this cost for equipment was added to the individual items of porcelain each time again.

> Items such as the barrows, clay paddles, wooden pails, and knives for sharpening the bodies, these have all been made with iron from here (*ben tie*), sturdy and durable, so why should they become unusable overnight? How is it that on the very day on which firing is completed, [the supervisors] do not account for the implements and materials used during the manufacture of the vessels, the place where these are being stored, the damaged ones amongst them, as well as the numbers of pieces worth storing?[16]

So instead of creating a detailed log that takes account of every single piece of equipment that had been used in the manufacturing and could be used again, the items disappeared, or at least out of sight of the supervisors.

The administrators identified this disappearance of resources as a kind of embezzlement of official funds: 'If you think lightly of official funds, then how can you respond appropriately to embezzlement?'[17] The supervisors who had allowed this kind of behaviour were charged with the responsibility for solving this disappearance of tools.

As we saw in the case of firewood, the method the administrators proposed for asserting control was to establish record books and logs. Everything stored in the warehouses, the size of the vessels, the quantities of materials used was to be entered in such logs. The quantities were to be checked by a foreman, so that if there were pieces missing, he could determine the price of filling the gaps and be held responsible for their replacement. Such measures were thought highly of: they 'could put a halt to the problems of embezzlement by the craftsmen and stop the false reporting of workers'.[18] In practice, however, the task of keeping track of every single piece of equipment in the hundreds of workshops that made up the imperial kiln complex was more difficult. The variety of materials used, the differences between the processes required for turning them into tools and equipment, and the physical distances between the workshops made this log-keeping task utterly impractical.

The use of hammers and pestles (*dui*) can serve as one example to illustrate this variety of materials and processes, and the challenges that full record keeping posed. The porcelain clay that was used to shape the bodies was made up of two raw materials: *kaolin* clay and white stone. Both were sourced from the nearby mountain ranges, and both needed refining by pulverization and purification in water. The best clays mined in the region contained mica and quartz, which made them extremely hard. 'The clay has blue-black seams [i.e. carbonaceous material] and spots like grains of sugar [i.e. quartz], as translucent as white jade and with golden spots like stars [i.e. mica]'.[19] To facilitate the pulverization of such raw materials, which involved repeated pounding with hammers, the workshops in sixteenth-century Jingdezhen manufactured a hand-powered piece of equipment. Largely made of wood, this equipment consisted of three parts: a single horizontal beam, one or more axles perpendicular to the main beam, and at the end of each axle a nozzle for pounding the clay. A rope attached to the beam allowed the operator to control the speed with which the pestle pounded the clay.[20]

In the seventeenth century, a waterwheel was used to drive the hammers for pounding, as we see in this illustration from Song Yingxing's 'The works of heaven and the inception of things' (*Tiangong kaiwu*) (Figure 8.2). The revolving water wheel rotated the horizontal beam, which in turn

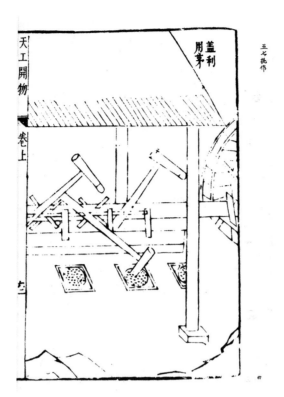

Figure 8.2 Water-powered hammers or mortars (*shui dui*) used, in this case, for pounding grain, but also used for refining clay. Song Yingxing, *Tiangong kaiwu* [Works of Heaven], *juan* 4.62a.

slammed the hammers on the end of axles onto the basin of clay or stone. The waterwheel and the hammers for pounding clay are also depicted in Figure 8.3. The need for hammerheads and pestles in different shapes and sizes throughout the production process was substantial. These wooden implements as well as the rope used for pulling the hammers down were all made in the dedicated workshops for this task. There were two whole work divisions with a total of 56 workstations tasked with their manufacture.[21] But beyond the hammers and pestles used in the purification of clay, there were many other kinds of pestles in circulation. The cobalt, for example, also needed to be pounded to make it as finely pulverized as possible, which required a pestle. This, too, was made on-site, and fell under the duties of the pestle-making workshops, but it was made from an entirely different material. Cobalt had to be pounded with a porcelain pestle. Moreover, it was used in an entirely different section of the kiln site.[22] The division of labour into separate tasks and the organization of production

Figure 8.3 Waterwheel and hammers pounding clay. Photo by the author, 2011.

into separate sections and responsibilities undoubtedly had advantages, but for the administrators it made keeping track of the circulation of pieces of equipment much more difficult.

The various wooden implements in use throughout the imperial kiln complex serves as another example of this challenge. The sheer endless quantity of vats, vessels, containers and buckets needed in the factory were all made within the imperial kiln complex. Not all of the vats were made from wood: the largest vats used for pounding the clay were made from stone, and the bowls used for the preparation of pigments were much smaller and made from porcelain.[23] But many of them were made from wood, and held together with strips made from bamboo, which was also sourced locally.[24] The wooden tubs in use throughout the production process had their own work division. It was comparatively small; it only had one named foreman, and eight workers, making it the same size as other small workshops, such as the dye workshop, the rope-making workshop and the lacquer workshop.[25] And like in the case of pestles, tubs and vats were in use throughout the production site. Keeping track of every single wooden vat and recording whether it could be reused or had to be replaced must have been an impractical task at best.

While many of the raw materials needed in each of the different work divisions could easily be resourced from the nearby mountains, some materials were more difficult to source from the immediate locality. One of those was metal. The kiln complex used a wide range of metal objects: metal bowls in which the clay was rinsed and some of the pigments were mixed; the heads or tips of the hammers used for pounding the clay; shovels, hoes and rakes for moving the clay; potters' wheels for shaping pots; knives and files for cleaning clay bodies; tongs for manoeuvring the pieces inside the kiln; clamps for pressing pieces together, and even for cooking pots.[26] Most of this metal was *shengtie*, usually translated as pig iron or cast iron, but literally meaning 'raw iron', as opposed to *shutie*, wrought iron, which literally means 'cooked iron'. From as early as the Han dynasty onwards, i.e. from the second century BCE, the iron and steel production formed part of the imperial state monopoly. As the historian Robert Hartwell already pointed out in 1966, however, almost every province had some iron mining during the eleventh century, and there were private iron works enterprises everywhere.[27] Access to iron, therefore, did not depend exclusively on access to supplies from the imperial ironworks. For example, archaeological excavations in south-eastern Anhui and north-eastern Jiangxi has revealed evidence of iron mining and blast-furnaces in the region from as early as the Song dynasty.[28] During the Ming dynasty, the state mainly asserted its monopoly rights over the production of steel for the arms industry, and the main ironworks that served the Ming imperial administration were located in Hebei province, east of Beijing, near the Great Wall.[29] But the fertile delta of the Yangzi river, known as Jiangnan, continued to produce iron in the late Yuan and early Ming dynasties, until, from the mid-Ming onwards, it was western Guangdong that produced most of the iron ore in use in coastal China.[30]

In principle, the process of making cast iron (or pig iron) from iron ore was simple: the iron ore was combined with charcoal, and smelted in a blast furnace, so that at high heat the oxygen and other impurities were removed. The melted substance poured out of the oven and into a mould made of sand, usually in the shape of a central artery with a series of small brick-shaped forms to the right and left of the central artery. Looking a bit like suckling pigs, hence the name pig iron, these small brick-shaped pieces of iron could be easily removed from the central artery, and used for a variety of purposes, including further refining to create wrought iron. Iron-smelting and ceramics manufacture clearly had some commonalities, and technologies may well have circulated between the two.[31] The imperial kilns in Jingdezhen used iron ore to produce the tools and equipment pieces required for the operation of the kilns. But here, too, metal objects had to be distributed for use to all parts of the kilns, and it was difficult to keep track of such items. It is not surprising, then, that the administrator in charge asked where all the items 'made with iron from here (*ben tie*), sturdy and durable' went, and why they should 'become unusable overnight'.[32] Such objects were simply too numerous, too varied in use, and too desirable for those working in other kilns to keep track of.

Cobalt for Adding Blue

Cobalt was undoubtedly the most expensive and difficult to obtain resource in Jingdezhen, yet it was used in large quantities in the production of blue and white ceramics. As we already saw in the previous chapter, the circulation of cobalt was carefully managed and access severely restricted. Despite such efforts to keep cobalt exclusively under the control of the imperial kiln administration, cobalt constantly flowed out of sight of the administrators and into the hands of those who worked in the private kilns.

The price of this commodity was indeed prohibitive. One of the reasons why cobalt was so expensive was that the best quality cobalt in use in Jingdezhen had to be sourced from distant locations. According to the administrative records of the early sixteenth century, these different types of blue (*qing*) were identifiable by their provenance. 'Potters use Muslim blue (*Hui qing*), which originally was tribute from outside the empire'.[33] But so-called Muslim blue was not the only cobalt in circulation; cobalt was mined in Yunnan, and there were several kinds of locally mined blues in circulation.[34] There was a locally mined 'stone blue' (*shizi qing*) from Ruizhou; another kind of colouring agent referred to as *pitang qing* was mined in Leping, the county that neighboured Fuliang. 'In the past, *pitang qing* was produced in Leping in this prefecture'.[35] To some extent, the circulation and use of these commodities were mutually dependent: 'Stone blue was produced in various places in Ruizhou, but while Muslim blue was in circulation, [the use of] stone blue declined'.[36] So Muslim blue was the most expensive because of its distant provenance, but despite its price it continued to be the most desirable. Other types of blue in circulation were only used when Muslim blue was not available.

It is extremely difficult, and probably a misguided enterprise, to try and match the various types of blue that are named in the sixteenth-century texts with specific material substances of which we know the chemical composition.[37] In the past, research on the different types of blue pigment in circulation has been led by the idea that there are two main forms of cobalt: one with high levels of arsenic, and one with high levels of manganese (another mineral). The assumption was that cobalt with high levels of arsenic matched the sources of cobalt in Saxony and Iran, while the high level of manganese without arsenic characterized 'native cobalt' that was mined in Leping.[38] More recent research, however, has shown that the presence of arsenic or manganese and other impurities in the cobalt has as much to do with the methods of mining, purification and firing as with the geological factors that shaped the different mines.[39] Moreover, as the exploitation of each mine progressed, and the supplies began to be exhausted, the composition of the cobalt ore also changed. It does not seem to be the case, then, that the composition of the cobalt serves as an unproblematic indication of where it was mined. On top of that, access to cobalt from Iran changed over time. During the Yuan dynasty, supplies may well have been delivered by Central Asian merchants via overland trade routes, and some have suggested that the voyages of Zheng He brought back supplies of cobalt from port cities in the Persian Gulf.[40] Over the course of the fifteenth century, however, these access routes were cut off and supplies dwindled. As a result, most of the cobalt that was used in the sixteenth-century kilns consisted of a combination of ingredients, mixed to specific proportion to achieve the best results.

It was, however, extremely difficult to keep the different types, qualities and grades of cobalt separate within the working environment of the kilns, because there were so many different processes involved. Once the cobalt had reached the workshops, the process of working the cobalt within the imperial factory consisted of several clearly separated stages:

> Pounding the cobalt. [The process] begins by breaking it up with a hammer. The best quality cobalt has flecks of vermilion in it. Middle quality cobalt has silver stars. Each pound yields three ounces of [this kind of] cobalt.
>
> Washing the cobalt. After pounding it, the small pieces are pulverised very finely, and poured into water. Using a magnet, they pull out the mixed stones, while the pure cobalt settles. Each pound yields five or six mace.
>
> Painting with cobalt. Each day, morning and midday, the workmen gather, and cobalt is allocated to them for [the purpose of] painting.

It was often only after the firing process was complete that the differences manifested themselves. 'If the cobalt is pure, then the colour distributes without pooling together. If one adds a lot of stone cobalt, then the colour is deep without clarity. The best cobalt has one mace of stone cobalt added to each pound. The middle grade of cobalt has four to six parts added'.[41] So, to produce the pigment that the painters could use, the workers had to grind the cobalt very finely, sometimes for many days in a row, and then mix the various grades together in the correct proportions. Whenever work was interrupted for food or sleep, the substance had to be accounted for and stored securely. 'At mealtimes, the workers disperse, but a close watch must be held over their comings and goings, to prevent people from bringing in *shiqing* and swapping it for *huiqing*'.[42] Even when the painters were working with cobalt, they had to be supervised:

> As for painting with cobalt, each day, morning and evening, the workmen gather, and cobalt is allocated to them for painting. Sometimes [the workers] are lazy and slow, and they conceal each other's faults, so that the master craftsmen have to keep constant watch. The master craftsmen also aid and abet the wrongdoers, so large numbers of people secretly pilfer [the cobalt].[43]

In short, it was almost impossible to keep cobalt under control. There were simply too many different hands and too many separate processes for the imperial administrators to be able to keep track of this resource.

Unsurprisingly, however, the imperial kiln administrators wanted to put a halt to the flow of cobalt and sought to keep it under tight wraps. Initially, the control was imposed by the provincial authorities.

> During the Jiajing reign (1522–1566), whenever they fired imperial wares, the [supervisors] sent a memorial to the storehouse of the Provincial Administration Commission of the Jiangxi Branch of the Ministry of Works, who then supplied it in a timely fashion.[44]

So, the kiln administrators themselves also had to petition to gain access to cobalt. But they had to hand over their supply to the kiln supervisors, who guarded the commodity equally keenly, as they 'asserted their control, tightly guarding the cobalt to prevent it from being traded. But as a rule, they only distributed the cobalt when they had received a financial incentive to open the storage box'.[45] Nonetheless, supervision and surveillance were the only means available to the administrators.

To combat the disappearance of cobalt during the various working processes, the administrators came up with the following solution:

> After discussions, it was suggested that during the pounding of the cobalt, individual small tables would be set up, and covered with a muslin cloth.

> Two holes would be made in the cloth and sewn into two sleeves to cap-
> ture the hands of the artisans. This way, these sleeves served to tie together
> the [workers'] elbows, so that they could not reach out and pull back to
> steal [cobalt]. This is referred to as 'securing the Muslim blue'.

The text offers a rather ingenious way of dealing with the thieving. The administrators proposed the making of a protective cover with narrow sleeves through which the workers have to work. Similarly, methods of surveillance were proposed for the painting stage. Painting scrolls were to be hung up (as guidance), divided into different subject groups, and then the pots were set out next to seats, to which the workers were allocated with a number. When they had completed their painting, they would get someone from the government office with good calligraphy to write the characters on the base, and then the pots went into the kiln. When they came out again, the objects were all to be entered into the ledger, and by these numbers matched up to the original workers who had applied the cobalt. That way, whenever the finished product revealed tampering with the cobalt, such as the replacement of the expensive, pure *huiqing* with a cheaper alternative, the worker could be held accountable and punished accordingly.

These were extremely complex measures, all aimed at stemming the flow of cobalt, and keeping track of this precious commodity at all times. Whatever the imperial administrators tried, however, the various stages and hands involved in working with the material, as the craftsmen and their supervisors did on a daily basis, created opportunities and posed a serious threat to the assumed superiority of the kiln administrators. Scholars of manufacturing processes in Europe, and especially of proto-industrialization, have made similar observations about embezzlement.[46] In the proto-industrial phase of development, when much of the manufacturing was done in small workshops by means of the 'putting-out' system rather than in a centralized workshop, preventing embezzlement and fraud proved difficult.[47] In Jingdezhen, in the end, it was not possible to control all movements of the workers, and the administrators had to acknowledge that cobalt would circulate well beyond the confines of the imperial kilns.

Recipes for Adding Colour

So far, we have seen the circulation and fluidity of natural resources and the anxiety this circulation caused the imperial kiln administrators. We have also discussed several methods applied by the administrators to seek to stem the flow. Record keeping was a tried and tested approach when the imperial state felt a lack of control over a certain situation. In the fifteenth century, for example, when the Ming emperors felt there were too many Buddhist monks who flouted the monastic codes, they ordered the creation of ledgers of registered monks.[48] In the Jingdezhen kiln administration, creating a detailed log was frequently thought to offer a solution. Price fixing was not always possible, but in the case of firewood, this was seen as a further option to keep a semblance of control over the circumstances. The case of cobalt suggested a third approach, which we might characterize as process management: the text suggests that workers' every move should be monitored so as to restrict their unsupervised access to cobalt. The example below adds one further method to the approaches tried by the kiln administration: using the textual record to claim ownership over knowledge. The knowledge in question concerned the manufacture of coloured glazes, which required very specific ingredients, quantities and methods to produce the right shade and brilliance of colour after firing. The ingredients themselves were not limited or out of bounds for the general public, in fact, some of these were cheap ingredients such as alum or oil. But the written descriptions of how to combine the ingredients, and in what quantities, in other words, the recipes for making colour glazes, was not accessible to the workers themselves or to the owners of private kilns. That information remained the preserve of the imperial kiln administrators, or at least this was their aspiration. As the discussion below demonstrates, the information provided in the gazetteer was not intended to teach artisans how to make glazes; this was not meant to be a handbook or manual. In fact, without detail on the right conditions in the kiln (such as oxidation or reduction, high or low temperatures), the kiln workers would have little chance of achieving the right colours, shine, surface texture, and so on. The information was simply provided so that the administrators could try keep track of the quantities of ingredients and help those in charge to shore up their positions of authority, precisely at the moment that their authority came under threat.

The number of colours and coloured glazes in use during the sixteenth century was in fact limited, especially compared with the wide range of colours that came into use over the course of the seventeenth century, after new technologies had been introduced via the European Jesuits and the court in Beijing. The coloured glazes current in sixteenth-century Jingdezhen included a grey-green celadon-style glaze (*youse*), a brown glaze known as burnished gold (*zijin*), turquoise or kingfisher blue (*cuise*), a bright yellow (*jinhuang*), a bright green (*jinlü*), an iron red (*fanhong*),

Table 8.1 Pigments and ingredients. From *Jiangxi sheng dazhi*, 7.26a.

Pinyin	Characters	Literal translation	Common English name	Chemical element
qianfen	鉛粉	Powdered lead	Lead powder[50]	Lead
yanxiao	焰硝	Flamed saltpetre	Saltpetre	Potassium nitrate
qingfan	青礬	Green alum	Copperas or green vitriol	Ferrous sulfate
dai zhe shi	黛赭石	Black ochre stone		Hematite (iron ore)
hei qian	黑鉛	Black lead	Lead	Lead
song xiang	松香	Fragrance of pine	(Oil of) turpentine	
bai tan	白炭	Whitened coal	Charcoal	
jin bo	金箔	Sheets of gold	Gold foil	Gold
gu tong	古銅	Old copper	Old copper	Copper

a purple (*zise*), a pale blue (*jiaoqing*), and a pure white (*chunbai*).[49] Such single-coloured (monochrome) glazed items were more difficult to make than the *qingbai* wares, which relied on the whiteness of the clay itself, and the transparent quality of the glaze. But monochromes were in high demand at the imperial court, as they played key roles in the performance of rituals in different parts of the imperial court. The bright yellow wares, for example, were used in the annual imperial ceremony held at the Temple of Earth, while bright blue wares were in use at the Temple of Heaven. Red was reserved for the Altar of the Sun, and white for the Altar of the Moon. The manufacture of coloured glazes was thus an essential part of the fulfilment of each imperial demand.

To make such monochrome glazes, the potters relied on only a small set of pigments and colouring agents that were used in different combinations and proportions to create the desired effect. Table 8.1 lists some of the ingredients used as fluxes and for creating colours, giving some indication of the different terms in circulation, their literal translation, and the equivalent term in the vocabulary in chemical terms, as we would know them in Europe.[51]

Recipes specified the combinations of ingredients and their relative proportions and detailed how to apply these colours. Sometimes, the recipe merely listed the combination of ingredients, as we see in the case of the celadon-style glaze: 'Combine bean green (i.e. an iron-based pigment known to produce green), water, ash, and yellow soil'.[52] The final three ingredients are the basic ingredients for making a glaze: clay, mixed with water and the ash from burning lime and ferns. Added to this was the colouring agent, bean (or pea) green in this case. To achieve the burnished gold or brown (*zijin*) glaze, a mixture was made of ash and water, but mixed with *zijin* clay, an iron-rich clay known literally as 'purple gold'.[53] Turquoise or kingfisher-green (*cuise*) glaze was produced by mixing water with old copper and salt-petre. Saltpetre worked here as the solving agent or flux, 'a material that rendered the insoluble soluble', as Wood and Kerr put it.[54] For a light blue glaze (*jiao qing*), the glaze clay was mixed with water and ash, together with a kind of cobalt that was found locally: *shizi qing*, literally, 'stone blue'.[55] This has also been translated as 'pebble cobalt', and was mined in the environs of Jingdezhen.[56] For a pure white glaze, the glaze clay was simply mixed with water and ash. No quantities or proportions are provided for these coloured glazes, which may suggest that the method used was close enough to the method used for clear glaze so that separate instructions were not necessary for the experienced glaze-makers.

For some of the other recipes, however, the administrators provided regulatory guidance about quantities and the relative proportions of the ingredients. 'For a bright yellow (*jinhuang*), use one catty of ground black lead (*heiqianmo*), and add 1.2 ounces of ochre stone (*zheshi*)'.[57] The add-ition of ground lead to the glaze, in addition to the iron-oxide element from the ochre stone helps enhance the brightness of the yellow.[58] 'For bright green (*jinlü*), use one ounce of ground black lead that has been refined, and combine it with 1.4 ounces of ground old copper, and 6 ounces of ground stone (*shimo*)'.[59] This final ingredient, translated here literally as ground stone, refers to sand powder or silica, the main mineral substance in many of the clays found in China.[60] In ground form, this is the substance that helps create the glass-like quality of Chinese glazes.[61] The ostensible simplicity of the recipe text hides a more complex series of processes. Some of the raw materials had to be refined by firing them first; many of the ingredients were used in ground or pulverized form. Sometimes a processed product was subsequently combined with a further ingredient to enhance or brighten the colour. 'For bright blue (*jinqing*), use one catty of the refined kingfisher blue with one ounce of stone blue (*shizi qing*)'.[62] This bright blue colour, then, combined two key ingredients: the kingfisher or turquoise colouring, which was a copper-based pigment, and the locally mined form of cobalt known as stone cobalt. Together, these two kinds of blue pigments combined to create a vibrant blue colour. 'For bright red (*fanhong*), use the red from refined alum (i.e. ferrous sulfate), and for each ounce, add five ounces of ground copper and combine it with Canton glue (*Guang jiao*)'. The so-called Canton glue worked as a base or binding agent for the pigment, much like the oil of turpentine did. 'For purple (*zise*), com-bine one catty of ground black lead, one ounce of stone blue, and six ounces of ground stone (i.e. silica)'.[63] As we see, lead powder was the key element to create the yellow, green and red glazes, while locally sourced stone cobalt was the key ingredient for the bluish-green and purple.

The glazes used for monochromes, covering the whole of the porcelain body before a single firing were used in conjunction with decorations that were applied either under or on top of a high-fired glaze. Golden yellow, for example, was 'applied onto the white body after firing, and subsequently fired in the "colour kiln"'.[64] This so-called colour kiln, usually translated as muffle kiln, served the specific purpose of second firing the glazed goods at a lower temperature, so as to fix the more delicate pigments onto the surface of the glaze. The decorative type known as 'five colours' (*wucai*) was also made this way: 'Use the wares that have already been fired to a pure white, then add the various colours, and fire these'.[65] Here, too, there were stages and processes to be mindful of: 'When you fire alum red wares, you add the gold colour in the second firing; when [the object] is fired a second time, no other colour can be put on top of the golden yellow'.[66] For other wares, a slightly different method was used for applying the decorations: 'Apply white slip to the ceramic bodies, and with a brush, add all kinds of dragons, phoenixes, flowers and bamboo. Then add glaze water and refined ash, and fire'.[67] These wares are described as 'layered wares', referring to the technique where the colour is applied on top of a first layer of slip, after which a clear glaze is added. Yet another kind of decorative process involved creating a pattern by piercing the wares after the leather-hard stage: 'For pierced wares, on all kinds of shapes you use a metal awl and pierce dragons, phoenixes, flowers and bamboo, and then add slip and ash and fire'.[68] The glaze filled the small holes created with the awl and gave such vessels a translucent effect.

The imperial court had delegated the entire manufacturing process to the administrators of the imperial kilns in Jingdezhen, and it was the responsibility of the local administrators to produce whatever the imperial court demanded. This required careful management of the available resources, whether this concerned the equipment for preparing the raw ingredients, tools for making decorative patterns, or sourcing the ingredients for making coloured glazes and applying underglaze decorations. The latter were extremely expensive. Gold leaf, according to a late sixteenth-century source, cost 0.25 tael per 100 strips. Considering that a single large vessel required about 22 of such strips of gold leaf, this was a large cost. Old copper, at 0.06 tael per catty was also a high expense, as was lead powder at 0.04 tael. Saltpeter was 0.02 tael, and the various metals all cost between 0.02 and 0.03 tael per catty. Perhaps it was precisely because of the high cost of these resources, and the exclusivity of these monochromes, which were required for very specific ritual purposes at court, that in the area of minerals for pigments, the exertion of imperial control seemed to achieve some measure of success, or at the very least the illusion of control.

Packing and Storing: The Final Stages of Jingdezhen Production

'Whenever the process of making the porcelain has been completed, [the goods] are divided into consignments for transport'.[69] Jingdezhen's imperial kilns were responsible for the process that started with the sourcing of the clay and ended with the safe delivery at the imperial court. Packing the goods for transport formed a key element in that chain. Of course, in a town focused on the production of porcelain, there was a great deal of know-ledge about how to protect what they produced from the rigours of travel. Packing porcelain and preparing it for travel required far more than merely putting items in boxes. The biggest objects produced at the imperial kilns were the so-called dragon jars (*da long gang*). Such pots took about a month to build up and shape gradually before they could go into the kiln.[70] For the packing of each individual jar of this size and value, a great deal of trouble was taken in preparation of its transportation.

First, one needed two long pieces of fir wood (*shanmu*) of a circumfer-ence of about 18 inches (or 46 cm) to make a suitable box. Then, using mixed (i.e. cheaper) wood, a frame was made for the box to sit in. Bamboo poles were then attached to the frame so that two or three men could carry and manoeuvre this heavy load along narrow mountain paths. To protect the porcelain during transport, the inside of the wooden box was covered with a protective paste, made from fibres such as ramie, palm leaves, bamboo leaves, rattan and hemp, which were boiled and turned into a pulp, bound with fish glue and alum, and dyed yellow by adding the seed pods of the Chinese scholar tree (also known as the Japanese pagoda tree, Sophora Japonica).[71] After the boxes had been constructed from wood and protected on the inside with this protective layer, the boxes had to be coated on the outside with a layer of red lacquer, made by combining vermilion (*yinzhu*) and red lead (*huangdan*) with a mixture of ash, lime, Tong-tree oil and Canton glue.[72] Layers of paper wrapped around the object inside the box created further protection, and the whole construction was secured with paper-coated iron nails and welded locks. Of course, the labour and materials already invested in the manufacture of such a large vat justified these extensive preparations and high material costs necessary for securing the object for transport, but almost all the same ingredients were also required for packing the smaller items.

The smaller pieces were wrapped in several layers of paper, as the following statement explains:

> For each set of two bowls and dishes (*wandie*), use a small piece of yellow paper. When you get to ten pieces, you wrap these [i.e. five bundles of two] with one medium-size piece of paper. Each box is packed with 120 small items in total, so you will need 72 sheets of middle and small-sized paper. If you have more pieces, then you use more paper, and if you have fewer pieces you use less paper.[73]

The supply of paper required for packing purposes was vast, as was the quantity of cotton cloth required for wrapping the boxes. While the imperial kilns often succeeded in sourcing what they needed locally, the required supply of paper and cotton came from further afield: 'The authorities deputise the Nanchang prefectural government to send across [supplies of] paper, while the cotton is sent from Nankang and Jiujiang'.[74] These two prefectures were located in the north of Jiangxi province, near the transport networks of the Yangzi and Lake Poyang, and therefore had access to the wide variety of goods traded along the Yangzi river, including supplies of cotton.

By now, we are familiar with the repertoire of methods of the kiln administrators. On the one hand, the administrators sought to fix the price of this part of the production process: 'In the case of land transport, both the expenses incurred in carriage and the costs of packaging have been fixed'.[75] On the other hand, the overseers were asked 'to estimate the overall cost of all materials such as oils, metal, hemp and cinnabar, to forward this in detail to the factory [management], who then add this estimate to the labour costs'.[76] The quantities were not necessarily large. For example, only 10 grams of alum was required for the packaging materials of one shipment, and the unit price of alum amounted only to 1/10th of a tael per kilo.[77] But because of the overall quantities of parcels prepared to fill the imperial orders, these prices mattered to keep the costs down. And as always, the creation of careful records and fixed prices gave the kiln administrators at least the sense of being in control in an otherwise highly fluid landscape of commodity flows.

Not everything flowed out of Jingdezhen, however, and in fact, the storage of (nearly) imperial-quality goods that were not shipped out of Jingdezhen was a significant cause of concern. In an ideal world, the produced goods were all allocated to consignments for shipping, wrapped and packed up, and sent by waterway or road transport to their designated destinies. The problem was, however, that a single firing of a kiln yielded more goods than could or would ever be shipped. This was a matter of necessity: not all the porcelains would come out of the firing process as intended, and only the best items were suitable for the payment of imperial tribute, and thus there was a large amount of overproduction. These non-selected but imperial-quality goods, naturally, had to be placed in storage, until further decisions would be made about their fate. This storage of a precious commodity created problems:

> Year after year, we have to store ceramics. They accumulate on a daily basis, which means that the clerks and runners of the storage facility avail themselves of the opportunity to steal goods. For those who are fond of such things, they simply make a selection, and use them as gifts. In this way, goods that belong to the state end up serving private greed.[78]

The contrast this quote underscores is the difference between the things that belong to the state (lit. the public realm: *gongjia*) and things that are 'vainly used for selfish covetousness' (*tuji tanbi zhi si*). The reason this theft of stored porcelain was such a cause for concern was not only that it concerned imperial property, but that it facilitated behaviour that was considered immoral.

In 1571, the local officials deliberated this issue, and came up with the following solution. An official should be appointed to investigate the matter closely: 'Of all the vessels placed in the storage facility, the ones with coarse bodies, or where the colour of the (blue) decorations has turned out too dark, or where we have many of the same kind, these are not good enough [to keep]'.[79] But of course, that immediately raised the next question: what to do with these rejects? 'On the basis of such deliberations, these are then either sold (*fa mai*) or exchanged (*dui*) for *min yao*'. The verb in this phrase, *dui*, means to exchange, or to barter, or to cash in, with a strong emphasis on the exchange of one thing for another. So, what is being exchanged here? It is unlikely that the managers of the storehouse were asking for wares from the private kilns 'in exchange' for their rejected imperial wares. More likely is that what is being swapped here is the status; once they were handed in, presumably in exchange for a financial transaction at the private kilns, they proceeded into the commercial streams of the private kilns. To keep track of this whole process of deciding which were and which were not allowed to be stored, record books were created in several copies, two of which were held at the factory official headquarters, and one of which was handed to the storehouse. 'They use this to check quantities and carry out strict investigations … hoping to dispense with the problems of stealing and pilfering'.[80] As usual, and in ways that are by now only too familiar, the administrators turned to making lists as a way of dealing with their anxieties over the flow of goods and creating the illusion of an administrative upper-hand.

This chapter has focused on the flows of natural resources and the desire of the administrators to stem those flows and assert their control over them. My reading of the text that has formed the main source of information for this chapter, *Taoshu*, has revealed the extent to which written documentation served as a way to assuage these anxieties. Far from offering descriptions of circumstances and procedures, the text showed attempts at imposing regulation on what was not only unregulated but impossible to regulate. The next chapter focuses on the other key necessity for the manufacture of a piece of porcelain: skilled hands. There, too, as we will see, control over those skilled hands was not easy to get; circulation and mobility characterized their presence in Jingdezhen. In fact, the more goods and people circulated and flowed between the various spaces, the more the administrators sought to assert their control over those flows, and probably the wider the discrepancies between the written representations of the idealized circumstances the administrators envisioned and the actual patterns of movement and flow of resources and skills.

9 | Skilled Hands: Managing Human Resources and Skill in the Sixteenth-Century Imperial Kilns

In sixteenth-century Jingdezhen, the imperial kilns produced extraordinary porcelains. As we saw in the previous chapter, the natural resources of the area provide part of the explanation for this high-quality production. Clay and firewood were available all over the world, but the clays available near Jingdezhen were finer and whiter than almost anywhere else. The quality of the clay meant that consecutive imperial administrations, starting with the Song, and continuing during the Yuan and Ming dynasties, used the kilns in Jingdezhen for the production of porcelains intended for use in the imperial household, in the imperial palaces, and in the performance of rituals at the imperial court. The identification of Jingdezhen as a site of imperial porcelain production meant that precious commodities like imported cobalt were available there, and thus that the finest blue-decorated wares could be made in Jingdezhen. So, the quality of the resources available in Jingdezhen undoubtedly helps to explain why the wares made there were so exceptional.

Without the highly skilled hands of a potter, however, even the most superior of all raw materials could never be turned into fine pieces of porcelain. This chapter will focus on the workers who made this possible, asking whose hands shaped the local clay into bowls and vases, whose fingers held the brushes that painted cobalt onto the white bodies, and whose eyes judged the temperature in the kilns. It will consider how the sixteenth-century imperial kiln administrators managed their workforce and ask why the issue of skill remained such a vexing problem within the imperial kilns. Just like we saw in the case of the material resources, skilled craftsmen were in high demand, but for the imperial administrators, they were difficult to control. Most of the workers were mobile; they could take their labour to the imperial kiln, but also find work in the private kilns. The repeated attempts of the kiln administrators to identify skilled workers and bind them to the imperial kilns, and their ongoing expressions of concern over the issue of skilled labour underscore precisely how difficult it was to get hold of good craftsmen. Like in the case of high-quality natural resources, acquiring and keeping skilled labour came at a high cost. Ultimately, the kiln administrators had to reconcile themselves to their

Figure 9.1 Workers in Jingdezhen, ca. 1920. Photo by Frank B. Lenz
© *National Geographic* Magazine.

inability in asserting control over the labour force. Material and human resources were fluid and flowed relatively freely through the mazelike veins of the Jingdezhen network.

Who Were the Workers in Jingdezhen?

In the first half of the sixteenth century, the workforce in Jingdezhen was made up of different constituencies (Figure 9.1). They were there for different reasons, for varying lengths of time, and served in different capacities, but they all worked in one or other part of the kiln complex. The artisans or craftsmen (*jiang*) formed one of these constituencies. The term artisan here refers not so much to a chosen profession or a level of skill, but to the registration of a kiln worker's household. The household (*hu*, literally 'door') formed the basic unit of the population.[1] Each household had a fixed registration in the imperial population records, which determined the obligations and duties the state demanded of that household.[2] The size of the landholdings of the household determined the annual tax obligations of the household, payable in kind. The number of able-bodied male adults in the household determined the extent of the per capita tax obligation, which could be a labour duty.[3] Each household that owned some kind of property was also liable for various (corvée) labour duties, including military service.[4] The entire population of households was divided into units of 110 households, known as village communities (*li*). These village communities were divided into 11 units of ten households, known as tithings (*jia*). The ten households that made up the most affluent of the tithings took year-long turns as community heads; the remaining ten tithings took year-long turns collecting taxes and taking care of the labour duties that were levied upon these households.[5] This system of communities and tithings (or the *lijia* system), put in place during the reign of the first emperor of the Ming, was intended as a kind of self-monitoring level of local governing below the county.

The household registration determined what kind of labour duty each household had to perform. Technically speaking, the registration of each household into a specific category of labour service was unchangeable; the *Great Ming Commandments* (*Da Ming ling*) confirmed that households had to remain permanently in their original category; in fact, all of the laws issued by the first emperor of the Ming were officially unchangeable.[6] There were at least 45 different categories of household registrations, including numerous small categories, such as physicians, geomancers, and butchers.[7] But the three main categories of household in Ming China were the farming households (*min*), military households (*jun*) and the craftsmen (*jiang*). These craftsmen were known as shift or rotation workers (*lun ban*).[8] Such rotation workers had to work one shift once every three or four years, and often had to travel to the imperial capital to perform their duties in the imperial workshops. Because of the location of the imperial kilns near the source of the clay, those who were allocated to service in the kilns came to Jingdezhen for their shift.[9] The group of artisans working in Jingdezhen, then, was made up of members of local households that had been registered as artisans and delivered workers for the kilns for many generations.

In the first half of the sixteenth century, there would have been as many as 300 craftsmen working in Jingdezhen at any one stage.[10] For the vast majority of tasks, however, the kilns employed not craftsmen but labourers. These were divided into two types: 'general' labourers (*gongfu*) and clay workers (*shatufu*). The supply of such labourers to the imperial kilns formed part of the tax obligations that were imposed upon the county-level administrations in the region of Jingdezhen. The proximity of Jingdezhen was thus a double-edged sword for the local population. The opportunities for individuals getting involved in the making, buying and selling of porcelain were significant, but the tax duties imposed upon the local residents were also prohibitive. More often than not, these obligations led people to flee the region to less developed agricultural regions in, for example, Hubei, where fewer taxes were levied. For the administrators of the prefecture in which Jingdezhen was located (Raozhou), and for the administrators of the various counties of Raozhou, the proximity of Jingdezhen meant the obligation to supply the kilns with labour.[11] In the early sixteenth century, the annual numbers of workers sent were relatively low. The *Taoshu* [Book of Ceramics], included in the sixteenth-century gazetteer specifies the following numbers:

Poyang county sends 97 ('general') labourers and 64 clay workers.
Yugan county sends 58 labourers, and 36 clay workers.
Leping county sends 72 labourers, and 38 clay workers.
Fuliang county sends 50 labourers, and 18 clay workers.
Wannian county sends 30 labourers, and 7 clay workers.
Anren county sends 30 labourers, and 10 clay workers.
Dexing county sends 30 labourers, and 17 clay workers.[12]

This comes to a total of 557 workers. On top of supplying workers, the county administrators also had to furnish these labourers with an annual set fee of 7 tael per worker to pay for their accommodation and subsistence.[13] These fees that accompanied the workers from the surrounding counties had to be paid to the office of the imperial kiln administration in Fuliang county. This amounted to an annual amount of 3,899 tael in income for the kiln office.[14] The responsibility for using this money to pay for the subsistence of the workers rested with the Fuliang imperial kiln officials. However, as we will see below, more often than not, these monies disappeared in the kiln administration coffers, and were used for entirely different purposes. In fact, it was in the interest of the kiln administration to try to increase the numbers of workers as much as possible, and to supplement the kiln administration income in that way.[15] But more about such illegal practices below. Both groups, craftsmen and labourers, came to work in the kilns of Jingdezhen because of their household labour duties or because of their tax obligations.

Over the course of the sixteenth century, the taxation structure of the Ming dynasty changed significantly due to the gradual implementation of the Single Whip Reforms (*yi tiao bian fa*). In a reform programme that was rolled out in stages across the whole empire, every household was eventually asked to pay a single annual payment in silver instead of the variety of tax obligations demanded at different times of the year and payable in kind and labour. This single tax demand included a fee to commute any labour duties to a payment of 1.8 silver tael once every four years (i.e. as often as they would have performed their labour duty).[16] The impact of these reforms was significant. Instead of using a proportion of the local harvest to pay off tax obligations, or sending bolts of silk to the capital, the tax collectors had to ensure all tax payments were made in silver. As a consequence of having to submit all taxes into a single payment in silver rather than in kind (grain or textiles, mainly), the monetization of the economy increased rapidly, as farmers and textile manufacturers had to take their goods to market in order to obtain silver for their goods.[17] The payment of wages for soldiers, too, was converted to silver.[18] The economy of the late Ming suddenly required vast quantities of silver because of this reform of the tax system. Only a small part of this silver bullion was sourced locally; most of the silver entered into the Ming economy from other parts of the world, most notably from Spanish America. The silver mined in Potosí, for example, was brought to China on the so-called Manila galleons, and used to purchase goods manufactured in China. Having started as an empire built on agricultural foundations with an officially declared distaste of trade, the Ming became an empire that had to rely on the export of textiles, tea and porcelain so as to gain access to a steady supply of Spanish-American silver. From the final decades of the sixteenth century onwards, the daily running of the Ming came to be heavily dependent on the global circulation of silver.[19]

The impact of the Single Whip Reforms and the silverization of the economy were also noticeable in Jingdezhen. Not all those who had labour duties and obligations to work in Jingdezhen came to work in the kilns in person. Already in the mid-fifteenth century, the option existed of paying off one's labour duties by means of a payment in copper or by hiring someone to serve in one's stead. By the middle of the sixteenth century, those with 'craftsman' household status also did not have to work in the kilns in person; as a consequence, fewer workers came regularly to Jingdezhen to perform labour duties.[20] Instead of craftsmen and workers who came to the imperial kilns with a certain regularity, the kilns had to resort to hiring workers to supplement the workforce. 'It is called hired labour when the factory hires workers with low and high skills, to supplement firing and colouring craftsmen, to perform such tasks as refining cobalt, making cotton wadding, and mounting paintings'.[21] These last tasks were all labour intensive and presumably facilitated gaining the required skills and experience on the job.

Over the course of the sixteenth century, then, the workforce in Jingdezhen changed from hereditary craftsmen and corvée labourers to hired hands who were paid for their service.

Unsurprisingly, the mixed nature of the workforce posed significant problems for the maintenance of the required skill levels within the workforce. Most of the workers were in Jingdezhen on a temporary basis, to dispatch their own labour obligations, to work in lieu of someone else's labour duties, or on a short-term basis in temporary employment. Sometimes, those who were in Jingdezhen on behalf of someone else were not paid for their work, enhancing the precariousness of the workforce. 'Those who lack the resources to make a straightforward payment in place of their service duty hire a labourer to take on the required duties in their place, but in the end often they are not able to pay [these workers for their service].'[22] Of course, there were no mechanisms in place to compensate these replacement workers for their labour. The work was also seasonal: the largest kilns were only fired at certain times of the year, and no work with clay could be done when the temperatures dropped below freezing. Most of the work in the imperial kilns was done between April and November.[23] When duties were completed, kiln firing ended, or winter arrived, most of the workers had to return to their villages to eke out an existence from the land. The implications of this constantly rotating workforce with little or no settled base in Jingdezhen are significant, most of all, as we will see below, because it was nearly impossible to maintain, let alone develop, the level of skill amongst the workers. This fluidity and rotation and the difficulties of developing reliable skill levels in the workforce combined to pose significant challenges for the imperial kiln administrators in Jingdezhen.

How Much Were the Workers Paid?

In the sixteenth century, the hired labourers in the imperial kilns were paid set fees for their labour on top of an allowance for their maintenance. The distinction between the different rates paid to the workers was made on the basis of the level of skill. The workers who made 'difficult to make large vessels', such as dragon vats, or moulded vessels, or large jars, received the highest daily rate of 0.03 tael and 5 copper cash (*li*). One copper cash equals 1/1000th of a tael. This daily payment, in other words, amounts to 35 copper cash, or 0.035 tael. 'Hired labourers who perform such tasks as beating and washing the cobalt receive 25 copper cash (0.025 tael); at times of high pressure, they are given an additional 5 copper cash.'[24] Those who were involved in such supplementary tasks as making cotton wadding, making frames and boxes or preparing paper received the lowest amount of money: a daily supply of 2.5 Chinese pints (*sheng*) of rice and 0.01 tael. One Chinese pint is the equivalent of one tenth of a peck of rice, or one hundredth of a *dan* of rice. According to contemporary sources, a man eats about one pint of rice per day, or 'if a big eater twice that amount'.[25] In other words, the pay for this kind of low-skilled labour could keep one man and perhaps one dependent, but not more than that. The key difference between the rates of pay, these figures show, was the level of skill required, and the rates were open to some modification depending on the amount of pressure. 'If those with high skill get 0.03 tael; and with mid-level skill 0.025 tael, then when the pressure is high because of an imminent order, and the work is harder, all those with high skill should go up to 0.04 tael per day, and those with middling skill 0.03 tael'.[26]

To make some sense of these figures, we need to contextualize them a bit further. According to Li Kangying, in the late Ming, a weaver's average daily wage was 0.01 tael.[27] This rate is low: lower than the rate paid to the workers with the lowest skill in Jingdezhen (who earned a daily supply of 2.5 pint of rice on top of the 0.01 tael they were paid daily). The weaver's daily wage is also lower than the figure quoted by Li Bozhong, who writes that the daily wage of a worker in Jiangnan went from 0.02 tael per day to 0.04 tael per day between 1573 and 1640.[28] Of course, we do not know exactly how many days a worker in Jingdezhen could work per year. In accounting daily wages for manual labour, William Guanglin Liu uses both the figure of 300 working days (i.e. one day off per week, as well as several days for celebrations) and the figure of 365 working days.[29] A daily wage of 0.01 tael amounts to 3 tael a year for working 300 days; the daily wage of 0.035 for the skilled worker amounts to 10.5 tael a year if he works for 300 days. These figures are significantly lower than the figure that Ray Huang uses. According to Ray Huang's sources, in the sixteenth century, army recruits were paid an annual wage of 18 tael.[30] If we assume they did not work over the Chinese New Year celebrations, and they worked a total of 360 days a year, then this would amount to a daily rate of 0.05 tael, which is significantly higher than any of the manual labourers in Jingdezhen. As William Guanglin Liu has pointed out, a peasant family in Huizhou could earn as much as 10–15 tael of silver each year from their land.[31] More significant, however, in all these calculations is that the work in Jingdezhen was seasonal. In the winter, it was too cold to work the clays, so production ground to a halt. As a consequence, those who earned daily wages would undoubtedly have had to supplement their income with other work, just at the time in the year when the agricultural production had also slowed down. In other words, these wages hint at circumstances that must have been difficult if not impossible to sustain.

The Division of Labour

The division of the production of porcelain into segregated processes has been hailed as one of the key innovations of the production in Jingdezhen. One might associate this division into several separate tasks with Henry Ford's assembly-line production, where one worker repeatedly performs the same small individual task, increasing the efficiency of the overall production process. In Jingdezhen, however, the division of labour was not so much an innovation to increase productivity, as a mechanism to cope with a mixed labour force, and a system that created a high tolerance of low skill in the workforce. To make a fine piece of porcelain from start to finish requires the hands of a highly skilled potter, who can feel whether the clay is well-enough prepared, who can reliably throw a pot and shape its form, knows about pigments and glazes, who has the painterly skills to decorate the pot with the finest patterns, and knows about firewood and oven temperatures. The more divided the tasks are, however, the lower the skill set required to complete the individual tasks. For example, the preparation of the raw material as a whole undoubtedly required the skill to identify the best sites for mining stone and clay, the best methods for pulverization and purification in water, and the necessary fineness of the materials. But once sites had been identified, water-powered mills and pits for pulverization had been built, and vats for washing the materials had been set up, the vast majority of the work tasks involved digging, beating, sieving, carrying, pouring, stirring and more carrying. Such tasks required and transmitted certain skills and strengths, but no extensive training or schooling. Similarly, the making of saggars required some skill, namely turning the clay to form roughly potted bowls, and firing these on a high enough temperature that they could withstand the high temperatures of the porcelain kilns without falling apart, but not the refined skills required to work the porcelain clay. Separating out the tasks created work for many more unskilled workers, while fewer individuals with high skill levels were needed, who could specialize in a single area of expertise.

A good example of this separation is the shaping of clay bodies. Pots that were thrown on a wheel accommodated workmen with varied levels of skill. The potter throwing the larger pieces, including bowls, cups and plates, was different from the potter who only worked on the smaller pieces (i.e. less

Figure 9.2 Shapes in Jingdezhen. Photo by the author.

than one foot in diametre).[32] While the larger pieces required the kind of skill acquired by experience, smaller pieces could also be made by potters with less skill. Shapes were also made by using moulds, which was a more reliable process for the production of numerous items of identical size and shape, and less dependent on the potter's hands (Figure 9.2). More unusual shapes, i.e. square or polygonal, fluted or ribbed, gourd-shaped or even animal or human shaped, were made by forming individually cut pieces in the required shape and connecting these with slip (i.e. the same material used for the body of the vessel but mixed with water to make it more mould-able). The demand for unusual shapes points to the kind of technological development that Kenneth Pomeranz has described as 'labour-absorbing, not only because labour was abundant, but because [it] took the form of creating new products which required producers to acquire new skills'.[33] The task of forming the required shape would have been performed by a skilled worker, able to add this new shape to his/her repertoire, while the multitude of tasks that prepared the ground for this one worker could still be completed by unskilled workers: making thin slabs, cutting these into pieces, preparing the slip, holding the pot, washing the pot down, moving it and drying it. All such tasks could be learned on the job and supervised by a worker with only a marginally higher level of skill than the unskilled workers.

Each task required a number of workers completing the connected set of tasks in conjunction. No worker was working in isolation, and no worker would have failed to acquire at least some of the skills of the tasks in his or her immediate surroundings. This last observation is important for two reasons. The required entry level of skill was low, so that new workers could be brought up to speed with the small area of work they were assigned to in a matter of days if not hours, and the transmission of knowledge happened simply through observation and mimicry. A worker with a very low skill level could not only pick up an individual task easily but could acquire enough skill from the tasks performed nearby to import that skill to his own area of work.

The division of labour not only accommodated a low-skill workforce but was also easier to manage from the perspective of the administrators of the imperial kiln. Each separate task could be described in detail and allocated a specific amount of materials and time. For example, each potter working on the largest type of vessel the kilns produced was instructed to work on five vessels at the same time: shaping them in clay took up to 18 days, tidying the edges of the leather-hard vessel with a knife at least two days, rinsing the vessel and smoothing the surface two days each, and adding slip glaze a further two days, with time calculated in between the different phases to allow the clay to dry and harden off.[34] In the case of the smaller vessels, there were also clear guidelines on the number of items a worker should produce each day. For mid-sized large vessels, a single worker could shape ten bodies a day, and then required a further day each for tidying the edges, rinsing and repairing, and slip glazing. One worker could make ten of these large vessels in three days. For the size below that, a worker could make 50 in three days; 100 in three days for the third variety, and so on and so forth.[35] Engraving or carving added significantly more time to the process, thereby increasing the labour costs. The point, however, is the desire to manage productivity and the potential for asserting pressure onto the workforce so as to force the achievement of higher yields. As we will see below, this pressure may have been desirable on the part of the administrators, but the fragmentation of labour tasks and the precise allocation of natural and human resources to these tasks could not mask the deep-seated problems in this manner of production.

Imperial Kilns, Private Kilns and the Flows of Skilled Labour

Regardless of the number of workers who performed unskilled or low-skilled labour in the imperial kiln complex, some of the tasks within the

Figure 9.3 Porcelain workshop in Jingdezhen. Photo by China Photos/Getty Images.

process of making fine pieces of porcelain always required a high level of skill, and skilled workers were difficult to find. 'There are more than 300 imperial craftsmen, who are recruited repeatedly, yet there are few craftsmen whose skills are refined, and this is especially problematic for the case of painting'.[36] The quality of the painting on any given piece surely requires extremely high skill and is perhaps the most immediately visible indicator of quality. 'If the technical skills and artistry [of the craftsmen] are both refined and based on extensive experience, then they will have no difficulty in achieving success in firing pots, and they can make anything from the largest vessels to saggars. If you have workers that are only just good enough, however, then the biggest vessels they can make are winecups'.[37]

The size of ceramic bowls will be a familiar issue for anyone who has ever tried their hand at throwing pots: the bigger the size, the higher the required skill (Figure 9.3). A beginner can only make small items; to make anything bigger requires skill and experience. The risk with workers with low skill levels was that their pots failed, and that one did not find this out until after the pots had already been fired. Much better, then, to supplement the workers with low skill with additional recruits with high skills, so none of the pots turned out a disaster.[38] The challenge, of course, was to identify those workers who had experience and skill. To find this out, the text proposed that the supervisors ask the various workers to start with small-sized bowls, plates, dishes and saggars, and only letting the craftsmen with some ability proceed to making large bowls and wine vessels.[39] 'In those cases, on the day the work starts you have to supplement your workers by hiring workers with some ability from the private kilns'.[40] It transpires from all this that skilled labourers were in short supply, and yet they were essential for the success of the production. To compensate for the absence of skilled workers, the administrators of the imperial kilns turned to the private kilns and hired their best potters.

The presence of private kilns in the vicinity of the imperial kiln complex had a significant impact, both on the management of resources, as we saw in the previous chapter, and on the management of the labour force. The difficulties in securing a skilled workforce for the imperial kilns in Jingdezhen were exacerbated by the existence of a parallel structure of private ceramics production in Jingdezhen. So how did these two systems operate in such close proximity? The imperial kilns were part of the empire-wide administrative structure. They formed an organizational unit that, in administrative terms, fell under the imperial manufacturing office of the empire. Hence the presence in Jingdezhen of a kiln supervisor, appointed by the imperial palace, and an imperial kiln administrative office that looked much like a county yamen. This official administration was responsible for the delivery to the imperial court of high-quality porcelain, in the shapes, styles and quantities that the imperial court demanded. To deliver the goods, the administration managed its own imperial kilns. To get a sense of the quantities: in one year in the early fifteenth century (1436), 50,000 porcelain vessels were delivered to the imperial court from Jingdezhen, and in 1459, an order was placed for 133,000 pieces, although in recognition of the excessive burden this placed on the workers in the kilns, that order was subsequently reduced by 80,000 pieces.[41] Over the course of the sixteenth century, the production quantities varied from year to year, ranging from just over 900 pieces in 1537 to 120,000 pieces in 1547.[42] Crucially, the imperial kilns often did not succeed at producing enough items, both in terms of quantity and in terms of quality. And when the quality was not good enough or the quantity not high enough, the imperial kiln administrators had the option of turning to the other kilns in the area and requisitioning their products. The imperial kilns co-existed with private kilns. As we will see below, that co-existence undoubtedly had some advantages for both imperial and private kilns, but in terms of the attraction of skilled workers to the imperial kilns, it had distinct disadvantages for the imperial kilns.

According to the *Taoshu*, there were a total of 58 imperial kilns in Jingdezhen. Some 30 of the 58 imperial kilns were for the firing of large cisterns, which might be as large as 86 cm high and 94 cm in diameter, and thus required a dedicated type of kiln. The remaining 28 imperial kilns were both for firing blue and white wares and for enamelware. According to the same document, there were another 20 private kilns.[43] One of the differences between the imperial and the private kilns was their size. Both used roughly the same quantity of firewood per firing (80–90 shoulder-loads of firewood), but the imperial kilns could only hold around 300 pieces, while more than 1,000 vessels would be fired in the private kilns in one firing.[44] This significantly brought down the unit price of each vessel fired at the private kilns. Moreover, the imperial kilns were more cautious in their firing methods. When the official kilns were fired, the kiln supervisors only allowed the placement of wares of one colour in the kiln, and these had to be protected from the flames by a row of empty saggars. In the private kilns, in contrast, every row was occupied, with some of the coarser wares placed in the very front and back protecting the good wares in the middle rows from the flames. Moreover, the brick walls of the imperial kilns were sturdier, and covered with a dense layer of mud, so that no air could get in or out during the firing process. 'The reason that the vessels from the imperial kilns are pure and the vessels from the private kilns are of a more mixed quality is because of this difference in systems'.[45] These procedural differences, as they were written down in *Taoshu*, were perhaps more fictional than the authors have us believe. The authors created an idealized division intended to safe-guard the quality of the production in the imperial kilns and to deliver pre-cisely the kind of goods listed on the imperial demand.

The problem was that the firing procedures proposed in this document were no guarantee for a successful outcome. More often than not, the imperial kilns could not produce sufficient quantities of high-quality goods to fulfil the order, and the imperial kilns had to turn to the private kilns. During the course of the Jiajing reign period, this became official policy, known as 'guan da min shao', often rendered as 'official partnership with private kilns', which was a means of 'broadening the base of procurement of porcelain for the court'.[46] When the production quotas for the imperial goods were too high to manage for the imperial kilns, then the ordinary wares for daily use in the palace could be fired at those private kilns that were deemed to produce wares of high enough quality.[47] In that sense, then, the system was beneficial for the imperial kilns; with the weight of the imperial administration behind them, the kiln supervisors could initiate an exchange that left the best pieces in the hands of the imperial court.

There were, however, also distinct disadvantages to the co-existence of imperial and private kilns, as this critical observer noted: 'The way of working at the imperial and private kilns is not the same. In the imperial workshops, they tend to work in a perfunctory manner'.[48] The accusation of imperial kiln workers performing their duties in a perfunctory manner comes up regularly in the written records of the imperial kiln. Mostly, this concerns workers who perform their corvée obligation in the kilns. 'They keep registering their name with the authorities, occupying [the same position] over and over again, following the old [way of doing things] without an open-minded attitude'.[49] The observation is hardly surprising; the workers have come to Jingdezhen to perform corvée labour duties and are asked to carry out repetitive tasks in a highly divided work structure. More interesting, however, is the observer's identification of the contrast with the private kilns:

> In the private enterprises, they work extremely hard to safeguard their employment, and that can make the difference between success and ruination. Nowadays, when the kilns are about to be fired, the workers at the imperial kilns can make arrangements [for firing goods] with the private kilns, while at the private kilns, this is not an option. The workers at the imperial kilns are only used to their own system, and they rely on high prices to sell [the wares].[50]

Private enterprises, according to this observer, mean that people work harder because their jobs are on the line, while the imperial kilns have the luxury of firing their wares under better conditions, and then supplementing the quantities with goods produced privately. The private kilns, in contrast, have no way of supplementing their goods, and 'are more likely to run into difficulties because of insufficient [production]'.[51] The sixteenth-century Chinese economy is often said to display the early signs of capitalism, but it is nonetheless surprising to hear the similarities between the observations of these sixteenth-century officials and the claims of twentieth-century defenders of the privatization of state manufactures, or twenty-first-century supporters of public–private partnerships.

Over the course of the century, the official partnership between the imperial kilns and the private kilns became well established. The imperial kilns tried their best to fulfil the demands issued by the emperor. This included such impossible to make things like large square platters, which could not be made on the wheel, and inevitably cracked while they were drying in the sun. In desperation, the administrators would replace the missing square dishes with large round dishes, and had the calligraphers write the words 'Always the fixed shape' on the side of these round dishes.[52] But it became a working principle that under pressure, when the imperial order needed to be filled urgently, unfired wares were distributed to the nearby kilns for firing.[53] It did not make sense, however, to distribute wares for firing to places further afield: 'As for the potters based in more distant villages, we merely recruit the workers with high skill, and bring them to the factory to help with the work'.[54] This well-established practice of recruitment, however, brought its own problems, identified as follows by one of the administrators of the imperial kilns:

> They are deceitful at the private kilns. Many people are tempted to make use of the fact that the time of the submission is approaching. They start to do sloppy work, producing uneven and imprecisely painted pieces. The kiln administrators are under pressure, they must collect pieces. In the end, when the time comes for the submission, they often miss the allotted deadline. To deal with this situation, would it not be better to establish more kilns, and to hire the highly skilled workers, who then work within our factory, so we take care of shaping and firing ourselves, in our own factory. This would be faster and better.[55]

The private kilns were commercial enterprises and could take advantage of the pressure imposed on the imperial kiln by the centrally issued porcelain demand. Interestingly, instead of demanding higher prices for their pieces, the private kilns started to produce lower quality goods. Of course, producing lower quality goods and selling these for the standard price achieves the same financial benefit for the private kilns as producing lower quality goods presumably means fewer work hours and cheaper materials. But the point here is that human skill is the most sought-after resource. Hence the desire of the imperial administrator to select the most skilled of the workers and attempt to bring them under the control of the imperial kilns, to appropriate their bodies and harness the skill in their hands for their own purposes. But as was the case for the natural resources: the movement of labour and the flexibility that emerged as a consequence of the different systems of production ultimately meant a loss of control for the imperial kiln administrators.

Managing the Workforce

In 1558, kiln supervisor Fan Yongguan carried out an investigation of the labour force in Jingdezhen.[56] His findings were that there was a significant discrepancy between the number of workers from the nearby counties who were registered for work in the various workshops of the imperial kilns, and the actual number of workers.

> The actual number of workers, 260 individuals, is 107 less than the reported number of workers, which is 367. [The discrepancy in the figures] from Poyang is 60, from Anren 26, from Leping 42, from Fuliang 36, from Dexing 35, from Yugan 37, and from Wannian 25. Each month, in each workshop, the allocated workers (*lun bo*) rotate between the tasks. This is not allowed. The workers must be allocated to one specific workshop so as to eradicate this over-reporting.[57]

The problem of over-reporting was directly related to the fees that had to be paid to the kiln administration office for every worker. If the same workers switched from one workshop to another, then that same worker would be counted twice. The supervisors of each workshop reported the number of workers in their workshop, and this number was then used to issue a claim to each of the supplying counties, who were responsible for the payment of a fee per worker required. The labour of each worker represented a fee that lined the pockets of the officials managing the imperial kiln office in Fuliang. In response, a decision was taken in the same year to establish limits on the number of workers per workshop and a cap on the fees that could be claimed for their labour.[58] This did not resolve the problem, however, and the issue of over-reporting continued throughout the sixteenth century.[59]

A subsequent investigation of the working practices in the imperial kilns was carried out a few years later. The person responsible for this investigation was a man named Xu Pu. Born in Pucheng in Fujian province, and since 1553 holder of the highest civil service degree of the empire, Xu Pu began his career as magistrate of Yiyang county (now in Shangrao, Jiangxi).[60] He gained a certain measure of respect for his suppression of the unrest in the kilns of Hengfeng county. Hengfeng county was located in the northeastern corner of Jiangxi, a place now surrounded by four different provinces: Jiangxi to the west, Anhui to the north, Fujian to the south and Zhejiang to the east. Located high up in the hills, the place was 'densely populated, and many people living here were involved in the pottery business. They had ties with Fujian and Guangdong, having settled here to escape their tax obligations.'[61] Various attempts had already been made to settle this unruly area full of migrant workers trying to make ends meet by labouring in the kilns. This had been without success, until Xu Pu personally captured the 'villainous' (*jian min*) rebel leader Ye Shihao and dispersed his followers. In recognition of this achievement, Xu Pu was promoted to the role of supervising secretary (*jishizhong*) in the Office of Scrutiny of the Department of Works (*gongke*).[62] During the Ming dynasty, each of the six departments had such Offices of Scrutiny, staffed by supervising secretaries, who had a so-called 'speaking role', meaning that it fell to them to share their critiques and observations of current practice with the highest echelon of officials.[63] Such supervising secretaries had a censorial role, and it was in this capacity that Xu Pu was asked to offer his observations of the situation in Jingdezhen, and submit his thoughts in the form of a memorial to the emperor.

This memorial forms a useful starting point for understanding the issues that the officials in charge of the imperial porcelain manufactures felt they faced in the mid-sixteenth century. As Xu Pu put it: 'While there is a great deal of profit (*li*) to be made in Jingdezhen, numerous 'villains' (*jian*) also gather here'.[64] With this opening sentence, the main issue is immediately put onto the table: precisely because there is money to be made here, the town attracts not only numerous visitors, workers and merchants, but inevitably also the 'wrong' people. Xu Pu was a highly educated scholar-official, and his use of the word 'profit' in his description of the kind of place he thought Jingdezhen was, is not coincidental. In the sayings and ideas attributed to Confucius and noted down by his followers, the *Lunyu*, often translated as the Analects, we find the sentence: 'To act with an eye to personal profit will incur a lot of resentment'.[65] It is the personal, private gain that is problematic, and according to Xu Pu, it is precisely the private in opposition to what belongs to the state (presented as 'the common good') that is causing resentment in the perception of the administrators based in Jingdezhen. Xu observes that the presence of personal profit in Jingdezhen means that villains gather here, who combine a wicked nature with being self-seeking. Xu Pu's biographers had used exactly the same term for the rebel leader Ye Shihao; quite possibly, Xu's biographers had encountered the term in Xu Pu's own writings.[66] Twice, the term is used in implicit contrast with Xu Pu's own moral high-ground, and it may not be too much of a stretch to conclude that Xu Pu was of the opinion that such *jian min*, often migrant workers in the ceramics industry, posed a threat to the fragile stability of the kiln environment.

The memorial lists the problems that Xu Pu found to have arisen over the years in Jingdezhen, all 'longstanding problems at this imperial factory', though not a complete list, as the author himself acknowledged: 'I wish to raise these issues, but it is hard to be complete'. It is a list of problems that he would like to see reformed: 'I want to draft [this list], but it is hard to eradicate [the problems] completely'.[67] The first issue that Xu Pu tackled in his memorial concerns his observations about the working methods with the most precious of the raw materials present in Jingdezhen: cobalt. He finds it problematic that '[t]here is no method when the cobalt is beaten, and no method for its distribution. The true cobalt is mixed in with other stones, and crafty villains steal it [by putting it] in the pockets of their clothes'.[68] Xu Pu's description confirms what other officials had already complained about. When the workers had to prepare this highly precious material for its use as pigment by smashing it into powder, the opportunities for squirreling it away in pockets and clothing was almost impossible to control. All of the prefectures contributed to the cost of the materials, and there should have been a surplus, but the figures kept falling short. Xu Pu proposed a two-pronged approach to resolve the problem. On the one hand, the quantity of materials in circulation must be limited to stop the practices of pilfering cobalt; but at the same time, the amount of silver currency in circulation that the managers used to be in charge of must also be severely limited.[69]

The next issue Xu Pu wished to tackle concerns the rotation of individuals through various duties, and the over-reporting of workers this caused: 'People make use of the fact that they can switch duties, and as a consequence, numerous cases of over-reporting have been exposed'.[70] As we saw above, over-reporting was a frequent problem. By reporting each individual worker separately as he took up a certain task, the prefectures were liable for double payments. The problem stemmed, as we saw, from the fact that the prefectures were not liable to pay for a certain amount of work to be completed, but that they were responsible for the salary and subsistence costs of the work completed by workers with inherited artisan status, for whom this was part of their tax duties. In other words, for a single task, several workers could dispatch their corvée obligation, while the prefecture paid the costs for each of the workers, providing a profit for the managers of the kilns. Of course good management through the appointment of reliable supervisors could take care of this problem of working in rotation (and hence over-reporting), but unfortunately, a different type of problem presented itself there: 'Those who have been appointed as supervisors do this while being close friends with the fraudsters, and so they report to their superiors fictional numbers of workers and potters'.[71] The perennial problem that external managers faced in appointing individuals to positions of leadership from amongst their peers was the existence of internal friendships and obligations.

Interestingly, it is not until the very end of the memorial that the author raises the issue of skill:

> In the case of the imperial fishbowl vessels, they are very finely made and highly fragile, and most difficult to complete. The government craftsmen merely obey the officials in charge of the manufactory, who distribute [the task of making fishbowls] to the private kilns. Year after year it is like this, and the private kilns are compensated for this cost. This custom has now become the norm.[72]

The problem, once again, is not new. The poor quality and low skill level of those with official 'artisan status' was raised before. Certain tasks could be performed by these workers, but as we saw in the case of square boxes, and in the case of these large fishbowl vessels, the skill levels were far lower at the imperial kilns than at the private kilns. As a result, for this work, the tasks had to be farmed out to the private kilns, which meant that the costs went up significantly. And, as we have seen before, what were initially considered to be exceptional practices had become such routine that they had become normative.

Xu's memorial does not merely raise the issues that form cause for concern, but he also proposes a solution. 'If one wishes to reform these problems, then nothing is more important than selecting the [right] official; if you wish to select the [right] official, then this depends especially on giving someone exclusive responsibility [for the task]'.[73] Whatever problems have emerged in the imperial kiln, they can be resolved, according to Xu Pu, by making the right appointment, and handing full responsibility to this individual.

> I request that an imperial edict be sent to the Department of Personnel, which specifies that the office of the prefectural judge (*tuiguan*) in Ji'an reduces their staff by one, while one staffer is additionally appointed in the office of the judge in this prefecture [i.e. Raozhou]. The yamen of the official who originally appointed him [in Ji'an] does without the work of this person, and this individual is instructed to be stationed at the [porcelain] factory, where he exclusively manages the governing of the kilns, reforming the bad practices and getting rid of the poor elements. He is appointed in an additional position together with those who come from a *jinshi* background. This is considered to be in accordance with the rules of appointment. It cannot be allowed that officials of the Censorate or the Surveillance Office charge this person with other tasks and duties. The officials of the Censorate and Surveillance Office have read and discussed this proposal and have agreed to it. The Provincial Administration is considering the matter but has not yet reported their response.[74]

Again, numerous intriguing issues are raised. Concretely, the proposal is clear. The relevant office in the nearby prefecture of Ji'an will be asked to cut one member of staff, and that same person, already in possession of the relevant competencies, will be added to the same office in Raozhou prefecture. Being an outsider, without close connections to the administrators and workers in the region, meant that it would be easier to make the difficult decisions that had to be made: sacking people where needed, appointing further capable individuals, and reforming the deep-seated malpractices that had become so much part of the norm here. The focus on social status is intriguing. Concentrate on those with proper official status, Xu Pu advises, and, implicitly, cut out the people who know the business well from local perspective or experience, but without official status.

In some ways, it is precisely this final insight that shows Xu Pu's true colours and helps us interpret his perspective. Xu Pu was writing from the point of view of the imperial administration and wanted to fix problems that were problems *for* the administration. His text was included in the *Taoshu* so that later administrators could learn from it and take away from it some guidance for the management of the problems they, too, would encounter. In fact, the conclusion we may well draw from this, is that these issues were *not* considered to be problems locally. They were, in fact, embedded practices that made the business work. It kept the wheels turning and helped churn out the required quantities. Precisely because the local practices were fluid and the material and human resources could flow in unexpected patterns through the local landscape, creating connections between the various production sites, production continued regardless of the ongoing attempt to assert control over these flows by the representatives of the imperial administration.

10 | Material Circulations in the Sixteenth Century

The previous chapters have shown the inner workings of the imperial kiln in sixteenth-century Jingdezhen. The sources that informed the discussion were almost all drawn from the administrative records. The imperial court of the Ming empire required porcelain. This need for porcelain transpired at all levels: from the vessels used in ritual performances at the Temples of Heaven and Earth that confirmed the uppermost position of power that the emperor embodied within the realm to the vast porcelain cisterns that held the water for use in case of fire that were positioned throughout the court buildings; from the finest vases that graced the private residence of the emperor to the terrines in which the cooks prepared the soup and the cups from which attendants sipped their daily tea. The procurement of porcelain, much of it, though by no means all of it, drawn from Jingdezhen and its environs, absorbed the attention of a small group of government officials, whose job was to ensure Jingdezhen's porcelain arrived in the appropriate quantities and qualities, shapes and designs. The extant sixteenth-century documentation provides fascinating insights; a careful reading of which allowed us to see both what was required in terms of raw materials and human resources and where the imperial system failed to assert effective control over such assets. What emerged, the previous two chapters have shown, was an extended ceramics production system that stretched across the wider Jingdezhen region, where not only natural and human resources but also technologies and skills moved in circulatory fashion between the various sites of production. However, much of the imperial kiln administration might have wished to create boundaries and separations between an imperial (*guan*) and a private (*min*) sphere of production, both were part of the same system. The sixteenth-century imperial kilns functioned as a kind of hub, which facilitated the mobility of labour, materials, designs and ideas between Jingdezhen and the imperial court, and between the kilns in Jingdezhen and the other production sites in Raozhou. The imperial kilns could not have functioned without this mobility, as they drew on human and material resources that stretched across the region. At the same time, the region benefited from the concentration of technological expertise, high-quality resources and skill that

Figure 10.1 Gourd-shaped bottle with deer. H 45 × D 24.2 cm. 1522–1566, Jingdezhen. Collection Gemeentemuseum Den Haag, 0319976.

the imperial kilns brought. In this chapter, I will explore how the objects themselves bear the traces of this mobility.

Communities of Knowing and Making

This bulbous, gourd-shaped bottle (Figure 10.1) was made in Jingdezhen in the middle of the sixteenth century. The object was made from several separate pieces, with almost entirely disguised seams indicating where the pieces were joined together. The two bulbs, for example, were made from two half-rounded cup-shaped bowls. Each of the bulbs features a seemingly naturalistic scene, with a pair of deer moving through the landscape on the lower half. There are several different kinds of trees in this landscape: a flowering peach tree that shelters the deer; a plumtree, and a bamboo with wispy leaves and knotty stems. There are birds and a tortoise on rocky mounds. The character *shou*, meaning long life, is featured on the upper part of the gourd. The plants and animals that decorate the vase are all there to convey a message to its imperial beholder; each of the decorative elements signifies longevity, apart from the deer (*lù*), which not only symbolizes

Figure 10.2 Porcelain dish with underglaze blue design of two deer in a landscape with a tree, flowering plants and rocks. H 6 × D 32 cm. 1500–1550, Jingdezhen. Rijksmuseum, Amsterdam, inv. no. AK-RAK-1974-1.

long life but also wealth, because its homonym (*lù*) means 'salary', 'blessing' and 'good fortune'.

This gourd-shaped bottle, made in the imperial kiln, under the circumstances we have discussed in the previous two chapters, represents the finest quality of imperial porcelain production of the mid-sixteenth century. But as we also saw, the skilled hands, the top-quality raw materials, and the knowledge and experience that combined to make this fine piece were by no means exclusive to the imperial kilns. Hands, materials and experience all circulated well beyond the imperial kiln complex, and informed practice at other sites in the area. The plate in Figure 10.2 is a good example.

The dish was made in Jingdezhen in the first half of the sixteenth century, and features two prancing deer, surrounded by a natural landscape. The two deer appear in the centre of the plate, with a pine tree providing shelter over them on the top half. With their long thin legs lifted in the air, cloven-hooved feet, tails pointed upwards, slender bodies with spotted coats, and alert ears turned to face each other, the deer look lively and playful.

The decorative elements are evenly spaced out on the surface of the plate, and in combination with the regularity of the patterns in the bands surrounding the central decoration, at first glance create the impression of a geometrically shaped pattern. As was the case with the gourd-shaped bottle, the naturalistic scene in the centre of the plate conveys a clear message to the trained eye: the deer suggest longevity and blessings, while the evergreen pine tree stands for longevity. The surface of the plate shows some irregularities, which suggests that this item was never approved for imperial use. Most likely, this object was made at one of the many kilns that surrounded the imperial kilns in Jingdezhen. The hands that shaped the object and held the brush to paint the decorations may well also have handled imperial goods; as we saw in the previous chapter, the two worlds of the imperial and the private kilns were closely connected to each other. But the intended customer of this object was not the emperor himself, nor anyone within the imperial household.

Auspicious symbols including deer also grace the sides of this tall-standing bottle with fluted sides and a long neck, probably intended for the consumption of wine. It was made in Jingdezhen, towards the end of the sixteenth century (Figure 10.3).

There are similarities between the first two examples: the deer stand on tall legs, with slender ears, and their heads turned in contrasting directions. This tall-necked bottle's decorations, as we saw with the gourd-shaped bottle (Figure 10.1) and the deep dish (Figure 10.2), also conveys good wishes by means of the auspicious symbolism of the deer. The decorative scheme, however, is quite different. Instead of moving through an open landscape, the deer are surrounded by dense foliage. The deer and the flower heads stand out in white, while almost every part of the surface apart from the neck is covered with blue dots, lines and leaves. And strikingly, the six deer all feature inside their own panel. Objects with such panelled decorations came to form a group of their own, intended for export, as indeed this object was. Again, it is easy to spot the difference in quality between the gourd-shaped bottle on the one hand, and the dish and the tall-necked bottle on the other. Compared to the latter two, the surface is smoother, the clay whiter, the blue more intense, and the painting characterized by a more

Figure 10.3 Tall-necked porcelain bottle with deer. The bottle has a pear-shaped body with fluted sides, long narrow neck. 1575–1600, Jingdezhen. Inv. no. C.567–1910. © Victoria and Albert Museum, London.

skilled refinement in the case of the gourd-shaped bottle. Yet, the repertoire of auspicious symbols, represented by way of animals in a naturalistic setting, is the same regardless of the consumer, and the representation of the deer similar.

The division of the space into framed panels also features in the large plate in Figure 10.4. The band around the edge is divided into eight panels, each with a different decoration inside the panel. The base of the plate features four deer, standing tall on thin legs, with craning necks, arched backs and wispy ears. The four deer are surrounded by rocks, plants, trees and clouds, so by now we recognize the naturalistic setting that contains a message to its beholder. The pine tree, the *lingzhi* mushroom-shaped clouds, and the rocks with the Y-shape carved out inside them are all symbols of longevity.

These examples were all produced in Jingdezhen in the sixteenth century. There are significant differences, of course: they vary in size, shape, quality, colour and design. But there are significant similarities, too. All

Figure 10.4 Kraak porcelain plate with four deer and Y-shaped rocks. 1580–1600, Jingdezhen. Museum of East Asian Art (BATEA: 896). Heritage Images/Getty Images.

of the objects have been made in Jingdezhen within a period of roughly 100 years; all have been made from locally sourced clay, decorated with a blue pigment under the glaze and fired at a high temperature; and all of the objects feature deer as part of their decorative schemes. The five objects share the same local origin of the resources and their makers draw on the same local know-how about firing porcelain objects. Moreover, the objects have all been made by drawing on a shared language of design. The use of the deer in a natural landscape as design feature is one example of this shared language, especially since the designs all draw on the same symbolic repertoire that assigns purpose and meaning to those design features. But that shared language is also visible in the use of contrast between blue and white spaces on the surface of the object. Each of the objects uses white spaces to its advantage, either to create the white back-ground in which the blue deer jump to the foreground (as in Figures 10.1, 10.2 and 10.4); or to highlight the white deer themselves, set in a blue background (as in Figures 10.3 and 10.5). That shared language is also manifest in the use of lines and bands to create separate spaces on the sur-face, which in turn serve to articulate the shape of the objects: bands that

Figure 10.5 Porcelain dish in the shape of Mount Fuji with a design of horses and deer. ca. 1620–1630, Jingdezhen. Metropolitan Museum, 2010.206.

enhance the rounded curves of the gourd-shaped bottle (Figure 10.1), the slope of the cavetto of a dish (Figures 10.2 and 10.4), or the vertical lines that enhance the thinness of the neck (Figure 10.3). These objects have all been created by groups of makers who operate in the wider Jingdezhen region, and who share the same knowledge and experience of making porcelain objects. It is a community that is formed by knowing and making.

Beyond the Local

The significance of seeing the Jingdezhen production site as a network of human and material resources that stretched across the region (Raozhou) is significant not only for the circulation of resources, designs and skills between the imperial court and Raozhou, but also because it is the existence of that network that facilitated the adjustment to demands from beyond the boundaries of the empire. In what follows, I will show how Jingdezhen served as a hub that could also serve far-flung locations and consumers that were themselves invisible to those working in the various Raozhou manufacturing sites.

Take, for example, this object: a shallow dish in the shape of Mount Fuji, featuring a landscape scene, with trees and mountains (Figure 10.5). Horses gallop towards the centre from the right, and three deer stand startled on the left. The composition of the scene and the movement of animals through space are reminiscent of the objects discussed earlier, though offered here with far more detail and intricacy. It was made slightly later than the other objects, in the early seventeenth century, although it shares the characteristics mentioned above, especially the resources, technologies and languages of design. But the shape sets it apart: the wide-based triangular shape with the white top is immediately recognizable as Mount Fuji to someone who is conversant with Japanese visual culture. Of course, that makes it particularly interesting: the maker of this object would unlikely have been familiar with that visual language. Yet, the requirements to make it recognizable were effectively communicated to this maker in Jingdezhen, and this Jingdezhen object thereby became part of the Japanese world of objects. In that process, the boundaries became blurred, and the network was extended from Raozhou across the East China Sea to Japan. What matters is not so much the difference between the shapes that were current within the Chinese empire and the unfamiliar shape of Mount Fuji. More important is the network that could accommodate this adjustment of shape without losing its coherence and sense of community.

To make this object for the Japanese market, the sequence of events that started with the preparation of the clay, the refinement of the cobalt, and the packing of the kilns did not need to be adjusted. The symbolic language of the deer in a natural environment with rocks, trees and birds also did not need to change, regardless of whether it effectively conveyed the same message of longevity and blessings to its beholders. And as always, the painters used the balance between the colour blue and whiteness to emphasize the sense of space in the landscape and the height of the neck (and the snowy mountain). By this time, the Japanese were producing their own fine ceramics. In Arita (in Kyushu), they had access to the required resources, including kaolin and cobalt, and they had highly skilled potters producing extraordinary pieces for imperial demand. But the early seventeenth-century Japanese potters made fewer of such creatively shaped objects. Perhaps it was the experience with making oddly shaped items for the imperial court that gave the Jingdezhen potters the courage to adjust their shapes to make such items for the Japanese market, giving the Chinese potters an initial competitive advantage over the Arita producers. The competitive advantage did not last; the Japanese potters soon started to make their own extraordinarily shaped objects to cater for imperial and popular demand. The point is that for the Jingdezhen potters, the experience with making unusually shaped objects, such as the ribbed, fluted, box-shaped and oversize items demanded by the imperial court translated within the network into the relatively simple adjustment to the demands for the Japanese consumers.

That flexibility extended from the greater Jingdezhen region to the sites of production in the coastal regions, especially in Fujian, and connected the two. The kilns in these coastal regions worked with different clays, and lacked the direct proximity to the imperial kilns, which meant that the products from these kilns were slightly more thickly potted, more roughly shaped, and not as finely decorated. But other characteristics were shared, such as the use of the decorative repertoire and the adaptability for different markets, including those in Southeast Asia. In fact, a significant part of the ceramics production in sixteenth-century Jingdezhen, and more broadly speaking the kilns in southern China, was intended for Southeast-Asian consumers. This Southeast-Asian market was by no means a unified place; it covered a wide geographical range, and diverse cultural regions in what is now Vietnam, Thailand, the Philippines, and the numerous islands that make up the nation of Indonesia. The jar in Figure 10.6 was manufactured in one of the kilns in Zhangzhou, also known as Swatow.[1] It is an example of a vessel intended for the market in Southeast Asia. It is a squat little jar, fairly roughly potted, without handle, probably made for pouring water or wine.[2]

Similar finds suggest these wares were made in Zhangzhou in vast quantities, and exported on a very large scale throughout Southeast Asia.[3] Their shapes, together with a type of vessel known as recessed-base (or 'hole-bottom') wares, were made specifically for consumers in Southeast Asia.[4] As we saw in the case of the Japanese dish, adjustments could easily be made to the production process to accommodate different kinds of shapes; everything else remained unchanged. The little jar could be seen as an extension of the network that connected the kilns in the region of Jingdezhen to the coastal kilns of Zhangzhou and the consumers distributed throughout Southeast Asia. The production technologies in use in southern China also extended into mainland Southeast-Asia, especially to kilns in coastal Vietnam and Thailand. They are undoubtedly distinct wares, but in terms of technology, they are also related to the southern Chinese kilns. Once again, we see the interaction between local and global. Manufacturing was always

Figure 10.6 Small porcelain potiche-shaped jar with wide shoulder. Four panels with a white deer in blue foliage, with ruyi pattern on the shoulder. H 7.5 × D 9 cm. Zhangzhou, 1600–1624. Rijksmuseum, Amsterdam, inv. no. AK-NM-12327.

local: it happened in a specific site, drawing on the skills and resources of that particular manufacturing site. But if that local production was adapted in some way – in design, technology or materials – for global consumers, then local and global become intertwined, and form part of a connected process.

The object in Figure 10.3, with its tall neck and busy design was made for the Middle Eastern market. Both in shape and design, the Chinese production worked the deer design into the decorative pattern, creating an object familiar in style, recognizably Chinese, yet specifically suited to the tastes and expectations of a remote consumer based in the Middle

East. Two significant collections have shaped our knowledge of the overland movement of Chinese porcelains to Central Asia and the Middle East. These two, the Ardabil and Topkapı collections, came into being in very different places and times, but their continued existence as collections is what makes them so important. Today, the finest ceramic pieces of the Ardabil collection are housed in the National Museum of Iran, while the Topkapı porcelains are in part on display in the kitchen area of the Topkapı Saray Muzesi, and in part locked away in storage. Neither collection is easily accessible for research, and for both, scholars continue to rely on the path-breaking work by scholars in the 1950s, notably John Pope (1906–1982).[5] On the basis of their scholarship, we know that the pieces in the shrine at Ardabil were collected over the course of the fifteenth and sixteenth centuries, through trade and the exchange of diplomatic gifts. In the early seventeenth century, Shah ʿAbbās (1571–1629) donated his own collection to the shrine at Ardabil. The Ottoman collection held at the Topkapı Palace similarly came into being gradually.[6] Some were acquired through diplomatic gift exchange, others through trade, but a significant portion arrived as the result of the relentless expansion of Ottoman territory. When new areas were incorporated into the centrally administered political structure based in Istanbul, the material goods were brought to Istanbul as evidence of this submission.

The significance of these two monumental collections is hard to overestimate but has perhaps distracted scholars too much from the stories that smaller finds have to tell. Numerous other sites in Central Asia, the Gulf regions and the lands that belonged to the Ottoman empire enrich our understanding of Chinese export to these regions. Archaeological research in this wide-ranging terrain varies in terms of quantity and quality, but there is enough constancy in the finds to confirm that overland trade in Chinese porcelain continued throughout the sixteenth century, as did the maritime trade that delivered Chinese porcelain into the Gulf and the various ports of the Islamic world. Places such as the historic port of Julfar, now known as Ras al-Khaimah, one of the United Arab Emirates, or Sadana Island near Egypt provide ample evidence of extensive interaction with Chinese production sites over extended periods of time. Julfar's location on a promontory jutting out into the Persian Gulf shifted repeatedly over time, due to a silting up of the port, but archaeological excavations show sustained evidence of a Chinese connection.[7] For Sadana Island, the evidence comes from an eighteenth-century shipwreck found off the Egyptian coast in the Red Sea, which had on board roughly 900 tons of cargo, of which substantial quantities were made up of Chinese export porcelain, destined for the

Ottoman court.⁸ The various museum collections and archaeological excavation records in Central Asia and the Middle East confirm the global consumption of Jingdezhen's ceramics.

The export of porcelain to markets in Japan, Southeast Asia and the
Middle East, extended Jingdezhen's porcelain production beyond the
boundaries of the empire. Jingdezhen's production network already
included the imperial court and kilns throughout the prefecture of
Raozhou; its consumer network stretched far wider, across the empire as a
whole, but also to Japan, Korea, Southeast Asia and the Middle East. The
examples of objects decorated with deer show the coherence of the network: the mode of production in separate stages made it relatively simple
to make a recognizably similar product that catered for very diverse consumers. The technology remained the same, while size, shape, design and
quality could be adjusted to suit a variety of preferences and tastes. The
agents who facilitated the movement of objects between producers and
consumers were, on the whole, Chinese merchants. It was Jingdezhen's
kiln workers who prepared the goods for transport by wrapping, packaging and boxing the wares; local merchants who transported the goods
from Jingdezhen's porcelain storehouses to local market towns; Huizhou
merchants who facilitated the transport of goods from the Jiangxi region
to the urban centres in the lower Yangzi delta and by Grand Canal to the
imperial court, and delivered the goods by river to the southern provinces.⁹
In the ports along the south-eastern coast, the goods were put on Chinese
junks, and delivered to entrepots and ports in Malaka, the Ryukyu islands,
the Philippines and Southeast Asia. Portuguese ships transported porcelain to Japan. Overland routes, too, were travelled by Chinese merchants,
who delivered the goods to the markets in western China, and from there
to Central Asian markets. Of course, none of these markets were serviced
by Chinese merchants alone; none of the commercial transactions could
have happened without collaboration with and active participation from
Japanese, Southeast Asian and Middle Eastern merchants. Nonetheless,
within these trade patterns, the Chinese merchants played active roles,
thereby facilitating the extension of the weblike connections between the
kiln sites in the immediate vicinity of Jingdezhen and in the wider region
to locations scattered around the globe. The key to this web of connections
is that its extension into a global network did not necessitate any fundamental transformation of its inner workings. Local, regional, imperial and
global patterns of production and consumption formed part of a single
network.

The Role of the Europeans in the Sixteenth Century

Thus far, all of the agency in this story about global circulations of porcelain, and about local and global interactions has originated with non-European actors. Neither the producers of porcelain, nor those driving patterns of consumption, nor those who moved goods between the producers and consumers were European. But that changed around 1500, when the first Europeans started to make their appearance in the trade networks of the Indian Ocean. Here, the Portuguese merchants, who were the first to sail into the Indian Ocean, having first rounded the southern tip of the African continent in 1488, came into contact with the Chinese, Indian and Arab merchants who had been active in this region for centuries. Porcelain was only one of many goods traded, but the archaeological record of the Indian Ocean shows that porcelain was traded throughout the Indian Ocean. Porcelain has been found among the islands of Indonesia, but especially in the port cities on Java (Batavia) and Sumatra, throughout the Malay peninsula but especially in Malacca, Bengal, along the Coromandel coast, on the island of Ceylon, in Goa, Surat and further south on the Malabar coast, in Hormuz, Muscat and Mocha in the southern regions of the Red Sea, and all along the African coast. Chinese porcelain has also been excavated in Maravi, a state established in the mid-fifteenth century in the area that now encompasses southern Mozambique, Malawi and Zambia.[10] As the Portuguese began to know the patterns and agents of Indian Ocean trade, they soon became aware of the commercial potential of porcelain.

The Portuguese were not entirely unaware of porcelain when they first arrived in the Indian Ocean. Individual, highly treasured pieces of Chinese porcelain had already arrived in Europe via the overland trade routes and as ambassadorial gifts during the European Middle Ages. Most famously, this included the afore-mentioned Fonthill vase, the white piece of fourteenth-century Chinese porcelain that travelled from China to Hungary in 1338, from there to Naples in 1381, and eventually came to its current location in Ireland. Few ordinary Portuguese, however, would have had the opportunity to see this material with their own eyes. Moreover, a number of the Portuguese explorers and sailors arriving in the Indian Ocean might have known about porcelain only from the written record. Marco Polo, for example, who had written a widely read account about his travels in China between 1271 and 1295, had described porcelain as having 'such beauty that nothing lovelier could be imagined'.[11] Polo's popular account contributed greatly to the reputation of the distant lands of the East, its fabulous wealth, and the spices, gems, pearls and silks that could be had there. Most Portuguese, however, like most other Europeans, had absolutely no understanding of how this unfamiliar material was manufactured. A Portuguese Dominican friar, Gaspar da Cruz (c. 1520–1570), observed that '[t]here are many opinions among the Portugals who have not been in China, about where this porcelain is made, and touching the substance of which it is made, some saying of oyster-shells, others of dung rotten for a long time'.[12] Da Cruz sought to describe the manufacturing process, including the grinding of the stone, its purification in water and its separation into a fine, lower and coarse grade of clay, and the decoration of this porcelain with what Da Cruz called 'azure'. Despite these early descriptions, porcelain remained a mysterious material, which certainly enhanced its appeal. When the Portuguese observed the presence of porcelain in the ports of the entire Indian Ocean littoral region, it did not take very long for the Portuguese to become one of the participants in its trade. Moreover, they were keen to access the site of production, which took the Portuguese to Ming China.

The Portuguese arrived via Goa and Malaka in the Chinese empire in 1517 with a fleet led by Fernão Peres de Andrade (d. 1523). This first expedition, which also brought Ambassador of Portugal Tomé Pires (1465?–1524) to China, was initially successful, and Pires was welcomed to Beijing. In the 1520s, however, negative reports to the imperial court about the Portuguese taking control of Malacca and the enslavement of Chinese children in Canton undertaken by Andrade's brother changed the mood towards the Portuguese. Pires was imprisoned and died in 1524, and thereafter, the Portuguese traders were banned from entering Chinese ports. A Portuguese merchant by the name of Antonio Peixoto arrived in Chinese waters in 1542 on a ship laden in a port in Siam, with goods to trade with the Chinese. While there, a typhoon caused heavy damage to their ship, which floated adrift for two weeks before it arrived in Japanese waters, from where it eventually returned to Malacca.[13] It seems likely that it was the Chinese merchants in Malacca who established and maintained communication with the potters in Jingdezhen on behalf of the Portuguese merchants.[14] It was not until 1557 that the Chinese government permitted the Portuguese to establish a base on the peninsula of Macau, from where they then carried out their trading activities.

The earliest material evidence we have of the Portuguese merchants successfully communicating their wishes to the potters in Jingdezhen dates from the 1540s.[15] Potters in Jingdezhen created items decorated with the arms of Portuguese royals and nobles, sometimes inscribed with Latin texts

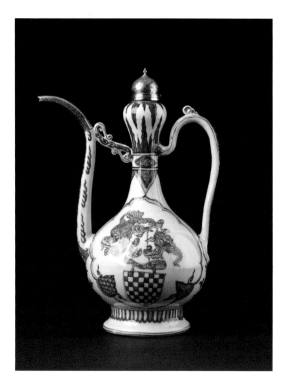

Figure 10.7 The Peixoto Ewer. Porcelain, with Iranian silver mounts. Jiajing reign period (1522–1566), Jingdezhen. Inv. no. C.567–1910. © Victoria and Albert Museum, London.

on the rim of the bowl.[16] One extraordinary example is a white porcelain ewer with cobalt blue decorations, held in the Victoria and Albert Museum collections and known as 'the Peixoto ewer' (Figure 10.7).[17] We know from the reign mark on the base that it was made in Jingdezhen between 1522 and 1566, when such ewers, modelled on Near Eastern brass pitchers, were made in large quantities.[18] The decorations on the ewer, a coat of arms painted in blue under the glaze, suggest it was custom-made for a Portuguese nobleman, perhaps even the merchant Antonio Peixoto, who was in the region at the time.[19] The silver mounts of the object, dated to the same time as the porcelain itself, are Persian in origin and must have been added to the object on its journey to Europe.[20] The object shows the spectacular ability of potters connected in some way to Jingdezhen to combine very varied knowledge about materials, markets and designs into a single high-quality object.

Sixteenth-century Portuguese 'chine de commande', porcelain made to order to Western specifications of the design, survives in much smaller quantities than its seventeenth-century equivalent. There is also much less documentation about the sixteenth-century porcelain trade than about the seventeenth century.[21] It is clear, however, that the Portuguese were not the only traders in porcelain for long. They were joined first by the Spanish, and then by the Dutch. Until 1580, when the Portuguese and the Spanish were unified under a single ruler, the Spanish and the Portuguese were in competition with each other, within Europe, but most of all in the wider world. The Treaty of Tordesillas, first signed in 1494, was intended to separate the world as it was then known to the Europeans into two spheres, one to be subject to influence by the Spanish, the other by the Portuguese. The lands to the east of the Iberian Peninsula, including part of the Brazilian and all of the African coasts, the Indian Ocean, the Spice Islands and southern China, were all allotted to the Portuguese, while the Spanish had access to the lands to the west, i.e. the Americas. A 1529 amendment to the treaty, signed at Zaragoza, sought to clarify the division of the Moluccan islands, which were considered the most valuable of all the overseas possession because of their spices.

The islands that make up what are now known as the Philippines were not considered as valuable, since no spices grew there. Their location meant that they fell squarely within the Portuguese realm, but the Spanish gambled, correctly, that the Portuguese would not prevent them from establishing an outpost of the Spanish Empire in the port of Manila in 1571. The reason why the Spanish were attracted to Manila was its location: between the Spice Islands, the southern ports of Japan, and the coast of Ming China, especially Fujian. The Chinese had long been engaged in trade with these islands, but after the Spanish established an entrepot here, vast quantities of silk and silver, lacquer and porcelain began to flow through the port of Manila from the late sixteenth century onward.[22] Gathered here from various sites of trade and manufacture, Asian goods were shipped from Manila to markets in Spanish America, including Acapulco, Mexico City and Veracruz.[23] From there, a selection of goods was sent onwards to Spain.

From 1580, the two Iberian empires became part of the same crown. Until 1640, when the Iberian Union came to an end, the Spanish kings also ruled over the Portuguese and all their overseas territories. In practice, the overseas possessions remained separate entities, but goods and people gained greater mobility during this time. The Iberian Union facilitated the flow of Spanish silver throughout the world. Chinese merchants who delivered Chinese goods including porcelain to Spanish and Portuguese ports, especially Malacca, Macau and Manila, were keen to return to Ming China with silver from the Spanish-controlled mines in Potosí.[24] The porcelain trade with the Spanish and Portuguese merchants brought New World silver into circulation in Ming China, precisely at a time when silver was in unprecedentedly high demand, as all taxes had been commuted to silver. Of course, that also meant that the ceramics producers were in a position to manufacture those goods that were considered desirable by consumers in the Iberian world.

The collection of Chinese porcelain amassed by Philip II (1527–1598) allegedly was one of the largest in the world, certainly in the sixteenth century. Despite that prominent collection, evidence from inventories and other archival materials recently explored by the Spanish scholar Cinta Krahe, demonstrates convincingly that amongst all the desirable Asian goods that were part of the global circulations, porcelain was not always treasured, at least in Habsburg Spain. It seems that most of the porcelain that was shipped from Manila to New Spain remained in the Americas; very little of that was further transhipped to Seville. As Krahe shows, in Spain, the porcelains were not stored in special cabinets or collections of precious goods; they were usually stored in rooms or cupboards where glasses, crockery and serving dishes were stored, the so-called *guardamangier*.[25]

In contrast, the porcelains shipped from Manila to New Spain met with enthusiastic consumers. The bright colour-scheme of blue and white porcelain was in high demand, especially when the wares were decorated with easily recognizable scenes such as animals in a natural landscape. The producers could easily cater for this taste: the scene of deer in a landscape with trees and rocks could easily be translated for a consumer with no knowledge or interest in the symbolic meaning of these elements. The framing of the scene with a band of more abstract decorative patterns, or the separation of the surface of the object into separate spaces for individual decorative elements worked well, as we see in the example illustrated in Figure 10.4. The adjustment to the demand for specific shapes was, as we have seen repeatedly, no obstacle for the producers working within the web of connections around Jingdezhen. The commodity that grew out of these developments in the late sixteenth century and came to be known as kraakware, quickly gained popularity throughout the New World.

The Spanish and Portuguese union under the crown of Philip II, established in 1580, also had significant consequences for the northern provinces of the Habsburg empire. These largely protestant provinces had been revolting against catholic Spanish rule since 1566, while maintaining peaceful relations with the Portuguese. This manifested itself especially in the exchange of goods and people through the hub of Antwerp. Portuguese shipments of Asian goods, for example, found their way to the markets and rich merchant homes of Antwerp in the second half of the sixteenth century. When the Portuguese joined forces with the Spanish, however, the Dutch declared war on the Portuguese as well as the Spanish. In 1581, the northern provinces finally managed to throw off what the northern Dutch felt to be the Spanish yoke, and established an independent political entity, known as the Republic of the Seven United Provinces, or, for short, the Dutch Republic. Over two decades later, in 1602, the Vereenigde Oostindische Compagnie (VOC for short) would be established, a chartered company, with investors from all seven provinces, and the right to establish a monopoly over goods traded from the east. In the seventeenth century, porcelain would go on to become one of the key commodities traded by the VOC. In the years before the VOC was founded, however, the Dutch were also exploring their options for access to the fabled goods of the east.

To facilitate their entry into this highly competitive trade, the Dutch took advantage of the knowledge about routes, ports and commodities that the Portuguese had accumulated over the course of the sixteenth century. When the city of Antwerp fell to Spanish control in 1585, many immigrants in the city fled Antwerp and moved to Amsterdam, especially the Calvinists, and the so-called new Catholics, Jews who had been forced to convert under the Spanish Inquisition. This influx not only grew the merchant population of the Dutch Republic, but also provided access to invaluable knowledge about Asia contained in travel records, maps and personal accounts.[26] After an initial attempt to reach Asia by means of the northern route, travelling along the Siberian coast in the Arctic Ocean, a group of merchants finally decided to travel southwards, despite the ongoing state of war with the Spanish and the Portuguese. They set off in April 1595, rounded the Cape of Good Hope and arrived at the island of Bantam in June 1596. This first expedition safely returned to Amsterdam in 1597, with a shipload full of spices. It was not until the second expedition, however, which left port in 1598, that a small quantity of porcelain was brought back from Asia. Spices were the main focus of these expeditions, and the VOC was established with the aim of creating a single company, so that the efforts in preparing such voyages could be combined, the costs of the spices could be kept low, and the profits could be maximized. Porcelain, however, soon emerged as a serious competitor for the trade in spices.[27]

Figure 10.8 shows a painting by Floris Claesz van Dijck (1574/ 1575–1651). Completed around 1615, the painting depicts fine damask tablecloths, a variety of fruit and nuts, three cheeses stacked on top of each other and several pieces of Chinese porcelain: a rimmed plate and a deep dish usually referred to as a 'klapmuts'. Both are decorated with a 'kraak'

Figure 10.8 Still life with cheese. Floris Claesz. Van Dijck, ca. 1615. 82.2 × 111.2 cm. Rijksmuseum, Amsterdam, SK-A-4821.

pattern: framed panels with individual decorations inside the panels, and narrow panels between the wider panels with pendants. Van Dijck was by no means the only painter who included pieces of Chinese porcelain in his still-life paintings. The painter Frans Snijders (1579–1657), who lived in Antwerp all his life, made several large still-life paintings with porcelain, as did the Antwerp painter Osias Beert (1580–1623). The depictions of Wanli porcelains in the still-life paintings produced in large numbers during this time suggest perhaps less their accessibility than their appeal and desirability.[28]

Concluding Thoughts

As we have seen in the previous chapter, the imperial kilns in Jingdezhen drew together a network of producers and consumers that encompassed the administrators and potters based at the imperial kilns, the diverse consumers based in the imperial court, and the private kilns scattered throughout the prefecture. What I have referred to as the weblike connections centred on Jingdezhen thrived in its diversity: consumers and producers, unskilled labourers and highly skilled painters, those based within Jingdezhen and those at the imperial court. Some parts of the network were local, other parts stretched to the regional and the empire-wide. The materials we have discussed in this chapter reflect both the network's cohesion and its diversity.

Three mechanisms served to facilitate circulation throughout the network, thereby enhancing its integration. The first of these was the variability of quality. The nature of the raw materials and the skill levels of the workers determined the quality of the goods produced and could easily be varied and adjusted to changing circumstances. For example, the quality of the raw materials and skilled hands determined the difference in quality between the gourd-shaped bottle for the imperial court (Figure 10.1), the round dish with deer (Figure 10.2) and the little jar for export (Figure 10.5). Despite the obvious differences, the objects also show that we are not talking about strict divisions but a spectrum or a continuum of quality. The Peixoto ewer is a good example of that spectrum. Its quality is extremely fine, closer to the gourd-shaped bottle than the little jar for export, yet it was made for an even more remote consumer than the little jar. Could some of the same hands that manufactured goods for the imperial palace also have touched an object made for export? In the past, studies of imperial porcelain and export-ware ceramics emphasized their differences over their similarities. Auctionhouse prices paid for what is considered to be imperial porcelain as opposed to export ware suggests the contemporary art market continues to see a difference. In recent years, however, the idea of movement between the two realms has started to gain currency. In light of our discussions in the previous chapter, it seems at least possible that a single pair of hands touched both kraak porcelain objects and imperial porcelains, even if the circumstances under which those hands laboured were different. Drawing on a shared set of raw resources and skills, workers throughout the network could easily adjust the quality of the goods they produced. By using more refined clay, higher quality cobalt, or more skilled painters, the quality could be more easily guaranteed; by using less carefully prepared clays, more diluted cobalt, less well-trained craftsmen, or by firing the goods in more densely packed kilns, one could save on expenses and produce lower quality goods. While the manufacturers catered to the demands of different consumers and diverse markets, they were able to create both cohesion and diversity.

The commonality of visual language was another mechanism that facilitated circulation and created cohesion throughout the network. The decorative motif of deer serves as a good example. Just like the spoken language, the language of visuality requires knowledge to facilitate full comprehension, but unlike in the case of the spoken word, visual communication is also possible without that shared knowledge. The image of a deer can communicate something even without establishing a shared linguistic repertoire. The image of a deer under a pine tree may well appeal for a variety of reasons and mean something different to each of its beholders, but it could still create a visual connection across social and cultural difference regardless of those distinctions.

Finally, the potters' ability to translate a variety of shapes and materials into porcelain objects strengthened the network's cohesion. Both the long-necked bottle (Figure 10.3) and the ewer (Figure 10.7) are shapes known in their metal form. Silver decanters for wine and silver ewers with a handle and a thin curved spout for pouring oil or rosewater were well-known in the Middle East. The process of translation into a new material seems effortless when looking at the successful outcomes in Figures 10.3 and 10.7 but involved a series of re-imaginations and experimentations that preceded this. Arguably, the process of translation across materials like silver and porcelain is closely related to the translation of shapes from nature into porcelain. The double gourd or the image of Mount Fuji formed the inspiration that led to the creative translation of an idea into a porcelain body. The ability to engage in this process of translation meant that the network could be accommodating and expansive at the same time as being coherent and integrated. The variability of quality and the translatability of shapes and materials meant that the participants in this web of connections could satisfy the desires of a wide range of consumers, and it was the commonality of the visual language that made this network both local and global.

11 | Local and Global in Jingdezhen's Long Seventeenth Century

In the last 15 years, the writing of history has been thoroughly transformed by what has been called 'the global turn'.[1] If we think of the practice of writing history as travelling along a path, then the concept of a 'turn' makes sense; many of its practitioners have moved into a new direction, where the view of the wider world is more visible.[2] The metaphor of a different direction or a turning off the path, however, also implies that the main direction of travel remains unchanged; the practice of history has remained the same, apart from the small group who have made the choice to move their work into a global direction. I would argue, instead, that the change is more profound; our historical awareness of interactions that cross boundaries has changed the field of history as a whole.[3] Of course, there is not a single reason that explains this transformation; the underlying factors are multiple and complex. They include the mobility and diversity of our contemporary world that forms the backdrop to our writing about history, which has made us more aware of diversity and boundary-crossings in the past. The fundamental challenge that globalization has posed to the authority and legitimacy of the nation state has also played its part in spurring on changes to the field of history, as has the powerful insight that space is not merely a static background or a given set of environmental features, but also a social construct as well as a historical agent in itself.[4] These factors have given scholars the impulse to think more critically about the units within which they explore the past, and to analyse patterns of change beyond pre-existing or constructed boundaries. Global history, in that sense, includes any historical practice that engages critically with the spatial units within which patterns of change occur, and all historical approaches that look beyond the spatial boundaries of the nation or geo-political region. Global history, thus, is by no means only the study of phenomena that occur all over the planet, or only the study of large-scale cross-cultural interactions. Just like microhistory, global history should be led by a close engagement with a wide range of primary sources. Ideally speaking, global history concerns a critical perspective on the role of space, a willingness to look beyond spatially determined and pre-existing boundaries such as regions or nation states, and a desire to identify patterns of change across boundaries of any kind.[5]

The approach of global history, then, has little to do with the size of the unit of analysis. It does not matter whether the unit is an individual town, a nation state or indeed a world region. If a study considers a unit to be closed, without challenging the legitimacy and permeability of its boundaries, regardless of whether these are physical, cultural or political, then that study thereby ignores the main insights provided by the scholarship on the notion of space. Anything that can be studied historically also has a spatial dimension; those spatial factors have historical agency, regardless of their size, and their analysis should always form some part of historical study. My approach to the history of porcelain takes the spatial dimension seriously; I analyse sources regardless of the size of the unit within which they have been produced. The terms 'global' and 'local' do not refer to opposing spatial units, such as the world as a whole or the town of Jingdezhen; in this approach, 'global' refers to historically mobile phenomena that move across boundaries, while 'local' refers to spatially bounded phenomena with limited movement across boundaries. The purpose of this spatial approach, then, is to trace such movements and their absences, and analyse the underlying factors that made movement and stasis possible and/or desirable or impossible and/or undesirable. Inevitably, then, global and local form part of the same spectrum; one cannot be studied in isolation from the other. Only when we consider local and global as part of the same process can we identify the fluctuations and wavering between global and local, highlight the significance of the impact of either globalizing or localizing trends, and see the unevenness in these developments.

Much of the history of Jingdezhen's porcelain to date has been written without this spatial perspective and without combining global and local. We see this both in studies of Jingdezhen as local site of ceramics production, and in studies of porcelain as global commodity. For example, Liang Miaotai's classic study of Jingdezhen presents the history of the town from its earliest beginnings in the Tang dynasty to its latter days under the communist regime, without questioning the ways in which Jingdezhen's past was connected to other sites of production.[6] Jingdezhen and its environs appear as a sealed unit, with a unique story that pertains only to Jingdezhen.[7] On the other end of the spectrum is a study like Robert Finlay's, which traces the global circulations of porcelain, in which Jingdezhen plays a major role.[8] But Jingdezhen itself, and the sources that reveal the inner workings of the production site do not form part of that story of global connections. In what follows below, I seek to make explicit where this spatial approach offers new perspectives to the study of Jingdezhen's porcelain, and challenge the ways in which the history of Jingdezhen has been written either as a global or as a local story, without integrating the two.

The 'Absence' of Jingdezhen

Chinese porcelain was traded all over the world, and yet place and space have received remarkably little attention in the study of its history. Where the focus is on the objects themselves, the use of place names as shorthand to identify the different types (or wares) of ceramics has had the effect of concealing from view their production sites and their complex histories. The geo-physical characteristics of a specific site and its socio-economic and technological patterns of change, in other words, the historical complexities of such sites are all collapsed into the single name of the site, and thereby removed from the analysis of the object itself. The term 'china' for porcelain is merely another example of the use of the toponym to take the place of the material; the term china refers to the place of its production, but at the same time makes the complexity of the place China less visible. Jingdezhen, in that line of reasoning, comes to mean 'blue and white porcelain', thereby rendering the town of Jingdezhen and its history invisible. In part, this is a feature of the object-centred approach; if we are interested in the formal aspects of the object, then we start with the object itself, not with the historical circumstances that preceded its emergence as object.[9] Jingdezhen, the place, is not part of our understanding of Jingdezhen, the wares.

The absence of Jingdezhen, the place, also characterizes the history of the consumption of ceramics. The different types of ceramics have discrete patterns of consumption.[10] The wares from the Ru kiln, for example, were produced around 1100 for the imperial court, and thus continued thereafter to be seen as highly desirable and consumed by the highest elites. Consumption studies of Ru wares, however, rarely make any mention of Ruzhou, the place.[11] Carswell's study of blue and white porcelain as it made its appearance all over the world is another example of the absence of Jingdezhen in studies of consumption. Jingdezhen features only as a name of the site where this consumer good emerged.[12] The history of its production is not part of the story of consumption. Porcelain's global consumption story often begins with the export of porcelain to the islands in Southeast Asia, or with the trade in porcelain to the African coast, documented in written records and archaeological traces from as early as the thirteenth century.[13] It highlights early contacts with the Portuguese in the Indian Ocean and the mediated trade that facilitated fine porcelains from Jingdezhen to reach the courts and noble-houses of sixteenth-century Europe, and discusses the turning point of the late sixteenth century. The founding of the British and Dutch East India Companies in 1600 and 1602 respectively represents a significant moment in this narrative. Most importantly, the arrival of the trading companies and the establishment of direct trade routes between Asia and Europe facilitated the movement of far larger quantities of porcelain goods than ever before. As a consequence, the history of porcelain consumption is considered to be a 'global' history, while the story of production remains largely a local story, embedded within the boundaries of the place itself.[14]

Studies of seventeenth- and eighteenth-century porcelain production fall into two distinct categories. On the one hand, there are studies that focus exclusively on Jingdezhen's production for the imperial court. These explore the ways in which the local kilns in Jingdezhen manufactured their finest pieces for the imperial court in Beijing. On the other, there are studies that focus on production for markets outside the Chinese empire. Very few explore the significance of the relationship between local production and global consumption. Scholars of imperial porcelain, especially during the Ming and Qing dynasties, largely ignore the history of porcelain made for export and their circulation in non-Chinese markets. Experts of imperial porcelain focus their expertise on the finest quality pieces intended for the imperial court and the particular technologies in terms of kilns, colour and decorations that serviced this production.[15] The manufacture of porcelain features in their studies in the form that relates to the imperial stream of porcelain production. Their outlook could be referred to as 'local' in the sense that looks only within a pre-established political and spatially bounded unit, without exploring wider connections or interactions beyond those boundaries of imperial porcelain.

Meanwhile, studies of the production for export rely to a great extent on non-Chinese language source material. Much of the scholarship on the global trade in porcelain has made use of the records of the East India trade companies, such as the VOC and the British EIC. Early attempts by T. Volker for the seventeenth century, and far more precise and footnoted studies by C.J.A. Jörg and others for the eighteenth century have charted the quantities of porcelains manufactured in and around Jingdezhen and exported via the port of Canton.[16] Ongoing work by Christine Ketel on porcelain for the Dutch market in the early seventeenth and the completed PhD thesis by Claire (Hui) Tang on enamel porcelain in the eighteenth century all rely on European documentation to reveal the quantities, sizes, shapes and styles of exported porcelains from Jingdezhen.[17] The increase in quantities of porcelain manufactured for export from the early seventeenth century to the late eighteenth century is undisputed. On the whole, however, the quality of what arrived in Europe did not go up over that period of 200 years. What were fine and exceptional pieces in the fifteenth century, brought to Europe as ambassadorial gifts, became specially manufactured pieces for Portuguese royals and noblemen in the sixteenth century. What were specifically described pieces in demand for the Dutch consumer, detailed in shape, size and decorative design by means of the *eisen* (demands), accompanied by drawings or wooden models in the seventeenth century, became in the eighteenth century consignments of mixed porcelain goods, described as 'of the kind available'. Porcelains provided ballast in the ships that sailed from Asia to Europe, were sold in batches in auctions and markets, and over the course of the eighteenth century, became part of every domestic interior in the Netherlands. Even the orphanage in Amsterdam had some Chinese porcelain.[18] Porcelain was no longer exceptional and special, but widely available for mass consumption. In short, these Dutch and English records show the making of mass commodity, available to the widest range of consumers. Without challenging any part of this story of mass consumption, I would argue that by failing to include the production side into this story of global consumption, the danger is that a false impression is created about production, which is seen as focused mainly on providing goods for mass production. So, production is considered in a binary fashion: fine quality goods manufactured for the imperial court, i.e. local, and low-quality goods manufactured solely for export. Far from being separate stories, of course these two are connected. The demand for quantity in Europe had an impact on the type of skills required in Jingdezhen.[19] The quantity of production in Jingdezhen for European markets had an impact on the desire for such manufactures and the development of new technologies and new ways of working in Europe. It is only when we combine both stories about skill, combine local and global, consumption and production that we see the full picture of these interconnections, and recognize the importance of the agency of Chinese manufacturers in the long seventeenth century.

Before we can explore that agency, however, we have to acknowledge how much changed over the course of the seventeenth century: the Ming regime came to an end, and the Manchu, who had been building momentum in the steppelands to the northeast of Beijing since the early seventeenth century, established the Qing dynasty in 1636. The northern part of Jiangxi province saw heavy fighting, the kilns were largely destroyed during this period, and for some years production was impossible.[20] But once the imperial kiln complex was restored around the 1680s, many innovations were brought in. It goes beyond the remit of this study to explore these developments in depth, but they include a new organizational structure for the production of craft at the imperial capital with the establishment of the Imperial Household Agency, from within which the supervision of the Jingdezhen kilns was directed. This meant, among other things that the supervision of production in Jingdezhen was carried out by trained men with extensive skills in ceramics production. The production of porcelain in Jingdezhen also saw the benefit of several technological innovations, such as the introduction of new glazes and enamels, the creation of porcelains that imitated wood, bamboo, leather, jade and metal, and the use of models created at the imperial workshops in Beijing to instruct the potters in Jingdezhen.[21] It is impossible, therefore, to understand the manufactures of Jingdezhen in the seventeenth and eighteenth centuries as continuous with the sixteenth-century kiln site we have discussed in previous chapters. Nevertheless, the documentary record of the late seventeenth and eighteenth centuries is helpful for putting the sixteenth-century developments in historical perspective.

Tang Ying and the Question of Skill

The history of Jingdezhen's ceramics is on the whole not a story of great individuals; few personal names associated with the work executed in Jingdezhen remain. The name of Tang Ying (1682–1756), however, stands out. The writings of Tang Ying, superintendent of the imperial kilns, form one of the most valuable sources for understanding the ways in which the production of porcelain in the last imperial dynasty catered for very specific markets.[22] Born in Fengtian, present day Shenyang in the northern province of Liaoning, Tang grew up in an elite family.[23] When he was still very young, Tang entered the Imperial Household Department, and began working at the Yangxin Hall, the Hall of Moral Cultivation, which housed a library and a painting collection. Here, Tang Ying gradually acquired extensive knowledge and skills in painting, design and creative writing, and where he gained administrative experience as Vice-Director in charge of painting.[24] Later, when he was working on specially commissioned pieces in Jingdezhen, he stated that he made these 'for the Hall of Moral Cultivation'.[25] When Tang Ying was first dispatched to Jingdezhen in 1728, Nian Xiyao (1671–1738) was still in charge.[26] Nian was also from an elite family, and in his early years in Beijing, he had received training in the Western principle of perspective in painting.[27] He was stationed at Jiujiang, and in charge of the customs paid on goods traded throughout Jiangnan, and in that capacity regularly visited

Jingdezhen to check on the production for the imperial court.[28] After 1735, when Nian left his position, Tang Ying remained in charge in Jingdezhen, until his death in 1756, serving for a short period in the Maritime Customs Service (*Yuehaiguan*) in Canton.[29]

During his time in Jingdezhen, Tang succeeded in making a significant impact across a number of areas. Firstly, the quality of the output in Jingdezhen developed significantly, as is testified by some of the finest individual pieces in Jingdezhen's history of imperial porcelain manufacture, crafted under his guidance. Secondly, the communication about technologies between the imperial court in Beijing and Jingdezhen was enhanced during his time. A close confidant of the Qianlong emperor, Tang Ying often understood easily what the emperor wanted, and communicated these demands effectively to the manufactures in Jingdezhen. Thirdly, Tang Ying's writings on the manufacture of porcelain provide us with invaluable information for eighteenth-century Jingdezhen.[30] Some years after Tang Ying's tenure in Jingdezhen, probably between 1767 and 1771, a man by the name of Zhu Yan arrived in Jiangxi to serve in the administration of the Jiangxi governor Wu Shaoshi (1698–1776).[31] The book he went on to write, *Taoshuo* 'On Ceramics', published probably in 1774, demonstrates detailed knowledge of the Jingdezhen industry.[32]

Texts by men like Tang Ying and Zhu Yan allow for an interesting comparison with the *Taoshu*, the sixteenth-century text on the administration of the kilns discussed in earlier chapters. Of course, such a comparison is fraught with difficulties. Much had changed between the sixteenth and eighteenth centuries. The production for overseas markets had perhaps declined, in part because what had been Jingdezhen's overseas markets were now producing high-quality ceramics themselves: Meissen in Germany, Delft in The Netherlands, Sèvres in France and the Wedgewood manufacturers in Britain all produced products that competed directly with Jingdezhen's ceramics in the eighteenth century. On the other hand, the growth in demand from the domestic market and the imperial court meant that the production itself did not decline. The existence of the extensive literature about the kilns in the eighteenth century, which in themselves are the subject of many current and several forthcoming studies, allow us to tease out some of the longer continuities.

The question of skill, a vexed question in both sixteenth- and eighteenth-century documents about the porcelain manufactures, was one such continuity.[33] But perceptions about that skill – what kind of skills were required, how they should be fostered and rewarded – were far from continuous.[34] As we will see below, it was not only Chinese reflections on the issue of skill that changed; European understandings of the skills of the porcelain workers also changed dramatically, as did Chinese reflections on the issue of skill. One of the first texts to introduce Chinese porcelain to readers of Western languages was Marco Polo's thirteenth-century travel account. Before that, the thirteenth-century account of William of Rubruck had already established European understanding of the Chinese as 'excellent craftsmen in whatever skill', but Rubruck had not mentioned porcelain specifically.[35] Polo was the first to describe this material called porcelain in some detail: made of a 'crumbly earth' that had to be dug, stacked and then left to mature for 30 to 40 years, that process of refinement allowed the creation of dishes 'of an azure tint with a very brilliant sheen'. He found porcelain bowls of 'incomparable beauty', and yet both 'plentiful and cheap'.[36] Polo's account was followed by several other authors, who all expressed amazement at the nature of the material itself and the skills required to make it, which were considered to be ingenious and astounding.[37] During the fourteenth and fifteenth centuries, when few individuals had ever seen porcelain with their own eyes, the material retained an almost magical quality. Even in the sixteenth century, when porcelains started to circulate in Europe in growing numbers because of the Portuguese trade, few understood how the material was made. Allegedly, the archbishop of Braga described blue and white porcelain to Pope Pius IV (1559–1565) as pieces that 'dumbfound the eyes, seeming a combination of alabaster and sapphires'.[38] The makers of such material, it was assumed, must possess extraordinary skill at manufacturing.

From the middle of the seventeenth century, however, there was a subtle shift in the ways in which European accounts described the Chinese manufacture of porcelain. The more detailed accounts written by Western observers in China led to a more comprehensive understanding in late seventeenth- and early eighteenth-century Europe of its methods and materials. Perhaps inevitably, the greater familiarity with the manufacturing process also reduced the sense of wonder and amazement, and gradually led to a sense of contempt. The French Jesuit Louis-Daniel le Comte (1655–1728) found it to be a 'mistake to think that … its Composition is so very difficult; if that were so, it would be neither so common, nor so cheap'.[39] In Le Comte's view, if the French could experiment with some of the raw materials available in France, then it 'might not be impossible to succeed' in making porcelain in France.[40] With the appearance of the famous letters by the French Jesuit Père d'Entrecolles (1664–1741) in the early eighteenth century, the production process lost all its mystery. The Jesuit emphasized the laborious processes and appalling conditions that characterized the work of making porcelain in Jingdezhen over the level of skill or craftsmanship of the potters. D'Entrecolles' letters set the tone for several other observations that followed, which depicted the manufacture of ceramics, as well as the arts more generally as 'nothing great', even 'second rate'.[41]

The rise in the quantity of imported goods and the influx in Europe of porcelains made in vast quantities specifically for the purpose of export seem to have gone hand-in-hand with a gradual decline in admiration for the levels of skill required to manufacture these goods.[42] Late seventeenth- and early eighteenth-century European accounts of the manufacture of porcelain made the process of manufacturing knowable, and the required skill less unfathomable for the European observers. The European manufactures of hard-paste porcelain at Meissen, Sèvres and Wedgwood posed a very serious challenge to the production for overseas markets in Jingdezhen. Individual pieces of porcelain made for royalty and nobility, followed by the reliable production of large quantities of European-made porcelain for growing consumer markets, soon competed with Chinese porcelain. When Lord Macartney visited China on his 1793 embassy, he confidently included British-made porcelains, and felt sure that even the Chinese Emperor would recognize its superiority over Chinese-made porcelain.[43] Macartney considered the skills of the Chinese potters to have declined, their machinery 'imperfect' and the porcelain manufactures as a whole 'precarious'.[44] Macartney's knowledge of the European production of high-quality ceramics led him to largely unfounded assumptions about the skill of the Chinese potters.

Meanwhile, for the Chinese manufacturers, especially those associated with the imperial kilns, the issues of skill and the retention of skilled workers remained crucial. As we saw in Chapter 9, in the late sixteenth century, a major cause for anxiety over skill was the lack of skilled workmen able and willing to carry out the numerous and varied duties across the whole spectrum of work associated with porcelain manufacture. To entice skilled workers into the imperial kilns, work tasks that required higher levels of skill had to be rewarded more highly than simpler tasks. For Tang Ying, the concern was not so much where workers came from, or how much they ought to be paid for each of the separate tasks. In his famous commentary on the 20 illustrations of porcelain manufacture, he rarely touches on wages paid. Only once does he reflect on the very low wages paid to the workers who grind down the ingredients for the pigments; grinding pigment was tedious work, as it took at least a month to create the required fineness. 'The workers' wage is three *qian* [i.e. three tenth of an ounce of silver] per month, but those who use both hands to work two pestles, and those who work through the night until the drum strikes once are paid double that'.[45]

Taken out of context, the statement means little, and there is not enough information to construct a detailed picture of labour wages in Jingdezhen at this time, although on the basis of some recent comparative work, it is clear that this is an extremely low wage.[46] Tang's final sentence is revealing: 'The old and young, the injured and the sick heavily rely on this work to provide themselves with a living'.[47] Grinding colour may have been mind-numbingly boring, but for those who were unable to earn a living any other way, this work may well have provided a lifeline. In a city full of migrant workers, who had to make do without the support of their extended families and access to even the smallest plot of agricultural land to grow basics, such lifelines were even more important. Tang cared about the circumstances under which the workforce had to produce the work.

Of course, the skills of the workers and the quality of the work they produced also mattered for Tang Ying. Just as we saw in the sixteenth century, in the eighteenth century, the manufacturing process was separated into a series of highly specialized, connected but individual tasks, carried out by 'specialised craftsmen' (*zhuanmen gongjiang*).[48] These, in turn, were divided into numerous smaller groups, depending on what seem like small differences in what they produced. For example, those who threw pots were divided into two groups. Those who threw the larger-size, round wares on the wheel, such as dishes, bowls, cups and plates between one and three *chi* in diameter, were in a different workshop (*zuo*) from those who made the exact same wares but in smaller dimensions, i.e. less than one *chi* in diameter.[49] There were saggar-makers (*xiabo zhi jiang*), moulders (*mojiang*), carpenters (*mujiang*) and kneaders (*nijiang*), lathe workers (*xuanjiang*), kiln workers (*yao zhi jiang*), crate makers (*zhuang tong jiang*) and mat makers (*jiaocao jiang*).[50] Others, not identified as craftsmen, included those who painted outlines (*huazhe*), who are distinct from those who filled in those outlines (*ranzhe*); those who embossed ceramic surfaces (*gong*) were different from those who made holes (*zhui*); those who carved (*diao*) were not the same as those who engraved (*lou*).[51] Undoubtedly, production on a large scale was done more efficiently by implementing a highly compartmentalized production line, but speed and cost of production were not the main concerns for Tang Ying. What mattered for Tang Ying was that this division of labour helped to safeguard the specific skills of the workers and the overall quality of the production. 'Those who draw the outlines (of the decorative patterns on porcelain) only study drawing, and do not learn (the techniques for) filling in; those who fill in only learn to do that, and do not study drawing. Thus, the [craftsmen] focus on their own skill without dividing their attention'.[52] While their specific skills were divided into these separate categories, they all worked in the same space, because ultimately, 'creating decorated [porcelain] was one and the same type of work'.[53]

What did concern Tang Ying, however, was the issue of consistency in quality across the large quantities that had to be produced. At this time of high-volume production, quality was about repetition and the ability to produce large numbers of items that were completely identical. 'In making round wares, every single shaped object is made hundreds or thousands of times. Without the use of a mould it would be extremely difficult to make each shaped object exactly the same'.[54] The use of a mould, which had to be 'like the original', but not exactly the same size, because of the shrinkage of the clay, allowed the potters to make identical (*wenhe*) objects. Each mould had to be perfected (*xiu*) rather than simply made (*zao*), and perfecting a mould always took several attempts, but ultimately, the goal was to make a series of objects of precisely the same size and shape, without even the tiniest of differences in size.[55] And it was not only the size and shape that had to be repeatable endlessly; the decorative patterns also had to be repeated *ad infinitum*: 'In painting the blue decorations on round wares, the same design element (*hao*) had to be repeated hundreds of thousands of times, and if the design was not painted in exactly the same way, then the result would be unevenness and mutual differences'. But here, of course, there was no mould or machine to guarantee sameness, only the highest level of skill.

This eighteenth-century vantage point has confirmed some of the long continuities that have characterized the porcelain manufactures in Jingdezhen: what was made locally was valued at great distances from that locality, but what was made locally also benefited from the mobility and flow of resources, goods, ideas and skills between places further afield, even if the distances had become far greater over the course of the centuries. Quantities of production mattered, as did the quality of what was produced, in the Song dynasty as it did in the Qing. Artisans moved between different sites of production, and so did the objects themselves, providing the inspiration for change, innovation and transformation. But that mobility and fluidity posed challenges for those in charge, and the written documentation created by those in power often served the attempt to order spaces, assert meaning onto those spaces, and regulate activity. Of course, continuity is not the only way to characterize what happened in Jingdezhen; far too much changed throughout the centuries, in terms of the spaces, the skills, the technologies and the objects; their meanings were recreated constantly. By applying both local and global lenses to the exploration of these continuities and changing meanings, we have been able to situate this city of blue and white in a new light: we have seen its place in the early modern world.

12 | Epilogue: Fragments of a Global Past

At first glance, the weekly market devoted only to the sale of broken pieces of ceramics that opened this book might have seemed an odd place to begin. How can dirty plastic sheets covered with odd assortments of broken bowls, fragments of plates and damaged pieces of porcelain have anything to offer to the historian? Officially known as the Porcelain and Antiques Market (Taoci guwan shichang), the Jingdezhen 'shard market' has in fact provided valuable insights for this study of the global history of China and the local impact of that global past.

Figure 12.1 shows the view from under the central arch of the shard market's large entrance gate, with its upturned eaves, wooden latticework and red painted beams, where the visitor encounters this odd collection of items. In the centre stands a strikingly white bust of Mao Zedong, surrounded by other Maos in something that looks like jade and in wood: a Mao waving, a Mao standing and a Mao sitting on a chair. Surrounding them are other Communist luminaries, children of the revolution, more Maos and statuettes of bearded Daoist and Confucian sages, standing side by side with small blue Buddhist lions and a motley selection of pots, vases, cups and plates. This display hints at the very wide range of materials, colours, periods, tastes and fashions that the goods for sale here represent.

Many of the goods are locally sourced. For example, the furniture sellers in the market sell the kinds of items that once filled village homes but are no longer considered desirable (Figure 12.2). There are kitchen implements like mooncake moulds and meat paddles, ashtrays, hand bellows made of wood and leather, coated baskets, carved pots for storing brushes, and a sheer endless quantity of stoneware pots for the storage of foodstuff and (alcoholic) beverages. More often than not, the wooden boxes and screens in Figure 12.2 come from the now abandoned wooden dwellings that once populated the Jiangxi countryside. Such wooden houses were often built around an open courtyard or 'heavenly well' (*tianjing*) that allows for natural light (and rainwater) to flow in.

Inevitably, such houses are now considered damp and impractical. Only the wooden items that have some decorative elements are salvaged. These are often further dismantled so that only the small pieces of carving remain,

Figure 12.1 Goods for sale at the entrance of the shard market. May 2013. Photograph by the author.

which are in turn sold on as decorative pieces, more easily accommodated in modern homes and apartments than the whole boxes, doors and screens. Unsurprisingly, the shard market, with its attractions to antiques traders and tourists from far beyond the region, seems an obvious place for selling such pieces. The porcelain shards for sale in the market, then, are surrounded by the typical kind of bric-a-brac or jumble that Jingdezhen, its environs and the wider region yield.

Many of the items for sale at the shard market are so-called kiln wasters (Figure 12.3). The extremely high temperatures inside the kilns meant that individual pieces could discolour or collapse during the firing process, or that whole stacks of tightly packed vessels or even an entire kiln load could fail. For example, in the middle of the sixteenth century, the emperor's annual demand for porcelains often included so-called 'fish bowls': large vats, up to 86 cm high and with a diameter of 94 cm. Such large objects often became unstable during the firing process and collapsed in the high heat, often causing further damage in their collapse. When individual pieces emerged from the kiln with brown spots or

Figure 12.2 Furniture sellers in the Jingdezhen shard market, with boxes, pots, baskets and wooden screens. May 2013. Photograph by the author.

Figure 12.3 Seller and her wares. Jingdezhen, May 2013. Photograph by the author.

discolouration, they were smashed and buried together with the broken pieces in pits near the kilns. Many were simply thrown into the river and washed downstream. Throughout the region, the ground is full of fragments and failed pieces, and whenever new foundations are dug, or new areas are developed, a fresh yield of shards is uncovered. Sometimes, a formal archaeological investigation is carried out, but more often than not, the excavating is left to what one might call guerrilla-archaeologists, and the fragmentary remains of Jingdezhen's production find their way to the market.[1] Of course, all historical sites in the People's Republic of China considered to have significant value in terms of cultural heritage fall under the auspices of the relevant state/provincial/county/city's heritage protection units (*wenwu baohu danwei*), which control access to and management of such sites.[2] There is, nonetheless, a great deal of informal (i.e. not funded by the state) and illicit (i.e. carried out with the intention of avoiding legal constraints) excavation in Jingdezhen. Building sites always yield new finds, and only rarely are they accompanied by formal excavations led by the local, regional or national heritage protection offices. More likely, a building site yields an informal excavation, partially led by locally based archaeologists, but rarely are such sites effectively controlled, creating opportunities for those based locally to engage in informal excavations. Such excavations are not likely to yield whole pieces, with kiln wasters and shards in the majority. It is these items that are sold in the Jingdezhen market.

Of course, all antiques markets attract a variety of visitors, ranging from discerning connoisseurs looking for a hidden gem amongst the jumble to bargain hunters and collectors of junk. More surprising is the interest in buying broken pieces of porcelain. What motivates the buyers in their search through shards? Intuitively, the buyers might be divided into two separate groups: those who collect porcelain for the purposes of heritage preservation, and those who are there for commercial purposes. The former stress the cultural values attached to porcelain, the latter see porcelain largely as a tradeable commodity. The first group includes, amongst others, collectors, enthusiasts, students and scholars, some of whom may well have come into contact with the pioneering work of the ceramics specialist Liu Xinyuan (1937–2013). Liu was for many years the director of the Jingdezhen Institute of Ceramic Archaeology, and widely regarded as one of the world's greatest authorities on Jingdezhen's archaeological heritage. Liu Xinyuan was born in 1937 and lived and worked through the most tumultuous decades in the history of the People's Republic of China. Without access to further education or specialized training, Liu forged his own path.

He taught himself and went from small-scale explorative investigations to excavations on a massive scale. He acquired not only an international reputation and close connections with overseas ceramics scholars, but also a substantial private collection, and a small army of collaborators, students and devotees.[3] Liu Xinyuan's mission was the preservation of Jingdezhen's material heritage for posterity, especially in light of what he considered to be the weakness of the heritage protection framework. For him, it was important that the legacy of the past was preserved, whether it was through officially sponsored archaeological excavations or by means of the individual actions of his students and followers. Scholars like Cao Jianwen and May Huang, trained by Liu Xinyuan, now based in Jingdezhen and faithful visitors to the weekly market, have built substantial private collections of shards purchased at the market or excavated on informal visits to sites in the environs of Jingdezhen.

Despite their best efforts, they can never compete with those who come to the market to buy shards, because they see the commercial potential of porcelain. The value of individual pieces of porcelain has sky-rocketed globally in recent years; press reports of record-breaking prices paid for pieces of imperial porcelain have circulated throughout the world. Inevitably, the high prices paid for perfect pieces of porcelain have affected the price of less perfect pieces, trickling down even to the smallest shards of porcelain. Not unlike a fragmentary piece of the Berlin wall, a shard of porcelain allows the beholder to be part of a much larger historical story. The fragment itself may seem worthless, but its association with the charismatic powers of the imperial court and the allure of the art market bestow it with historical and economic value. In a city down on its economic fortunes, the art market offers attractive opportunities for locals keen to make the most of the material legacy of the city's past.[4] Shards are available in large, though not endless, quantities, making it possible for enterprising locals to participate in this economic activity. Participation as seller in this market is easy, because access to the goods for sale here is only partially controlled. Unsurprisingly, a percentage of the buyers are also local. The shopping streets of Jingdezhen are full of small businesses that sell a mixture of low-value antiques, copies of imperial and fine pieces, contemporary pieces in a variety of styles, and shards of a wide variety of size and styles. The shard market provides these local traders with ample opportunity to replenish their stock. Some of these shops are run by very knowledgeable specialists with extensive knowledge of porcelain, others by locally based craftsmen and -women with their own workshops, who supplement the sale of their own work with the sale of striking shards or 'up-cycled' pieces that integrate shards into new pieces of jewellery or items for domestic design purposes. Porcelain shards have become big business in Jingdezhen.

Parallels between Past and Present

One of the interesting aspects of the weekly antiques market in Jingdezhen is that it allows us to see some of the parallels between premodern Jingdezhen and the city of the early twenty-first century. Today, the city of Jingdezhen is dominated by the sight of porcelain shops. The streets are lined with shops that sell all kinds of contemporary pieces; from large statuettes and oversize vases for the decoration of gardens and hotels to industrially made crockery and bespoke pieces to celebrate the wedding of a British royal, Jingdezhen's factories can make almost anything in porcelain. Small-scale workshops like the one in Figure 12.4 continue to produce hand-made 'antiques', imitating closely the shapes, colours and decorations of their historical predecessors.

Traders in search of goods to sell continue to flock to Jingdezhen, visiting the large-scale exhibition space on the outskirts of the city, the upmarket shops in the new malls, or indeed the antiques market on Monday morning. Today's capital of porcelain production is no longer Jingdezhen but Chaozhou in Guangdong, but Jingdezhen continues to manufacture porcelain, and the trade in porcelain continues to be the main driver of the local economy, just as it was in the sixteenth and seventeenth centuries. Then, it was the river and the river-side ferries and quays that provided the traders with access to the town and the network of connections in the region and beyond; nowadays, it is the road, coach, rail and airport networks that facilitate that same trade. Jingdezhen's porcelain production continues to create opportunities for commerce and profit.

Interestingly, both in the past and in the present, the local residents, who are actively involved in both the production and the trade of porcelain, are rarely taken into consideration as consumers. Specifications of size, colour, shape and quality, possibly accompanied by a model or prototype, arrive from a distant location, the goods are produced in accordance, and shipped out of town again. There is no evidence in the past or in the present that such goods manufactured for global consumers resonated in any way with the local community, in fact, there is no historical record at all of consumption patterns of porcelain within the town. Jingdezhen was and is a site for global production, but not a site of global consumption. It is perhaps this disconnect between producer and consumer that made it easier

Figure 12.4 Making pots. Jingdezhen, September 2009. Photograph by the author.

for the production of what we might refer to as counterfeits and fakes. These terms refer to objects that are sold to a buyer on the understanding they are one thing, while the seller knows these to be something different. Scholarly studies have referred to this as deceptive counterfeiting, in contrast to non-deceptive counterfeiting.[5] As Maris Gillette has shown, such issues most certainly form part of Jingdezhen's landscape.[6] On the basis of months of fieldwork in Jingdezhen between 2003 and 2006, Gillette was able to show the extent of copying and counterfeiting in porcelain production in Jingdezhen.[7] Gillette describes the production of replicas of the fine porcelains of previous eras and sold as authentic objects of art as deception, fraudulent behaviour, cheating and dishonesty, using descriptive terms that echo much of the concern about counterfeiting in the premodern era. It is not inconceivable that these practices were so widespread both in the past and in the present precisely because of the disconnect between production and consumption. If producer and consumer form part of the same socio-cultural space, then the production of fakes carries an ongoing risk of discovery and reputation damage. If production is for a distant, invisible consumer, then it may be easier to deceive or behave dishonestly.

The production of porcelain clearly created opportunities in Jingdezhen, but this came with a high price. The environmental damage done by the production of porcelain, the damaging conditions under which the labour force had to work, and the long-term impact of the global porcelain (art) market on the tangible heritage of Jingdezhen itself are all examples of this. To begin with the first, the environmental cost of the porcelain industry in Jingdezhen has long been observed. The polluting smoke that bellowed out of the chimneys, the never-ending noise of the factories, the bare mountains that had been hollowed out to yield clay and shaved to yield trees for firewood and ferns for glazes, all of these were glaringly obvious to visitors. The exploitation of the natural resources around Jingdezhen started long before the eighteenth century.[8] It was in the eighteenth century, however, that the environmental damage started to have an impact on Jingdezhen's ability to function effectively. As Anne Osborne observed: 'The decline of Jingdezhen in the eighteenth century coincides with the deforestation of the surrounding territory and a serious shortage of charcoal and fuel-wood, as well as deterioration of river transport because of siltation and disruption of streamflow', speculating that environmental degradation was to blame for the decline of Jingdezhen.[9] Despite the decline of the industry in Jingdezhen, production continued and was modernized, but environmental damage continued. Even when the production systems changed from using wood to coal from fuelling the kilns, wood continued to be used in large quantities. In 1923, a visitor to Jingdezhen described the supply of wood to the city, 'utterly devoid of green itself', as follows: 'the wood radius for a hundred miles around is constantly exploited, and as the forests are denuded, the source of supply gets farther and farther away'.[10] By the 1970s, the kilns were fuelled exclusively by coal, leading to further environmental damage. In 1974, when Mr and Mrs Boehm visited Jingdezhen, they observed that 'industrial cities like Ching-te-Chen have severe pollution problems caused by energy and heat produced solely from coal'.[11] Today's Jingdezhen is no different, although serious efforts are made to establish effective measures to counter the ongoing degradation of the landscape. Jingdezhen is a 'resource exhausted' city, where environmental damage and a decline of economic opportunities go hand in hand.[12] Today, as in the past, the trade in locally produced goods, such as the shards that the depleted soil still continues to yield, forms the only, but surely only temporary, way out of this situation.

Environmental destruction is not the only price Jingdezhen has paid; the damaging impact of the labour conditions on the local population is, equally, a constant through time. A recent study has shown that long-term exposure to silica dust increases the mortality of ceramics factory workers significantly.[13] Lung cancer and pneumocordiosis are well-known outcomes of life-long labour in the porcelain kiln factory environment.[14] The last decade has seen extensive research on the health and labour conditions of the workers in Jingdezhen, but observations about the impact of these conditions go back many centuries. Père d'Entrecolles noted that the workers were on the whole low skilled, poorly paid and destitute.[15] He described a deep pit surrounded by high walls where the bodies of workers were thrown if they did not have the resources to pay for a funeral. Especially in times of disease spreading through the city, the bodies were piled high and had to be covered with quicklime to dispose of the flesh.[16] The ongoing demands of consumers in the global market, in past and present, meant that production continued in Jingdezhen, and thus that labour continued to be attracted to the opportunities of work in the factories, despite the fact that labour never brought riches to more than a few and damaged the health of everyone else.

Finally, it is worth reflecting briefly on the impact of the porcelain trade on Jingdezhen's material heritage. Jingdezhen was always a site of production, not a space for the consumption, collection or display of porcelains. The beauty of Jingdezhen's porcelains was always for others to enjoy; the fruit of their labour was (and is) rarely on display for the workers themselves. This is eminently visible when one visits Jingdezhen's museums. Compared to the stunning collections of the Shanghai Museum or the Suzhou Museum, the museums in Jingdezhen have very little to boast about. There is a wide range of museums related to the sites of ancient kilns, the archaeological excavations carried out in the region, and the reclaimed and restored pieces of broken imperial wares, but individual pieces of significant value are difficult to find among the museum collections in today's Jingdezhen. Jingdezhen's porcelain left Jingdezhen, today as it did in the past. The sale of fragments in the shard market, depicted in Figure 12.5, is further testimony of the same, despite the argument made by some that the sale of shards to local 'artisans, scholars, shopkeepers and vendors' helps to build a particular local cultural identity in Jingdezhen.[17] There are no laws that prevent the buying and selling of second-hand goods or bric-a-brac.

On the other hand, of course, China's material heritage enjoys a certain amount of legal protection.[18] The material heritage laws are intended to preserve China's material legacy and to prevent the sale of valuable goods, yet in Jingdezhen, shards are sold in the semi-legality of the shard market. It may not be officially legitimized as a site for selling antiques, but it is most certainly condoned and tolerated by officials. It seems that what is available for sale in the shard market in Jingdezhen falls precisely between these categories; both sellers and buyers operate at the edges of the law, in the spaces

Figure 12.5 Shards for sale in the shard market. Jingdezhen, 2013. Photograph by the author.

between authenticity and fake, between legal and illegal. Laurence Massy has described this category of antiquities as follows:

> [They come from] excavations carried out by people who were not authorised to do so. The artefacts have long been removed from their original context and they are either on the art market or they are in private collections and are likely to enter the market in the future. This category is tolerated by those in the legal profession interested in the trade in stolen artefacts. It is difficult to quantify this category made up of antiquities which were originally illicit but have become legitimate over time.[19]

With the full knowledge and permission of precisely those authorities that determine the difference between legal and illegal, official/imperial and private, the local heritage is sold off and enters into the global market, where it disappears from public sight. In that sense, the price the population pays for their local site of production is the loss of their own material heritage.

Lessons for Writing Global History

The case of the Jingdezhen shard market and the parallels it highlights between past and present points to a number of useful lessons for the writing of global history. The history of the global has been written in many different ways, of course. For some, global history has to be written on the basis of comparison. Scholars like Patrick O'Brien or Chris Wickham are interested in understanding the particularities of a specific place and argue persuasively that an insight into what makes a place different can only be gained by comparing it to other places.[20] Of course, comparison relies on measurement of some kind, and reliable and comparable measurements are not always easy to find, meaning that only places with excellent records make an appearance in such global histories. For others, global history can also be the history of connections. Many excellent studies have been written about the connections between different parts of the world. It is in this context that the study of material culture has gained the attention of several scholars, including my fellow historians at Warwick. Giorgio Riello's study of cotton, for example, has shown the rich potential of this approach, showing the different kinds of connections that the focus on cotton can reveal, including the dissemination of production technologies, the circulatory movements of design, the integration of the political and economic structures presided over by the European trading companies, and the movement of the commodity itself.[21] This and other studies have clearly shown the range of possibilities offered by a focus on individual commodities for global history, especially where the approach integrates the insights from material culture studies to show how meanings associated with commodities both changed and remained part of the changed commodity as it moved across boundaries of time and space.[22] In conclusion, I would like to mention some issues that should be taken into consideration in future studies of global material culture. Past and present are once again remarkably parallel.

One of these concerns the importance of connecting the stories of objects and human actors. The study of material culture, and the focus on objects and their itineraries, suggests a shift from human to non-human actors. Non-human actors, including objects, but also animals, microbes, plants and food, have long been popular subjects in global historical studies.[23] By isolating a single crop or pathogen, the sheer endless complexities of global connections can be reduced to manageable proportions. The linguistic and conceptual concerns are also reduced: a potato is still a potato, whether it appears in Spanish, French or Chinese sources, even if it means very different things in those contexts. Similarly, we can follow the bacterium that gave rise to the plague, Yersinia pestis and use scientific methods of isolation and testing to establish a theory about the spread of the Black Death that bypasses the difficulties associated with learning Mongolian and other Central Asian languages required for understanding the cultural context from which it emerged. But if global histories are written without people, and material culture studies are produced without the linguistic knowledge of the context, we will remain hampered in our understanding. To some extent, the history of non-human actors will always be dependent on human actors, whose stories have to be understood through their own languages, rather than the homogenizing forces of any single language. I have attempted here to tell the history of making porcelain in connection with the various records that the makers, traders and beholders of porcelain left behind. Global history can never be written on the basis of objects alone, but need to reflect human and non-human together, both in all their rich diversities and in their overlaps and commonalities.

The second issue concerns the importance of combining past and present. It is entirely possible to write a global history of sixteenth-century Jingdezhen and its porcelains without connecting the relevance of those historical developments to today's context. All too often, historians take to heart the famous quote from L. P. Hartley, who said in *The Go-Between* that 'The past is a foreign country, they do things different there'.[24] As an encouragement to pay extra attention to the strangeness of the past, the statement can unintentionally lead to an approach to studies of (objects of) the past as having little to do with today's world. One might write a study of Jingdezhen and its magnificent porcelains without ever visiting the rather less glamorous site of its production. The art market, and the powerful impact of the global art market even on the sale of shards in a semi-legal market in Jingdezhen reminds us how important it is to connect the past to the present, and to use the significance of the past as a way of highlighting the importance of protecting this legacy today.

Finally, this epilogue, as well as the book as a whole, has sought to illustrate that global history can only be written by taking the local seriously. Porcelain, both in its production and its consumption, has to be studied in a global perspective, because its cross-cultural materials and designs, its transnational movements and its multi-layered meanings demand it. But the global can never be studied at the expense of the thickness of local description and the engagement with local sources. The history of Jingdezhen, in fact, is never only a global story, as it is never only a local story. But in the long perspective that I have taken here, it is clear that at times it is the local factors that explain better why important changes and transitions occurred, at times it is the regional factors, and at times the explanations have to come from much further afield. It is the wavering between local and global that has most characterized the history of this city of blue and white.

Notes

Chapter 1 The Shard Market of Jingdezhen

1 Regina Krahl, 'Tang Blue-and-White', in *Shipwrecked: Tang Treasures and Monsoon Winds*, ed. Regina Krahl, John Guy, J. Keith Wilson, and Julian Raby (Washington and Singapore: Arthur M. Sackler Gallery, Smithsonian Institution; National Heritage Board, Singapore Tourism Board, 2010), 209–211.

2 Oliver Watson, 'Ceramics and Circulation', in *A Companion to Islamic Art and Architecture* (Hoboken, NJ: Wiley-Blackwell, 2017), 489; see also Krahl, 'Tang Blue-and-White'.

3 The best study of technological change in Jingdezhen's manufactures remains Rose Kerr and Nigel Wood, *Ceramic Technology*, Science and Civilisation in China, Vol 5: Chemistry and Chemical Technology, Part XII (Cambridge University Press, 2004).

4 The precise starting point of blue and white ceramics production continues to be discussed. A recent and very fulsome discussion of the subject can be found in Adam T. Kessler, *Song Blue and White Porcelain on the Silk Road* (Leiden: Brill, 2012).

5 Robert Tichane, *Ching-Te-Chen: Views of a Porcelain City* (Painted Post, NY: New York State Institute for Glaze Research, 1983).

6 Robert Finlay, *The Pilgrim Art: Cultures of Porcelain in World History* (Berkeley: University of California Press, 2010); Michael Dillon, 'Transport and Marketing in the Development of the Jingdezhen Porcelain Industry during the Ming and Qing Dynasties', *Journal of the Social and Economic History of the Orient* 35, 3 (1992): 278–290; Stephen Little, 'Economic Change in Seventeenth-Century China and Innovations at the Jingdezhen Kilns', *Ars Orientalis* 26 (1996): 47–54; Anne Gerritsen, 'Ceramics for Local and Global Markets: Jingdezhen's Agora of Technologies', in *Cultures of Knowledge: Technology in Chinese History*, ed. Dagmar Schäfer and Francesca Bray (Leiden: Brill, 2012), 164–186.

7 One of the most extensive overviews can be found in Kerr and Wood, *Ceramic Technology*.

8 A few illustrative examples are merely intended to give an impression of the field. See, for example, Margaret Medley, 'The Yuan-Ming Transformation in the Blue and Red Decorated Porcelains of China', *Ars Orientalis* 9 (1973): 89–101; Beijing daxue kaogu wenbo xueyuan and Jiangxi sheng wenwu kaogu yanjiusuo, *Jingdezhen chutu Mingdai yuyao ciqi* 景德镇出土明代御窑瓷器 [*Porcelain from*

the Ming imperial kilns excavated in Jingdezhen] (Beijing: Wenwu chubanshe, 2009); Regina Krahl, 'Export Porcelain Fit for the Chinese Emperor. Early Chinese Blue-and-White in the Topkapı Saray Museum, Istanbul', *Journal of the Royal Asiatic Society of Great Britain & Ireland* 118, 1 (1986): 68–92; Stacey Pierson, *Designs as Signs: Decoration and Chinese Ceramics* (London: Percival David Foundation of Chinese Art: School of Oriental and African Studies, University of London, 2001); Fang Lili 方李莉, *Jingdezhen Minyao* 景德鎮民窑 *[The Folk Kilns of Jingdezhen]* (Beijing: Renmin meishu chubanshe, 2002).

9 A few examples of this scholarship may suffice. Robert Finlay, 'The Pilgrim Art: The Culture of Porcelain in World History', *Journal of World History* 9, 2 (1998): 141–187; Finlay, *The Pilgrim Art*, 2010; Liu Zhaohui 刘朝晖, *Ming Qing yilai Jingdezhen ciye yu shehui* 明清以来景德镇瓷业与社会 (Shanghai shudian chubanshe, 2010); Maris Gillette, 'Copying, Counterfeiting, and Capitalism in Contemporary China: Jingdezhen's Porcelain Industry', *Modern China* 36, 4 (2010): 367–403; Maris Boyd Gillette, 'Labor and Precariousness in China's Porcelain Capital', *Anthropology of Work Review* 35, 1 (2014): 25–39; Tsing Yuan, 'The Porcelain Industry and Ching-Te-Chen, 1550–1700', *Ming Studies* 1978, 1 (1978): 45–54; Dillon, 'Transport and Marketing in the Development of the Jingdezhen Porcelain Industry During the Ming and Qing Dynasties'.

10 A few examples of the kinds of things that are referred to as global by historians: Ina Baghdiantz McCabe, *A History of Global Consumption: 1500–1800* (London: Routledge, 2015); Francesca Bray et al., eds., *Rice: Global Networks and New Histories* (Cambridge University Press, 2015); Robert K. Batchelor, *London: The Selden Map and the Making of a Global City, 1549–1689* (University of Chicago Press, 2014).

11 Robert J. Charleston, *World Ceramics: An Illustrated History* (Harmondsworth, Middlesex, UK: P. Hamlyn, 2002).

12 Maxine Berg, *Writing the History of the Global: Challenges for the 21st Century* (Oxford University Press, 2013); Giorgio Riello, *Cotton: The Fabric That Made the Modern World* (Cambridge University Press, 2013); Patrick O'Brien, 'Historiographical Traditions and Modern Imperatives for the Restoration of Global History', *Journal of Global History* 1, 1 (2006): 3–39.

13 Some continue to write the history of the Chinese empire as a separate story. See for example Frederick W. Mote, *Imperial China, 900–1800* (Cambridge, MA: Harvard University Press, 1999); others situate the history of the empire in broader context: Morris Rossabi, *A History of China* (Malden, MA: John Wiley and Sons, 2014); Valerie Hansen, *The Open Empire: A History of China to 1800*, 2nd. (New York: W. W. Norton & Co., 2015).

14 Dennis O. Flynn and Arturo Giráldez, 'Born with a "Silver Spoon": The Origin of World Trade in 1571', *Journal of World History* 6, 2 (1995): 201–221.

15 Dennis O. Flynn and Arturo Giráldez, *China and the Birth of Globalization in the 16th Century* (Farnham: Ashgate Variorum, 2010); André Gunder Frank, *ReOrient: Global Economy in the Asian Age* (Berkeley: University of California Press, 1998).

16 Beijing wenwu jiansheng bianweihui, *Porcelains of the Yuan dynasty* 元代瓷器 (Beijing meishu sheying chubanshe, 2005); Margaret Medley, *Illustrated Catalogue of Underglaze Blue and Copper Red Decorated Porcelains* (University of London, Percival David Foundation of Chinese Art, 2004); Xiong Liao 熊寥 and Ma Xigui 馬希桂, *Gems of the official kilns* 官窑名瓷 (Taibei: Yishu tushu gongsi, 1993).

17 He Li, *Chinese Ceramics: The New Standard Guide* (London: Thames & Hudson, 1996).

18 Kerr and Wood, *Ceramic Technology*.

19 Richard von Glahn, *An Economic History of China: From Antiquity to the Nineteenth Century* (Cambridge University Press, 2016), 247–248, 298, 372.

20 Kessler, *Song Blue and White Porcelain on the Silk Road*; John N. Miksic, *Singapore and the Silk Road of the Sea, 1300–1800* (Singapore: Nus Press, 2014); Zhao Bing, 'Global Trade and Swahili Cosmopolitan Material Culture: Chinese-Style Ceramic Shards from Sanje Ya Kati and Songo Mnara (Kilwa, Tanzania)', *Journal of World History* 23, 1 (2012): 41–85; Meha Priyadarshini, 'From the Chinese Guan to the Mexican Chocolatero: A Tactile History of the Transpacific Trade, 1571–1815' (PhD, Columbia University, 2014).

21 Krahl, 'Tang Blue-and-White'.

22 Roxanna M. Brown and Sten Sjostrand, *Turiang: A Fourteenth-Century Shipwreck in Southeast Asian Waters* (Pasadena, CA: Pacific Asia Museum, 2000); Sten Sjostrand and Claire Barnes, 'The "Turiang": A Fourteenth-Century Chinese Shipwreck Upsetting Southeast Asian Ceramic History', *Journal of the Malaysian Branch of the Royal Asiatic Society* 74, 1 (2001): 71–109; Barbara Harrisson, 'The Ceramic Trade across the South China Sea, c. AD 1350–1650', *Journal of the Malaysian Branch of the Royal Asiatic Society* 76, 1 (2003): 99–114.

23 C. J. A. Jörg, *Porcelain and the Dutch China Trade* (The Hague: M. Nijhoff, 1982); George Kuwayama, *Chinese Ceramics in Colonial Mexico* (Los Angeles; Honolulu, Hawaii: Los Angeles County Museum of Art, 1997).

24 Maris Boyd Gillette, *China's Porcelain Capital: The Rise, Fall and Reinvention of Ceramics in Jingdezhen* (London: Bloomsbury Academic, 2016).

25 As Gillette mentions, Fang Lili has written extensively about the makers that worked in Jingdezhen. Ibid., 3; Fang Lili 方李莉, *Jingdezhen Minyao*.

26 Finlay's final chapter is entitled 'The Decline and Fall of Chinese Porcelain: The West and the World, 1500–1800', Finlay, *The Pilgrim Art*, 2010, 253–296.

27 Franklin Mendels, 'Proto-Industrialization: The First Phase of the Industrialization Process', *The Journal of Economic History* 32, 1 (1972): 241–261.

28 Riello, *Cotton*, 64–66.

Chapter 2 City of Imperial Choice: Jingdezhen, 1000–1200

1 I refer to the illustrated and annotated edition of this text. Lan Pu 蓝浦 and Zheng Tinggui 郑廷桂, *Jingdezhen tao lu tushuo* 景德镇陶录图说 (Jinan Shi: Shandong

huabao chubanshe, 2004), 118; an unillustrated version of the same text can be found in the standard anthology that brings together historical writings about porcelain: Xiong Liao 熊寥 and Xiong Wei 熊微, eds., *Zhongguo taoci guji jicheng* 中国陶瓷古籍集成 *[Anthology of ancient texts about China's porcelain]* (Shanghai wenhua chubanshe, 2006), 507. For a range of translations of this passage, see, for example, Lan Pin-nan and Cheng T'ing-kuei, *Ching-Te-Chen T'ao-Lu or The Potteries of China*, trans. Geoffrey Robley Sayer (London: Routledge & Kegan Paul, 1951), 39–40; He Yimin, 'Prosperity and Decline: A Comparison of the Fate of Jingdezhen, Zhuxianzhen, Foshan and Hankou in Modern Times', *Frontiers of History in China* 5, 1 (2010): 52–85.

2 For studies of the text, see Lu Jiaming, 'Lüelun Jingdezhen Tao Lu Ji Qi Xueshu Jiazhi' [Brief Discussion of Jingdezhen Taolun and Its Scholarly Value]', *Nanchang Zhiye Jishu Shifan Xueyuan Xuebao*, 1996, 52–58; see also Margaret Medley, 'Ching-Tê Chên and the Problem of the "Imperial Kilns"', *Bulletin of the School of Oriental and African Studies* 29, 2 (1966): 326–338; Ellen Huang, 'China's China: Jingdezhen Porcelain and the Production of Art in the Nineteenth Century' (San Diego: PhD, University of California, 2008), 88–89.

3 James Hargett has discussed the occurrence of a place being named after a reign period for Shaoxing in the twelfth century. James M. Hargett, '會稽: Guaiji? Guiji? Huiji? Kuaiji? Some Remarks on an Ancient Chinese Place-Name', *Sino-Platonic Papers*, 234 (2013).

4 Gillette, *China's Porcelain Capital*, 14; Liang Miaotai 梁淼泰, *Ming Qing Jingdezhen chengshi jingji yanjiu* 明清景德鎮城市經濟研究 *[Study of the urban economy of Jingdezhen during the Ming-Qing period]*, 2nd ed. (1991; repr., Nanchang: Jiangxi renmin chubanshe, 2004), 6. Sakuma Shigeo 佐久間重男, *Keitokuchin Yōgyōshi Kenkyū* 景德鎮窯業史研究 (Tōkyō: Daiichi Shobō, 1999) is perhaps the exception that proves the rule.

5 'Ceramics Today – Jingdezhen 2004', accessed 30 January 2017, www.ceramicstoday.com/articles/jingdezhen.htm.

6 For a vivid description of life during the Five Dynasties, see Glen Dudbridge, *A Portrait of Five Dynasties China: From the Memoirs of Wang Renyu (880–956)* (Oxford University Press, 2013).

7 Peter Lorge, *The Reunification of China: Peace through War under the Song Dynasty* (Cambridge University Press, 2015), 5–20.

8 On art patronage, see Heping Liu, '"The Water Mill" and Northern Song Imperial Patronage of Art, Commerce, and Science', *The Art Bulletin* 84, 4 (2002): 566; on historiography, see Johannes L. Kurz, 'The Consolidation of Official Historiography during the Early Northern Song Dynasty', *Journal of Asian History* 46, 1 (2012): 13–35.

9 The document has been preserved in *Song huiyao*, the largest collection of documents dated to the Song dynasty. Xu Song 徐松 (1781–1848), ed., *Song Huiyao Jigao* 宋會要輯稿 *[Draft of an Institutional History of the Song Dynasty]*, 'Shihuo' 52.37a; see also *Zhongguo taoci guji jicheng*, 4.

10 Tracy Miller, *The Divine Nature of Power: Chinese Ritual Architecture at the Sacred Site of Jinci* (Cambridge, MA: Harvard University Press, 2007).

11 *Song Huiyao Jigao*, 'Shihuo' 52.37a.

12 Ibid.

13 Xiang Kunpeng 项坤鹏, 'Songdai gongting yongci laiyuan shenxi 宋代宫廷用瓷来源探析 [Research on the Sources of Porcelain Used by the Court of the Song Dynasty]', *Kaogu yu wenwu*, 1 (2015): 55.

14 Robert M. Hartwell, 'The Imperial Treasuries: Finance and Power in Song China', *Bulletin of Sung and Yüan Studies*, 20 (1988): 18–89; Christian Lamouroux, *Fiscalité, comptes publics et politiques financières dans la Chine des Song: le chapitre 179 du Songshi* (Paris: Institut des hautes études chinoises, 2004); see also Patricia Buckley Ebrey, *Emperor Huizong* (Cambridge, MA: Harvard University Press, 2014), 9, 89–91.

15 See, for an example of an excavation report, Sun Xinmin 孙新民, 'Songling Chutu de Dingyao Gongci Shixi 宋陵出土的定窑贡瓷试析 [Trial Division of Tribute Porcelain from the Ding Kilns Excavated from Song Imperial Graves]', *Wenwu Chunqiu* 3 (1994): 47–51.

16 Krahl writes that '[s]everal hundred Yue kilns have been discovered along the Bay of Hangzhou, in particular around the shores of Shanglin Lake (Shanglinhu) southeast of Cixi, in close vicinity to Ningbo'. Regina Krahl, 'Green Wares of Southern China', in *Shipwrecked: Tang Treasures and Monsoon Winds*, ed. Regina Krahl et al. (Washington, DC; Singapore: Arthur M. Sackler Gallery, Smithsonian Institution; National Heritage Board: Singapore Tourism Board, 2010), 187.

17 Chuimei Ho, ed., *New Light on Chinese Yue and Lonquan Wares: Archaeological Ceramics Found in Eastern and Southern Asia, A.D. 800–1400* (Centre of Asian Studies, The University of Hong Kong, 1994).

18 The wares produced in this region during the Tang dynasty are known as Xing wares. William Watson, *The Arts of China 900–1620* (New Haven: Yale University Press, 2000), 25. A stunning example of a Xing jar of glossy white porcelain made in the late seventh century is in the Metropolitan Museum of Art in New York, inv. no. 2013.231.

19 Kerr and Wood, *Ceramic Technology*, 11; Nigel Wood, *Chinese Glazes: Their Origins, Chemistry and Re-Creation* (London: A. & C. Black, 2007), 21.

20 The 'Regulatory office for trade and taxation of the porcelain kilns' is mentioned in a locally excavated stele. See Meng Fanfeng 孟繁峰 and Huang Xin 黄信, 'Tang houqi de Dingyao shi fanzhen yiwu junguan yao 唐后期的定窑是藩镇义武军官窑', *Palace Museum Journal*, 2 (2014): 39–51. See also Kerr and Wood, *Ceramic Technology*, 159.

21 These were regularly sized vessels. For their dimensions, see Sun Xinmin 孙新民, 'Songling Chutu de Dingyao Gongci Shixi', 47.

22 Li Zhiyan 李知宴 and Guan Shanming 關善明, *Songdai taoci* 宋代陶瓷 *[Song ceramics]* (Hong Kong: Muwentang meishu chubanshe, 2012), 70–72; He Li, *Chinese Ceramics*, 134–135. See numbers 217–228 for examples of Ding ware.

23 Jiangxisheng wenwu kaogu yanjiusuo and Fuliangxian bowuguan, 'Jiangxi Fuliang Fenghuangshan Songdai yaozhi fajue jianbao 江西浮梁凤凰山宋代窑址发掘简报 [Brief Report of the Excavation of the Song Kilns at Fenghuangshan in Fuliang, Jiangxi]', *Wenwu*, 12 (2009): 25–38.

24 Kerr and Wood, *Ceramic Technology*, 214, 219. For illustrations of excavated pieces of both Yue-type ware and white porcelain dated to the tenth century, see page 551.

25 *Song Huiyao Jigao*, juan 192, 'Fangyu', 12.17a.

26 'Shihuo' 52.37a.

27 Qin Yu 秦彧, 'Qingzhou yao kao "青州窑"考 [An examination of the 'Qingzhou kilns']', *Dongnan wenhua*, 7 (2001): 71–73.

28 Hin-Cheung Lovell, 'Sung and Yüan Monochrome Lacquers in the Freer Gallery', *Ars Orientalis* 9 (1973): 124–125, especially footnote 12a.

29 James C. Y. Watt, *East Asian Lacquer: The Florence and Herbert Irving Collection* (New York: Metropolitan Museum of Art, 1991), 22–23.

30 Xie Min 謝旻 (fl. 18th c.), ed., *Jiangxi tong zhi* 江西通志, Yingyin Wenyuange Siku quanshu (1732; repr., Taipei: Taiwan shangwu yinshuguan, 1983), juan 93 (Taozheng).

31 宋景德中，置镇，始遣官制瓷贡京师，应官府之需，命陶工书建年景德于器，于是天下咸称景德镇. Zhao Zhiqian 趙之謙 (1829–1884), ed., *(Guangxu) Jiangxi Tongzhi* 江西通志, Zhongguo Fangzhi Ku (1881; repr., Beijing: Beijing Airusheng shuzihua jishu yanjiu zhongxin, 2009), 93.5a.

32 Joseph P. McDermott and Shiba Yoshinobu, 'Economic Change in China, 960–1279', in *Sung China, 960–1279*, ed. John Chaffee and Denis Twitchett, vol. 5 Pt 2, *The Cambridge History of China* (Cambridge University Press, 2015), 321–436.

33 Ibid.

34 A forthcoming study by Christian de Pee deals with the intellectual aspects of urbanization especially in Kaifeng during the tenth and eleventh centuries.

35 Ouyang Xiu 歐陽修, *Gui tian lu* 歸田録 (Beijing: Zhonghua shuju, 1997), juan 1, 1–2.

36 Meng Yuanlao 孟元老, *Dongjing menghua lu* 東京夢華錄 *[A Dream of Splendour in the Eastern Capital]*, Wenyuange Siku quanshu, n.d., accessed 17 January 2017. The French sinologist Jacques Gernet also drew on this work in his descriptions of Kaifeng 'on the eve of the Mongol invasion'. See Jacques Gernet, *Daily Life in China on the ve of the Mongol Invasion, 1250–1276* (Stanford University Press, 1995).

37 Meng Yuanlao 孟元老, *Dongjing menghua lu*, 4.4b–5a.

38 Wood, *Chinese Glazes*, 90–92.

39 Rose Kerr's work illustrates this beautifully. See, for example, Rose Kerr, *Song Dynasty Ceramics* (London: V & A, 2004); Rose Kerr, *Song China Through 21st Century Eyes: Yaozhou and qingbai Ceramics* = 今之视昔:宋代耀州窑及青白瓷 (Netherlands: Meijering Art Books, 2009).

40 Sabrina Rastelli, 'The Concept of the Five Famous Wares of the Song Dynasty – A Modern Invention', in *Songdai Wuda Mingyao Kexue Jishu Guoji Xueshu Taolunhui Lunwenji* 宋代五大名窑科学技术国际学术讨论会论文集

[*Proceedings of International Symposium on Science and Technology of Five Great Wares of the Song Dynasty*], ed. Shi Ningchang 史宁昌 and Miao Jianmin 苗建民 (Beijing: Kexue chubanshe, 2016), 460–466.

41 Sun Xinmin, 'Recent Excavations at the Ru Kiln: Qingliangsi', in *Song Ceramics: Art History, Archaeology and Technology*, ed. Stacey Pierson, trans. Benedetta Mottino, Colloquies on Art & Archaeology in Asia 22 (London: Percival David Foundation of Chinese Art, School of Oriental and African Studies, 2004), 214.

42 Regina Krahl and Jessica Harrison-Hall, *Chinese Ceramics: Highlights of the Sir Percival David Collection* (London: British Museum, 2009).

43 Tao Zongyi 陶宗儀 (fl. 1360–68), *Nancun chuogeng lu* 南村輟耕錄 (Beijing: Zhonghua shuju, 1959), 363. See also *Zhongguo taoci guji jicheng*, 173.

44 Lu You 陸游, *Lao xue'an biji* 老學庵筆記, Yingyin Wenyuange Siku quanshu (Taipei: Shangwu yinshuguan, 1983), 2.11a. See also *Zhongguo taoci guji jicheng*, 171.

45 Shane McCausland, 'An Art Historical Perspective on the Guan-Ge Controversy', in *Song Ceramics: Art History, Archaeology and Technology*, ed. Stacey Pierson, Colloquies on Art & Archaeology in Asia 22 (London: Percival David Foundation of Chinese Art, School of Oriental and African Studies, 2004), 30.

46 Li Jiazhi 李家治, ed., *Jianlun Guan Ge Er Yao: Keji Yanjiu Wei Guan, Ge Deng Yao Shi Kong Ding Wei* 简论官哥二窑: 科技研究为官, 哥等窑时空定位 (Beijing: Kexue chubanshe, 2007).

47 Suzanne Kotz, ed., *Imperial Taste: Chinese Ceramics from the Percival David Foundation* (San Francisco: Chronicle Books, 1989), 32.

48 Tuo tuo, *Song shi* 宋史 [*Song history*] (Beijing: Zhonghua shuju, 2011), juan 87, 2146. The evidence for the Yaozhou bureau comes from an inscription dated 1008 for a temple dedicated to the Kiln god, which refers to two officials of this office. Feng Xianming 冯先铭, *Zhongguo taoci shi* 中国陶瓷史 [*The history of Chinese porcelain*] (Beijing: Wenwu chubanshe, 1982), 250.

49 Wood, *Chinese Glazes*, 129; Guo Xuelei 郭学雷, *Mingdai Cizhou yao ciqi* 明代磁州窑瓷器 (Beijing: Wenwu chubanshe, 2005).

50 For some specific examples, see He Li, *Chinese Ceramics*, 148 image no 222. Another example is in the Victoria and Albert Museum, inv. no. C.43–1968. See also Qin Dashu 秦大树, 'Lun Cizhouyao yu Dingyao de guanxi he xianghu yingxiang 论磁州窑与定窑的联系和相互影响 [The connection and mutual influence of the Cizhou and Ding Kilns', *Palace Museum Journal*, 4 (1999): 43–56.

51 Yang Yumin 杨玉敏, 'Changzhou bowuguan cang Cizhou yao ciqi 常州博物馆藏磁州窑瓷器 [Cizhou ceramics from the Changzhou Museum collection]', *Nanfang wenwu*, 1 (2001): 81–82+86.

52 Kerr and Wood, *Ceramic Technology*, 41–49.

53 Wood, *Chinese Glazes*, 56; Kerr and Wood, *Ceramic Technology*, 552–553.

54 Ibid., 51.

55 Ibid., 55; Kerr and Wood, *Ceramic Technology*, 552.

56 Wang Xiaomeng 王小蒙, 'Yaozhou Yao Qingci de Meixue Linian Ji Fengge Bianqian 耀州窑青瓷的美学理念及风格变迁 [The Aesthetics and Stylistic

Transformations of Green Porcelain from Yaozhou]', *Sichuan Cultural Relics*, 5 (2009): 49.

57 *Song Huiyao Jigao*, juan 142, 'Shihuo' 41.40b–41a.

58 Sun Xinmin 孙新民, 'Shilun bei Song zaoqi de Yueyao mise ci 试论北宋早期的越窑秘色瓷 [Secret colour porcelain from the Yue kilns from the early Northern Song]', *Jiangxi wenwu*, 4 (1991): 28–30. See also the National Palace Museum exhibition on this subject, 'Mise Porcelain: Impressive Discovery and Mysterious Tribute', http://en.dpm.org.cn/exhibitions/current/2017-05-23/2650.html, consulted on 3 September 2018. See Ding Yinzhong 丁银忠 et al., 'Shanglinhu housi'ao yao zhi ci zhi xiabo de gongyi tezheng yanjiu 上林湖后司岙窑址瓷质匣钵的工艺特征研究 [The Processing characteristic of Porcelain Saggar of Shanglinhu Housi'ao Kiln Site]', *Palace Museum Journal*, 6 (2017): 142–150+161.

59 Kessler, *Song Blue and White Porcelain on the Silk Road*, 59, 141, 160.

60 Regina Krahl, 'The "Alexander Bowl" and the Question of Northern Guan Ware', *Orientations* 25,11 (1993): 72–75; Nigel Wood and Sabrina Rastelli, 'Parallel Developments in Chinese Porcelain Technology in the 13th-14th Centuries AD', in *Craft and Science: International Perspectives on Archaeological Ceramics*, ed. Marcos Martinón-Torres (Doha: Bloomsbury Qatar Foundation, 2014), 225–234.

61 N. Wood and He Li, 'A Study of the Techniques Used to Make Laohudong Guan Ware in China in the Southern Song Dynasty', *Archaeometry* 57, 4 (2015): 617–635.

62 James A. Benn, *Tea in China: A Religious and Cultural History* (Honolulu: University of Hawai'i Press, 2015), 117ff; John Kieschnick, *The Impact of Buddhism on Chinese Material Culture* (Princeton University Press, 2002).

63 James Marshall Plumer and Caroline Plumer, *Temmoku: A Study of the Ware of Chien* (Tokyo, 1972).

64 K. S. Lo, *The Stonewares of Yixing from the Ming Period to the Present Day* (Hong Kong, 1986); Rose Kerr, 'Yixing', in *Grove Art Online* (Oxford University Press, 1996), www.oxfordartonline.com/subscriber/article/grove/art/T092881.

65 Huang Yijun 黄义军, *Songdai qingbai ci de lishi dili yanjiu* 宋代青白瓷的历史地理研究 *[The historical geography of Song period bluish-white porcelain* (Beijing: Wenwu chubanshe, 2010).

66 *Song Huiyao Jigao*, juan 129 ('Shihuo' 16: Taxes, part II).

67 Xiao Fabiao 肖发标, 'Bei Song Jingdezhen Yao de Gongci Wenti 北宋景德镇窑的贡瓷问题 [The Problem of Porcelain Tribute from Jingdezhen during the Northern Song]', *Zhongguo Gutaoci Yanjiu* 7 (2001): 256.

68 William Guanglin Liu, 'The Making of a Fiscal State in Song China, 960–1279: The Making of a Fiscal State in Song China', *The Economic History Review* 68, 1 (2015): 54; Charles O. Hucker, *A Dictionary of Official Titles in Imperial China* (Stanford University Press, 1985), 426.

69 Peter Golas, 'The Sung Fiscal Administration', in *The Cambridge History of China* Volume 5 Part 2, ed. John W. Chaffee and Denis Twitchett (Cambridge University Press, 2015).

70 Richard von Glahn, *An Economic History of China: From Antiquity to the Nineteenth Century* (Cambridge University Press, 2016), 238–239.

71 *Song shi*, zhi, juan 139, Shihuo, lower part, number 8. page 4553.; *ZGTC*, 5.

72 Li Tao (1115–1184), *Xu Zizhi Tongjian Changbian* 續資治通鑑長編, Yingyin Wenyuange Siku Quanshu, vols 414-322 (Taipei: Taiwan shangwu yinshuguan, 1983), 329.5a–b.

Chapter 3 Circulations of White

1 景德陶昔三百余座埏埴之器洁白不疵故鬻于他所皆有饒玉之称. Fu Zhenlun 傅振伦, *Zhongguo gu taoci luncong* 中国古陶瓷论丛 (Beijing: Zhongguo guangbo dianshi chubanshe, 1994), 171.

2 Dai Junliang, *Zhongguo Gujin Diming Dacidian* 中国古今地名大词典 (Shanghai: Shanghai cishu chubanshe, 2005), 2239. In 1277, this prefecture was raised to the status of circuit.

3 Zhao Bing, 'Érudition, expertise, technique et politique autour de la querelle de la datation du Taoji', *Arts asiatiques*, 61 (2006): 143–164.

4 Liu Xinyuan 刘新园, 'Jiang Qi "Taoji" Zhuzuo Shidai Kaobian 蒋祈《陶记》著作时代考辨 [Consideration of the Dating of Jiang Qi's Taoji]', *Jingdezhen Taoci* S1 (1981): 5–35; Kerr and Wood, *Ceramic Technology*, 24. In footnote 11 on this page, the authors list the main studies in Chinese on this debate. Kessler also follows Liu Xinyuan in dating Taoji to the Southern Song dynasty. Kessler, *Song Blue and White Porcelain on the Silk Road*, 354–360.

5 Zhao Bing bases her argument on a careful study of the Qing superintendant based in Jingdezhen, Tang Ying. She concludes that it was his doing that the text would be read as a product of the Yuan dynasty. Zhao Bing, 'Érudition, expertise, technique et politique'; Kessler agrees that the dating of Taoji to the Yuan dynasty is a Qing intervention. Kessler, *Song Blue and White Porcelain on the Silk Road*.

6 The scholar Ma Wenkuan 马文宽 recently reviewed the available evidence in a detailed and meticulous study, and concluded that the Yuan date of 1325 is most likely. Ma Wenkuan 马文宽, 'Ping "Jiang Qi Taoji Zhuzuo Shidai Kaobian": Yu Liu Xinyuan Xiansheng Shangque 评《蒋祈〈陶记〉著作时代考辨》－与刘新园先生商榷 [Critique of "A Consideration of the Date of Jiang Qi's Taoji": A Discussion with Liu Xinyuan]', *Kaogu Xuebao* 3 (2008): 395–414; The Palace Museum scholar Fa Zhenlun assumed the text dated to the Yuan dynasty. Fu Zhenlun 傅振伦, *Zhongguo gu taoci luncong* 中国古陶瓷论丛, 171.

7 For an illustration of such a mould, see Shelagh Vainker, 'Ceramics for Use', in Jessica Rawson, *The British Museum Book of Chinese Art*, 2nd ed. (London: British Museum Press, 2007), 227; Kerr and Wood, *Ceramic Technology*, 443.

8 Wood, *Chinese Glazes*, 57.

9 Porcelain bowl with *qingbai* glaze and straight copper-bound rim. There is an incised lily design on the interior. H 6 cm. Jingdezhen, 12–13th century. British Museum, PDF.460. See also Wood, *Chinese Glazes*.

10 On monochromes of this period, see Monika Kopplin, ed., *The Monochrome Principle: Lacquerware and Ceramics of the Song and Qing Dynasties* (Munich: Hirmer Verlag, 2008).

11 浮梁巧燒瓷 / 顏色比瓊玖. Hong Mai 洪邁, *Rongzhai suibi* 容齋隨筆, Sibu congkan xubian (Shanghai: Shangwu yinshuguan, 1934), 4.13a.

12 Wu Zimu 吳自牧, *Mengliang lu* 夢梁錄, Zhibu zuzhai congshu, 1814, 13.5b.

13 若夫浙之東西器尚黃黑出於湖田之窯. Fu Zhenlun 傅振倫, *Zhongguo gu taoci luncong*, 172.

14 Jiang Qi 蔣祈, 'Song Jiang Qi "Taoji" Jiaozhu 宋蔣祈《陶記》校注', ed. Bai Kun 白焜, *Jingdezhen Taoci* S1 (1981): 45n20.

15 江湖川廣器尚青白出於鎮之窯. Fu Zhenlun 傅振倫, *Zhongguo gu taoci luncong*, 172.

16 Ibid., 172.

17 必地有擇焉者. Ibid.

18 其色澤不美而在可棄. Ibid.

19 所謂器之品數大略有如此者. Ibid.

20 Janet Lippman Abu-Lughod, *Before European Hegemony: The World System A.D. 1250–1350* (New York: Oxford University Press, 1989).

21 Colleen Ho, 'Thirteenth and Fourteenth Century European-Mongol Relations', *History Compass* 10, 12 (2012): 946–968; Michal Biran, *Chinggis Khan* (Oxford: Oneworld, 2007); Christopher I. Beckwith, *Empires of the Silk Road: A History of Central Eurasia from the Bronze Age to the Present* (Princeton University Press, 2011); William W. Fitzhugh, Morris Rossabi and William Honeychurch, *Genghis Khan and the Mongol Empire* (Washington, DC; Media: Arctic Studies Center, Smithsonian Institution; Mongolian Preservation Foundation, 2013).

22 M. N. Pearson, *The Indian Ocean* (London: Routledge, 2007).

23 Marco Polo, *The Travels of Marco Polo.*, ed. R. E. Latham (Harmondsworth, Middlesex: Penguin Books, 1958).

24 John Larner, *Marco Polo and the Discovery of the World* (New Haven; London: Yale University Press, 1999); Thomas T. Allsen, 'The Cultural Worlds of Marco Polo', *Journal of Interdisciplinary History* 31, 3 (2001): 375–383; Debra Strickland makes the important point that the text and its illustrations represent quite diverse interpretations of these largely unfamiliar worlds, with the text conveying a nuanced understanding of the diversity and sophistication of the Eastern 'other', and the illustrations fulfilling the expectations popular

especially at court of an uncivilized, barbarian East. D. H. Strickland, 'Artists, Audience, and Ambivalence in Marco Polo's Divisament Dou Monde', *Viator* 36 (2005): 493–530.

25 Edmund de Waal, *The White Road: A Pilgrimage of Sorts* (Random House, 2015), 12–13. De Waal provides a good description of the enduring allure of the object.

26 Wood, *Chinese Glazes*, 60.

27 Chaofang Ming et al., 'Archaeometric Investigation of the Relationship between Ancient Egg-White Glazed Porcelain (Luanbai) and Bluish White Glazed Porcelain (Qingbai) from Hutian Kiln, Jingdezhen, China', *Journal of Archaeological Science* 47 (2014): 83.

28 Kessler, *Song Blue and White Porcelain on the Silk Road*, 230.

29 I have discussed my understanding of the meaning of these inscriptions in greater detail elsewhere. See Anne Gerritsen, 'Porcelain and the Material Culture of the Mongol-Yuan Court', *Journal of Early Modern History* 16, 3 (2012): 241–273.

30 Kessler, *Song Blue and White Porcelain on the Silk Road*, 358.

31 Lin Cheng et al., 'The Study of Ancient Porcelain of Hutian Kiln Site from Five Dynasty (902–979) to Ming Dynasty (1368–1644) by INAA', *Journal of Radioanalytical and Nuclear Chemistry* 304, 2 (2015): 822.

32 Ming et al., 'Archaeometric Investigation', 84.

33 Kessler, *Song Blue and White Porcelain on the Silk Road*, 398. Kessler refers here to the scholars who have made this claim.

34 Thomas T. Allsen, *Commodity and Exchange in the Mongol Empire: A Cultural History of Islamic Textiles* (Cambridge University Press, 1997), 58–59.

35 This is the argument Kessler also makes. Kessler, *Song Blue and White Porcelain on the Silk Road*, 398.

36 Kerr and Wood, *Ceramic Technology*, 220.

37 Wood, *Chinese Glazes*, 58.

38 Haydn H. Murray, Wayne Bundy and Colin C. Harvey, eds., *Kaolin Genesis and Utilization: A Collection of Papers Presented at the Keller '90 Kaolin Symposium* (Boulder: Clay Mineral Society, 1993); Haydn H. Murray, 'Traditional and New Applications for Kaolin, Smectite, and Palygorskite: A General Overview', *Applied Clay Science* 17, 5–6 (2000): 209; Georges-Ivo E. Ekosse, 'Kaolin Deposits and Occurrences in Africa: Geology, Mineralogy and Utilization', *Applied Clay Science* 50, 2 (2010): 212–236.

39 Old and new archaeological excavations with finds of southern porcelains in the territories of the Xixia and Jin regimes are extensively discussed in Kessler, *Song Blue and White Porcelain on the Silk Road*.

40 Susan Whitfield, *Life Along the Silk Road*, 2015; Susan Whitfield and Ursula Sims-Williams, *The Silk Road: Trade, Travel, War and Faith* (Chicago, IL: Serindia Publications, 2004); Lokesh Chandra and Radha Banerjee, *Xuanzang and the Silk Route* (New Delhi: Munshiram Manoharlal Publishers, 2008).

41 The fictional account of the Journey to the West (*Xi you ji*) by Wu Cheng'en (c. 1500-c. 1582) has been translated by Anthony Yu. It tells the story of the monk who went from China to India in search of Buddhist scriptures. Wu Cheng'en, *The Journey to the West*, trans. Anthony C. Yu (University of Chicago Press, 1977); see also Chun Mei, *The Novel and Theatrical Imagination in Early Modern China* (Leiden: Brill, 2011).

42 Xinru Liu, *Ancient India and Ancient China: Trade and Religious Exchange AD 1–600* (Delhi: Oxford University Press, 1988).

43 A number of scholars have written about the topic of mutual dependency between the nomadic peoples and sedentary agriculturalists from a variety of perspectives. See, for example, Liu Xinru, *The Silk Road in World History* (Oxford University Press, 2010); Liu Xinru, 'Migration and Settlement of the Yuezhi-Kushan: Interaction and Interdependence of Nomadic and Sedentary Societies', *Journal of World History* 12, 2 (2001): 261–292; Valerie Hansen and Oxford University Press, *The Silk Road: A New History* (Oxford University Press, 2015).

44 For an extensive exploration of the exotica that came into the Tang empire from the Silk Routes, see the classic study by Edward H. Schafer, *The Golden Peaches of Samarkand: A Study of T'ang Exotics* (Berkeley: University of California Press, 1963).

45 Shiba Yoshinobu, 'Sung Foreign Trade: Its Scope and Organization', in *China Among Equals: The Middle Kingdom and Its Neighbors, 10th-14th Centuries*, ed. Morris Rossabi (Berkeley: University of California Press, 1983), 106; Yong-i Yun and Regina Krahl, *Korean Art from the Gompertz and Other Collections in the Fitzwilliam Museum: A Complete Catalogue* (Cambridge University Press, 2006), 119.

46 The full title of the catalogue is 'Special Exhibition of Cultural Relics found off Sinan Coast'. Kungnip Chungang Pangmulgwan (Korea), *Sinan haejŏ munmul: Sinan haejŏ munhwajae t'ŭkpyŏl chŏn torok* (Sŏul: Samhwa Ch'ulp'ansa, 1977).

47 Youn Moo-byong, 'Recovery of Seabed Relics at Sinan and Its Results from the Viewpoint of Underwater Archaeology', in *Shin'an Kaitei Hikiage Bunbutsu = The Sunken Treasures off the Sinan Coast*, ed. Tōkyō Kokuritsu Hakubutsukan (Nagoya: Chūnichi Shinbunsha, 1983), 82; see also Jeremy Green, 'The Shinan Excavation, Korea: An Interim Report on the Hull Structure', *The International Journal of Nautical Archaeology and Underwater Exploration* 12, 4 (1983): 293–301; Michael Flecker, 'The South-China-Sea Tradition: The Hybrid Hulls of South-East Asia', *The International Journal of Nautical Archaeology* 36, 1 (2007): 75–90; Pierre-Yves Manguin, 'Trading Ships of the South China Sea', *Journal of the Economic and Social History of the Orient* 36, 3 (1993): 253–280.

48 John G. Ayers, 'Discovery of a Yuan Ship at Sinan, Southwest Korea – 1st Report', *Oriental Art* 24, 1 (1978): 79–85.

49 Li Dejin, Jiang Zhongyi and Guan Jiakun, 'Chaoxian Xin'an Haidi Chenchuan Zhong de Zhongguo Ciqi 朝鲜新安海底沉船中的中国瓷器 [The Chinese Ceramics in the Shipwreck on the Sinan Seabed in Korea]', *Kaogu Xuebao* 2 (1979): 245–254.

50 Ibid., 245.

51 According to Youn Moo-byong, the bronze coin recovered by suction hose amounted to more than 18 tons. This was still an underestimate. Youn Moo-byong, 'Recovery of Seabed Relics at Sinan and its Results from the Viewpoint of Underwater Archaeology', 82–83.

52 Tōkyō Kokuritsu Hakubutsukan, *Shin'an Kaitei Hikiage Bunbutsu = The Sunken Treasures off the Sinan Coast* (Nagoya: Chūnichi Shinbunsha, 1983).

53 Derek Thiam Soon Heng, 'Export Commodity and Regional Currency: The Role of Chinese Copper Coins in the Melaka Straits, Tenth to Fourteenth Centuries', *Journal of Southeast Asian Studies* 37, 2 (2006): 179–203.

54 Little, 'Economic Change in Seventeenth-Century China', 53n5.

55 Charlotte von Verschuer, *Le commerce entre le Japon, la Chine et la Corée à l'époque médiévale: VIIe-XVIe siècle*, 2014.

56 Ibid., 118–119.

57 Moon Whan Suk and Kim Minkoo, 'Tracking 800-Year-Old Shipments: An Archaeological Investigation of the Mado Shipwreck Cargo, Taean, Korea', *Journal of Maritime Archaeology* 6, 2 (2011): 129–149.

58 Zhao Rugua 趙汝适, *Zhufanzhi* 諸蕃志 (Taibei: Taiwan shangwu yinshuguan, 1983). See also the discussion in Shiba Yoshinobu, 'Sung Foreign Trade: Its Scope and Organization'.

59 Some have suggested this term should be understood as meaning 'blue decorations on a white background', but there is very little evidence that cobalt blue was already in use at this moment for the decoration of white ceramics. Kessler, *Song Blue and White Porcelain on the Silk Road*, 351n330.

60 Zhou observed that Chinese gold and silver is held 'in the highest regard', silk is next, then pewter and lacquer, and only then celadon. Zhou Daguan, *A Record of Cambodia: The Land and Its People*, trans. Peter Harris (Chiang Mai: Silkworm Books, 2007), 71.

61 On Wang Dayuan, see Hyunhee Park, *Mapping the Chinese and Islamic Worlds: Cross-Cultural Exchange in Pre-Modern Asia* (Cambridge University Press, 2012), 91, 176.

62 Wang Dayuan 汪大淵, *Daoyi zhilüe jiaoshi* 島夷誌略校釋 *[Annotated edition of the 'Report of the Island Barbarians']*, ed. Su Jiqing 蘇繼廎 (Ming dyn.; repr., Beijing: Zhonghua shuju, 1981); Roderich Ptak, 'Wang Dayuan on Kerala', in *China, the Portuguese, and the Nanyang: Oceans and Routes, Regions and Trades (c. 1000–1600)*, ed. Roderick Ptak (Aldershot: Ashgate, 2004), 39–52.

63 F. C. Cole and B. Laufer, *Chinese Pottery in the Philippines* (Chicago, IL: Field Museum of Natural History, 1912); Dekun Zheng, *Studies in Chinese Ceramics* (Hong Kong: The Chinese University Press, 1984), 107–108.

64 Robert Fox, 'The Archeological Record of Chinese Influences in the Philippines', *Philippine Studies* 15, 1 (1967): 57–60; Leandro Locsin and Cecilia Locsin, *Oriental Ceramics Discovered in the Philippines* (Rutland [Vt], 1967); Eleanor von Erdberg-Consten, 'The Manila Trade Pottery Seminar', *Philippine*

Studies 16, 3 (1968): 545–557; J. M. Addis, 'The Dating of Chinese Porcelain Found in the Philippines: A Historical Retrospect', *Philippine Studies* 16, 2 (1968): 371–380.

65 Janice Stargardt, 'Behind the Shadows: Archaeological Data on Two-Way Sea-Trade between Quanzhou and Satingpra, South Thailand, 10th-14th Century', in *The Emporium of the World: Maritime Quanzhou, 1000–1400*, ed. Angela Schottenhammer (Leiden; Boston: Brill, 2001), 350.

66 Sten Sjostrand and Claire Barnes, 'The "Turiang"'.

67 Senake Bandaranayake and Madhyama Saṃskṛtika Aramudala (Sri Lanka), *Sri Lanka and the Silk Road of the Sea* (Colombo: Sri Lanka Institute of International Relations, 2003).

68 Kenneth R. Hall, *A History of Early Southeast Asia: Maritime Trade and Societal Development, 100–1500* (Lanham, MD: Rowman & Littlefield, 2011).

69 Pierre-Yves Manguin, 'Early Coastal States of Southeast Asia: Funan and Srivijaya', in *Lost Kingdoms: Hindu-Buddhist Sculpture of Early Southeast Asia*, ed. John Guy (New York: Metropolitan Museum of Art, 2014), 111–115; James C. M. Khoo, ed., *Art & Archaeology of Fu Nan: Pre-Khmer Kingdom of the Lower Mekong Valley* (Bangkok: Orchid Press, 2003).

70 Sebastian R. Prange, *Monsoon Islam: Trade and Faith on the Medieval Malabar Coast* (Cambridge University Press, 2018), 11–13; Ronit Ricci, 'Islamic Literary Networks in South and Southeast Asia', *Journal of Islamic Studies* 21, 1 (2010): 1–28; M. C. Ricklefs, *A History of Modern Indonesia since c. 1200* (Stanford University Press, 2008).

71 Prange, *Monsoon Islam*.

72 Ibn Batuta, *Travels in Asia and Africa, 1325–1354*, trans. H. A. R. Gibb (London: Routledge & Kegan Paul, 1983); Ross E. Dunn, *The Adventures of Ibn Battuta a Muslim Traveler of the 14th Century* (Berkeley: University of California Press, 2012); Stewart Gordon, *When Asia Was the World* (Cambridge, MA: Da Capo Press, 2008).

73 Karl Jahn, *Die Chinageschichte des Rašīd ad-Dīn* (Wien [etc.], 1971); Paul Kahle, 'Eine Islamische Quelle über China um 1500 (Das Khitayname des Ali Ekber)', *Acta Orientalia* 12 (1934): 91–110; Kaveh Hemmat, 'A Chinese System for an Ottoman State: The Frontier, the Millennium, and Ming Bureaucracy in Khatayi's Book of China' (PhD, The University of Chicago, 2014); Nile Green, 'From the Silk Road to the Railroad (and Back): The Means and Meanings of the Iranian Encounter with China', *Iranian Studies* 48, 2 (2015): 165–192.

74 For a translation of the full text of Ibn Battuta's travels, see Ibn Battuta, *The Travels of Ibn Battuta, A.D.1325–54*, trans. H. A. R. Gibb and C. F. Beckingham, 4 vols (London: Hakluyt Society, 1958). This passage is taken from the abridged translation. Battuta, *Travels in Asia and Africa, 1325–1354*, 282–283.

75 Anne Gerritsen and Stephen McDowall, 'Material Culture and the Other: European Encounters with Chinese Porcelain, ca. 1650–1800', *Journal of World History* 23, 1 (2012): 87–113.

76 Alain George, 'Direct Sea Trade Between Early Islamic Iraq and Tang China: From the Exchange of Goods to the Transmission of Ideas', *Journal of the Royal Asiatic Society* 25, 4 (2015): 579–624.

77 Zhou Qufei 周去非, *Lingwai daida* 嶺外代答 (Taibei: Taiwan shangwu yinshuguan, 1983), 3.7a.

78 On the relationship between Islamic and Chinese ceramics, see Watson, 'Ceramics and Circulation'.

79 Elizabeth Lambourn and Phillip Ackerman-Lieberman, 'Chinese Porcelain and the Material Taxonomies of Medieval Rabbinic Law: Encounters with Disruptive Substances in Twelfth-Century Yemen', *The Medieval Globe* 2, 2 (2017): 199–238.

80 Marcus Milwright, *The Fortress of the Raven: Karak in the Middle Islamic Period, 1100–1650* (Leiden: Brill, 2008), 242.

81 Axelle Rougeulle, 'Excavations at Sharmah, Ḥaḍramawt: The 2001 and 2002 Seasons', *Proceedings of the Seminar for Arabian Studies* 33 (2003): 287–307; Axelle Rougeulle and Vincent Bernard, eds., *Sharma: un entrepôt de commerce médiéval sur la côte du Ḥaḍramawt (Yémen, ca 980–1180)* (Oxford: Archaeopress, 2015).

82 Éric Vallet, *L'Arabie marchande: état et commerce sous les sultans Rasūlides du Yémen (626–858/1229–1454)* (Paris: Publications de la Sorbonne, 2010). I am grateful to my student Victor Xu (Xu Guanmian) for pointing this out.

83 Zhao, 'Global Trade and Swahili Cosmopolitan Material Culture'.

84 Zhao Bing, 'Chinese-Style Ceramics in East Africa from the 9th to 16th Century: A Case of Changing Value and Symbols in the Multi-Partner Global Trade', *Afriques. Débats, Méthodes et Terrains d'histoire*, 6 (2015), https://afriques. revues.org/1836.

85 Sam Nixon, 'Excavating Essouk-Tadmakka (Mali): New Archaeological Investigations of Early Islamic Trans-Saharan Trade', *Azania: Archaeological Research in Africa* 44, 2 (2009): 241.

Chapter 4 From Cizhou to Jizhou

1 According to the currency converter of the National Archives (www.nationalarchives.gov.uk/currency/, consulted on 21 December 2017), the amount of £360 would have been worth £13,312.80 in 2005. According to 'Measuring Worth', the same object would have cost £22,930.00 in 2016. See www.measuringworth.com/, consulted on 21 December 2017.

2 Peter Lam, 'The David Vases Revisited: Annotation Notes of the Dedicatory Inscriptions', *Orientations* 40, 8 (2009): 70–77.

3 Translation from Peter Way, who commented on Peter Lam's translation of the inscriptions (see previous footnote). Peter Way, 'Some Further Notes on the Percival David Ritual Vases and Their Inscriptions', *The Percival David Ritual*

Vases (blog), 16 February 2013, http://percivaldavidritualvases.blogspot.com/. Consulted on 21 December 2017.

4 Kessler, *Song Blue and White Porcelain on the Silk Road*. For Kessler's discussion of the David vases, see section III.1, entitled 'Regarding the Percival David Collection Vases' (pp. 213–226).

5 Ibid., 348–354.

6 'Chemistry of Cobalt', Chemistry LibreTexts, 3 October 2013, https://chem. libretexts.org/Core/Inorganic_Chemistry/Descriptive_Chemistry/Elements_ Organized_by_Block/3_d-Block_Elements/Group_09%3A_Transition_Metals/ Chemistry_of_Cobalt.

7 Even after the conquest of Yunnan by the Ming army, Yunnan remained a remote part of the empire, largely populated by non-Han groups. Bin Yang, *Between Winds and Clouds: The Making of Yunnan (Second Century BCE to Twentieth Century CE)*, (New York: Columbia University Press, 2014).

8 This point is also made by Nancy Shatzman Steinhardt, 'Review of *Song Blue and White Porcelain on the Silk Road*. By Adam T. Kessler', *Journal of the Royal Asiatic Society (Third Series)* 25, 1 (2015): 184–187.

9 Cao Zhao 曹昭 (fl. 14th c.), *Gegu yaolun* 格古要論, Yingyin Wenyuange Siku quanshu (Taipei: Taiwan shangwu yinshuguan, 1983).

10 It was made, for example, at Yaozhou. See, Wang Xiaomeng 王小蒙, 'Tang Yaozhou Yao Tai Heicai Ci de Gongyi Tedianji Qi Yuanyuan, Yingxiang 唐耀州窑素胎黑彩瓷的工艺特点及其渊源、影响 [Origin of the Technique of Porcelain with Black Drawings from the Yaozhou Kiln during the Tang Period and Its Influence]', *Kaogu Yu Wenwu* 3 (2013): 73–79.

11 Kerr and Wood, *Ceramic Technology*, 170. The early tomb finds are on display in the Handan Museum (www.hdmuseum.org/); see also Wang Qingzheng and Kelun Chen Kelun, *A Dictionary of Chinese Ceramics* (Singapore: Sun Tree Publishing, 2002), 153.

12 Kerr and Wood, *Ceramic Technology*, 170; Beijing daxue kaogu xuexi, *Guantai Cizhou yao zhi* 观台磁州窑址 (Beijing: Wenwu chubanshe, 1997).

13 Song-dynasty Cizhou wares have been found in Shanxi province in Jiexiu County, Gaoping County, and Taiyuan city. Song dynasty Cizhou wares in Shandong have been found in De County. Mino Yutaka and Patricia Wilson, *An Index to Chinese Ceramic Kiln Sites from the Six Dynasties to the Present* (Toronto: Royal Ontario Museum, 1973), 30.

14 Mino Yutaka and Wilson, 30; Wang Xing 王兴, *Cizhou yao shihua* 磁州窑史话 (Tianjin: Tianjin guji chubanshe, 2004); Guo Xuelei 郭学雷, *Mingdai Cizhou yao*.

15 On the fermentation of wine in this region, see H. T. Huang, *Fermentations and Food Science*, Science and Civilisation in China, Vol 6: Biology and Biological Technology, Part V. (Cambridge University Press, 2000).

16 For the British Museum Cizhou objects, see Jessica Harrison-Hall, 'The Taste for Cizhou', *Apollo* 174, 592 (2011): 48–54.

17 The Neolithic wares with painted decorations have been left out of consideration here. Suzanne G. Valenstein, *Handbook of Chinese Ceramics* (New York: Metropolitan Museum of Art, 2012).

18 Rawson, *The British Museum Book of Chinese Art*; Wood, *Chinese Glazes*, 169; see Kerr and Wood, *Ceramic Technology*, 531–534 for a discussion of the Qionglai and Changsha glazes, and 653–656 on painted decorations on these wares; Li Weidong et al., 'Study on the Phase-Separated Opaque Glaze in Ancient China from Qionglai Kiln', *Ceramics International* 29, 8 (2003): 933–937.

19 Kerr and Wood, *Ceramic Technology*, 653.

20 Ibid., 655.

21 Rawson, *The British Museum Book of Chinese Art*, xxx.

22 Li Zhiyan 李知宴 and Guan Shanming 關善明, *Songdai taoci*, 82.

23 Song Donglin 宋東林, 'Bei Song Jindai Jiaocang Ciqi Kaoshu 北宋金代窖藏瓷器考述 [Ceramics from Northern Song and Jin Hoards]', *Journal of Gugong Studies* 1 (2012): 8–54. The discussion of Cizhou finds is on pp. 22–24.

24 Wang Bo 汪勃 et al., 'Jiangsu Yangzhou Song dacheng beimen shuimen yizhi fajue jianbao 江苏扬州宋大城北门水门遗址发掘简报 [Excavation on the Water Valve Site at the Northern Gate of the Great Song City in Yangzhou, Jiangsu]', *Kaogu*, 12 (2005): 24–40+97+100–101+103+2; see also the short version in English: 'Excavation on the Water Valve Site at the Northern Gate of the Great Song City in Yangzhou, Jiangsu', *Chinese Archaeology* 6, 1 (n.d.): 120–127. Between 2003 and 2007, archaeological research was carried out here by the Joint Archaeological Team of IA, CASS, the Nanjing Museum and Yangzhou Municipal Institute of Cultural Relics and Archaeology.

25 Cao Guoqing 曹国庆, *Zhongguo chutu ciqi quanji* 中國出土瓷器全集, ed. Zhang Bai, vol. 14: Jiangxi (Beijing: Kexue chubanshe, 2008), 64; Liu Lichun 刘礼纯, 'Ruichang Song Mu Chutu Cizhou Yaoxi Ciping 江西瑞昌宋墓出土磁州窑系瓷瓶 [Cizhou Type Vases Excavated from a Song Tomb in Ruichang, Jiangxi]', *Wenwu*, 8 (1987): 89–90.

26 Similar designs are known from Cizhou vases in various other collections: the Atkins Museum of Fine Arts in Kansas City, the Fogg Art Museum, and a private Japanese collection. Yutaka Mino and Katherine R. Tsiang, *Freedom of Clay and Brush through Seven Centuries in Northern China: Tz'u-Chou Type Wares, 960–1600 A.D.* (Indianapolis; Bloomington: Indianapolis Museum of Art; Indiana University Press, 1981), 160–161; see also Wang Jianzhong 王建中, *Cizhou yaoci jianding yu jianshang* 磁州窑瓷鉴定与鉴赏 (Nanchang: Jiangxi meishu chubanshe, 2002), 146 (illustration 37) for a similar object.

27 Cao Guoqing 曹国庆, *Zhongguo chutu ciqi quanji* 中國出土瓷器全集, 14: Jiangxi: 64; during the Song and Yuan dynasties, these kilns in Yuzhou were amongst the more significant sites of Cizhou production. Mino and Tsiang, *Freedom of Clay and Brush through Seven Centuries in Northern China*.

28 Fan Fengmei 范凤妹, 'Ji Jiangxi Chutu de Beifang Mingyao Ciqi 记江西出土 的北方名窑瓷器 [Famous Porcelains from the North in Jiangxi Excavations]', *Jiangxi Lishi Wenwu* 2 (1986): 120–122.

29 These items were found in the tomb of a Lady Shi, wife of Xiong Ben (d. 1091), a high minister of Song who hailed from Poyang in Jiangxi. Fan Fengmei 范凤 妹, 122.

30 The British Museum shard is listed as 1947,0717.4-5.

31 Fan Fengmei 范凤妹, 'Ji Jiangxi Chutu de Beifang Mingyao Ciqi', 120.

32 The Gao'an hoard has been the subject of a great deal of discussion. The most useful is a recent study by Liu Jincheng and Liu Jingbang, which provides a useful overview of older scholarship on the hoard and presents the most up to date understandings of the hoard and its possible original owner. Liu Jincheng 刘金成 and Liu Jingbang 刘璟邦, 'Gao'an Yuandai Jiaocang zhi zai yanjiu – jiaocang maicang niandai ji qi zhuren shenfen kao 高安元代窖藏之再研究—— 窖藏埋藏年代及其主人身份考 [Revisiting the Gao'an Hoard of the Yuan Dynasty – the date of its burial and the identity of its owner]', *Nanfang wenwu*, 4 (2013): 101–118; Liu Yuhei 刘裕黑 and Xiong Lin 熊琳, 'Guanyu Gao'an Yuanci jiaocang de jige wenti 关于高安元瓷窖藏的几个问题 [Several Questions Regarding the Hoard of Yuan Porcelain at Gao'an in Jiangxi]', *Nanfang wenwu*, 2 (1990): 49–53; Yi Gu 依谷, 'Jiangxi Gao'an Yuanci jiaocang faxian jishi 江西 高安元瓷窖藏发现纪实 [The discovery of a Yuan-dynasty hoard at Gao'an in Jiangxi]', *Nanfang wenwu*, 1 (2002): 120–126.

33 Fan Fengmei 范凤妹, 'Ji Jiangxi Chutu de Beifang Mingyao Ciqi', 121.

34 Yang Houli 杨后礼, 'Jiangxi Yongxin Faxian Yuandai Jiaocang Ciqi 江西永 新发现元代窖藏瓷器 [Porcelains Discovered in the Yuan Dynasty Hoard in Yongxin, Jiangxi]', *Wenwu* 4 (1983): 47–49.

35 Chen Peng 曾庆生 and Zeng Qingsheng 曾庆生, 'Quanzhou Fuhoushan Chutu de Jiangxi Taoqi 泉州府后山出土的江西陶器', *Jiangxi Lishi Wenwu* 4 (1983): 73–77.

36 Ren Yashan 任亚珊, 'Yuandai Zhang Honglüe Ji Furen Mu Qingli Baogao 元代 张弘略及夫人墓清理报告 [Excavation Report of the Tomb of Zhang Honglüe and His Wife of the Yuan Dynasty]', *Wenwu Chunqiu* 5 (2013): 28–41.

37 Ibid., 39.

38 The classic study of migration in Chinese history is Wu Songdi 吴松弟, *Zhongguo yimin shi* 中国移民史, vol. 4: Liao, Song, Jin, Yuan shiqi (Fuzhou: Fujian renmin chubanshe, 1997); see also Ruth Mostern, *'Dividing the Realm in Order to Govern': The Spatial Organization of the Song State (960–1276 CE)* (Cambridge, MA: Harvard University Asia Center, 2011) especially 222–228, 248 and 253; Zhou Zhenhe and Kathy Lo write that the precise pattern of migration southwards in the twelfth century is not easy to verify, especially in Jiangxi, although 'the best deduction is that many migrants from Henan […] travelled to Jiangxi'. Zhou Zhenhe and Kathy Lo, 'Migrations in Chinese History and Their Legacy on Chinese Dialects', *Journal of Chinese Linguistics*, 3 (1991): 41.

39 Zhao Bing, 'Apport de l'étude céramologique à la compréhension de la culture matérielle de la région de Jizhou au Jiangxi (Xe-XIVe siècles)', *Études Chinoises* XXI, 1–2 (2002): 185–196.

40 Liu Xitao has established that of the 5,751 successful Song-dynasty *jinshi* graduates that hailed from Jiangxi, 940 came from Jizhou. Liu Xitao 刘锡涛, 'Ji'an Songdai wenhua fazhan chengjiu lüeshuo 吉安宋代文化发展成就略说 [The Development of Culture in Ji'an in the Song Dynasty]', *Journal of Jinggangshan Normal College* 26, 1 (2005): 61.

41 Huang Yangxing 黄阳兴, 'Nan Song Jizhou Yao Chazhan Zhuangshi de Chanqu 南宋吉州窑茶盏装饰的禅趣 [Zen-Gusto on Decorations of Tea Sets in Jizhou Kiln of Southern Song Dynasty]', *Shouzang* 8 (2012): 60.

42 Liu Xitao has compiled the information available in a number of different sources, and reaches the conclusion that there were 135 Buddhist temples in Song-dynasty Jizhou, and 59 Daoist. Liu Xitao 刘锡涛 , 'Ji'an Songdai wenhua fazhan', 63.

43 The main studies of the Jizhou kilns are the following: Gao Liren 高立人, *Jizhou Yonghe yao* 吉州永和窑 (Shanghai: Wenhui chubanshe, 2002); Robert D. Mowry, Eugene Farrell and Nicole Coolidge Rousmaniere, *Hare's Fur, Tortoiseshell, and Partridge Feathers: Chinese Brown-and Black-Glazed Ceramics, 400–1400* (Cambridge, MA: Harvard University Art Museums, 1997); Peng Minghan 彭明瀚, *Ya su zhi jian: Jizhou yao* 雅俗之间: 吉州窑 (Beijing: Wenwu chubanshe, 2007); Yu Jiadong 余家栋, *Jiangxi Jizhou yao* 江西吉州窑 (Guangzhou: Lingnan meishu chubanshe, 2002).

44 Hence the title of this book: Mowry, Farrell and Coolidge Rousmaniere, *Hare's Fur, Tortoiseshell, and Partridge Feathers*.

45 A. D. Brankston, 'Ceramics from the Eumorfopoulos Collection. Two Vases from Chi-Chou', *The British Museum Quarterly* 13, 2 (1939): 46–47.

46 Guo Xuelei 郭学雷, 'Chanzong Sixiang Dui Nan Song Jizhou Yao Ciqi Zhuangshi de Yingxiang 禅宗思想对南宋吉州窑瓷器装饰的影响 – The Influence of Buddhist Thought on Decoration of Porcelains from the Jizhou Kilns of the Southern Song Dynasty', *Shoucang*, 7 (2012): 52–63; Huang Yangxing 黄阳兴, 'Nan Song Jizhou Yao Chazhan'.

47 See the discussion of this process of Jizhou imitation of Ding wares in Zhao Bing, 'Les imitations de porcelaines de Ding du Xe au XIVe siècle: le cas des officines de potiers de Jizhou au Jiangxi', *Arts asiatiques* 56 (2001): 61–80; Xie Mingliang, *Dingyao baici tezhan tulu* 定窯白瓷特展圖錄 *[Catalogue of the special exhibition of Ting ware white porcelain]* (Taibei: Guoli gugong bowuguan, 1987); quoted in Kessler, *Song Blue and White Porcelain on the Silk Road*, 305.

48 Huang Nianfeng 黄年凤, 'Jizhou yao fang Ding ci yu Nanbei wenhua jiaoliu 吉州窑仿定瓷与南北文化交流 [The Jizhou imitation of Ding ware and the cultural exchange between North and South]', *Nanfang wenwu*, 1 (2002): 68–69.

49 Li Baoping, 'Application of ICP-MS Trace Element Analysis in Study of Ancient Chinese Ceramics', *Chinese Science Bulletin* 48, 12 (2003): 1219–1224; Jang Namwon writes: 'Kilns that imitated Cizhou-yao can be found in Shanxi,

Shandong, Sichuan, Hunan, Anhui, Jiangxi, Guangdong, Guangxi Zhuangzu Zizhiqu, and Fujian provinces'. Jang Namwon, 'The Origin and Development of Ceramics with Underglaze Iron Decoration and White Porcelain in the Goryeo Dynasty', trans. Kim Hyun Kyung, *Misulsa Nondan (Art History Forum)* 18 (2004): 41–71; Huang Nianfeng 黄年风, 'Cong Jizhouyao ci kan nanbei taoci wenhua jiaoliu 从吉州窑瓷看南北陶瓷文化交流 – Porcelain Cultural Exchange between the South and the North as Evidenced by the Jizhou Kiln Porcelain', *Shoucang Jia*, 11 (2006): 13–16; the same point is made by Kang Yu 康煜 and Zeng Qiong 曾琼, 'Chuyi Cizhouyaohe Jizhouyao youxia baidi caihui zhuangshi wenyang 刍议磁州窑和吉州窑釉下白地彩绘装饰纹样 [An insight into the decorative types of under-glazed colour painted porcelain from Cizhou and Jizhou]', *China ceramics* 44, 9 (2008): 78; Beijing daxue kaogu xuexi, *Guantai Cizhou yao zhi* 观台磁州窑址; Ōsaka Shiritsu Bijutsukan 大阪市立美術館, *Shiro to kuro no kyōen: Chūgoku Jishū yōkei tōki no sekai* 白と黒の競演: 中国磁州窯系陶器の世界 (Ōsaka Shiritsu Bijutsukan, 2002).

50 John Guy, *Oriental Trade Ceramics in South-East Asia, Ninth to Sixteenth Centuries.* (Oxford University Press, 1986), 73.

51 Wang Qingzheng and Chen Kelun, *A Dictionary of Chinese Ceramics*, 161.

52 John Hay, 'Questions of Influence in Chinese Art History', *Res: Anthropology and Aesthetics* 35 (1999): 240–262; see also Jonathan Hay, 'Toward a Theory of the Intercultural', *Res: Anthropology and Aesthetics* 35 (1999): 5–9.

53 Mino and Tsiang, *Freedom of Clay and Brush through Seven Centuries in Northern China*, plate 35. For other examples, see in the Rijksmuseum, a white bowl with abstract pattern AK-MAK-504, or a meiping vase with a sgraffito decoration of flowers, made in Cizhou in the 11th–early 12th century. Metropolitan Museum of Art, 23.54.2.

54 Many more examples of abstract patterns filling backgrounds and empty spaces have been included in Ren Shuanghe 任双合 and Yang Jianguo 杨建国, *Cizhouyao huapu* 磁州窑画谱 *[Designs from Cizhou kilns]* (Beijing: Wenhua yishu chubanshe, 2009). See, for example, pp. 13, 25, 28–29, 58–59, 83, etc.

55 For an example, see a Jizhou vase in the Metropolitan Museum of Art in New York, inv. no. 2015.500.7.1. A very similar object is in the Changshu municipal museum, and was included in the Chanfeng yu Ruyun exhibition. See item 084 in the catalogue. Shenzhen bowuguan 深圳博物馆, *Chan feng yu ru yun: Song Yuan shidai de Jizhou yaoci qi*, 1st ed. (Beijing: Wenwu chubanshe, 2012).

56 For further examples of such abstract pattern filling the surface of Jizhou wares, see Gao, *Jizhou Yonghe yao*, 82; Shenzhen bowuguan, *Chan feng yu ru yun*, 108 plate 091.

57 For further examples of stylized flowers in Jizhou wares, see Gao, *Jizhou Yonghe yao*, 154, 165.

58 A striking example of a light-coloured Cizhou jar with flower decorations is in the Victoria and Albert Museum, C.32-1935. See also C.68-1935 and

C.443–1928. In the San Francisco Museum of Asian Art, see Object B60P427, a covered jar with brown floral sprays and calligraphy, and B60P1+, a jar with floral sprays. For further examples of dark flower sprays on a light surface made in Jizhou, see Gao, 146 (illustration 5–45); 154 (illustration 5–51), 158 (illustration 5-54b).

59 Gao, 147, 148, 152.

60 Gao, *Jizhou Yonghe yao.*

61 Jessica Harrison-Hall, *Catalogue of Late Yuan and Ming Ceramics in the British Museum* (London: British Museum Press, 2001), 438–439.

62 Wang Ching-Ling, 'Re-considering a Cizhou-type jar in the VVAK collection', *Aziatische Kunst* 45.1 (2015): 38–44.

63 Wang Ning 王宁, *Jizhou Yinghe yao zuopin ji* 吉州永和窑作品集 *[A collection of Jizhou ceramics from the Yonghe kiln]* (Wuhan: Hubei meishu chubanshe, 2005), 94.

64 Gao, *Jizhou Yonghe yao*, 147–148. See also Guo Xuelei, *Chanfeng yu Ruyun*, items 62, 63, 64, 66.

65 Further evidence can be gleaned from the line drawings of decorative features on Song ceramics from the major kilns provided in Li Yucang 李雨苍, *Songdai taoci wenshi jingcui hui lu* 宋代陶瓷纹饰精粹绘录 *[Selected collection of the ceramic decorative patterns in the Song dynasty]*, (Shanghai: Shanghai guji chubanshe, 2004); see also the useful drawings of designs and shapes in Wang Jianzhong 王建中, *Cizhou yaoci jianding yu jianshang* 磁州窑瓷鉴定与鉴赏. Page 146 features a Cizhou object for which there is a close parallel amongst Jizhou wares (a pair of vases).

66 Fan Fengmei 范凤妹, 'Ji Jiangxi Chutu de Beifang Mingyao Ciqi', 121.

67 Ling Zhang, *The River, the Plain, and the State: An Environmental Drama in Northern Song China, 1048–1128*, 2016.

68 Valerie Hansen and Ken Curtis, *Voyages in World History*, 3rd ed. (Cengage Learning, 2016), 321.

69 Wu Songdi 吴松弟, *Zhongguo yimin shi*, 4: Liao, Song, Jin, Yuan shiqi: 328–330.

70 Zhou Bida 周必大, *Wenzhong ji* 文忠集, Yingyin Wenyuange Siku quanshu (Taipei: Taiwan shangwu yinshuguan, 1983), 74.9b–11a; John W. Chaffee, *Branches of Heaven: A History of the Imperial Clan of Sung China*, (Cambridge, MA: Harvard University Asia Center, 1999), 155–156. See also 344n57.

71 Chaffee, *Branches of Heaven*, 156, 159. Zhou Bida and Yang Wanli both wrote epitaphs for Zhao Gongheng, confirming, as Chaffee points out, his high status in Jizhou. Zhao Gongheng was buried in Jizhou together with two other clansmen: Zhao Gongyu and Zhao Yanwu (1137–1201). See 344n71.

72 Zhou Bida 周必大, *Wenzhong ji*, 75.6a-8b; Chaffee, *Branches of Heaven*, 161.

73 These include Zhao Shiyi (1149–1217), who served in Jizhou as magistrate, and Zhao Xiguan (1176–1233), who only served as Jizhou magistrate nominally, as by then he had become a courtier. Chaffee, *Branches of Heaven*, 196, 199, 352n78.

Chapter 5 From Jizhou to Jingdezhen

1 Herbert Giles, *A Chinese Biographical Dictionary* (New York: Paragon Book Gallery, 1975), 874–875.

2 In Jiangxi, there are memorials in Ji'an, where he was born, and in the ancestral town of Futian. There was a Ming-era memorial to Wen Tianxiang in Beijing, and today there is a memorial near his site of execution. There are several large memorials to Man Tin Cheung (Wen Tianxiang in Cantonese) in Hong Kong, including in San Tin village, where Wen Tianxiang is revered as ancestor. The Singapore statue of Wen Tianxiang is in the Chinese Garden (Jurong).

3 Cao Zhao, *Xinzeng Gegu yaolun* 新增格古要論 (1459; repr., Changsha: Shangwu chubanshe, 1939), juan 7.23b–24a.

4 Fang Yizhi 方以智 (1611–1671), *Wuli xiaoshi* 物理小識, vol. 131–132, Siku quanshu (Taipei: Taiwan shangwu yinshuguan, 1981), juan 8.25a–b.

5 Lan Pu 蓝浦 and Zheng Tinggui 郑廷桂, *Jingdezhen taolu*, 176.

6 On the emergence of 'ink plum' as a genre of paintings, see Maggie Bickford, *Ink Plum: The Making of a Chinese Scholar-Painting Genre* (Cambridge University Press, 1996), 29. She mentions several Jiangxi natives who were prominent practitioners of plum texts and images.

7 Hou-mei Sung Ishida, 'The Early Ming Ink Plum Blossom Painter Xu Jing', *Oriental Art* 35, 2 (1989): 97–109.

8 Mary Gardner Neill, 'The Flowering Plum in the Decorative Arts', in *Bones of Jade, Soul of Ice: The Flowering Plum in Chinese Art*, ed. Maggie Bickford (New Haven, CN: Yale University Art Gallery, 1985), 193–243. The discussion of the theme on Jizhou wares can be found on pp. 198–204.

9 Bickford, *Ink Plum*; Patricia Bjaaland Welch, *Chinese Art: A Guide to Motifs and Visual Imagery* (North Clarendon, VT: Tuttle, 2008), 38–39.

10 See, for example, a brown Jizhou bowl with a design in cream-coloured slip in the collection of the New South Wales Art Gallery, inv. no. 519.1988. Gao, *Jizhou Yonghe yao*, 144 Image 5–41. Wang Ning 王宁, *Jizhou Yinghe yao zuopin ji* 吉州永和窑作品集 *[A collection of Jizhou ceramics from the Yonghe kiln]*, 61. A dark-glazed teabowl dating to the thirteenth or early fourteenth century, now in the Metropolitan Museum of Art (Metropolitan Museum of Art inv. no. 24.100.1) shows that this theme continued to be popular during the Yuan dynasty in Jizhou.

11 For a general introduction to the transformations that occurred during this time, see Herbert Franke and Denis Crispin Twitchett, eds., *Alien Regimes and Border States, 907–1368*, vol. 6, Cambridge History of China (Cambridge University Press, 2008); for a succinct statement of the administrative changes, see Elizabeth Endicott, *Mongolian Rule in China: Local Administration in the Yuan Dynasty*, Council on East Asian Studies (Cambridge, MA: Harvard University Press, 1989).

12 On the Song imperial attempt to regulate trade, and on the significance of overseas trade for the Song polity, see Brian Thomas Vivier, 'Chinese Foreign Trade, 960–1276' (PhD, Yale University, 2009).

13 For more on this, see Gerritsen, 'Porcelain and the Material Culture of the Mongol-Yuan Court'.

14 Linda Walton's study of the significance of academies as part of elite strategies to survive the Song-Yuan transition is very useful here. Linda Walton, 'Family Fortunes in the Song-Yuan Transition: Academies and Chinese Elite Strategies for Success', *T'oung Pao* 97, 1–3 (2011): 37–103.

15 The civil service examinations were re-established in 1315. Benjamin A. Elman, *A Cultural History of Civil Examinations in Late Imperial China* (Berkeley, CA: University of California Press, 2000), 32.

16 Before the completion of much archaeological research, scholars generally agreed with a Southern Song-early Yuan date for the end of production in Jizhou. See Tang Changpu 唐昌朴, 'Jiangxi Jizhou Yao Faxian Song Yuan Qinghua Ci 江西吉州窑发现宋元青花瓷', *Wenwu*, 4 (1980): 4.

17 James C. Y. Watt and Maxwell K. Hearn, *The World of Khubilai Khan: Chinese Art in the Yuan Dynasty* (New York: Metropolitan Museum of Art, 2010), 36, 269.

18 Ibid., 269.

19 Yu Jiadong 余家栋, *Jiangxi Jizhou yao*.

20 Geng Sheng 耕生, 'Yuan Jizhou yao jinian zhen ci liang zhong 元吉州窑纪年珍瓷两种 [Two pieces of chronological porcelain created by Jizhou kiln]', *Shoucang*, 13 (2013): 70–71.

21 The Palace Museum in Beijing has a small lidded jar (H 6.5 cm) in its collections with underglaze line drawings, made in Jizhou, and dated to 1209. Another piece decorated with underglaze brush-lines is illustrated on Cao Guoqing 曹国庆, *Zhongguo chutu ciqi quanji* 中國出土瓷器全集, 14: Jiangxi: 56. See also K. H. Koh, 'Jizhou ware', created on 14 April 2008, www.koh-antique.com/jizhou/jizhou.htm. Consulted on 13 November 2013.

22 Geng Sheng 耕生, 'Yuan Jizhou yao jinian zhen ci liang zhong 元吉州窑纪年珍瓷两种 [Two pieces of chronological porcelain created by Jizhou kiln]'; Shenzhen bowuguan, *Chan feng yu ru yun*.

23 The object number of the British Museum vase is 1936,1012.158. There is also a Jizhou vase from the Eumorfopoulos collection dated by Brankston to the 'late Yuan or early Ming', but there is no external evidence to confirm the early Ming date, and late Yuan seems more likely. Brankston, 'Ceramics from the Eumorfopoulos Collection. Two Vases from Chi-Chou', 47.

24 To give just a few examples: The Harvard Art Museums have 30 pieces of Jizhou ceramics, of which 11 are dated to the Southern Song, and 19 to the Southern-Song/Yuan period. The fact that none of these are confidently dated to the Yuan, let alone to the Ming is instructive. The collection of the Ackland Art Museum at the University of North Carolina at Chapel Hill includes 18 items of Jizhou

ware, 11 of which are dated to the Song (as a whole) and a further seven specifically to the Southern Song. The collection does not include Yuan pieces. The Victoria and Albert Museum has 17 pieces; 10 of which are dated to the Southern Song, five to the Southern Song/Yuan period and only two to the Yuan dynasty. The Metropolitan Museum of Art has 12 Jizhou pieces, three of which are dated to the Song as a whole, eight to the Southern Song/Yuan period and one to the Yuan.

25 Zhang Wenjiang 张文江, Li Yuyuan 李育远 and Yuan Shengwen 袁胜文, 'Jizhou yizhi jin jinian kaogu diaocha fajue de zhuyao shouhuo 吉州窑遗址近几年考古调查发掘的主要收获 [Archaeological Excavations of Jizhou Kiln Sites in Recent Years]', *Journal of National Museum of Chinese History*, 6 (2014): 40.

26 Many of these are described in the Jiangxi volume of the Zhongguo chutu ciqi quanji. Cao Guoqing 曹国庆, *Jiangxi* 江西, vol. 14, 中国出土瓷器全集 (Beijing: Kexue chubanshe, 2008). See, for examples, pages 54–56, 74, 79–80, 83, 86.

27 Cao Guoqing 曹国庆, 14: 124.

28 Wu Ke 武可, 'Liuzi yizhi chutu de Jizhou yao ciqi 柳孜遗址出土的吉州窑瓷器', *Shoucang jie*, 12 (2008): 60–61; Zhang Hui 张辉 and Gong Xicheng 宫希成, 'Sui Tang Dayunhe Tongjiqu (Bianhe) Tang Song Chenchuan Yu Yan'an Guwenhua Yicun 隋唐大运河通济渠（汴河）唐宋沉船与沿岸古文化遗存', *Journal of National Museum of Chinese History*, 6 (2010): 24–32; Li Weiran 李蔚然, 'Nanjing Chutu Jizhou Yao Cizhen 南京出土吉州窑瓷枕', *Wenwu*, 1 (1977): 95; Zhuang Wenbin 庄文彬, 'Sichuan Suining Jinyucun Nan Song Jiaocang 四川遂宁金鱼村南宋窖藏', *Wenwu*, 4 (1994): 4–28; Li Huibing 李辉柄, 'Suining Jiaocang Ciqi Qianyi 遂宁窖藏瓷器浅议——兼谈成都附近县市窖藏瓷器', *Wenwu*, 4 (1994): 29–31; Chen Defu 陈德富, 'Suining Jinyu Cun Jiaocang Song Ci San Yi 遂宁金鱼村窖藏宋瓷三议', *Sichuan Wenwu*, 5 (1997): 44–51.

29 John W. Dardess, *Ming China, 1368–1644: A Concise History of a Resilient Empire* (Lanham, MD: Rowman & Littlefield, 2012), 103.

30 Hok-lam Chan, 'The Rise of Ming T'ai-Tsu (1368–1398): Facts and Fictions in Early Ming Official Historiography', *Journal of the American Oriental Society* 95, 4 (1975): 703, quoting TTSL, 13/165. This refers to *(Ming) Taizu shilu* (1418), ed. Yao Kuang-hsiao (1335–1418) et al., 257 juan. Academia Sinica, Taipei 1962; Edward L. Dreyer, 'The Poyang Campaign of 1363: Inland Naval Warfare in the Founding of the Ming Dynasty', in *Chinese Ways in Warfare*, ed. John King Fairbank and Frank Kierman (Cambridge, MA: Harvard University Press, 1974), 202–242; see also Stephen R. Turnbull and Wayne Reynolds, *Fighting Ships of the Far East (1): China and Southeast Asia 202 BC–AD 1419* (Oxford: Osprey, 2002).

31 Anne Gerritsen, *Ji'an Literati and the Local in Song-Yuan-Ming China* (Leiden; Boston: Brill, 2007), 123–124; Hok-lam Chan, 'Xie Jin (1369–1415) as Imperial Propagandist: His Role in the Revisions of the "Ming Taizu Shilu"', *T'oung Pao* 91, 1–3 (2005): 58–124.

32 The point has been made by a number of scholars, of which He Bingdi, author of the classic study of social mobility through examination success is perhaps the best known. See Ping-ti Ho, *The Ladder of Success in Imperial China: Aspects of Social Mobility, 1368–1911* (New York: Columbia University Press, 1964), 231, 246–248. Dardess, *Ming China, 1368–1644*, 168.

33 宋末土盡窯變故移之浮梁. Ding Xiang 定祥 and Liu Yi 劉繹, eds., *[Guangxu] Ji'an Fuzhi* [光緒] 吉安府志 *[Prefectural Gazetteer of Ji'an]*, Zhongguo Fangzhi Congshu (Taibei: Chengwen chubanshe, 1875), 53.82a–b; see also Gao, *Jizhou Yonghe yao*, 19.

34 For a superb discussion of yaobian during the Qing dynasty, see Ellen Huang, 'An Art of Transformation: Reproducing *Yaobian* Glazes in Qing-Dynasty Porcelain' (2017), *Archives of Asian Art* (2018) 68 (2): 133–156.

35 Zhou Hui 周煇 (1126-), *Qingbo zazhi* 清波雜志, Sibu congkan xubian (Shanghai: Shangwu yinshuguan, 1934), 5.6b–7a.

36 Cao Zhao, *Gegu yaolun*, 7.23b–24a.

37 宋末土盡窯變故移之浮梁. Ding Xiang 定祥 and Liu Yi 劉繹, *Ji'an Fuzhi*, 53.82a–b; see also Gao, *Jizhou Yonghe yao*, 19.

38 Wang Bu 王補 and Zeng Cancai 曾燦材, eds., *Minguo Luling xian zhi* 民國廬陵縣志, Zhongguo difangzhi jicheng (Nanjing: Jiangsu guji chubanshe, 1996), 28.42b.

39 Wang Bu 王補 and Zeng Cancai 曾燦材, 28.42b.

40 Ibid., 28.42b.

41 Chen Boquan 陈柏泉, 'Jizhou yao shaoci lishi chushen 吉州窑烧瓷历史初探', *Jiangxi lishi wenwu*, 3 (1982): 32.

42 Shi Runzhang 施閏章, *Juzhai zaji* 矩齋雜記, Congshu jicheng xu bian (Shanghai: Shanghai shudian, 1994), 19.10a–b; see also Anne Gerritsen, 'Jizhou as Kiln Town: Writing the History of a Forgotten Past', 2009, www. humanities.uci.edu/eastasian/SungYuan/Downloads/ideas_networks _places/; and Liu Yi 刘毅, 'Yaobian ji qi ciye wenhua yi 窑变及其瓷业文化意义 [Kiln transmutation and its significance for porcelain culture]', *Nanfang wenwu*, 2 (2014): 110–115.

43 Shi Runzhang's literary collection has been included in the *Siku quanshu*. Shi Runzhang 施閏章, *Xueyutang wenji* 學餘堂文集, Yingyin Wenyuange Siku quanshu (Taipei: Taiwan shangwu yinshuguan, 1983).

44 Chen Boquan 陈柏泉, 'Jizhou yao shaoci'; Chen Lili 陈立立, 'Jizhou Yao Gongjiang Zai Jingdezhen Cidu Diwei Queli Guochengzhong de Zuoyong 吉州窑工匠在景德镇瓷都地位确立过程中的作用', 江西社会科学, *Jiangxi Social Sciences*, 8 (2011): 160–161.

45 Cao Zhao *Gegu yaolun*, 下 3a.

46 Ibid.

47 Wang Rui 王睿, 'Jizhou Yao Zhi Yonghe Yao Yu Linjiang Yao Chubu Bijiao 吉州窑之永和窑与临江窑初步比较', *Nanfang Wenwu*, 2 (2015): 151.

48 Tang Changpu 唐昌朴, 'Jiangxi Jizhou Yao Faxian Song Yuan Qinghua Ci'.

49 Kessler, *Song Blue and White Porcelain on the Silk Road*, 337.

50 Wu Rui 吴瑞 et al., 'Hutian Yao Chutu Heiyouci de Chandi Yanjiu 湖田窑出土黑釉瓷的产地研究 [Research on the Provenance of Black-Glazed Ceramics Excavated from the Hutian Kiln Site]', *Zongguo Taoci* 41, 2 (2005): 77–81; Xiao Fabiao 肖发标, 'Shilun Hutian Yao Chutu de Heyouci 试论湖田窑出土的黑釉瓷', *Shanghai Wen Bo Lun Cong*, 1 (2007): 40–44.

51 Shih Ching-fei 施靜菲, 'Jingdezhen Yuan Qinghua Qiyuan Zhi Bendi Yinsuo Kaocha 景德鎮元青花起源之本地因素考察 [Local Origins of the Beginnings of Jingdezhen Yuan Blue-and-White]', *Zhejiang University Journal of Art and Archaeology* 1 (2014): 183–217.

52 Chen Defu 陈德富, 'Suining Jinyu Cun Jiaocang Song Ci San Yi'.

53 Wang Xiaoying 王小迎 and Wang Rui 王睿, 'Jiangsu Yangzhou Nan Song Baoyoucheng xicheng menwai chutu taoci qi 江苏扬州南宋宝祐城西城门外出土陶瓷器 [Porcelain Unearthed Outside West Gate of Southern Song Baoyou City Site]', *Journal of the National Museum of China* 146 (2015): 93–111. For the discussion of the excavated Jizhou wares, see 94–97.

54 'A special institution – the Hutian Kiln Site Protection Office (also the Hutian Kiln Site Museum) was established in 1979 for the protection of the site. In 1982, the 40 ha site entered the list of Major Cultural Heritage under State-level Protection'. Jiangxi Provincial Institute of Cultural Relics and Archaeology and Jingdezhen Museum of Civilian Kiln, 'Report on Excavations from 1988 to 1999: Hutian Kiln Site in Jingdezhen', Chinese Archaeology, accessed 23 March 2017, www.kaogu.net.cn/html/en/Publication/New_books/2013/1025/30009.html.

55 He presented a report of this trip to the Oriental Ceramics Society in London, published as A. D. Brankston, 'An Excursion to Chingte-Chen and Chi-an-Fu in Kiangsi', *Transactions of the Oriental Ceramic Society* 16 (1938): 19–32; the information he gleaned from this visit was also included in Archibald Dooley Brankston, *Early Ming Wares of Chingtechen* (Hong Kong: Oxford University Press, 1982), 55–60; the trip also included India, Thailand and Cambodia. See also 'A D Brankston (Biographical Details)', British Museum, accessed 23 March 2017, www.britishmuseum.org/research/search_the_collection_00database/term_details.aspx?bioId=141986.

56 Brankston, *Early Ming Wares of Chingtechen*, 57.

57 Ibid., 57–58.

58 Ibid., 57.

59 Kessler, *Song Blue and White Porcelain on the Silk Road*, 336; Feng Xianming 冯先铭, 'Woguo taoci fazhanzhong de jige wenti 我国陶瓷发展中的几个问题', *Wenwu* 7 (1973): 20–27; see also Zhu Boqian 朱伯谦, 'Zhejiang Liangchu Taji Chutu Song Qinghuaci 浙江两处塔基出土宋青花瓷', *Wenwu*, 4 (1980): 1–3; this is also discussed in Kessler, *Song Blue and White Porcelain on the Silk Road*, 336.

60 Anne Gerritsen, 'Fragments of a Global Past: Ceramics Manufacture in Song-Yuan-Ming Jingdezhen', *Journal of the Social and Economic History of the Orient* 52 (2009): 120.

61 Shenzhen bowuguan, *Chanfeng yu ruyun: Song Yuan shidai de Jizhou yao ciqi* 禅風与儒韻: 宋元时代的吉州窑瓷器 (Beijing: Wenwu chubanshe, 2012), 96, 134–135.

62 For a blunter example than the plantain leaves of the David vases, see *Chanfeng yu ruyun* images 31, page 195.

63 Gao, *Jizhou Yonghe yao*, 73; *Chanfeng yu ruyun*, 161, 212; Wang Ning 王宁, *Jizhou Yinghe yao zuopin ji* 吉州永和窑作品集 *[A collection of Jizhou ceramics from the Yonghe kiln]*, 52.

64 The dragon is a feature on many underglaze painted wares made in Cizhou. See, for example, the dragon-covered Cizhou jar dated to the Yuan dynasty in the Umezawa Memorial Gallery in Tokyo, Japan. It is also published in Gao, *Jizhou Yonghe yao*, 76 illustrations 4–5. For another Yuan example, see the collection of the Rijksmuseum, AK-MAK-110.

65 A large plate (D 45.5 cm) with the dragon curling from left to right is in the National Museum of Iran and illustrated in Shanghai Museum, *Splendors in smalt: art of Yuan blue-and-white porcelain* 幽蓝神采: 元代青花瓷器特集 (Shanghai: Shanghai Museum, 2012), Image 33. An example of the head-meets-toe dragon is Image 38 in the same catalogue. The pair of dragons chasing pearls is Image 46 (from the Idemitsu Museum). See also the dragon on an early fourteenth-century stem cup in the collection of the University of California in San Diego in Artstor.

66 See, for example, the Ding dish with dragon pattern in Tōwakai 陶話会, ed., *Tōwakai sōji tenkan zufu* 陶話会宋瓷展観図譜 *[Catalogue of the exhibition of Song stoneware of the Tokyo Ceramics Society]* (Tōkyō: Ootsuka Kōgeisha, 1929), Plate 29. There is a Ding plate with imprinted dragons in the collection of the Rijksmuseum, dated before 1300. AK-MAK-532. See also the Ding-ware dragon dish from a private collection displayed at Eskenazi in 2015. Eskenazi Ltd, *Principal wares of the Song period from a private collection: 8–29 May 2015* (London: Eskenazi, 2015), 48.

67 Alain R. Truong, 'Decorated Porcelains of Dingzhou: White Ding Wares from the Collection of the National Palace Museum', 18 June 2014, www.alaintruong.com/archives/2014/06/18/30098378.html.

68 Susanne Kotz, *In Pursuit of the Dragon: Traditions and Transitions in Ming Ceramics. An Exhibition from the Idemitsu Museum of Arts* (Seattle Art Museum, 1988), 56 Illustration 1.

69 A Cizhou-type dragon jar from the Tangut (Western) Xia dynasty (1038–1227) can be found in Artstor, ID RL01268. A Cizhou storage jar in cream slip with a brown-slip dragon dated to the early fourteenth century has been published in Kotz, *In Pursuit of the Dragon* illustration 1; a similar jar was also recovered from the Sinan shipwreck. Kotz, 56.

70 My translation. Feng Xianming 冯先铭, 'Woguo taoci fazhanzhong de jige wenti'.

Chapter 6 Blue and White Porcelain

1 Kenneth R. Robinson, 'Chosŏn Korea in the Ryūkoku "Kangnido": Dating the Oldest Extant Korean Map of the World (15th Century)', *Imago Mundi* 59, 2 (2007): 177–192.

2 The original version of this map, thought to have been made in 1402, is not in existence today. Map 6.1 is one of two early copies, both of which have been preserved in Japan. Park, *Mapping the Chinese and Islamic worlds*, 104–107. Two state councillors of the early Choson (or Joseon) period (1392–1910), Kim Sahjong and Yi Mu, proposed the making of this map, while yet another high-ranking official by the name of Yi Hoe was the main creator of the 1402 map; Robinson, 'Chosŏn Korea in the Ryūkoku "Kangnido"', 179.

3 Yŏng-u Han, Hwi-jun An and U-sŏng Pae, *The Artistry of Early Korean Cartography*, trans. Byonghyon Choi, 2008, 9–11.

4 Han, An and Pae, 11.

5 Ibid., 11.

6 These two maps are 'Map of the Vast Reach of Civilization's Resounding Teaching' (*Shengjiao guangbei tu*) by Li Zemin, and the 'Map of Integrated Regions and Terrains' (*Hunyi jiangli tu*) by the monk Qingjun. Han, An and Pae, 9.

7 Kenneth R. Robinson, 'Gavin Menzies, 1421, and the Ryūkoku Kangnido World Map', *Ming Studies* 61 (2010): 56–70. The *Da Ming hunyi tu* is now in the First Historical Archives in Nanjing.

8 Robinson refers to the map as a 'heteroglossic artefact'. Robinson, 'Chosŏn Korea in the Ryūkoku "Kangnido"', 179.

9 Park, *Mapping the Chinese and Islamic Worlds*, especially Chapter 3. See also Kuei-Sheng Chang, 'Africa and the Indian Ocean in Chinese Maps of the Fourteenth and Fifteenth Centuries', *Imago Mundi* 24, 1 (1970): 21–30.

10 S. Arasaratnam, 'Recent Trends in the Historiography of the Indian Ocean, 1500 to 1800', *Journal of World History*, 2 (1990): 236–237.

11 Riello, *Cotton*, 17–19.

12 See Craig Clunas, Jessica Harrison-Hall and Yu Ping Luk, eds., *Ming China: Courts and Contacts, 1400–1450* (London: The British Museum, 2016). Several of the chapters in this volume discuss the extension of Ming maritime power.

13 Paul Pelliot, 'Les grands voyages maritimes chinois au debut du XVe siecle', *T'oung Pao* 30 (1933): 237–452; J. J. L. Duyvendak, 'The True Dates of the Chinese Maritime Expeditions in the Early Fifteenth Century', 34 (1939): 341–413; Edward L. Dreyer, *Zheng He: China and the Oceans in the Early Ming Dynasty, 1405–1433* (New York: Pearson Longman, 2007).

14 Historical sources for the seventh voyage, for example, confirm that the fleet had 27,550 personnel. Dreyer, *Zheng He*, 128; see also Sally K. Church, 'Zheng He: An Investigation into the Plausibility of 450-Ft Treasure Ships', *Monumenta Serica* 53, 1 (2005): 1–43.

15 *Xuanzong Shilu*, juan 114, Xuande 9.11.丁丑. Quoted in Han Zhenhua 韩振华, 'Lun Zheng He Xia Xiyang de Xingzhi 论郑和下西洋的性质 [On the Nature of Zheng He's Voyages to the Western Oceans]', *Xiamen Daxue Xuebao*, 1 (1958): 184.

16 Han Zhenhua 韩振华, 184.

17 Sally K. Church, 'Review of Ming Dynasty Baochuanchang Shipyard in Nanjing – by Nanjing Municipal Museum', *International Journal of Nautical Archaeology* 37, 1 (2008): 198.

18 Robert Finlay, 'The Voyages of Zheng He: Ideology, State Power, and Maritime Trade in Ming China', *Journal of The Historical Society* 8, 3 (2008): 327–347.

19 For a recent bibliography, see Ying Liu, Zhongping Chen and Gregory Blue, *Zheng He's Maritime Voyages (1405–1433) and China's Relations with the Indian Ocean World A Multilingual Bibliography* (Leiden: Brill, 2014).

20 See, for example, the following statement taken from a global history textbook: 'For reasons that are still debated, the Ming emperor suddenly ordered all overseas activity halted and China turned inward, beginning an isolation that ended only in the 1800s'. Craig Lockard, *Societies, Networks, and Transitions, A Global History*, vol. II: Since 1450 (Boston: Wadsworth, 2011), 288.

21 The exception that proves the rule is perhaps Zheng He's appearance in Felipe Fernández-Armesto, *Pathfinders: A Global History of Exploration* (New York: W.W. Norton, 2007).

22 Yasuhiro Yokkaichi, 'Chinese and Muslim Diasporas and the Indian Ocean Trade Network under Mongol Hegemony', in *The East Asian Mediterranean: Maritime Crossroads of Culture, Commerce and Human Migration*, ed. Angela Schottenhammer (Wiesbaden: Harrassowitz, 2008), 73–102; Tansen Sen, 'Maritime Interactions between China and India: Coastal India and the Ascendancy of Chinese Maritime Power in the Indian Ocean', *Journal of Central Eurasian Studies* 2 (2011): 41–82; Lin Meicun and Ran Zhang, 'Zheng He's Voyages to Hormuz: The Archaeological Evidence', *Antiquity* 89, 344 (2015): 417–432.

23 Ivy Maria Lim, 'From Haijin to Kaihai: The Jiajing Court's Search for a Modus Operandi along the South-Eastern Coast (1522–1567)', *Journal of the British Association for Chinese Studies* 2 (2013): 1–26.

24 Hoàng Anh Tuấn, 'Regionalising National History: Ancient and Medieval Vietnamese Maritime Trade in the East Asian Context', *Medieval History Journal* 17, 1 (2014): 96.

25 Roxanna M. Brown, *The Ming Gap and Shipwreck Ceramics in Southeast Asia: Towards a Chronology of Thai Trade Ware* (Bangkok: Siam Society, 2009); Tai Yew Seng, 'Ming Gap and the Revival of Commercial Production of Blue and White Porcelain in China', *Bulletin of the Indo-Pacific Prehistory Association* 31 (2011): 85–92.

26 Ursula Sims-Williams, 'An Illustrated 14th Century Khamsah by Khvaju Kirmani', *Asian and African Studies Blog* (blog), 1 August 2013, http://britishlibrary.typepad .co.uk/asian-and-african/2013/07/an-illustrated-14th-century-khamsah-by-khvaju-kirmani.html; Teresa Fitzherbert, 'Khwājū Kirmānī (689–753/1290–1352): An Éminence Grise of Fourteenth Century Persian Painting', *Iran* 29 (1991):

137–151; J. T. P. de Bruijn, 'Ḵᵛāju Kermāni', Encyclopaedia Iranica, 20 July 2009, www.iranicaonline.org/articles/kvaju-kerman-poet-and-mystic.

27 Fitzherbert, 'Khwājū Kirmānī', 145.

28 Kulliyáti Khwájú Karmání, 'The poetical works of Khwájú of Karmán. British Library Manuscript Add. 18,113' (1396).

29 Jonathan Bloom and Sheila S. Blair, eds., 'Junayd', in *The Grove Encyclopedia of Islamic Art and Architecture*, accessed 8 May 2015, www.oxfordislamicstudies.com/article/opr/t276/e454.

30 Fitzherbert, 'Khwājū Kirmānī', 137; Norah M. Titley, *Persian Miniature Painting and its Influence on the Art of Turkey and India* (London: The British Library, 1983), 26–32.

31 A. L. B. Ashton, 'Early Blue and White in Persian Mss.', *Transactions of the Oriental Ceramic Society* 1934–1935 (1936): 23.

32 Image of blue vase with white dragon: www.gettyimages.no/detail/photo/meiping-vase-decorated-with-a-white-dragon-high-res-stock-photography/150099913. See the object in the Guimet collection: www.guimet.fr/en/home/92-anglais/collections/china/386-meiping-vase.

33 Shanghai Museum, *Splendors in Smalt*.

34 Paul Kahle, 'Chinese Porcelain in the Lands of Islam', in *Opera Minora* (Leiden: Brill, 1956), 326–361.

35 Priscilla Soucek, 'Ceramic Production as Exemplar of Yuan-Ilkhanid Relations', *Res: Anthropology and Aesthetics* 35 (1999): 125.

36 Yuka Kadoi, *Islamic Chinoiserie: The Art of Mongol Iran* (Edinburgh University Press, 2009).

37 Basil Gray, 'Blue and White Vessels in Persian Miniatures of the 14th and 15th Centuries Re-Examined', *Transactions of the Oriental Ceramic Society* 24 (1948–49): 23–30.

38 Ibid., 24.

39 Ibid., 28.

40 Harriet Zurndorfer, 'Wanli China versus Hideyoshi's Japan: Rethinking China's Involvement in the Imjin Waeran', in *The East Asian War, 1592–1598: International Relations, Violence and Memory*, ed. James Bryant Lewis (London: Routledge, 2015), 197–235.

41 I have learned a great deal from the MA dissertation of a recent graduate at Leiden University: Karwin Cheung, 'Journeys to the Past: Travel and Painting as Antiquarianism in Joseon Korea', MA thesis, Leiden University, 2017.

42 The collection of the Dongguk University Museum in Seoul holds a porcelain jar that was made in 1498 during the Joseon Dynasty under the reign of King Seongjong. The jar is identified as National Treasure 176 on the Cultural Heritage Administration website. On the same website, National Treasure 219 represents an early fifteenth-century example of a blue and white porcelain jar with plum and bamboo designs. This jar, now in the Leeum, Samsung Museum of Art, seems to have been based on a fifteenth-century Ming model. Ewha Women's University Museum also holds a number of jars of the same kind. See http://english.cha.go.kr, consulted on 22 December 2017.

43 Kwon Sohyun, 'Establishing and Practicing Propriety', in *In Blue and White: Porcelain of the Joseon Dynasty*, ed. Kang Tae-gyu (Seoul: National Museum of Korea, 2015), 69. A decree was issued in 1407, during the reign of Taejong, stating that instead of gold and silver, porcelain and lacquer should be used for ritual objects.『金銀器皿, 除內用國用外, 下令 中外, 一切禁止, 國中皆用沙漆器』(Taejong Sillok, year 7, 1st month, 19th day).

44 Ibid., 69.

45 Franck Goddio, 'The Wreck on the Lena Shoal', in *Lost at Sea: The Strange Route of the Lena Shoal Junk* (London: Periplus, 2002), 8.

46 Peter Lam, 'Maritime Trade in China during the Middle Ming Period Circa 1500 AD', in *Lost at Sea: The Strange Route of the Lena Shoal Junk* (London: Periplus, 2002), 43–57. The various chapters provide an in-depth overview of the wreck and its cargo.

47 Bobby C. Orillaneda, 'Maritime Trade in the Philippines During the 15th Century CE', *Moussons. Recherche En Sciences Humaines Sur l'Asie Du Sud-Est* 27 (2016): 84. The route was also included in a fifteenth-century Chinese compilation entitled *Shunfeng xiangsong*, c. 1430. The Bodleian Library has an early printed copy. Laud MS, Or. 145. See also Goddio, 'The Wreck on the Lena Shoal', 6–7.

48 Leonard Blussé, 'Port Cities of South East Asia: 1400–1800', in *The Oxford Handbook of Cities in World History*, ed. Peter Clark (Oxford University Press, 2013).

49 Michael Pearson, 'Spain and Spanish Trade in Southeast Asia', *Journal of Asian History* 2, 2 (1968): 109–129.

50 Blussé, 'Port Cities of South East Asia'; Kirti N. Chaudhuri, *Trade and Civilisation in the Indian Ocean: An Economic History from the Rise of Islam to 1750* (Cambridge University Press, 1985).

51 Laura Lee Junker, *Raiding, Trading, and Feasting: The Political Economy of Philippine Chiefdoms* (Honolulu: University of Hawai'i Press, 1999).

52 Fox, 'The Archeological Record of Chinese Influences in the Philippines', 41; 56.

53 Bobby C. Orillaneda, 'Of Ships and Shipping: The Maritime Archaeology of Fifteenth Century CE Southeast Asia', in *Early Navigation in the Asia-Pacific Region: A Maritime Archaeological Perspective*, ed. Chunming Wu (Springer Singapore, 2016), 29–57.

54 Orillaneda, 'Maritime Trade in the Philippines During the 15th Century CE'.

55 Ibid., 87–88.

56 Ibid., 88.

57 Ibid., 89.

58 Ibid., 93.

59 Miklós Boskovits and David Alan Brown, *Italian Paintings of the Fifteenth Century* (Oxford University Press, 2003), 95.

60 Rosamond E. Mack, *Bazaar to Piazza: Islamic Trade and Italian Art, 1300–1600* (Berkeley: University of California Press, 2002), 104; Karl-Heinz Spiess, 'Asian Objects and Western European Court Culture in the Middle Ages', in *Artistic and Cultural Exchanges between Europe and Asia, 1400–1900: Rethinking Markets, Workshops and Collections*, ed. Michael North (Farnham, Surrey, England; Burlington, VT: Ashgate, 2010), 9–28.

61 Stacey Pierson, *Collectors, Collections and Museums: The Field of Chinese Ceramics in Britain, 1560–1960* (Oxford; New York: Peter Lang, 2007), 17.

62 Ibid.; Lauren Arnold, *Princely Gifts and Papal Treasures: The Franciscan Mission to China and Its Influence on the Art of the West, 1250–1350* (San Francisco: Desiderata Press, 1999).

63 Mack, *Bazaar to Piazza*, 104; Galeazzo Cora, *La Porcellana Dei Medici* (Milano: Fabbri Editori, 1986); Marco Spallanzani, *Ceramiche alla corte dei Medici nel Cinquecento* (Modena: Panini, 1994).

64 A. I. Spriggs, 'Oriental Porcelain in Western Paintings, 1450–1700', *Transactions of the Oriental Ceramic Society* 36 (1964–1966): 73.

65 The bowl she has identified is Plate 8.2: a blue and white porcelain bowl, Xuande mark and period, 1426–1435, Jingdezhen. H 9 cm × D 15.9 cm. Sir Percival David Collection, PDF 681. Jessica Harrison-Hall, 'Early Ming Ceramics: Rethinking the Status of Blue-and-White', in *Ming China: Courts and Contacts, 1400–1450*, ed. Craig Clunas, Jessica Harrison-Hall and Yu Ping Luk (London: The British Museum, 2016), 77.

66 Harrison-Hall, 77.

Chapter 7 The City of Blue and White

1 Stephen McDowall, *Qian Qianyi's Reflections on Yellow Mountain: Traces of a Late-Ming Hatchet and Chisel* (Hong Kong University Press, 2009).

2 Wang Zongmu 王宗沐 and Lu Wan'gai 陸萬垓, eds., *(Wanli) Jiangxi sheng dazhi* 江西省大志, Nanjing tushuguan guben shanben congkan (1597 Beijing: Xianzhuang shuju, 2003), juan 7.4a. Hereafter *Jiangxi sheng dazhi*

3 The river had several different names, and was only called Chang from the point at which it crossed into Jiangxi. Lai Jinming 赖金明 and Zhang Wenjiang 张文江, '"Cuncun yaohuohuhu taoyan": Changjiangbian de yaozhi "村村窑火, 户户陶埏"——昌江边的窑址', *China Cultural Heritage*, 3 (2014): 23.

4 Joseph McDermott describes a sixteenth-century Qimen magistrate who forbade the population from digging up clay, 'presumably for the pottery kilns in Jingdezhen'. Joseph McDermott, *The Making of a New Rural Order in South China*, vol. 1, Village, lineage and land in Huizhou: c. 960–1540 (Cambridge University Press, 2013), 338n80.

5 For transport to Huizhou, to the north of Jingdezhen, the merchants used the Chang, taking the goods upriver. Xiao Fabiao 肖发标, 'Yicheng shanshui shihua, qiannian guzhen yaoli 一城山水诗画,千年古镇瑶里', *China Cultural Heritage*, 3 (2014): 40–45+10.

6 Lu Fangqi 卢方琦, 'Ming Qing Nanchangcheng fuyuan yanjiu 明清南昌城复原研究 [Restoration Research on Nanchang City in the Ming and Qing Dynasties]' (MA thesis, Peking University, 2013), 7.

7 John Naley Johnston, 'Jiangxi Landmarks on Jingdezhen Porcelain With Special Reference to Tengwang Ge' (PhD, SOAS, 2016); Lu Fangqi, Ming Qing Nanchangcheng', 30–31.

8 Ling Lichao 凌礼潮, '"Jiangxi tian Huguang" yu "Huguang tian Sichuan" bijiao yanjiu chuyi "江西填湖广"与"湖广填四川"比较研究刍议', *Beijing keji daxue xuebao*, 1 (2014): esp. 52–53.

9 According to one of the region's foremost historians, Fuliang's mountainous lands constituted 79 per cent of the area. Liang Miaotai 梁淼泰, 'Ming-Qing shiqi Fuliang de nonglin shangpin 明清时期浮梁的农林商品', *Zhongguo shehui jingjishi yanjiu*, 1 (1988): 28.

10 Qiao Gui 乔湽, He Xiling 贺熙齡, and You Jisheng 游際盛, eds., *[Daoguang] Fuliang xian zhi* 道光浮梁縣志, Zhongguo difangzhi jicheng. [3], Jiangxi fuxian zhi ji; 7 (Nanjing: Jiangsu guji chubanshe, 1996), 4.a–5a. For the reign of the Hongwu emperor, the gazetteer gives the figure of 104,970; but for Daoguang the figure drops steeply to 92,595. During the Tianshun, Hongzhi and Zhengde reign periods, the figure is stable at 99,000; from Jiajing, the figure remains at 100,000. See also Liang Miaotai 梁淼泰, 'Ming-Qing shiqi Fuliang de nonglin shangpin', 33.

11 The full list of office holders in Fuliang county during the Ming dynasty can be found in *[Daoguang] Fuliang xian zhi*, 10.16a–36a.

12 Liu Xinyuan 刘新园, 'Jiangxi Jingdezhen Guanyinge Mingdai yaozhi fajue jianbao 江西景德镇观音阁明代窑址发掘简报', *Wenwu*, 12 (2009): 39–58+1.

13 Yu Rirong 余日蓉, 'Ming Jiajing 'Jiangxi tongzhi' banben kao 明嘉靖《江西通志》版本考', *Jiangxi Social Sciences*, 12 (1998): 49–51.

14 Zhou Guang 周廣, ed., *(Jiajing) Jiangxi tong zhi* 嘉靖江西通志, Zhongguo fangzhiku (Beijing: Beijing Airusheng shuzihua jishu yanjiu zhongxin, 2009), juan 8.20a.

15 Ibid., juan 8.20a.

16 Liu Tao 刘陶 et al., 'Jiyu yuanbao zidongji de Jingdezhen nanhe liuyu yaozhi jingguan yanbian 基于元胞自动机的景德镇南河流域窑址景观演变 [The Kiln Landscape Evolvement of Jingdezhen Nanhe River Basin Based on Cellular Automation]', *Zhongguo Taoci*, 8 (2012): 35–38.

17 Dai Yihui 戴仪辉 et al., 'Jiangxi Jingdezhen Liyang ciqi shan Mingdai yaozhi fajue jianbao 江西景德镇丽阳瓷器山明代窑址发掘简报', *Wenwu*, no. 03 (2007): 17–33+1; Zhong Hua 钟华, 'Jingdezhen Liyang Mingdai ci yaozhi shidai kao–jian tan xingshuai yuanyin 景德镇丽阳明代瓷窑址时代考——兼谈兴衰原因', *Nanfang wenwu*, 3 (2013): 77–82.

18 Zhong Hua 钟华, 'Jingdezhen Liyang Mingdai ci yaozhi shidai kao', 77.

19 Ouyang Shilin 欧阳世彬, 'Shiwu shiji Jingdezhen minyao yanjiu 十五世纪景德镇民窑研究', *Taoci xuebao*, 2 (2000): 72–85.

20 See the discussion of the notion of an 'extended court' in the introduction in David M. Robinson, ed., *Culture, Courtiers, and Competition: The Ming Court (1368–1644)* (Cambridge, MA: Harvard University Asia Center, 2008), 14. These members of the imperial clan, variously referred to as princes or kings, are the

subject of Craig Clunas' book, *Screen of Kings: Royal Art and Power in Ming China* (Honolulu: University of Hawai'i Press, 2013).

21 According to Lu Wan'gai's preface, the Wanli edition was expanded with material drawn from Assistant Magistrate Chen Xueqian's 陳學乾 *Taozheng lu* 陶政錄. This text is no longer extant. *Jiangxi sheng dazhi*, juan 7.

22 As James Akerman writes in the introduction to a recent collection of articles, 'The connection between cartography and the exercise of imperial power is an ancient one.' James R. Akerman, *The Imperial Map: Cartography and the Mastery of Empire* (University of Chicago Press, 2009), 1.

23 Joseph Dennis, *Writing, Publishing, and Reading Local Gazetteers in Imperial China, 1100–1700* (Cambridge, MA: Harvard University Asia Center, 2015), 3–4.

24 *Jiangxi sheng dazhi*, 7.3b.

25 7.18b.

26 7.17a–b.

27 7.5b–6a.

28 7.11b ff.

29 7.24b.

30 7.25a.

31 7.3b.

32 7.23a.

33 7.12a.

34 7.27b.

35 The phrase 'heaven and earth, dark and yellow', or 'heaven is dark, the soil is yellow' are the opening four characters of the 'Ten Thousand Character primer' used to teach children a basic set of characters. It implies the most fundamental division between what is above and what is below. Xingsi Zhou, *Ch'ien Tzu Wen. The Thousand Character Classic: A Chinese Primer*, ed. Francis W. Paar (New York: F. Ungar Pub. Co., 1963).

36 *Jiangxi sheng dazhi*, 7.12b.

37 By far the best study of this book is the following study: Dagmar Schäfer, *The Crafting of the 10,000 Things Knowledge and Technology in Seventeenth-Century China* (University of Chicago Press, 2011).

Chapter 8 Anxieties over Resources in Sixteenth-Century Jingdezhen

1 Pat Hudson, *The Industrial Revolution* (London: Edward Arnold, 1992), 27.

2 Ibid., 27; Hudson references Mendels, 'Proto-Industrialization'.

3 *Jiangxi sheng dazhi*, 7.24b.

4 Kerr and Wood refer to a family pottery in Singapore, which used six tonnes of fuel to fire a 42-metre dragon kilns to a temperature of 1,280 degrees Celsius. Kerr and Wood, *Ceramic Technology*, 353n141.

5 *Jiangxi sheng dazhi*, 7.24b.

6 7.24b and 25a.

7 7.25a.

8 7.24b; One hundred fen made up one tael. I use catty as translation for the Chinese term *jin*. One catty was made up of 16 ounces (*liang*). For details, see Endymion Porter Wilkinson, *Chinese History: A Manual* (Cambridge, MA: Harvard University Asia Center, 2000), 237.

9 This comment appears in an additional note. See *Jiangxi sheng dazhi*, 7.25b. The Chinese steelyard consisted of an arm or beam of about 1.5 metres, graduated with weight units (*jin* and *liang*, and on smaller versions also the *qian*), a hook to lift the items to be weighed and a loose weight unit. For a recent discussion of Yuan dynasty weights and measures, see Hans Ulrich Vogel, *Marco Polo Was in China: New Evidence from Currencies, Salts and Revenues* (Leiden: Brill, 2012). See Appendix 6, especially table 6: 'Weights and weight measures of the Yuan period, 1295–1306' (p. 479). For illustrations of Chinese weights and measures, see Qiu Long 邱隆, *Zhongguo gudai duliangheng tuji* 中國古代度量衡圖集 *[Weights and measures in China through the ages]* (Beijing: Wenwu chubanshe, 1981).

10 *Jiangxi sheng dazhi*, 7.25a.

11 7.25a.

12 7.25b.

13 7.25b.

14 7.25b.

15 7.28b.

16 7.28b.

17 7.28b.

18 7.28b–29a.

19 *Jiangxi sheng dazhi*; the insertions in this translation indicate the present-day equivalent of the sixteenth-century Chinese terms. Kerr and Wood, *Ceramic Technology*.

20 *Jiangxi sheng dazhi*, 7.28b.

21 7.3b.

22 7.28b.

23 7.28b.

24 7.28a.

25 7.22b.

26 7.27b–28a.

27 Robert Hartwell, 'Markets, Technology, and the Structure of Enterprise in the Development of the Eleventh-Century Chinese Iron and Steel Industry', *The Journal of Economic History* 26, 1 (1966): 35, 38.

28 Donald B. Wagner, *Ferrous Metallurgy*. Science and Civilisation in China, vol. 5: Chemistry and Chemical Technology, Pt. XI. (Cambridge University Press, 2008), 296–297; 308.

29 The state ironworks were officially located in Zunhua, Hebei, from 1403 to 1581. Wagner, 5: Chemistry and Chemical Technology, Pt. XI:326–327. The discussion of the decision to leave iron production in private hands is on page 338.

30 Ibid.

31 Kerr and Wood, *Ceramic Technology*, 308.

32 *Jiangxi sheng dazhi*, 7.28b.

33 7.11b.

34 Shi Ching-fei 施靜菲, 'Yunnan diqu qinghuaci qi de bianqian-jian tan qi yu jiangxi jingdezhen he yuenan qinghuaci de guanlian 雲南地區青花瓷器的變遷－兼談其與江西景德鎮和越南青花瓷的關連 [The Transformation of Blue-and-White Porcelain in Yunnan, with Consideration of the Relationship between the Blue-and-White Porcelains of Jingdezhen and Vietnam]', *Taiwan National University Journal of Art History*, 25 (2008): 171–270+275.

35 *Jiangxi sheng dazhi*, 7.11b.

36 7.11b.

37 James Watt, who has written on cobalt, has suggested that locally mined cobalt is not cobalt but azurite. J. C. Y. Watt, 'Notes on the Use of Cobalt in Later Chinese Ceramics', *Ars Orientalis* 11 (1979): 63–85.

38 The most detailed discussion of the literature on cobalt and its sources up to 2012 can be found in Chapter 4 of Kessler, *Song Blue and White Porcelain on the Silk Road*, 503–541.

39 Ibid., 527–536.

40 Finlay, 'The Voyages of Zheng He', 337; quoting Han Zhenhua 韩振华, 'Lun Zheng He Xia Xiyang de Xingzhi 论郑和下西洋的性质 [On the Nature of Zheng He's Voyages to the Western Oceans]'.

41 *Jiangxi sheng dazhi*, 7.13a.

42 7.12b.

43 7.11b.

44 7.11b.

45 7.11b.

46 See, for example, the study by John Styles on the widespread occurrence of embezzlement. John Styles, 'Embezzlement, Industry and the Law in England, 1500–1800', in *Manufacture in Town and Country before the Factory*, ed. Maxine Berg, Pat Hudson and Michael Sonenscher (Cambridge University Press, 1983), 173–210.

47 Peter Kriedte, Hans Medick and Jürgen Schlumbohm, *Industrialization before Industrialization: Rural Industry in the Genesis of Capitalism*, Past and Present Publications (Cambridge University Press, 1981), 112.

48 Anne Gerritsen, 'The Hongwu Legacy: Fifteenth-Century Views on Zhu Yuanzhang's Monastic Policies', in *Long Live the Emperor!: Uses of the Ming Founder across Six Centuries of East Asian History*, ed. Sarah Schneewind (Minneapolis: Society for Ming Studies, 2008), 55–72.

49 *Jiangxi sheng dazhi*, 7.26a; Chinese University of Hong Kong Art Museum, *Shimmering Colours: Monochromes of the Yuan to Qing Periods: The Zhuyuetang*

Collection (五色瓊霞: 竹月堂藏元明清一道釉瓷器) (The Chinese University of Hong Kong Art Museum, 2005); Margaret Medley, *Illustrated Catalogue of Ming and Qing Monochrome Wares* (University of London, Percival David Foundation of Chinese Art, School of Oriental and African Studies, 1989).

50 It is possible that this term, powdered lead, refers to lead oxide, which would be easier to render into powder than metallic lead. This ingredient is used to lower the firing temperature and to produce shine and brilliance. Personal communication from Dr Saul Guerrero (15 December 2018).

51 *Jiangxi sheng dazhi*, 7.26a.

52 7.26a.

53 7.26a; Kerr and Wood describe the clay as 'purple gold'. Kerr and Wood, *Ceramic Technology*, 439.

54 Ibid., 633.

55 On *shiziqing*, see R. Wen et al., 'The Chemical Composition of Blue Pigment on Chinese Blue-and-White Porcelain of the Yuan and Ming Dynasties (1271–1644)', *Archaeometry* 49, 1 (2007): 101–115.

56 Lan Pin-nan and Cheng T'ing-kuei, *Ching-Te-Chen T'ao-Lu or The Potteries of China*, 26.

57 *Jiangxi sheng dazhi*, 7.26a.

58 Kerr and Wood, *Ceramic Technology*, 563.

59 *Jiangxi sheng dazhi*, 7.26a.

60 Kerr and Wood, *Ceramic Technology*, 43.

61 Ibid., 631.

62 *Jiangxi sheng dazhi*, 7.26a.; On *shizi qing*, see further below. Wen et al., 'The Chemical Composition of Blue Pigment on Chinese Blue-and-White Porcelain'.

63 *Jiangxi sheng dazhi*, 7.26a; see also the translation on Lan Pin-nan and Cheng T'ing-kuei, *Ching-Te-Chen T'ao-Lu or The Potteries of China*, 25.

64 *Jiangxi sheng dazhi*, 7.26a.

65 7.26a.

66 7.26a.

67 7.26a.

68 7.26a.

69 7.29a.

70 7.23a.

71 7.29a.

72 7.29b.

73 7.31b.

74 7.31b.

75 7.29a.

76 7.31b.

77 For the unit price, see 7.29b; for the specification of the quantity, see 7.31b.

78 *Jiangxi sheng dazhi*, 7.32b.

79 7.32b.

80 7.32b.

Chapter 9 Skilled Hands

1 Francesca Bray, *Technology and Gender: Fabrics of Power in Late Imperial China* (Berkeley: University of California Press, 1997), 93.

2 When the first emperor of the Ming, Zhu Yuanzhang, came to the throne in 1368, he ordered that 'each household must enrol with the authorities just as they had previously been enrolled. Any change of their registers is forbidden'. The first order to register the population was issued on the first day of the 11th month of the 18th year of the Zhizheng reign (i.e. 1 December 1358). See *Ming shilu*, vol. 1, 70. See also Wang Yuquan, 'Some Salient Features of the Ming Labor Service System', *Ming Studies*, 1 (1986): 3. Wang refers to *Da Ming huidian* (1587: rpt. Taiwan, 1964), vol. 1, 350.

3 The impact of this variety of tax obligations on the villages in Huizhou is insightfully analysed in McDermott, *The Making of a New Rural Order in South China*.

4 Heinz Friese, *Das Dienstleistungs-System der Ming-Zeit, 1368–1644* (Hamburg: Gesellschaft für Natur- und Völkerkunde Ostasiens, 1959).

5 Ray Huang, 'The Ming Fiscal Administration', in *Cambridge History of China*, ed. Denis Twitchett and Frederick W. Mote, vol. 8: The Ming Dynasty, 1368–1644, Part 2 (Cambridge University Press, 1998), 134–135.

6 Edward M. Farmer, *Zhu Yuanzhang & Early Ming Legislation* (Leiden: Brill, 1995), 161. On the unchangeable laws, see also page 17. Friese, *Das Dienstleistungs-System*, 28–29; on the status of Zhu Yuanzhang's laws under subsequent Ming emperors, see some of the studies in Sarah Schneewind, ed., *Long Live the Emperor!: Uses of the Ming Founder across Six Centuries of East Asian History* (Minneapolis: Society for Ming Studies, 2008).

7 For a full listing of these 45 categories, see Wang Yuquan, 'Some Salient Features of the Ming Labor Service System', 25–29.

8 *Lun ban* literally means work in rotation. The other category were the settled artisans, the *zhuzuojiang*, who were all registered in and around the capital, and all served within the imperial household, and fell under the jurisdiction of the eunuchs in the imperial palace. Friese, *Das Dienstleistungs-System*, 118–122.

9 The same was true for those who worked in the silk or textile industries, which were largely located in the Suzhou and Hangzhou area, where the climate was suitable for raising silk worms. Most other manufactures, however, were located within reach of the imperial capital.

10 *Jiangxi sheng dazhi*, 7.21a.

11 Workers for the imperial kiln were dispatched from seven counties in the region: Poyang, Yugan, Leping, Fuliang, Wannian, Anren and Dexing.

12 *Jiangxi sheng dazhi*, 7.6b.

13 7.6b.

14 7.6b.

15 7.6b.

16 The artisans that were resident in or near the capital and served in the *Jiangzuoyuan* (artisans known as residential artisans or *zhuzuo renjiang*) were not allowed to commute their service to payment. Friese, *Das Dienstleistungs-System*, 129; see also Robert Lee, 'The Artisans of Ching-Tê-Chên in Late Imperial China' (MA thesis, University of British Columbia, 1980), 4, 8–13.

17 Martin Heijdra, 'The Socio-Economic Development of Rural China during the Ming', in *The Cambridge History of China. Vol. 8, The Ming Dynasty, 1368–1644, Pt. 2*, ed. Denis Crispin Twitchett and Frederick W. Mote (Cambridge University Press, 1998), 456–457; von Glahn, *An Economic History of China*, 307, 346.

18 William Guanglin Liu, *The Chinese Market Economy, 1000–1500* (Albany: State University of New York Press, 2015).

19 The demand for silver in China from the sixteenth century onwards has been widely documented. The work of Dennis Flynn and Giráldez is a good starting point, and a number of their studies have been brought together in Flynn and Giráldez, *China and the Birth of Globalization in the 16th Century*; for a strong argument in favour of seeing China's demand for silver as shaping factor for the world economy, see Frank, *ReOrient*.

20 Heijdra, 'The Socio-Economic Development of Rural China during the Ming', 456; Friese, *Das Dienstleistungs-System*, 18, 128–129.

21 *Jiangxi sheng dazhi*, 7.21a.

22 7.21b.

23 Kerr and Wood, *Ceramic Technology*, 212.

24 *Jiangxi sheng dazhi*, 7.22a–b.

25 Li Bozhong, *Agricultural Development in Jiangnan, 1620–1850* (Basingstoke: Macmillan, 1998), 208n30.

26 *Jiangxi sheng dazhi*, 7.22b.

27 Li Kangying, *The Ming Maritime Trade Policy in Transition, 1368 to 1567* (Wiesbaden: Harrassowitz, 2010), 66. Li's source is a text by the sixteenth-century Jiang Yihua, *Xitai manji*, 4.5a.

28 Li Bozhong, *Agricultural Development in Jiangnan, 1620–1850*, 92.

29 Liu, *The Chinese Market Economy*, 3.

30 Ray Huang, *Taxation and Governmental Finance in Sixteenth-Century Ming China* (Cambridge University Press, 1974), 263.

31 Liu, *The Chinese Market Economy*, 264.

32 Tichane, *Ching-Te-Chen*, 144.

33 Kenneth Pomeranz, 'Labour-Intensive Industrialization in the Rural Yangzi Delta: Late Imperial Patterns and Their Modern Fates', in *Labour-Intensive Industrialization in Global History*, ed. Gareth Austin and Kaoru Sugihara (London, New York: Routledge, 2013), 122.

34 *Jiangxi sheng dazhi*, 7.23a.

35 7.23a–b.

36 7.21a. The Chinese text reads 官匠凡三百餘名而復招募蓋工緻之匠少而繪事 尤難.

37 7.23b–24a.

38 The term for highly skilled workers is *gao shou* 高手. The term for the failed pots is *kuyu* 苦窳. 7.24a.

39 8.23b–24a. Workers with some ability is rendered as 有堪用之匠.

40 7.24a.於起工之日多雇堪用民匠分補.

41 Kerr and Wood, *Ceramic Technology*, 198.

42 Ibid., 199; Lee, 'The Artisans of Ching-Te-Chen', 29.

43 *Jiangxi sheng dazhi*, 7.3a.

44 7.17a.

45 7.17a–b.

46 Kerr and Wood, *Ceramic Technology*, 200.

47 Lee, 'The Artisans of Ching-Te-Chen'; Tsing Yuan, 'The Porcelain Industry and Ching-Te-Chen, 1550–1700'; Hon Ming Yip, 'The Kuan-Ta-Min-Shao System and Ching-Te-Chen's Porcelain Industry', in *Zhongguo Jinshi Shehui Wenhua Shi Lunwen Ji [Papers on Society and Culture of Early Modern China]* (Taipei: Institute of History and Philology, Academia Sinica, 1992).

48 *Jiangxi sheng dazhi*, 7.17b.

49 7.21b.

50 7.17b.

51 7.17b.

52 7.19a.

53 7.19a–b.

54 7.19b.

55 7.19b.

56 7.7a; Fan Yongguan, *zi* Shuxiu, *hao* Sizhai and Zhoushan, held as his highest position the responsibility for the grain tax circuit (*liangchudao*) in the northern and southern capitals. Fan served in Jingdezhen between 1557 and 1558. See Peng Tao 彭涛, 'Mingdai huanguan zhengzhi yu Jingdezhen de taozheng 明代宦官政治与景德镇的陶政 [The eunuch system of the Ming dynasty and the governance of Jingdezhen]', *Nanfang wenwu*, 2 (2006): 119.

57 *Jiangxi sheng dazhi*, 7.7a. The total number of workers listed here actually comes to 261, not 260, but presumably this is a simple accounting error on the part of the gazetteer compilers.

58 7.7a.

59 Chen Dian's comparison between different editions of Taoshu shows clearly that later revisions merely added later iterations of the same problem, without finding adequate solutions. Chen Dian 陈殿, 'Wang Zongmu zuan yu Lu Wan'gai zengxiu *Jiangxisheng dazhi – Taoshu* de bijiao yanjiu 王宗沐纂与陆万垓增修 《江西省大志·陶书》的比较研究 [Comparison of the editions of Taoshu in Jiangxisheng dazhi by Wang Zongmu and the enlarged revision by Lu Wan'gai]', *Dongfang bowu* 4 (2012): 16–22.

60 Mei Yantao 梅彦騊 and Li Baozhen 李葆貞, eds., *(Shunzhi) Pucheng xianzhi (順治)浦城縣志*, Shunzhi 8 nian (1651) keben (Beijing: Airusheng, 2009), 8 (zhong). 24a–b. His biography can be also found in Weng Tianhu 翁天祐, Lü Weiying 吕渭英, and Weng Zhaotai 翁昭泰, eds., *Guangxu xuxiu Pucheng xianzhi* 光緒續修浦城縣志, Reprint of blockprint edition of 1900, Zhongguo difangzhi jicheng (Shanghai shudian, 2000), juan 22.39a–b.

61 *Jiangxi sheng dazhi*, 6.20a; see also *Pucheng xianzhi*, 8 (zhong). 24a.

62 *Pucheng xianzhi*, 8 (zhong) 24b. On the Office of Scrutiny, see Daniel Bryant, 'A Note on the Yi-Yüan Jen-Chien', *Ming Studies* 2011, 63 (2011): 69–72; see also the insightful discussion of this administrative role within the central government in Ka-chai Tam, 'Favourable Institutional Circumstances for the Publication of Judicial Works in Late Ming China', *Études Chinoises* 28 (2009): 51–71.

63 The classic study of the censorial system is Charles O. Hucker, *The Censorial System of Ming China* (Stanford University Press, 1966). See there for a general discussion of the role of supervising secretaries.

64 *Jiangxi sheng dazhi*, 7.10a.

65 *Lunyu* 4.12. The translation is by Ames. See Roger T. Ames and Henry Rosemont, trans., *The Analects of Confucius: A Philosophical Translation* (New York: Ballantine, 1998), 91.

66 Xu Pu used the very term in his memorial sent to the emperor about the reforms of the administration in Jingdezhen, discussed below.

67 *Jiangxi sheng dazhi*, 7.10a.

68 7.10a.

69 7.10a.

70 7.10a.

71 7.10a.

72 7.10a.

73 7.10a.

74 7.10b.

Chapter 10 Material Circulations in the Sixteenth Century

1 See inventory number AK-NM-15327.

2 Known as 'jarlets', such small jars were in popular demands throughout Southeast Asia, but particularly in Vietnam. Dr John Johnston (Academy of Visual Arts, Hong Kong Baptist University) is at present engaged in research on this topic.

3 Hung-Guk Cho, 'The Trade between China, Japan, Korea and Southeast Asia in the 14th Century through the 17th Century Period', *International Area Studies Review* 3, 2 (2000): 67–107.

4 Dawn Rooney, 'The Recessed Base (Hole-Bottom) Saucer: A Type of Chinese Export Ware', *Arts of Asia* 12, 1 (1982): 114–118. Such wares with a recessed base

are part of the collection of ceramics from mainland Southeast Asia in the Freer Gallery of Art and Arthur M. Sackler Gallery. Curatorial remarks by Louise Cort confirm that this type of ware was made in Fujian or Guangdong in the fifteenth and sixteenth centuries, for export to the Philippines. See https://seasianceramics.asia.si.edu, consulted on 21 January 2014.

5 John Alexander Pope, *Fourteenth-Century Blue-and-White: A Group of Chinese Porcelains in the Topkapu Sarayi Müzesi, Istanbul*, Freer Gallery of Art. Occasional Papers; 1952, 2, 1 (Washington: Smithsonian Institution, 1952); John Alexander Pope, *Chinese Porcelains from the Ardebil Shrine* (Washington, DC: Smithsonian Institution, 1956).

6 Krahl, 'Export Porcelain Fit for the Chinese Emperor'.

7 Derek Kennet, 'Julfar and the Urbanisation of Southeast Arabia', *Arabian Archaeology and Epigraphy* 14, 1 (2003): 103–125; see also the ethnological study by William Lancaster and Fidelity Lancaster, 'Pottery Makers and Pottery Users: In Ras Al-Khaimah Emirate and Musandam Wilayat of Oman, and around Ra's Al-Junayz in the South-east of Ja'alan Wilayat, Oman', *Arabian Archaeology and Epigraphy* 21, 2 (2010): 199–255.

8 Cheryl Ward, 'The Sadana Island Shipwreck: An Eighteenth-Century AD Merchantman off the Red Sea Coast of Egypt', *World Archaeology* 32, 3 (2001): 368–382; Cheryl Ward, 'Chinese Porcelain for the Ottoman Court: Sadana Island, Egypt', in *Beneath the Seven Seas: Adventures with the Institute of Nautical Archaeology*, ed. George Fletcher Bass (London: Thames & Hudson, 2005), 186–191.

9 McDermott, *The Making of a New Rural Order in South China*, 378.

10 Archaeological excavations at the Maravi capital, Mankhamba, have yielded substantial quantities of Chinese porcelain, dated to the last decades of the sixteenth century. Yusuf M. Juwayeyi, 'Archaeological Excavations at Mankhamba, Malawi: An Early Settlement Site of the Maravi', *Azania: Archaeological Research in Africa* 45, 2 (2010): 179. On the basis of the shards of Chinese porcelains, a minimum number could be established: four plates in the first and second layer, and a further 19 cups of bowls in layers three and four. See Juwayeyi, page 188.

11 Polo, *The Travels of Marco Polo*, 238; see also Gerritsen and McDowall, 'Material Culture and the Other'.

12 Galeote Pereira, Gaspar da Cruz and Martín de Rada, *South China in the Sixteenth Century: Being the Narratives of Galeote Pereira, Fr. Gaspar da Cruz, Fr. Martín de Rada (1550–1575)*, trans. C. R. Boxer (London: Hakluyt Society, 1953), 126–127.

13 This information comes from the 1597 account by the official historian of Portuguese India, Diogo do Couto, who lived in India between 1559 and 1616. It has been translated and included in Charles Ralph Boxer, *The Christian Century in Japan: 1549–1650* (Berkeley: University of California Press, 1951), 24.

14 Christiaan Jörg, 'The Portuguese and the trade in Chinese porcelain: from the beginning until the end of the Ming dynasty', in *Portugal na porcelana da China: 500 andos de comércio (Portugal in porcelain from China: 500 years of trade)*, ed. Alberto Varela Santos, vol. 1 (Lisboa: Artemágica, 2007), 47–71.

15 The standard work on the history of the 'first orders' in the trade in porcelain between Portugal and China is Alberto Varela Santos, ed., *Portugal na porcelana da China*.

16 Teresa Canepa, 'Silk, Porcelain and Lacquer: China and Japan and Their Trade with Western Europe and the New World 1500–1644: A Survey of Documentary and Material Evidence' (PhD, Leiden University, 2015).

17 The object, which has museum number C.222–1931, came from the late nineteenth-century collection of William Giuseppe Gulland, who spent much of his life as a merchant in Asia. It is discussed in Craig Clunas, ed., *Chinese Export Art and Design* (London: Victoria and Albert Museum, 1987), figure 12; Reino Liefkes and Hilary Young, eds., *Masterpieces of World Ceramics in the Victoria and Albert Museum* (London: V&A Publishing, 2008), 68–69. In 2012, the piece featured in an exhibition at the National Museum of China, entitled 'Passion for Porcelain: masterpieces of ceramics from the British Museum and the Victoria and Albert Museum'.

18 Harrison-Hall, *Catalogue of Late Yuan and Ming Ceramics*, 9–10.

19 Varela Santos, *Portugal na porcelana da China*, 1:160. As all Portuguese merchants were forbidden from entering China at this time, Peixoto and his two partners conducted their trade at sea in the port of Quanzhou. Jörg, 'The Portuguese and the trade in Chinese porcelain', 63.

20 The shape of the shield is 'peninsular' (also known as Portuguese), and is chequered. There is a barred helmet, turned to the left, with straps on the side of the helmet, and decorative mantling fluttering around the helmet. Varela Santos, *Portugal na porcelana da China*, 1:160.

21 Jörg, 'The Portuguese and the trade in Chinese porcelain', 63; Pereira, Cruz and Rada, *South China in the Sixteenth Century*, xix–xxxvii; Zhidong Hao, *Macau History and Society* (Hong Kong University Press, 2011), 11.

22 Dana Leibsohn, 'Made in China, Made in Mexico', in *At the Crossroads: The Arts of Spanish America & Early Global Trade, 1492–1850*, ed. Donna Pierce and Ronald Y. Otsuka (Denver Art Museum, 2012), 11–40.

23 See the chapter entitled 'From Junk to Galleon: Commercial Activity in Manila' in Meha Priyadarshini, *Chinese Porcelain in Colonial Mexico: The Material Worlds of an Early Modern Trade* (London: Palgrave Macmillan, 2018), 63–96.

24 Francisco Bethencourt, 'The Iberian Atlantic: Ties, Networks, and Boundaries', in *Theorising the Ibero-American Atlantic*, ed. Harald E. Braun and Lisa Vollendorf (Leiden: Brill, 2013), 25–30.

25 Cinta Krahe, *Chinese Porcelain in Habsburg Spain* (Madrid: Centro de Estudios Europa Hispanica, 2016).

26 One example is the travel account of Jan Huygen van Linschoten, *Itinerario voyage ofte schipvaert van Jan Huygen van Linschoten naer Oost ofte Portugaels Indien 1579–1592* ('s-Gravenhage: M. Nijhoff, 1955).

27 Karina Corrigan, Jan van Campen and Femke Diercks, eds., *Asia in Amsterdam: The Culture of Luxury in the Golden Age* (Salem, MA: Peabody Essex Museum, 2015), 261.

28 Thijs Weststeijn, 'Cultural Reflections on Porcelain in the Seventeenth-Century Netherlands', in *Chinese and Japanese Porcelain for the Dutch Golden Age*, ed. Jan van Campen and Titus M. Eliëns (Zwolle: Waanders, 2014), 213–229.

11 Local and Global in Jingdezhen's Long Seventeenth Century

1 The following are just a small selection of the large volume of publications that engage with what I call here a 'global turn'. Kenneth Pomeranz, *The Great Divergence: China, Europe, and the Making of the Modern World Economy* (Princeton University Press, 2000); Hans Medick, 'Turning Global? Microhistory in Extension', *Historische Anthropologie* 24, 2 (2016): 241–252; D. R. Woolf, *A Global History of History* (Cambridge University Press, 2011); Berg, *Writing the History of the Global*; Anne Gerritsen, 'From Long-Distance Trade to the Global Lives of Things: Writing the History of Early Modern Trade and Material Culture', *Journal of Early Modern History* 20, 6 (2016): 526–544; Dominic Sachsenmaier, *Global Perspectives on Global History: Theories and Approaches in a Connected World* (Cambridge University Press, 2011); O'Brien, 'Historiographical Traditions and Modern Imperatives for the Restoration of Global History'; Giorgio Riello, 'The Globalization of Cotton Textiles: Indian Cottons, Europe, and the Atlantic World, 1600–1850', in *The Spinning World: A Global History of Cotton Textiles, 1200–1850*, ed. Giorgio Riello and Prasannan Parthasarathi (Oxford University Press, 2009), 261–287; James Belich et al., eds., *The Prospect of Global History* (Oxford University Press, 2016).

2 The phrase 'turn' was first used as part of the linguistic turn. See Gabrielle M Spiegel, ed., *Practicing History: New Directions in Historical Writing after the Linguistic Turn* (London: Routledge, 2005); and especially Geoff Eley, 'Is All the World a Text? From Social History to the History of Society Two Decades Later', in *Practicing History: New Directions in Historical Writing after the Linguistic Turn*, ed. Gabrielle M. Spiegel (London: Routledge, 2005), 35–61.

3 For a fuller discussion of this, see Anne Gerritsen and Christian De Vito, 'Micro-Spatial Histories of Labour: Towards a New Global History', in *Micro-Spatial*

Histories of Global Labour, ed. Christian G. De Vito and Anne Gerritsen (Cham: Palgrave MacMillan, 2018), 1–28.

4 One of the most influential texts bringing this 'spatial turn' about is Doreen B. Massey, *For Space* (London; Thousand Oaks, CA: Sage, 2005); see also more recent publications like Barney Warf, *The Spatial Turn: Interdisciplinary Perspectives* (London: Routledge, 2014); Marijn Nieuwenhuis and David Crouch, eds., *The Question of Space: Interrogating the Spatial Turn between Disciplines* (London: Rowman & Littlefield, 2017).

5 Gerritsen and De Vito, 'Micro-Spatial Histories of Global Labour'.

6 Liang Miaotai 梁淼泰, *Ming Qing Jingdezhen chengshi jingji yanjiu.*

7 This is also the case, for example, in the classic study of Jingdezhen in Japanese: Sakuma Shigeo 佐久間重男, *Keitokuchin Yōgyōshi Kenkyū* 景德鎮窯業史研究; see also Jingdezhen shi difangzhi bianzuan weiyuanhui, ed., *Zhongguo cidu: Jingdezhen shi* 中国瓷都 ·景德镇市 *[Porcelain capital of China: The City of Jingdezhen]*, 2 vols (Beijing: Fangzhi chubanshe, 2004).

8 Finlay, *The Pilgrim Art*, 2010; see also his earlier article on the same topic: 'The Pilgrim Art', 1998.

9 Rosemary E. Scott, ed., *The Porcelains of Jingdezhen* (London: Percival David Foundation of Chinese Art, 1993); Wang Xiaofeng, *Jingdezhen: qiannian cidu* 景德鎮：千年瓷都 (Nanchang: Jiangxi renmin chubanshe, 2015); Qianshen Bai, 'Inscriptions, Calligraphy and Seals on Jingdezhen Porcelains from the Shunzhi Era', in *Treasures from an Unknown Reign: Shunzhi Porcelain, 1644–1661*, ed. Michael Butler, Julia B. Curtis and Stephen Little (Alexandria, VA: Art Services International in Association with the University of Washington Press, Seattle, 2002), 56–67.

10 Stacey Pierson is one of the scholars who have worked on this extensively. See, for two examples, Stacey Pierson, *From Object to Concept: Global Consumption and the Transformation of Ming Porcelain* (Hong Kong University Press, 2013); and 'The Movement of Chinese Ceramics: Appropriation in Global History', *Journal of World History* 23, 1 (2012): 9–39.

11 Gugong bowu yuan (Taiwan), *Ru yao* 汝窯 *[Ru wares]* (Hong Kong: Kaifa gufen youxian gongsi, 1961); Percival David, *A Commentary on Ju Ware* (London: Shenval Press, 1937); more recent studies, especially archeological studies, begin to sketch a different picture. See, for example, Sun Xinmin, 'Recent Excavations at the Ru Kiln: Qingliangsi'.

12 John Carswell, *Blue & White: Chinese Porcelain around the World* (London: British Museum Press, 2007).

13 On the export of porcelain to Southeast Asia, see Wang Dayuan 汪大淵, *Daoyi zhilüe jiaoshi* 島夷誌略校釋 *[Annotated edition of the 'Report of the Island Barbarians']*; Zhao Bing, 'Global Trade and Swahili Cosmopolitan Material Culture'; Gerritsen and McDowall, 'Material Culture and the Other'.

14 The foundational work of Rose Kerr and Nigel Wood is an interesting example. Their work addresses both the history of production for the various sites, and what they call 'ceramic transfer', where the story of porcelain is traced beyond the Chinese cultural context. But the sections of the book are firmly separate. Kerr and Wood, *Ceramic Technology.*

15 A recent example is Yan Chongnian 阎崇年, *Yu yao qian nian* 御窑千年 *[A thousand years of imperial kilns]* (Beijing: Sanlian, 2017).

16 T. Volker, *Porcelain and the Dutch East India Company, as Recorded in the Dagh-Registers of Batavia Castle, Those of Hirado and Deshima and Other Contemporary Papers 1602–1682* (Leiden: Brill, 1954); C. J. A. Jörg, *Porcelain and the Dutch China Trade* (The Hague: M. Nijhoff, 1982); for more recent studies on the topic, see Jan van Campen and Titus M Eliëns, eds., *Chinese and Japanese Porcelain for the Dutch Golden Age* (Zwolle: Waanders Uitgevers, 2014).

17 Christine L. van der Pijl-Ketel and Johannes Bastiaan Kist, *The Ceramic Load of the 'Witte Leeuw' (1613)* (Amsterdam: Rijksmuseum, 1982); see also Christine Ketel's ongoing PhD research at the University of Leiden; Hui (Claire) Tang, ' "The Colours of Each Piece": Production and Consumption of Chinese Enamelled Porcelain, c.1728–c.1780' (PhD, University of Warwick, 2017).

18 Anne E. C. McCants, 'Exotic Goods, Popular Consumption, and the Standard of Living: Thinking about Globalization in the Early Modern World', *Journal of World History* 18, 4 (2007): 433–462; Anne E. C. McCants, 'Asiatic Goods in Migrant and Native-Born Middling Households', in *Goods from the East, 1600–1800: Trading Eurasia*, ed. Maxine Berg (Basingstoke: Palgrave Macmillan, 2015), 197–215.

19 Winnie Wong has explored such issues for the contemporary case of the painters' village, Dafen. See Winnie Won Yin Wong, *Van Gogh on Demand: China and the Readymade* (University of Chicago Press, 2013).

20 Liang Miaotai 梁淼泰, *Ming Qing Jingdezhen chengshi jingji yanjiu*, 93; Shigeo Sakuma 佐久間重男, *Keitokuchin yōgyōshi kenkyū*, 232–233.

21 Ibid.

22 His writings exist in many editions. I have mostly used the edition of his texts included in *Zhongguo taoci guji jicheng*, 288–306.

23 Tang Ying was a member of a Chinese banner family. His biography was included in the draft of the Qing History. For a biography in English, see Arthur W. Hummel, ed., *Eminent Chinese of the Ch'ing Period, 1644–1912* (Washington: US Government Printing Office, 1943), 442; see also Peter Lam, 'Tang Ying (1682–1756): The Imperial Factory Superintendent at Jingdezhen', *Transactions of the Oriental Ceramics Society* 63 (1999 1998): 65–82.

24 Kerr and Wood, *Ceramic Technology*, 27n124.

25 See the inscription on a series of alter vessels, which starts with the statement 'Made by the Chief Superintendent of Works for the Yangxin Hall'. Ibid., 196.

26 See also the discussion of the relationship between Nian and Tang in Kristina Kleutghen, *Imperial Illusions: Crossing Pictorial Boundaries in the Qing Palaces* (Seattle: University of Washington Press, 2015), 62.

27 Catherine Jami, *The Emperor's New Mathematics Western Learning and Imperial Authority during the Kangxi Reign (1662–1722)* (Oxford University Press, 2012), 322–323. In 1735, Nian Xiyao published an expanded version of his 1729 book entitled *Shixue* [A study of vision], a study he had worked on with the famous Qing court painter Giuseppe Castiglione (1688–1766), as he states in the preface. John Finlay, ' "40 Views of Yuanming Yuan": Image and Ideology in a Qianlong Imperial Album of Poetry and Paintings' (PhD, Yale University, 2011); John Finlay, 'The Qianlong Emperor's Western Vistas: Linear Perspective and Trompe l'Oeil Illusion in the European Palaces of the Yuanming Yuan', *Bulletin de l'École Française d'Extrême-Orient* 94 (2007): 159–193; Kleutghen, *Imperial Illusions*.

28 Kerr and Wood, *Ceramic Technology*, 196.

29 Peter Lam uses 1756 as the date of his death. Lam, 'Tang Ying (1682–1756): The Imperial Factory Superintendent at Jingdezhen'; so does Zhao Bing, 'Érudition, expertise, technique et politique', 143ff.; A much earlier scholar, Hsu Wen-chin uses 1755. Wen-Chin Hsu, 'Social and Economic Factors in the Chinese Porcelain Industry in Jingdezhen during the Late Ming and Early Qing Period, Ca. 1620–1683', *Journal of the Royal Asiatic Society (New Series)* 120, 1 (1988): 146; on Tang Ying's time in Canton, see Huang Chao and Paul A. Van Dyke, 'Hoppo Tang Ying 唐英 (1750–1751) and the Development of the Guangdong Maritime Customs', *Journal of Asian History* 51, 2 (2017): 223–256.

30 Perhaps Tang Ying's most famous text on porcelain is his 1743 *Taoye tu bian ci* (Illustrated Explanation of Ceramics Production). It has been published in numerous forms and was included in the late nineteenth-century edition of Zhao Zhiqian 趙之謙 (1829–1884), *(Guangxu) Jiangxi Tongzhi*; it was also included in *Zhongguo taoci guji jicheng*, 299–306; and in Lan Pu 蓝浦 and Zheng Tinggui 郑廷桂, *Jingdezhen taolu*; it was translated in Stephen Bushell, *Description of Chinese Pottery and Porcelain* (Oxford: Clarendon Press, 1910), 7–30. For an illustrated translation, see Tichane, *Ching-Te-Chen*, 134–171; the references below refer to this edition: Tang Ying 唐英, 'Tao ye tu bian ci 陶冶图编次', in *Zhongguo taoci guji jicheng*, 299–306.

31 Wu Shaoshi, *zi* Ernan, was a man from Haifeng in Shandong. Wu Shaoshi and his son Wu Tan feature extensively in Philip A. Kuhn, *Soulstealers: The Chinese Sorcery Scare of 1768* (Cambridge, MA: Harvard University Press, 1990); see also Hsiung Ping-chen 熊秉真, 'Qing zhengfu dui Jiangxi de jingying 清政府對江西的經營 [The management of Jiangxi under the Qing government]', *Jindai shi yanjiusuo jikan* 18 (1989): 37–74.

32　Percival David, 'The T'ao Shuo and "The Illustrations of Pottery Manufacture": A Critical Study and a Review Reviewed', *Artibus Asiae* 12, 3 (1949): 166.

33　Christine Moll-Murata, 'Guilds and Apprenticeship in China and Europe: The Jingdezhen and European Ceramics Industries', in *Technology, Skills and the Pre-Modern Economy in the East and the West*, ed. Stephan R. Epstein, Maarten Prak and Jan Luiten van Zanden (Leiden: Brill, 2013), 225–257; for an anthropological perspective, see Tim Ingold, *The Perception of the Environment: Essays on Livelihood, Dwelling and Skill* (London: Routledge, 2000).

34　On the issue of craft and skill in Qing China, see Dorothy Ko, *The Social Life of Inkstones: Artisans and Scholars in Early Qing China* (Seattle: University of Washington Press, 2017), e.g. 231n5.

35　Peter Jackson, trans., *The Mission of Friar William of Rubruck: His Journey to the Court of the Great Khan Möngke 1253–1255* (London: Hakluyt Society, 1990), 203; Gerritsen and McDowall, 'Material Culture and the Other', 87.

36　Polo, *The Travels of Marco Polo*, 238.

37　For a more detailed discussion of these descriptions and their authors, see Gerritsen and McDowall, 'Material Culture and the Other', 94.

38　Quoted in Robert Finlay, 'Weaving the Rainbow: Visions of Color in World History', *Journal of World History* 18, 4 (2007): 426.

39　Louis le Comte, *Memoirs and Observations Typographical, Physical, Mathematical, Mechanical, Natural, Civil, and Ecclesiastical, Made in a Late Journey through the Empire of China, and Published in Several Letters: Particularly upon the Chinese Pottery and Varnishing, the Silk and Other Manufactures, the Pearl Fishing, the History of Plants and Animals, Description of Their Cities and Publick Works, Number of People, Their Language, Manners and Commerce, Their Habits, Oeconomy, and Government, the Philosophy of Confucius, the State of Christianity: With Many Other Curious and Useful Remarks* (London: Printed for BenjTooke, 1697), 158–159.

40　Le Comte, 160.

41　Gerritsen and McDowall, 'Material Culture and the Other', 108.

42　On the specifics of the quantities, see Jörg, *Porcelain and the Dutch China Trade*, 1982.

43　Gerritsen and McDowall, 'Material Culture and the Other', 111–112.

44　Ibid., 110–111.

45　Comment to illustration 10. Tang Ying 唐英, 'Tao ye tu bian ci', 302.

46　A recent study sheds some light on the issue of labour wages in eighteenth-century China. From a range of sources, they identify a daily wage of 0.08 of a tael in Canton, and 0.1 of a tael in Suzhou in 1730. See Robert C. Allen et al., 'Wages, Prices, and Living Standards in China, 1738–1925: In Comparison with Europe, Japan, and India', *The Economic History Review* 64, S1 (2011): 8–38. The 3/10th of a tael per month for grinding work in Jingdezhen amounts to just over 0.01 of a tael per day.

47　Comment to Illustration 10. Tang Ying 唐英, 'Tao ye tu bian ci', 302.

48 Ibid., 301.

49 There is a missing sentence in the Zhongguo taoci guji jicheng edition of the text. The sentence referring to the size of the smaller items has, however, been included in Xie Min 謝旻 (fl. 18th c.), *Jiangxi tong zhi*, 135.83a.

50 Tang Ying 唐英, 'Tao ye tu bian ci', 300–305.

51 Ibid., 303.

52 Comment on Illustration 11. Tang Ying 唐英, 303.

53 Ibid., 11. Ibid., 303.

54 Ibid., 5. Ibid., 301.

55 Ibid., 6. Ibid., 301.

Chapter 12 Epilogue

 1 He Ding and Zhang Jie, 'Vernacular Uses and Cultural Identity of Heritage: Trade of Antique Fragments in the Chinese Porcelain Capital', *International Journal of Heritage Studies* 22, 10 (2016): 849.

 2 Wang Yunxia, 'Enforcing Import Restrictions of China's Cultural Objects: The Sino–US Memorandum of Understanding', in *Enforcing International Cultural Heritage Law*, ed. Francesco Francioni and James Gordley (Oxford University Press, 2013), 240–255.

 3 Liu Xinyuan 刘新园, 'Jiangxi Jingdezhen Guanyinge'.

 4 The work by Maris Gillette addresses some of these issues. Gillette, *China's Porcelain Capital*; see also Gillette, 'Labor and Precariousness in China's Porcelain Capital'; Yu Bin and Xiao Xuan, 'The Ecological Protection Research Based on the Cultural Landscape Space Construction in Jingdezhen', *Procedia Environmental Sciences* 10 (2011): 1829–1834.

 5 Piyush Sharma and Ricky Y. K. Chan, 'Counterfeit Proneness: Conceptualisation and Scale Development', *Journal of Marketing Management* 27, 5–6 (2011): 602–626.

 6 Gillette, 'Copying, Counterfeiting, and Capitalism in Contemporary China'.

 7 Ibid., 368.

 8 Anne Rankin Osborne, 'Barren Mountains, Raging Rivers: The Ecological and Social Effects of Changing Land Use on the Lower Yangzi Periphery in Late Imperial China' (PhD, Columbia University, 1989), 92.

 9 Anne Osborne, 'Highlands and Lowlands: Economic and Ecological Interactions in the Lower Yangzi Region under the Qing', in *Sediments of Time: Environment and Society in Chinese History*, ed. Mark Elvin and Cuirong Liu (Cambridge University Press, 2009), 220.

10 Harry A. Franck, 'A Journey from Kuling to Ching-te-chen', in Tichane, *Ching-Te-Chen*, 378.

11 Frank J. Cosentino, *The Boehm Journey to Ching-Te-Chen, China, Birthplace of Porcelain* (Trenton, NJ: Edward Marshall Boehm, Inc., 1984), 122.

12 Luo Xuan 罗璇 et al., 'Ziyuan kujiexing chengshi tudi zonghe chengzai shuiping fenxi--yi Jiangxisheng Jingdezhen wei lie 资源枯竭型城市土地综合承载水平分析——以江西省景德镇市为例   – Comprehensive Carrying Capacity of Land of Resource-Exhausted Cities——A Case of Jingdezhen, Jiangxi Province', *Jiangxi nongye daxue xuebao: shehui kexue bao* 11, 3 (2012): 101–106.

13 Weihong Chen et al., 'Long-Term Exposure to Silica Dust and Risk of Total and Cause-Specific Mortality in Chinese Workers: A Cohort Study', *PLOS Medicine* 9, 4 (2012).

14 Mike McKiernan, 'La Maladie de Porcelaine', *Occupational Medicine* 61, 3 (2011): 146–147; Xiaokang Zhang et al., 'Cohort Mortality Study in Three Ceramic Factories in Jingdezhen in China', *Journal of Huazhong University of Science and Technology [Medical Sciences]* 28, 4 (2008): 386–390; Satiavani Poinen-Rughooputh et al., 'Occupational Exposure to Silica Dust and Risk of Lung Cancer: An Updated Meta-Analysis of Epidemiological Studies', *BMC Public Health* 16, 1 (2016).

15 Pere d'Entrecolles, 'Letter I' in Tichane, *Ching-Te-Chen*, 77, 97.

16 'On jette de la chaux vive pour consumer les chairs'. Père d'Entrecolles, 'Lettre au Père Orry', in Bushell, *Description of Chinese Pottery and Porcelain*, 209.

17 He Ding and Zhang Jie, 'Vernacular Uses and Cultural Identity of Heritage'.

18 Wang Yunxia, 'Enforcing Import Restrictions'.

19 Laurence Massy, 'The Antiquity Art Market: Between Legality and Illegality', ed. Paul Ponsaers, *International Journal of Social Economics* 35, 10 (2008): 729.

20 O'Brien, 'Historiographical Traditions and Modern Imperatives for the Restoration of Global History'.

21 Riello, *Cotton*.

22 For some of the collaborative work we have done in this area, see Zoltán Biedermann, Anne Gerritsen and Giorgio Riello, eds., *Global Gifts: The Material Culture of Diplomacy in Early Modern Eurasia* (Cambridge University Press, 2018); Gerritsen and McDowall, 'Material Culture and the Other'; Giorgio Riello and Anne Gerritsen, eds., *Writing Material Culture History* (London: Bloomsbury, 2015); Anne Gerritsen and Giorgio Riello, eds., *The Global Lives of Things: The Material Culture of Connections in the Early Modern World*, 2016; for a historiographical overview of this subject, see Gerritsen, 'From Long-Distance Trade to the Global Lives of Things'.

23 One example is this classic study: Alfred W. Jr Crosby, *The Columbian Exchange: Biological and Cultural Consequences of 1492* (Westport, CO: Greenwood Press, 1972).

24 L. P. Hartley, *The Go-Between* (1953; repr., Camberwell: Penguin Books, 2010).

Bibliography

'A D Brankston (Biographical Details)'. British Museum. Accessed 23 March 2017. www.britishmuseum.org/research/search_the_collection_database/term_details.aspx?bioId=141986.

Abu-Lughod, Janet L. *Before European Hegemony: The World System A.D. 1250–1350*. Oxford University Press, 1989.

Addis, J. M. 'The Dating of Chinese Porcelain Found in the Philippines: A Historical Retrospect'. *Philippine Studies* 16, no. 2 (1968): 371–380.

Akerman, James R. *The Imperial Map: Cartography and the Mastery of Empire*. University of Chicago Press, 2009.

Allen, Robert C., Jean-Pascal Bassino, Debin Ma, Christine Moll-Murata and Jan Luiten van Zanden. 'Wages, Prices, and Living Standards in China, 1738–1925: In Comparison with Europe, Japan, and India'. *The Economic History Review* 64, no. S1 (2011): 8–38.

Allsen, Thomas T. *Commodity and Exchange in the Mongol Empire: A Cultural History of Islamic Textiles*. Cambridge University Press, 1997.

'The Cultural Worlds of Marco Polo'. *Journal of Interdisciplinary History* 31, no. 3 (2001): 375–383.

Ames, Roger T. and Henry Rosemont, trans. *The Analects of Confucius: A Philosophical Translation*. New York: Ballantine, 1998.

Arasaratnam, S. 'Recent Trends in the Historiography of the Indian Ocean, 1500 to 1800'. *Journal of World History* 1, no. 2 (1990): 225–248.

Arnold, Lauren. *Princely Gifts and Papal Treasures: The Franciscan Mission to China and its Influence on the Art of the West, 1250–1350*. San Francisco: Desiderata Press, 1999.

Ashton, A. L. B. 'Early Blue and White in Persian Mss'. *Transactions of the Oriental Ceramic Society* 1934–1935 (1936): 21–25.

Ayers, John G. 'Discovery of a Yuan Ship at Sinan, Southwest Korea – 1st Report'. *Oriental Art* 24, no. 1 (1978): 79–85.

Baghdiantz McCabe, Ina. *A History of Global Consumption: 1500–1800*. London: Routledge, 2015.

Bai, Qianshen. 'Inscriptions, Calligraphy and Seals on Jingdezhen Porcelains from the Shunzhi Era'. In *Treasures from an Unknown Reign: Shunzhi Porcelain, 1644–1661*, edited by Michael Butler, Julia B. Curtis and Stephen Little, 56–67. Alexandria, VA: Art Services International in association with the University of Washington Press, Seattle, 2002.

Bandaranayake, Senake and Madhyama Saṃskṛtika Aramudala (Sri Lanka). *Sri Lanka and the Silk Road of the Sea*. Colombo: Sri Lanka Institute of International Relations, 2003.

Batchelor, Robert K. *London: The Selden Map and the Making of a Global City, 1549–1689*. University of Chicago Press, 2014.

Beckwith, Christopher I. *Empires of the Silk Road: A History of Central Eurasia from the Bronze Age to the Present*. Princeton University Press, 2011.

Beijing daxue kaogu wenbo xueyuan, and Jiangxi sheng wenwu kaogu yanjiusuo. *Jingdezhen chutu Mingdai yuyao ciqi* 景德镇出土明代御窑瓷器 [Porcelain from the Ming imperial kilns excavated in Jingdezhen]. Beijing: Wenwu chubanshe, 2009.

Beijing daxue kaogu xuexi. *Guantai Cizhou yao zhi* 观台磁州窑址 [The Cizhou kiln site at Guantai]. Beijing: Wenwu chubanshe, 1997.

Beijing wenwu jiansheng bianweihui. *Porcelains of the Yuan dynasty* 元代瓷器. Beijing: Beijing meishu sheying chubanshe, 2005.

Belich, James, John Darwin, Margret Frenz and Chris Wickham, eds. *The Prospect of Global History*. Oxford University Press, 2016.

Benn, James A. *Tea in China: A Religious and Cultural History*. Honolulu: University of Hawai'i Press, 2015.

Berg, Maxine. *Writing the History of the Global: Challenges for the 21st Century*. Oxford University Press, 2013.

Bethencourt, Francisco. 'The Iberian Atlantic: Ties, Networks, and Boundaries'. In *Theorising the Ibero-American Atlantic*, edited by Harald E. Braun and Lisa Vollendorf, 15–36. Leiden: Brill, 2013.

Bickford, Maggie. *Ink Plum: The Making of a Chinese Scholar-Painting Genre*. Cambridge University Press, 1996.

Biedermann, Zoltán, Anne Gerritsen and Giorgio Riello, eds. *Global Gifts: The Material Culture of Diplomacy in Early Modern Eurasia*. Cambridge University Press, 2018.

Bin, Yu and Xiao Xuan. 'The Ecological Protection Research Based on the Cultural Landscape Space Construction in Jingdezhen'. *Procedia Environmental Sciences* 10 (2011): 1829–1834.

Biran, Michal. *Chinggis Khan*. Oxford: Oneworld, 2007.

Bloom, Jonathan and Sheila S. Blair, eds. 'Junayd'. In *The Grove Encyclopedia of Islamic Art and Architecture*. Accessed 8 May 2015. www.oxfordislamicstudies.com/article/opr/t276/e454.

Blussé, Leonard. 'Port Cities of South East Asia: 1400–1800'. In *The Oxford Handbook of Cities in World History*, edited by Peter Clark. Oxford University Press, 2013.

Boskovits, Miklós and David Alan Brown. *Italian Paintings of the Fifteenth Century*. Oxford University Press, 2003.

Boxer, Charles Ralph. *The Christian Century in Japan: 1549–1650*. Berkeley: University of California Press, 1951.

Brankston, Archibald Dooley. 'An Excursion to Chingte-Chen and Chi-an-Fu in Kiangsi'. *Transactions of the Oriental Ceramic Society* 16 (1938): 19–32.

'Ceramics from the Eumorfopoulos Collection. Two Vases from Chi-Chou'. *The British Museum Quarterly* 13, no. 2 (1939): 46–47.

Early Ming Wares of Chingtechen. 1938. Reprint, Oxford University Press, 1982.

Bray, Francesca. *Technology and Gender: Fabrics of Power in Late Imperial China*. Berkeley: University of California Press, 1997.

Bray, Francesca, Peter A. Coclanis, Edda L. Fields-Black and Dagmar Schäfer, eds. *Rice: Global Networks and New Histories*. Cambridge University Press, 2015.

Brown, Roxanna M. *The Ming Gap and Shipwreck Ceramics in Southeast Asia: Towards a Chronology of Thai Trade Ware*. Bangkok: Siam Society, 2009.

Brown, Roxanna M. and Sten Sjostrand. *Turiang: A Fourteenth-Century Shipwreck in Southeast Asian Waters*. Pasadena, CA: Pacific Asia Museum, 2000.

Bruijn, J. T. P. de. 'Ḵᵛāju Kermāni'. Encyclopaedia Iranica, 20 July 2009. www.iranicaonline.org/articles/kvaju-kerman-poet-and-mystic.

Bryant, Daniel. 'A Note on the Yi-yüan Jen-chien'. *Ming Studies* 2011, no. 63 (2011): 69–72.

Bushell, Stephen. *Description of Chinese Pottery and Porcelain*. Oxford: Clarendon Press, 1910.

Campen, Jan van and Titus M Eliëns, eds. *Chinese and Japanese Porcelain for the Dutch Golden Age*. Zwolle: Waanders Uitgevers, 2014.

Canepa, Teresa. 'Silk, Porcelain and Lacquer: China and Japan and Their Trade with Western Europe and the New World 1500–1644: A Survey of Documentary and Material Evidence'. PhD, Leiden University, 2015.

Cao Guoqing 曹国庆. *Zhongguo chutu ciqi quanji* 中國出土瓷器全集 [Porcelain excavated in China]. Edited by Zhang Bai. Vol. 14: Jiangxi. Beijing: Kexue chubanshe, 2008.

Cao Zhao 曹昭 (14th c.). *Xinzeng Gegu yaolun* 新增格古要論 [Newly enlarged Gegu yaolun]. 1459. Reprint, Changsha: Shangwu chubanshe, 1939.

Gegu yaolun 格古要論 [Essential criteria of antiquities]. Yingyin Wenyuange Siku quanshu. Taipei: Taiwan shangwu yinshuguan, 1983.

Carswell, John. *Blue & White: Chinese Porcelain Around the World*. London: British Museum Press, 2007.

'Ceramics Today – Jingdezhen 2004'. Accessed 30 January 2017. www.ceramicstoday.com/articles/jingdezhen.htm.

Chaffee, John W. *Branches of Heaven: A History of the Imperial Clan of Sung China*. Cambridge, MA: Harvard University Asia Center, 1999.

Chan, Hok-Lam. 'The Rise of Ming T'ai-tsu (1368–98): Facts and Fictions in Early Ming Official Historiography'. *Journal of the American Oriental Society* 95, no. 4 (1975): 679–715.

'Xie Jin (1369–1415) as Imperial Propagandist: His Role in the Revisions of the "Ming Taizu Shilu"'. *T'oung Pao* 91, no. 1–3 (2005): 58–124.

Chang, Kuei-Sheng. 'Africa and the Indian Ocean in Chinese Maps of the Fourteenth and Fifteenth Centuries'. *Imago Mundi* 24, no. 1 (1970): 21–30.

Charleston, Robert J. *World Ceramics: An Illustrated History.* Harmondsworth, Middlesex, UK: P. Hamlyn, 2002.

Chaudhuri, Kirti N. *Trade and Civilisation in the Indian Ocean: An Economic History from the Rise of Islam to 1750.* Cambridge University Press, 1985.

'Chemistry of Cobalt'. Chemistry LibreTexts, 3 October 2013. https://chem. libretexts.org/Core/Inorganic_Chemistry/Descriptive_Chemistry/Elements_ Organized_by_Block/3_d-Block_Elements/Group_09%3A_Transition_ Metals/Chemistry_of_Cobalt.

Chen Boquan 陈柏泉. 'Jizhou yao shaoci lishi chushen 吉州窑烧瓷历史初探 [Preliminary investigation into the history of firing ceramics at the Jizhou kiln]'. *Jiangxi lishi wenwu*, no. 3 (1982): 25–36.

Chen Defu 陈德富. 'Suining Jinyu cun Jiaocang Song Ci San Yi 遂宁金鱼村窖藏 宋瓷三议. [Three remarks about the Song porcelain in the Jinyu village hoard in Suining]'. *Sichuan wenwu*, no. 5 (1997): 44–51.

Chen Dian 陈殿. 'Wang Zongmu zuan yu Lu Wan'gai zengxiu *Jiangxisheng dazhi* - Taoshu de bijiao yanjiu 王宗沐纂与陆万垓增修《江西省大志·陶书》的比 较研究 [Comparison of the editions of Taoshu in *Jiangxisheng dazhi* by Wang Zongmu and the enlarged revision by Lu Wan'gai]'. *Dongfang bowu* 4 (2012): 16–22.

Chen Lili 陈立立. 'Jizhou Yao Gongjiang Zai Jingdezhen Cidu Diwei Queli Guochengzhong de Zuoyong 吉州窑工匠在景德镇瓷都地位确立过程中的 作用'. *Jiangxi shehui kexue*, no. 8 (2011): 160–165.

Chen Peng 曾庆生 and Zeng Qingsheng 曾庆生. 'Quanzhou Fuhoushan Chutu de Jiangxi Taoqi 泉州府后山出土的江西陶器'. *Jiangxi lishi wenwu* 4 (1983): 73–77.

Chen, Weihong, Yuewei Liu, Haijiao Wang, Eva Hnizdo, Yi Sun, Liangping Su, Xiaokang Zhang, et al. 'Long-Term Exposure to Silica Dust and Risk of Total and Cause-Specific Mortality in Chinese Workers: A Cohort Study'. *PLOS Medicine* 9, no. 4 (2012).

Cheng, Lin, Meitian Li, Junling Wang and Rongwu Li. 'The Study of Ancient Porcelain of Hutian Kiln Site from Five Dynasty (902–979) to Ming Dynasty (1368–1644) by INAA'. *Journal of Radioanalytical and Nuclear Chemistry* 304, no. 2 (2015): 817–822.

Chinese University of Hong Kong Art Museum. *Shimmering Colours: Mono-chromes of the Yuan to Qing Periods: The Zhuyuetang Collection* (五色瓊霞: 竹月堂藏元明清一道釉瓷器). The Chinese University of Hong Kong Art Museum, 2005.

Cho, Hung Guk. 'The Trade Between China, Japan, Korea and Southeast Asia in the 14th Century through the 17th Century Period'. *International Area Studies Review* 3, no. 2 (2000): 67–107.

Church, Sally K. 'Review of Ming Dynasty Baochuanchang Shipyard in Nanjing – by Nanjing Municipal Museum'. *International Journal of Nautical Archaeology* 37, no. 1 (2008): 198–200.

'Zheng He: An Investigation into the Plausibility of 450-Ft Treasure Ships'. *Monumenta Serica* 53, no. 1 (2005): 1–43.

Clunas, Craig. *Chinese Export Art and Design*. London: Victoria and Albert Museum, 1987.

   Screen of Kings: Royal Art and Power in Ming China. Honolulu: University of Hawaiʻi Press, 2013.

Clunas, Craig, Jessica Harrison-Hall and Yu Ping Luk, eds. *Ming China: Courts and Contacts, 1400–1450*. London: The British Museum, 2016.

Cole, F. C. and B. Laufer. *Chinese Pottery in the Philippines*. Chicago, IL: Field Museum of Natural History, 1912.

Cora, Galeazzo and Angiolo Fanfani. *La Porcellana dei Medici*. Milano: Fabbri Editori, 1986.

Corrigan, Karina, Jan van Campen and Femke Diercks, eds. *Asia in Amsterdam: The Culture of Luxury in the Golden Age*. Salem, MA: Peabody Essex Museum, 2015.

Cosentino, Frank J. *The Boehm Journey to Ching-Te-Chen, China, Birthplace of Porcelain*. Trenton, NJ: Edward Marshall Boehm, Inc., 1984.

Crosby, Alfred W. Jr. *The Columbian Exchange: Biological and Cultural Consequences of 1492*. Westport, CN: Greenwood Press, 1972.

Dai Junliang 戴均良. *Zhongguo Gujin Diming Dacidian* 中国古今地名大词典 [Dictionary of old and new placenames in China]. 3 vols. Shanghai cishu chubanshe, 2005.

Dai Yihui 戴仪辉 et al. 'Jiangxi Jingdezhen Liyang ciqi shan Mingdai yaozhi fajue jianbao 江西景德镇丽阳瓷器山明代窑址发掘简报 [Brief excavation report of a Ming kiln site at Liyang in Jingdezhen in Jiangxi]'. *Wenwu*, no. 03 (2007): 17–33+1.

Dardess, John W. *Ming China, 1368–1644: A Concise History of a Resilient Empire*. Lanham, MD: Rowman & Littlefield, 2012.

David, Percival. *A Commentary on Ju Ware*. London: Shenval Press, 1937.

   'The T'ao Shuo and "The Illustrations of Pottery Manufacture": A Critical Study and a Review Reviewed'. *Artibus Asiae* 12, no. 3 (1949): 165–183.

Dennis, Joseph. *Writing, Publishing, and Reading Local Gazetteers in Imperial China, 1100–1700*. Cambridge, MA: Harvard University Asia Center, 2015.

Dillon, Michael. 'Transport and Marketing in the Development of the Jingdezhen Porcelain Industry during the Ming and Qing Dynasties'. *Journal of the Social and Economic History of the Orient* 35, no. 3 (1992): 278–290.

Ding Xiang 定祥 and Liu Yi 劉繹, eds. *[Guangxu] Ji'an Fuzhi* [光緒] 吉安府志 [Prefectural Gazetteer of Ji'an]. 53 vols. 1875.

Ding Yinzhong 丁银忠, Dan Yingying 单莹莹, Xie Chunlong 谢纯龙, Shen Yueming 沈岳明 and Zheng Jianming 郑建明. 'Shanglinhu housi'ao yao zhi ci zhi xiabo de gongyi tezheng yanjiu 上林湖后司岙窑址瓷质匣钵的工艺特征研究 [The characteristics of the porcelain saggars of Shanglinhu Housi'ao kiln site]'. *Palace Museum Journal*, no. 06 (2017): 142–150+161.

Dreyer, Edward L. 'The Poyang Campaign of 1363: Inland Naval Warfare in the Founding of the Ming Dynasty'. In *Chinese Ways in Warfare*, edited by John King Fairbank and Frank Kierman, 202–42. Cambridge, MA: Harvard University Press, 1974.

Zheng He: China and the Oceans in the Early Ming Dynasty, 1405–1433. New York: Pearson Longman, 2007.

Dudbridge, Glen. *A Portrait of Five Dynasties China: From the Memoirs of Wang Renyu (880–956)*. Oxford University Press, 2013.

Dunn, Ross E. *The Adventures of Ibn Battuta: A Muslim Traveler of the 14th Century*. Revised edition. Berkeley: University of California Press, 2012.

Duyvendak, J. J. L. 'The True Dates of the Chinese Maritime Expeditions in the Early Fifteenth Century'. *T'oung Pao* 34 (1939): 341–413.

Ebrey, Patricia Buckley. *Emperor Huizong*. Cambridge, MA: Harvard University Press, 2014.

Ekosse, Georges-Ivo E. 'Kaolin Deposits and Occurrences in Africa: Geology, Mineralogy and Utilization'. *Applied Clay Science* 50, no. 2 (2010): 212–236.

Eley, Geoff. 'Is All the World a Text? From Social History to the History of Society Two Decades Later'. In *Practicing History: New Directions in Historical Writing after the Linguistic Turn*, edited by Gabrielle M. Spiegel, 35–61, London: Routledge, 2005.

Elman, Benjamin A. *A Cultural History of Civil Examinations in Late Imperial China*. Berkeley: University of California Press, 2000.

Endicott, Elizabeth. *Mongolian Rule in China: Local Administration in the Yuan Dynasty*. Council on East Asian Studies. Cambridge, MA: Harvard University Press, 1989.

Eskenazi Ltd. *Principal Wares of the Song Period from a Private Collection*. London: Eskenazi, 2015.

'Excavation on the Water Valve Site at the Northern Gate of the Great Song City in Yangzhou, Jiangsu'. *Chinese Archaeology* 6, no. 1 (n.d.): 120–127.

Fan Fengmei 范凤妹. 'Ji Jiangxi Chutu de Beifang Mingyao Ciqi 记江西出土的北方名窑瓷器 [Famous Porcelains from the North in Jiangxi Excavations]'. *Jiangxi lishi wenwu* 2 (1986): 120–122.

Fang Lili 方李莉. *Jingdezhen minyao* 景德鎮民窑 [The Folk Kilns of Jingdezhen]. Beijing: Renmin meishu chubanshe, 2002.

Fang Yizhi 方以智 (1611–1671). *Wuli xiaoshi* 物理小識 [Small encyclopedia of the principles of things]. Vol. 131–132. Siku quanshu. Taipei: Taiwan shangwu yinshuguan, 1981.

Farmer, Edward M. *Zhu Yuanzhang & Early Ming Legislation*. Leiden: Brill, 1995.

Feng Xianming 冯先铭. *Zhongguo taoci shi* 中国陶瓷史 [The History of Chinese Porcelain]. Beijing: Wenwu chubanshe, 1982.

'Woguo taoci fazhanzhong de jige wenti: cong Zhongguo chutu wenwu zhanlan taoci zhanpin tanqi 我国陶瓷发展中的几个问题：从中国出土文物展览陶瓷展品谈起. [Several problems in the development of Chinese porcelain, discussed from the perspective of some excavated pieces]'. *Wenwu* 7 (1973): 20–27.

Fernández-Armesto, Felipe. *Pathfinders: A Global History of Exploration*. New York: W.W. Norton, 2007.

Finlay, John. '"40 Views of Yuanming Yuan": Image and Ideology in a Qianlong Imperial Album of Poetry and Paintings'. PhD, Yale University, 2011.

'The Qianlong Emperor's Western Vistas: Linear Perspective and Trompe l'Oeil Illusion in the European Palaces of the Yuanming Yuan'. *Bulletin de l'École Française d'Extrême-Orient* 94 (2007): 159–193.

Finlay, Robert. *The Pilgrim Art: Cultures of Porcelain in World History*. Berkeley, CA: University of California Press, 2010.

'The Pilgrim Art: The Culture of Porcelain in World History'. *Journal of World History* 9, no. 2 (1998): 141–187.

'The Voyages of Zheng He: Ideology, State Power, and Maritime Trade in Ming China'. *Journal of The Historical Society* 8, no. 3 (2008): 327–347.

'Weaving the Rainbow: Visions of Color in World History'. *Journal of World History* 18, no. 4 (2007): 383–431.

Fitzherbert, Teresa. 'Khwājū Kirmānī (689–753/1290–1352): An *Éminence Grise* of Fourteenth Century Persian Painting'. *Iran* 29 (1991): 137–151.

Fitzhugh, William W., Morris Rossabi and William Honeychurch. *Genghis Khan and the Mongol Empire*. Washington, DC; Media: Arctic Studies Center, Smithsonian Institution; Mongolian Preservation Foundation, 2013.

Flecker, Michael. 'The South-China-Sea Tradition: The Hybrid Hulls of South-East Asia'. *The International Journal of Nautical Archaeology* 36, no. 1 (2007): 75–90.

Flynn, Dennis O. and Arturo Giráldez. 'Born with a "Silver Spoon": The Origin of World Trade in 1571'. *Journal of World History* 6, no. 2 (1995): 201–221.

China and the Birth of Globalization in the 16th Century. Farnham, UK: Ashgate Variorum, 2010.

Fox, Robert. 'The Archeological Record of Chinese Influences in the Philippines'. *Philippine Studies* 15, no. 1 (1967): 41–62.

Frank, André Gunder. *ReOrient: Global Economy in the Asian Age*. Berkeley: University of California Press, 1998.

Franke, Herbert and Denis Crispin Twitchett, eds. *Alien Regimes and Border States, 907–1368*. Vol. 6. Cambridge History of China. Cambridge University Press, 2008.

Friese, Heinz. *Das Dienstleistungs-System der Ming-Zeit, 1368–1644*. Hamburg: Gesellschaft für Natur- und Völkerkunde Ostasiens, 1959.

Fu Zhenlun 傅振伦. *Zhongguo gu taoci luncong* 中国古陶瓷论丛 [Essays in ancient Chinese pottery and porcelain]. Beijing: Zhongguo guangbo dianshi chubanshe, 1994.

Gao Liren 高立人. *Jizhou Yonghe yao* 吉州永和窑 [The Yonghe kilns at Jizhou]. Shanghai: Wenhui chubanshe, 2002.

Geng Sheng 耕生. 'Yuan Jizhou yao jinian zhen ci liang zhong 元吉州窑纪年珍瓷两种 [Two pieces of chronological porcelain created in the Jizhou kiln]'. *Shoucang*, no. 13 (2013): 70–71.

George, Alain. 'Direct Sea Trade Between Early Islamic Iraq and Tang China: From the Exchange of Goods to the Transmission of Ideas'. *Journal of the Royal Asiatic Society* 25, no. 4 (2015): 579–624.

Gernet, Jacques. *Daily Life in China on the Eve of the Mongol Invasion, 1250–1276.* Stanford University Press, 1995.

Gerritsen, Anne. 'Ceramics for Local and Global Markets: Jingdezhen's Agora of Technologies'. In *Cultures of Knowledge: Technology in Chinese History*, edited by Dagmar Schäfer and Francesca Bray, 164–186. Leiden: Brill, 2012.

'Fragments of a Global Past: Ceramics Manufacture in Song-Yuan-Ming Jingdezhen'. *Journal of the Social and Economic History of the Orient* 52 (2009): 117–152.

'From Long-Distance Trade to the Global Lives of Things: Writing the History of Early Modern Trade and Material Culture'. *Journal of Early Modern History* 20, no. 6 (2016): 526–544.

Ji'an Literati and the Local in Song-Yuan-Ming China. Leiden: Brill, 2007.

'Jizhou as Kiln Town: Writing the History of a Forgotten Past', 2009. www.humanities.uci.edu/eastasian/SungYuan/Downloads/ideas_networks_places/.

'Porcelain and the Material Culture of the Mongol-Yuan Court'. *Journal of Early Modern History* 16, no. 3 (2012): 241–273.

'The Hongwu Legacy: Fifteenth-Century Views on Zhu Yuanzhang's Monastic Policies'. In *Long Live the Emperor!: Uses of the Ming Founder Across Six Centuries of East Asian History*, edited by Sarah Schneewind, 55–72. Minneapolis, MN: Society for Ming Studies, 2008.

Gerritsen, Anne and Christian De Vito. 'Micro-Spatial Histories of Labour: Towards a New Global History'. In *Micro-Spatial Histories of Global Labour*, edited by Christian De Vito and Anne Gerritsen, 1–28. London: Palgrave Macmillan, 2018.

Gerritsen, Anne and Giorgio Riello, eds. *Writing Material Culture History*. London: Bloomsbury, 2015.

Gerritsen, Anne and Stephen McDowall. 'Material Culture and the Other: European Encounters with Chinese Porcelain, ca. 1650–1800'. *Journal of World History* 23, no. 1 (2012): 87–113.

Gerritsen, Anne and Giorgio Riello, eds. *The Global Lives of Things: The Material Culture of Connections in the Early Modern World*, 2016.

Giles, Herbert. *A Chinese Biographical Dictionary*. New York: Paragon Book Gallery, 1975.

Gillette, Maris. 'Copying, Counterfeiting, and Capitalism in Contemporary China: Jingdezhen's Porcelain Industry'. *Modern China* 36, no. 4 (2010): 367–403.

China's Porcelain Capital: The Rise, Fall and Reinvention of Ceramics in Jingdezhen. London: Bloomsbury Academic, 2016.

'Labor and Precariousness in China's Porcelain Capital'. *Anthropology of Work Review* 35, no. 1 (2014): 25–39.

Goddio, Franck. 'The Wreck on the Lena Shoal'. In *Lost at Sea: The Strange Route of the Lena Shoal Junk*, edited by Franck Goddio and Josephine Bacon 1–41. London: Periplus, 2002.

Golas, Peter. 'The Sung Fiscal Administration'. In *Sung China*, edited by John W. Chaffee and Denis Twitchett. Vol. 5 Part 2. Cambridge History of China. Cambridge University Press, 2015.

Gordon, Stewart. *When Asia Was the World*. Cambridge, MA: Da Capo Press, 2008.

Gray, Basil. 'Blue and White Vessels in Persian Miniatures of the 14th and 15th Centuries Re-Examined'. *Transactions of the Oriental Ceramic Society* 24 (1948–49): 23–30.

Green, Jeremy. 'The Shinan Excavation, Korea: An Interim Report on the Hull Structure'. *The International Journal of Nautical Archaeology and Underwater Exploration* 12, no. 4 (1983): 293–301.

Green, Nile. 'From the Silk Road to the Railroad (and Back): The Means and Meanings of the Iranian Encounter with China'. *Iranian Studies* 48, no. 2 (2015): 165–192.

Gugong bowu yuan (Taiwan). Ru yao 汝窯 [Ru wares]. Hong Kong: Kaifa gufen youxian gongsi, 1961.

Guo Xuelei 郭学雷. 'Chanzong Sixiang Dui Nan Song Jizhou Yao Ciqi Zhuangshi de Yingxiang 禅宗思想对南宋吉州窑瓷器装饰的影响 – The Influence of Buddhist Thought on Decoration of Porcelains from the Jizhou Kilns of the Southern Song Dynasty'. *Shoucang*, no. 7 (2012): 52–63.

    Mingdai Cizhou yao ciqi 明代磁州窑瓷器 [Ceramics from the Ming dynasty Cizhou kilns]. Beijing: Wenwu chubanshe, 2005.

Guy, John. *Oriental Trade Ceramics in South-East Asia, Ninth to Sixteenth Centuries*. Oxford University Press, 1986.

Hall, Kenneth R. *A History of Early Southeast Asia: Maritime Trade and Societal Development, 100–1500*. Lanham, MD: Rowman & Littlefield, 2011.

Han, Yŏng-u, Hwi-jun An and U-sŏng Pae. *The Artistry of Early Korean Cartography*. Translated by Byonghyon Choi. Larkspur, CA: Tamal Vista Publications, 2008.

Han Zhenhua 韩振华. 'Lun Zheng He Xia Xiyang de Xingzhi 论郑和下西洋的性质 [On the Nature of Zheng He's Voyages to the Western Oceans]'. *Xiamen Daxue Xuebao*, no. 1 (1958): 172–188.

Hansen, Valerie. *The Open Empire: A History of China to 1800*. 2nd ed. New York: W. W. Norton & Co., 2015.

Hansen, Valerie and Ken Curtis. *Voyages in World History*. 3rd ed. Boston, MA: Cengage Learning, 2016.

Hansen, Valerie. *The Silk Road: A New History*. Oxford University Press, 2015.

Hao, Zhidong. *Macau History and Society*. Hong Kong University Press, 2011.

Hargett, James M. '會稽: Guaiji? Guiji? Huiji? Kuaiji? Some Remarks on an Ancient Chinese Place-Name'. *Sino-Platonic Papers*, no. 234 (2013).

Harrison-Hall, Jessica. *Catalogue of Late Yuan and Ming Ceramics in the British Museum*. London: British Museum Press, 2001.

'Early Ming Ceramics: Rethinking the Status of Blue-and-White'. In *Ming China: Courts and Contacts, 1400–1450*, edited by Craig Clunas, Jessica Harrison-Hall and Yu Ping Luk, 77–86. London: British Museum Press, 2016.

'The Taste for Cizhou'. *Apollo* 174, no. 592 (2011): 48–54.

Harrisson, Barbara. 'The Ceramic Trade across the South China Sea c. AD 1350–1650'. *Journal of the Malaysian Branch of the Royal Asiatic Society* 76, no. 1 (2003): 99–114.

Hartley, L. P. *The Go-Between*. 1953. Reprint, London: Penguin Books, 2010.

Hartwell, Robert. 'Markets, Technology, and the Structure of Enterprise in the Development of the Eleventh-Century Chinese Iron and Steel Industry'. *The Journal of Economic History* 26, no. 1 (1966): 29–58.

'The Imperial Treasuries: Finance and Power in Song China'. *Bulletin of Sung and Yüan Studies*, no. 20 (1988): 18–89.

Hay, John. 'Questions of Influence in Chinese Art History'. *Res: Anthropology and Aesthetics* 35 (1999): 240–262.

'Toward a Theory of the Intercultural'. *Res: Anthropology and Aesthetics* 35 (1999): 5–9.

He Ding and Zhang Jie. 'Vernacular Uses and Cultural Identity of Heritage: Trade of Antique Fragments in the Chinese Porcelain Capital'. *International Journal of Heritage Studies* 22, no. 10 (2016): 844–856.

He, Yimin. 'Prosperity and Decline: A Comparison of the Fate of Jingdezhen, Zhuxianzhen, Foshan and Hankou in Modern Times'. *Frontiers of History in China* 5, no. 1 (2010): 52–85.

Heijdra, Martin. 'The Socio-Economic Development of Rural China during the Ming'. In *The Ming Dynasty, 1368–1644*, edited by Denis Crispin Twitchett and Frederick W. Mote, 417–578. Vol. 8 Part 2. Cambridge History of China. Cambridge University Press, 1998.

Hemmat, Kaveh. 'A Chinese System for an Ottoman State: The Frontier, the Millennium, and Ming Bureaucracy in Khatayi's Book of China.' PhD, The University of Chicago, 2014.

Heng, Derek Thiam Soon. 'Export Commodity and Regional Currency: The Role of Chinese Copper Coins in the Melaka Straits, Tenth to Fourteenth Centuries'. *Journal of Southeast Asian Studies* 37, no. 2 (2006): 179–203.

Ho, Chuimei, ed. *New Light on Chinese Yue and Lonquan Wares: Archaeological Ceramics Found in Eastern and Southern Asia, A.D. 800–1400*. Centre of Asian Studies, The University of Hong Kong, 1994.

Ho, Colleen. 'Thirteenth and Fourteenth Century European-Mongol Relations'. *History Compass* 10, no. 12 (2012): 946–968.

Ho, Ping-ti. *The Ladder of Success in Imperial China: Aspects of Social Mobility, 1368–1911*. New York: Columbia University Press, 1964.

Hong Mai 洪邁. *Rongzhai suibi* 容齋隨筆. Sibu congkan xubian. Shanghai: Shangwu yinshuguan, 1934.

Hsiung Ping-chen 熊秉真. 'Qing zhengfu dui Jiangxi de jingying 清政府對江西 的經營 [The management of Jiangxi under the Qing government]'. *Jindai shi yanjiusuo jikan* 18 (1989): 37–74.

Hsu, Wen-Chin. 'Social and Economic Factors in the Chinese Porcelain Industry in Jingdezhen during the Late Ming and Early Qing Period, ca. 1620–1683'. *Journal of the Royal Asiatic Society (New Series)* 120, no. 01 (1988): 135–159.

Huang, Chao and Paul A. Van Dyke. 'Hoppo Tang Ying 唐英 (1750–1751) and the Development of the Guangdong Maritime Customs'. *Journal of Asian History* 51, no. 2 (2017): 223–256.

Huang, Ellen. 'An Art of Transformation: Reproducing *Yaobian* Glazes in Qing-Dynasty Porcelain'. *Archives of Asian Art* 68, no. 2 (2018): 133–156.

'China's China: Jingdezhen Porcelain and the Production of Art in the Nineteenth Century'. PhD, University of California at San Diego, 2008.

Huang, H. T. *Fermentations and Food Science*. Science and Civilisation in China, Vol 6: Biology and Biological Technology, Part V. Cambridge University Press, 2000.

Huang Nianfeng 黄年凤. 'Jizhou yao fang Ding ci yu Nanbei wenhua jiaoliu 吉州窑 仿定瓷与南北文化交流 [The Jizhou Imitation of Ding Ware and the Cultural Exchange Between North and South]'. *Nanfang wenwu*, no. 1 (2002): 68–69.

'Cong Jizhouyao ci kan nanbei taoci wenhua jiaoliu 从吉州窑瓷看南北陶瓷文化交流 – [Porcelain Cultural Exchange between the South and the North as Evidenced by the Jizhou Kiln Porcelain]'. *Shoucang Jia*, no. 11 (2006): 13–16.

Huang, Ray. *Taxation and Governmental Finance in Sixteenth-Century Ming China*. Cambridge University Press, 1974.

'The Ming Fiscal Administration'. In *The Ming Dynasty, 1368-1644*, edited by Denis Twitchett and Frederick W. Mote, 106–71. Vol. 8 Part 2. Cambridge History of China. Cambridge University Press, 1998.

Huang Yangxing 黄阳兴. 'Nan Song Jizhou Yao Chazhan Zhuangshi de Chanqu 南 宋吉州窑茶盏装饰的禅趣 [Zen-Gusto on Decorations of Tea Sets in Jizhou Kiln of Southern Song Dynasty]'. *Shoucang* 8 (2012): 60–67.

Huang Yijun 黄义军. *Songdai qingbai ci de lishi dili yanjiu* 宋代青白瓷的历史地 理研究 [The Historical Geography of Song Period Bluish-White Porcelain]. Beijing: Wenwu chubanshe, 2010.

Hucker, Charles O. *A Dictionary of Official Titles in Imperial China*. Stanford University Press, 1985.

The Censorial System of Ming China. Stanford University Press, 1966.

Hudson, Pat. *The Industrial Revolution*. London: Edward Arnold, 1992.

Hummel, Arthur W., ed. *Eminent Chinese of the Ch'ing Period, 1644–1912*. Washington: US Government Printing Office, 1943.

Ibn Battuta. *The Travels of Ibn Battuta, A.D. 1325–54*. Translated by H. A. R. Gibb and C. F. Beckingham. 4 vols. London: Hakluyt Society, 1958.

Travels in Asia and Africa, 1325–1354. Translated by H. A. R. Gibb. London: Routledge & Kegan Paul, 1983.

Ingold, Tim. *The Perception of the Environment: Essays on Livelihood, Dwelling and Skill*. London: Routledge, 2000.

Ishida, Hou-mei Sung. 'The Early Ming Ink Plum Blossom Painter Xu Jing'. *Oriental Art* 35, no. 2 (1989): 97–109.

Jackson, Peter, trans. *The Mission of Friar William of Rubruck: His Journey to the Court of the Great Khan Möngke 1253–1255*. London: Hakluyt Society, 1990.

Jahn, Karl. *Die Chinageschichte des Rašīd ad-Dīn*. Wien Böhlaus, 1971.

Jami, Catherine. *The Emperor's New Mathematics Western Learning and Imperial Authority During the Kangxi Reign (1662–1722)*. Oxford University Press, 2012.

Jang, Namwon. 'The Origin and Development of Ceramics with Underglaze Iron Decoration and White Porcelain in the Goryeo Dynasty'. Translated by Kim Hyun Kyung. *Misulsa Nondan (Art History Forum)* 18 (2004): 41–71.

Jiang Qi 蔣祈. 'Song Jiang Qi "Taoji" Jiaozhu 宋蔣祈《陶記》校注 [Annotated edition of Jiang Qi's 'Taoji']'. Edited by Bai Kun 白焜. *Jingdezhen Taoci* S1 (1981): 36–52.

Jiangxi Provincial Institute of Cultural Relics and Archaeology, and Jingdezhen Museum of Civilian Kiln. 'Report on Excavations from 1988 to 1999: Hutian Kiln Site in Jingdezhen'. Chinese Archaeology. Accessed 23 March 2017. www.kaogu.net.cn/html/en/Publication/New_books/2013/1025/30009.html.

Jiangxisheng wenwu kaogu yanjiusuo and Fuliangxian bowuguan. 'Jiangxi Fuliang Fenghuangshan Songdai yaozhi fajue jianbao 江西浮梁凤凰山宋代窑址发掘简报 [Brief Report of the Excavation of the Song Kilns at Fenghuangshan in Fuliang, Jiangxi]'. *Wenwu*, no. 12 (2009): 25–38.

Jingdezhen shi difangzhi bianzuan weiyuanhui, ed. *Zhongguo cidu: Jingdezhen shi* 中国瓷都·景德镇市 [Porcelain capital of China: The City of Jingdezhen]. 2 vols. Beijing: Fangzhi chubanshe, 2004.

Johnston, John Naley. 'Jiangxi Landmarks on Jingdezhen Porcelain With Special Reference to Tengwang Ge'. PhD, SOAS, 2016.

Jörg, Christiaan. *Porcelain and the Dutch China Trade*. The Hague: M. Nijhoff, 1982.

'The Portuguese and the Trade in Chinese Porcelain: From the Beginning Until the End of the Ming Dynasty'. In *Portugal na porcelana da China: 500 andos de comércio (Portugal in Porcelain from China: 500 Years of Trade)*, edited by Alberto Varela Santos, 1:47–71. Lisboa: Artemágica, 2007.

Junker, Laura Lee. *Raiding, Trading, and Feasting: The Political Economy of Philippine Chiefdoms*. Honolulu: University of Hawai'i Press, 1999.

Juwayeyi, Yusuf M. 'Archaeological Excavations at Mankhamba, Malawi: An Early Settlement Site of the Maravi'. *Azania: Archaeological Research in Africa* 45, no. 2 (2010): 175–202.

Kadoi, Yuka. *Islamic Chinoiserie: The Art of Mongol Iran*. Edinburgh University Press, 2009.

Kahle, Paul. 'Chinese Porcelain in the Lands of Islam'. In *Opera Minora*, 326–361. Leiden: Brill, 1956.

'Eine islamische Quelle über China um 1500 (Das Khitayname des Ali Ekber)'. *Acta Orientalia* 12 (1934): 91–110.

Kang Yu 康煜 and Zeng Qiong 曾琼. 'Chuyi Cizhouyaohe Jizhouyao youxia baidi caihui zhuangshi wenyang 刍议磁州窑和吉州窑釉下白地彩绘装饰纹样 [An Insight into the Decorative Types of Under-Glazed Color Painted Porcelain from Cizhou and Jizhou]'. *China Ceramics* 44, no. 9 (2008): 79–81.

Kennet, Derek. 'Julfar and the Urbanisation of Southeast Arabia'. *Arabian Archaeology and Epigraphy* 14, no. 1 (2003): 103–125.

Kerr, Rose. *Song China Through 21st Century Eyes: Yaozhou and Qingbai Ceramics* = 今之视昔: 宋代耀州窑及青白瓷. Netherlands: Meijering Art Books, 2009.

    Song Dynasty Ceramics. London: V & A, 2004.

    'Yixing'. In *Grove Art Online*. Oxford University Press, 1996. www.oxfordartonline.com/subscriber/article/grove/art/T092881.

Kerr, Rose and Nigel Wood. *Ceramic Technology*. Science and Civilisation in China, Vol 5: Chemistry and Chemical Technology, Part XII. Cambridge University Press, 2004.

Kessler, Adam T. *Song Blue and White Porcelain on the Silk Road*. Leiden: Brill, 2012.

Khoo, James C. M., ed. *Art & Archaeology of Fu Nan: Pre-Khmer Kingdom of the Lower Mekong Valley*. Bangkok: Orchid Press, 2003.

Kieschnick, John. *The Impact of Buddhism on Chinese Material Culture*. Princeton University Press, 2002.

Kleutghen, Kristina. *Imperial Illusions: Crossing Pictorial Boundaries in the Qing Palaces*. Seattle: University of Washington Press, 2015.

Ko, Dorothy. *The Social Life of Inkstones: Artisans and Scholars in Early Qing China*. Seattle: University of Washington Press, 2017.

Kopplin, Monika, ed. *The Monochrome Principle: Lacquerware and Ceramics of the Song and Qing Dynasties*. Munich: Hirmer Verlag, 2008.

Kotz, Suzanne, ed. *Imperial Taste: Chinese Ceramics from the Percival David Foundation*. San Francisco: Chronicle Books, 1989.

Krahe, Cinta. *Chinese Porcelain in Habsburg Spain*. Madrid: Centro de Estudios Europa Hispanica, 2016.

Krahl, Regina. 'Export Porcelain Fit for the Chinese Emperor. Early Chinese Blue-and-White in the Topkapı Saray Museum, Istanbul'. *Journal of the Royal Asiatic Society of Great Britain & Ireland* 118, no. 01 (1986): 68–92.

    'Green Wares of Southern China'. In *Shipwrecked: Tang Treasures and Monsoon Winds*, edited by Regina Krahl et al., 184–199. Washington, DC; Singapore: Arthur M. Sackler Gallery, Smithsonian Institution; National Heritage Board: Singapore Tourism Board, 2010.

    'Tang Blue-and-White'. In *Shipwrecked: Tang Treasures and Monsoon Winds*, edited by Regina Krahl, et al., 209–211. Washington and Singapore: Arthur M. Sackler Gallery, Smithsonian Institution; National Heritage Board, Singapore Tourism Board, 2010.

'The "Alexander Bowl" and the Question of Northern Guan Ware'. *Orientations* 25, no. 11 (1993): 72–75.

Krahl, Regina and Jessica Harrison-Hall. *Chinese Ceramics: Highlights of the Sir Percival David Collection*. London: British Museum Press, 2009.

Kriedte, Peter, Hans Medick and Jürgen Schlumbohm. *Industrialization before Industrialization: Rural Industry in the Genesis of Capitalism*. Past and Present Publications. Cambridge University Press, 1981.

Kuhn, Philip A. *Soulstealers: The Chinese Sorcery Scare of 1768*. Cambridge, MA: Harvard University Press, 1990.

Kulliyáti Khwájú Karmání. 'The poetical works of Khwájú of Karmán'. British Library Manuscript Add. 18,113' 1396.

Kungnip Chungang Pangmulgwan (Korea). *Sinan haejŏ munmul: Sinan haejŏ munhwajae t'ŭkpyŏl chŏn torok*. Sŏul: Samhwa Ch'ulp'ansa, 1977.

Kurz, Johannes L. 'The Consolidation of Official Historiography during the Early Northern Song Dynasty'. *Journal of Asian History* 46, no. 1 (2012): 13–35.

Kuwayama, George. *Chinese Ceramics in Colonial Mexico*. Los Angeles; Honolulu, Hawaii: Los Angeles County Museum of Art, 1997.

Kwon, Sohyun. 'Establishing and Practicing Propriety'. In *In Blue and White: Porcelain of the Joseon Dynasty*, edited by Kang Tae-gyu, 68–89. Seoul: National Museum of Korea, 2015.

Lai Jinming 赖金明 and Zhang Wenjiang 张文江. '"Cuncun yaohuohuhu taoyan": Changjiangbian de yaozhi "村村窑火,户户陶埏"——昌江边的窑址'. *China Cultural Heritage*, no. 03 (2014): 22–30+10.

Lam, Peter. 'Maritime Trade in China during the Middle Ming Period Circa 1500 AD'. In *Lost at Sea: The Strange Route of the Lena Shoal Junk*, 43–57. London: Periplus, 2002.

'Tang Ying (1682–1756): The Imperial Factory Superintendent at Jingdezhen'. *Transactions of the Oriental Ceramics Society* 63 (1998–1999): 65–82.

'The David Vases Revisited: Annotation Notes of the Dedicatory Inscriptions'. *Orientations* 40, no. 8 (2009): 70–77.

Lambourn, Elizabeth and Phillip Ackerman-Lieberman. 'Chinese Porcelain and the Material Taxonomies of Medieval Rabbinic Law: Encounters with Disruptive Substances in Twelfth-Century Yemen'. *The Medieval Globe* 2, no. 2 (2017): 199–238.

Lamouroux, Christian. *Fiscalité, comptes publics et politiques financières dans la Chine des Song: le chapitre 179 du Songshi*. Paris: Institut des hautes études chinoises, 2004.

Lan, Pin-nan and Cheng T'ing-kuei. *Ching-Te-Chen T'ao-Lu or The Potteries of China*. Translated by Geoffrey Robley Sayer. London: Routledge & Kegan Paul, 1951.

Lan Pu 蓝浦 and Zheng Tinggui 郑廷桂. *Jingdezhen tao lu tushuo* 景德镇陶录图说[Illustrated explanations on the Jingdezhen porcelain kilns]. Jinan Shi: Shandong huabao chubanshe, 2004.

Lancaster, William and Fidelity Lancaster. 'Pottery Makers and Pottery Users: In Ras Al-Khaimah Emirate and Musandam Wilayat of Oman, and around Ra's

Al-Junayz in the South-east of Ja'alan Wilayat, Oman'. *Arabian Archaeology and Epigraphy* 21, no. 2 (2010): 199–255.

Larner, John. *Marco Polo and the Discovery of the World*. New Haven; London: Yale University Press, 1999.

Le Comte, Louis. *Memoirs and Observations Typographical, Physical, Mathematical, Mechanical, Natural, Civil, and Ecclesiastical, Made in a Late Journey through the Empire of China, and Published in Several Letters: Particularly upon the Chinese Pottery and Varnishing, the Silk and Other Manufactures, the Pearl Fishing, the History of Plants and Animals, Description of Their Cities and Publick Works, Number of People, Their Language, Manners and Commerce, Their Habits, Oeconomy, and Government, the Philosophy of Confucius, the State of Christianity: With Many Other Curious and Useful Remarks*. London: Printed for BenjTooke, 1697.

Lee, Robert. 'The Artisans of Ching-Tê-Chên in Late Imperial China'. MA thesis, University of British Columbia, 1980.

Leibsohn, Dana. 'Made in China, Made in Mexico'. In *At the Crossroads: The Arts of Spanish America & Early Global Trade, 1492–1850*, edited by Donna Pierce and Ronald Y. Otsuka, 11–40. Denver Art Museum, 2012.

Li, Baoping. 'Application of ICP-MS Trace Element Analysis in Study of Ancient Chinese Ceramics'. *Chinese Science Bulletin* 48, no. 12 (2003): 1219–1224.

Li, Bozhong. *Agricultural Development in Jiangnan, 1620–1850*. Basingstoke: Macmillan, 1998.

Li Dejin 李德金, et al., 'Chaoxian Xin'an Haidi Chenchuan Zhong de Zhongguo Ciqi 朝鲜新安海底沉船中的中国瓷器 [The Chinese Ceramics in the Shipwreck on the Sinan Seabed in Korea]'. *Kaogu Xuebao* 2 (1979): 245–254.

Li, He. *Chinese Ceramics: The New Standard Guide*. London: Thames & Hudson, 1996.

Li, Huibing 李辉柄. 'Suining Jiaocang Ciqi Qianyi 遂宁窖藏瓷器浅议 [Some comments on the porcelain in the Suining hoard]'. *Wenwu*, no. 4 (1994): 29–31.

Li Jiazhi 李家治, ed. *Jianlun Guan Ge Er Yao: Keji Yanjiu Wei Guan, Ge Deng Yao Shi Kong Ding Wei* 简论官哥二窑：科技研究为官，哥等窑时空定位 [The Guan and Ge kilns: using scientific research to evaluate the time and place of the Guan, Ge and other kilns]. Beijing: Kexue chubanshe, 2007.

Li, Kangying. *The Ming Maritime Trade Policy in Transition, 1368 to 1567*. Wiesbaden: Harrassowitz, 2010.

Li Tao 李燾 (1115–1184). *Xu Zizhi Tongjian Changbian* 續資治通鑑長編. Yingyin Wenyuange Siku Quanshu, vols 414–322. Taipei: Taiwan shangwu yinshuguan, 1983.

Li Weidong, Li Jiazhi, Wu Jun and Guo Jingkun. 'Study on the Phase-Separated Opaque Glaze in Ancient China from Qionglai Kiln'. *Ceramics International* 29, no. 8 (2003): 933–937.

Li Weiran 李蔚然. 'Nanjing Chutu Jizhou Yao Cizhen 南京出土吉州窑瓷枕 [A Jizhou kiln ceramic pillow excavated in Nanjing]'. *Wenwu*, no. 1 (1977): 95.

Li Yucang 李雨苍. *Songdai taoci wenshi jingcui hui lu* 宋代陶瓷纹饰精粹绘录 [Selected Collection of the Ceramic Decorative Patterns in the Song Dynasty]. Shanghai guji chubanshe, 2004.

Li Zhiyan 李知宴 and Guan Shanming 關善明. *Songdai taoci* 宋代陶瓷 [Song Ceramics]. Hong Kong: Muwentang meishu chubanshe, 2012.

Liang Miaotai 梁淼泰. *Ming Qing Jingdezhen chengshi jingji yanjiu* 明清景德鎮城市經濟研究 [Study of the Urban Economy of Jingdezhen during the Ming-Qing period]. 1991. Reprint, Nanchang: Jiangxi renmin chubanshe, 2004.

'Ming-Qing shiqi Fuliang de nonglin shangpin 明清时期浮梁的农林商品 [Farming and forestry products from Ming-Qing Fuliang]'. *Zhongguo shehui jingjizhi yanjiu*, no. 01 (1988): 28–38.

Liefkes, Reino and Hilary Young, eds. *Masterpieces of World Ceramics in the Victoria and Albert Museum*. London: V&A Publishing, 2008.

Lim, Ivy Maria. 'From Haijin to Kaihai: The Jiajing Court's Search for a Modus Operandi along the South-Eastern Coast (1522–1567)'. *Journal of the British Association for Chinese Studies* 2 (2013): 1–26.

Lin, Meicun and Ran Zhang. 'Zheng He's Voyages to Hormuz: The Archaeological Evidence'. *Antiquity* 89, no. 344 (2015): 417–432.

Ling Lichao 凌礼潮. '"Jiangxi tian Huguang" yu "Huguang tian Sichuan" bijiao yanjiu chuyi "江西填湖广"与"湖广填四川"比较研究刍议 [Comparative research on 'Jiangxi fills Huguang' and 'Huguang fills Sichuan']'. *Beijing keji daxue xuebao*, no. 1 (2014): 48–54.

Linschoten, Jan Huygen van. *Itinerario voyage ofte schipvaert van Jan Huygen van Linschoten naer Oost ofte Portugaels Indien 1579–1592*. 's-Gravenhage: M. Nijhoff, 1955.

Little, Stephen. 'Economic Change in Seventeenth-Century China and Innovations at the Jingdezhen Kilns'. *Ars Orientalis* 26 (1996): 47–54.

Liu, Heping. '"The Water Mill" and Northern Song Imperial Patronage of Art, Commerce, and Science'. *The Art Bulletin* 84, no. 4 (2002): 566–595.

Liu Jincheng 刘金成 and Liu Jingbang 刘璟邦. 'Gao'an Yuandai Jiaocang zhi zai yanjiu – jiaocang maicang niandai ji qi zhuren shenfen kao 高安元代窖藏之再研究——窖藏埋藏年代及其主人身份考 [Revisiting the Gao'an Hoard of the Yuan Dynasty – the Date of its Burial and the Identity of its Owner]'. *Nanfang wenwu*, no. 4 (2013): 101–118.

Liu Lichun 刘礼纯. 'Ruichang Song Mu Chutu Cizhou Yaoxi Ciping 江西瑞昌宋墓出土磁州窑系瓷瓶 [Cizhou Type Vases Excavated from a Song Tomb in Ruichang, Jiangxi]'. *Wenwu*, no. 8 (1987): 89–90.

Liu Tao 刘陶, Xiao Xuan 肖绚, Yan Lianghua 严亮华 and Jiang Nanwei 江南伟. 'Jiyu yuanbao zidongji de Jingdezhen nanhe liuyu yaozhi jingguan yanbian 基于元胞自动机的景德镇南河流域窑址景观演变 [The Kiln Landscape Evolvement of Jingdezhen Nanhe River Basin Based on Cellular Automation]'. *Zhongguo Taoci*, no. 8 (2012): 35–38.

Liu, William Guanglin. *The Chinese Market Economy, 1000–1500*. Albany: State University of New York Press, 2015.

'The Making of a Fiscal State in Song China, 960–1279: The Making of a Fiscal State in Song China'. *The Economic History Review* 68, no. 1 (2015): 48–78.

Liu, Xinru. *Ancient India and Ancient China: Trade and Religious Exchange AD 1–600*. Oxford University Press, 1988.

'Migration and Settlement of the Yuezhi-Kushan: Interaction and Interdependence of Nomadic and Sedentary Societies'. *Journal of World History* 12, no. 2 (2001): 261–292.

The Silk Road in World History. Oxford University Press, 2010.

Liu Xinyuan 刘新园. 'Jiang Qi "Taoji" Zhuzuo Shidai Kaobian 蒋祈《陶记》著作时代考辨 [Consideration of the Dating of Jiang Qi's Taoji]'. *Jingdezhen Taoci* S1 (1981): 5–35.

'Jiangxi Jingdezhen Guanyinge Mingdai yaozhi fajue jianbao 江西景德镇观音阁明代窑址发掘简报 [Excavation report of the Ming Guanyinge kilnsite in Jingdezhen]'. *Wenwu*, no. 12 (2009): 39–58+1.

Liu Xitao 刘锡涛. 'Ji'an Songdai wenhua fazhan chengjiu lüeshuo 吉安宋代文化发展成就略说 [The Development of Culture in Ji'an in the Song Dynasty]'. *Journal of Jinggangshan Normal College* 26, no. 1 (2005): 61–64.

Liu Yi 刘毅. 'Yaobian ji qi ciye wenhua yii 窑变及其瓷业文化意义 [Kiln Transmutation and its Significance for Porcelain Culture]'. *Nanfang wenwu*, no. 2 (2014): 110–115.

Liu, Ying, Zhongping Chen and Gregory Blue. *Zheng He's Maritime Voyages (1405–1433) and China's Relations with the Indian Ocean World: A Multilingual Bibliography*. Leiden: Brill, 2014.

Liu Yuhei 刘裕黑 and Xiong Lin 熊琳. 'Guanyu Gao'an Yuanci jiaocang de jige wenti 关于高安元瓷窖藏的几个问题 [Several Questions Regarding the Hoard of Yuan Porcelain at Gao'an in Jiangxi]'. *Nanfang wenwu*, no. 2 (1990): 49–53.

Liu Zhaohui 刘朝晖. *Ming Qing yilai Jingdezhen ciye yu shehui* 明清以来景德镇瓷业与社会 [The Jingdezhen ceramics industry and society from the Ming-Qing]. Shanghai shudian chubanshe, 2010.

Lo, K. S. *The Stonewares of Yixing from the Ming Period to the Present Day*. Hong Kong University Press, 1986.

Lockard, Craig. *Societies, Networks, and Transitions, A Global History*. Vol. II: Since 1450. Boston, MA: Wadsworth, 2011.

Locsin, Leandro and Cecilia Locsin. *Oriental Ceramics Discovered in the Philippines*. Rutland, VT: Tuttle, 1967.

Lokesh, Chandra and Radha Banerjee. *Xuanzang and the Silk Route*. New Delhi: Munshiram Manoharlal Publishers, 2008.

Lorge, Peter. *The Reunification of China: Peace through War under the Song Dynasty*. Cambridge University Press, 2015.

Lovell, Hin-Cheung. 'Sung and Yüan Monochrome Lacquers in the Freer Gallery'. *Ars Orientalis* 9 (1973): 121–130.

Lu Fangqi 卢方琦. 'Ming Qing Nanchangcheng fuyuan yanjiu 明清南昌城复原研究 [Restoration Research on Nanchang City in the Ming and Qing Dynasties]'. MA thesis, Peking University, 2013.

Lu Jiaming. 'Lüelun Jingdezhen Tao Lu Ji Qi Xueshu Jiazhi' 略论《景德镇陶录》及其学术价值 [Brief Discussion of Jingdezhen Taolun and Its Scholarly Value]'. *Nanchang Zhiye Jishu Shifan Xueyuan Xuebao*, 1996, 52–58.

Lu You 陸游. *Lao xue'an biji* 老學庵筆記. Yingyin Wenyuange Siku quanshu. Taipei: Shangwu yinshuguan, 1983.

Luo Xuan 罗璇, Xia Min 夏敏, Wen Bo 文博 and Jiang Xiangyun 姜翔云. 'Ziyuan kujiexing chengshi tudi zonghe chengzai shuiping fenxi–yi Jiangxisheng Jingdezhen wei lie 资源枯竭型城市土地综合承载水平分析——以江西省景德镇市为例 – Comprehensive Carrying Capacity of Land of Resource-Exhausted Cities——A Case of Jingdezhen, Jiangxi Province'. *Jiangxi nongye daxue xuebao: shehui kexue bao* 11, no. 03 (2012): 101–106.

Ma Wenkuan 马文宽. 'Ping "Jiang Qi Taoji Zhuzuo Shidai Kaobian": Yu Liu Xinyuan Xiansheng Shangque 评《蒋祈〈陶记〉著作时代考辨》一与刘新园先生商榷 [Critique of "A Consideration of the Date of Jiang Qi's Taoji": A Discussion with Liu Xinyuan]'. *Kaogu Xuebao* 3 (2008): 395–414.

Mack, Rosamond E. *Bazaar to Piazza: Islamic Trade and Italian Art, 1300–1600*. Berkeley, CA: University of California Press, 2002.

Manguin, Pierre-Yves. 'Early Coastal States of Southeast Asia: Funan and Srivijaya'. In *Lost Kingdoms: Hindu-Buddhist Sculpture of Early Southeast Asia*, edited by John Guy, 111–115. New York: Metropolitan Museum of Art, 2014.

    'Trading Ships of the South China Sea'. *Journal of the Economic and Social History of the Orient* 36, no. 3 (1993): 253–280.

Massey, Doreen B. *For Space*. London; Thousand Oaks, CA: Sage, 2005.

Massy, Laurence. 'The Antiquity Art Market: Between Legality and Illegality'. *International Journal of Social Economics* 35, no. 10 (2008): 729–738.

McCants, Anne E. C. 'Asiatic Goods in Migrant and Native-Born Middling Households'. In *Goods from the East, 1600–1800: Trading Eurasia*, edited by Maxine Berg, 197–215. Basingstoke: Palgrave Macmillan, 2015.

    'Exotic Goods, Popular Consumption, and the Standard of Living: Thinking about Globalization in the Early Modern World'. *Journal of World History* 18, no. 4 (2007): 433–462.

McCausland, Shane. 'An Art Historical Perspective on the Guan-Ge Controversy'. In *Song Ceramics: Art History, Archaeology and Technology*, edited by Stacey Pierson, 29–47. Colloquies on Art & Archaeology in Asia 22. London: Percival David Foundation of Chinese Art, School of Oriental and African Studies, 2004.

McDermott, Joseph. *The Making of a New Rural Order in South China*. Vol. 1, Village, lineage and land in Huizhou: c. 960–1540. 2 vols. Cambridge University Press, 2013.

McDermott, Joseph and Shiba Yoshinobu. 'Economic Change in China, 960–1279'. In *Sung China, 960–1279*, edited by John Chaffee and Denis Twitchett, 321–436. Vol. 5 Part 2. Cambridge History of China. Cambridge University Press, 2015.

McDowall, Stephen. *Qian Qianyi's Reflections on Yellow Mountain: Traces of a Late-Ming Hatchet and Chisel*. Hong Kong University Press, 2009.

McKiernan, Mike. 'La Maladie de Porcelaine'. *Occupational Medicine* 61, no. 3 (2011): 146–147.

Medick, Hans. 'Turning Global? Microhistory in Extension'. *Historische Anthropologie* 24, no. 2 (2016): 241–252.

Medley, Margaret. 'Ching-Tê Chên and the Problem of the "Imperial Kilns"'. *Bulletin of the School of Oriental and African Studies* 29, no. 02 (1966): 326–338.

    Illustrated Catalogue of Ming and Qing Monochrome Wares. London: University of London, Percival David Foundation of Chinese Art, School of Oriental and African Studies, 1989.

    Illustrated Catalogue of Underglaze Blue and Copper Red Decorated Porcelains. London: University of London, Percival David Foundation of Chinese Art, 2004.

    'The Yuan-Ming Transformation in the Blue and Red Decorated Porcelains of China'. *Ars Orientalis* 9 (1973): 89–101.

Mei, Chun. *The Novel and Theatrical Imagination in Early Modern China.* Leiden: Brill, 2011.

Mei Yantao 梅彥駒 and Li Baozhen 李葆貞, eds. *(Shunzhi) Pucheng xianzhi* (順治)浦城縣志. Shunzhi 8 (1651) keben. Beijing: Airusheng, 2009.

Mendels, Franklin. 'Proto-Industrialization: The First Phase of the Industrialization Process'. *The Journal of Economic History* 32, no. 1 (1972): 241–261.

Meng Fanfeng 孟繁峰 and Huang Xin 黄信. 'Tang houqi de Dingyao shi fanzhen yiwu junguan yao 唐后期的定窑是藩镇义武军官窑 [The Late-Tang Ding Kiln's supervision by the Yiwu Army under the Tang military governor]'. *Palace Museum Journal*, no. 2 (2014): 39–51.

Meng Yuanlao 孟元老. *Dongjing menghua lu* 東京夢華錄 [A Dream of Splendour in the Eastern Capital]. Wenyuange Siku quanshu edition.

Miksic, John N. *Singapore and the Silk Road of the Sea, 1300–1800.* Singapore: NUS Press, 2014.

Miller, Tracy. *The Divine Nature of Power: Chinese Ritual Architecture at the Sacred Site of Jinci.* Cambridge, MA: Harvard University Press, 2007.

Milwright, Marcus. *The Fortress of the Raven: Karak in the Middle Islamic Period, 1100–1650.* Leiden: Brill, 2008.

Ming, Chaofang, Yimin Yang, Jian Zhu, Li Guan, Changsheng Fan, Changqing Xu, Zhengquan Yao, Jonathan Mark Kenoyer, Guoding Song and Changsui Wang. 'Archaeometric Investigation of the Relationship between Ancient Egg-White Glazed Porcelain (Luanbai) and Bluish White Glazed Porcelain (Qingbai) from Hutian Kiln, Jingdezhen, China'. *Journal of Archaeological Science* 47 (2014): 78–84.

Mino, Yutaka and Katherine Tsiang. *Freedom of Clay and Brush through Seven Centuries in Northern China: Tz'u-Chou Type Wares, 960–1600 A.D.* Indianapolis; Bloomington: Indianapolis Museum of Art; Indiana University Press, 1981.

Mino, Yutaka and Patricia Wilson. *An Index to Chinese Ceramic Kiln Sites from the Six Dynasties to the Present.* Toronto: Royal Ontario Museum, 1973.

Moll-Murata, Christine. 'Guilds and Apprenticeship in China and Europe: The Jingdezhen and European Ceramics Industries'. In *Technology, Skills and the Pre-Modern Economy in the East and the West*, edited by Stephan R. Epstein, Maarten Prak and Jan Luiten van Zanden, 225–257. Leiden: Brill, 2013.

Moon, Whan Suk and Kim Minkoo. 'Tracking 800-Year-Old Shipments: An Archaeological Investigation of the Mado Shipwreck Cargo, Taean, Korea'. *Journal of Maritime Archaeology* 6, no. 2 (2011): 129–149.

Mostern, Ruth. *'Dividing the Realm in Order to Govern': The Spatial Organization of the Song State (960–1276 CE)*. Cambridge, MA: Harvard University Asia Center, 2011.

Mote, Frederick W. *Imperial China, 900–1800*. Cambridge, MA: Harvard University Press, 1999.

Mowry, Robert D., Eugene Farrell and Nicole Coolidge Rousmaniere. *Hare's Fur, Tortoiseshell, and Partridge Feathers: Chinese Brown- and Black-Glazed Ceramics, 400–1400*. Cambridge, MA: Harvard University Art Museums, 1997.

Murray, Haydn H. 'Traditional and New Applications for Kaolin, Smectite, and Palygorskite: A General Overview'. *Applied Clay Science* 17, no. 5–6 (2000): 207–221.

Murray, Haydn H., Wayne Bundy and Colin C. Harvey, eds. *Kaolin Genesis and Utilization: A Collection of Papers Presented at the Keller '90 Kaolin Symposium*. Boulder, CO: Clay Mineral Society, 1993.

Neill, Mary Gardner. 'The Flowering Plum in the Decorative Arts'. In *Bones of Jade, Soul of Ice: The Flowering Plum in Chinese Art*, edited by Maggie Bickford, 193–243. New Haven, CN: Yale University Art Gallery, 1985.

Nieuwenhuis, Marijn and David Crouch, eds. *The Question of Space: Interrogating the Spatial Turn between Disciplines*. London: Rowman & Littlefield, 2017.

Nixon, Sam. 'Excavating Essouk-Tadmakka (Mali): New Archaeological Investigations of Early Islamic Trans-Saharan Trade'. *Azania: Archaeological Research in Africa* 44, no. 2 (2009): 217–255.

O'Brien, Patrick. 'Historiographical Traditions and Modern Imperatives for the Restoration of Global History'. *Journal of Global History* 1, no. 1 (2006): 3–39.

Orillaneda, Bobby C. 'Maritime Trade in the Philippines During the 15th Century CE'. *Moussons. Recherche en sciences humaines sur l'Asie du Sud-Est* 27 (2016): 83–100.

   'Of Ships and Shipping: The Maritime Archaeology of Fifteenth Century CE Southeast Asia'. In *Early Navigation in the Asia-Pacific Region: A Maritime Archaeological Perspective*, edited by Chunming Wu, 29–57. Springer Singapore, 2016.

Ōsaka Shiritsu Bijutsukan 大阪市立美術館. *Shiro to kuro no kyōen: Chūgoku Jishū yōkei tōki no sekai* 白と黒の競演: 中国磁州窯系陶器の世界 [The charm of black & white ware: the transition of Cizhou type wares]. Ōsaka Shiritsu Bijutsukan, 2002.

Osborne, Anne. 'Highlands and Lowlands: Economic and Ecological Interactions in the Lower Yangzi Region under the Qing'. In *Sediments of Time: Environment and Society in Chinese History*, edited by Mark Elvin and Cuirong Liu, 203–234. Cambridge University Press, 2009.

   'Barren Mountains, Raging Rivers: The Ecological and Social Effects of Changing Land Use on the Lower Yangzi Periphery in Late Imperial China'. PhD, Columbia University, 1989.

Ouyang Shilin 欧阳世彬. 'Shiwu shiji Jingdezhen minyao yanjiu 十五世纪景德镇民窑研究 [The popular kilns of Jingdezhen during the fifteenth century]'. *Taoci xuebao*, no. 2 (2000): 72–85.

Ouyang Xiu 欧陽修. *Gui tian lu* 歸田録. Beijing: Zhonghua shuju, 1997.

Park, Hyunhee. *Mapping the Chinese and Islamic Worlds: Cross-Cultural Exchange in Pre-Modern Asia*. Cambridge University Press, 2012.

Pearson, Michael. *The Indian Ocean*. London: Routledge, 2007.

'Spain and Spanish Trade in Southeast Asia'. *Journal of Asian History* 2, no. 2 (1968): 109–129.

Pelliot, Paul. 'Les grands voyages maritimes chinois au debut du XVe siecle'. *T'oung Pao* 30 (1933): 237–452.

Peng Minghan 彭明瀚. *Ya su zhi jian: Jizhou yao* 雅俗之间: 吉州窑 [Between elegance and vulgarity: the Jizhou kilns]. Beijing: Wenwu chubanshe, 2007.

Peng Tao 彭涛. 'Mingdai huangguan zhengzhi yu Jingdezhen de taozheng 明代宦官政治与景德镇的陶政 [The Eunuch System of the Ming dynasty and the Governance of Jingdezhen]'. *Nanfang wenwu*, no. 2 (2006): 114–120+111.

Pereira, Galeote, Gaspar da Cruz and Martín de Rada. *South China in the Sixteenth Century: Being the Narratives of Galeote Pereira, Fr. Gaspar da Cruz, Fr. Martín de Rada, (1550–1575)*. Translated by C. R. Boxer. London: Hakluyt Society, 1953.

Pierson, Stacey. *Collectors, Collections and Museums: The Field of Chinese Ceramics in Britain, 1560–1960*. Oxford; New York: Peter Lang, 2007.

Designs as Signs: Decoration and Chinese Ceramics. London: Percival David Foundation of Chinese Art: School of Oriental and African Studies, University of London, 2001.

From Object to Concept: Global Consumption and the Transformation of Ming Porcelain. Hong Kong University Press, 2013.

'The Movement of Chinese Ceramics: Appropriation in Global History'. *Journal of World History* 23, no. 1 (2012): 9–39.

Pijl-Ketel, Christine L. van der and Johannes Bastiaan Kist. *The Ceramic Load of the 'Witte Leeuw' (1613)*. Amsterdam: Rijksmuseum, 1982.

Plumer, James Marshall and Caroline I. Plumer. *Temmoku: A Study of the Ware of Chien*. Tokyo: Idemitsu Art Gallery, 1972.

Poinen-Rughooputh, Satiavani, Mahesh Shumsher Rughooputh, Yanjun Guo, Yi Rong and Weihong Chen. 'Occupational Exposure to Silica Dust and Risk of Lung Cancer: An Updated Meta-Analysis of Epidemiological Studies'. *BMC Public Health* 16, no. 1 (2016): 1137.

Polo, Marco. *The Travels of Marco Polo*. Edited by R. E. Latham. Harmondsworth, Middlesex: Penguin Books, 1958.

Pomeranz, Kenneth. 'Labour-Intensive Industrialization in the Rural Yangzi Delta: Late Imperial Patterns and Their Modern Fates'. In *Labour-Intensive Industrialization in Global History*, edited by Gareth Austin and Kaoru Sugihara, 122–143. London, New York: Routledge, 2013.

The Great Divergence: China, Europe, and the Making of the Modern World Economy. Princeton University Press, 2000.

Pope, John Alexander. *Chinese Porcelains from the Ardebil Shrine*. Washington, DC: Smithsonian Institution, 1956.

    Fourteenth-Century Blue-and-White: A Group of Chinese Porcelains in the Topkapu Sarayi Müzesi, Istanbul. Washington, DC: Smithsonian Institution, 1952.

Prange, Sebastian R. *Monsoon Islam: Trade and Faith on the Medieval Malabar Coast*. Cambridge University Press, 2018.

Priyadarshini, Meha. *Chinese Porcelain in Colonial Mexico: The Material Worlds of an Early Modern Trade*. London: Palgrave Macmillan, 2018.

    'From the Chinese Guan to the Mexican Chocolatero: A Tactile History of the Transpacific Trade, 1571–1815'. PhD, Columbia University, 2014.

Ptak, Roderich. 'Wang Dayuan on Kerala'. In *China, the Portuguese, and the Nanyang: Oceans and Routes, Regions and Trades (c. 1000–1600)*, edited by Roderich Ptak, 39–52. Aldershot: Ashgate, 2004.

Qiao Gui 喬湺, He Xiling 賀熙齡 and You Jisheng 游際盛, eds. *[Daoguang] Fuliang xian zhi* 道光浮梁縣志. Nanjing: Jiangsu guji chubanshe, 1996.

Qin Dashu 秦大树. 'Lun Cizhouyao yu Dingyao de guanxi he xianghu yingxiang 论磁州窑与定窑的联系和相互影响 [The Connection and Mutual Influence of the Cizhou and Ding Kilns]'. *Palace Museum Journal*, no. 4 (1999): 43–56.

Qin Yu 秦彧. 'Qingzhou yao kao "青州窑"考 [An Examination of the 'Qingzhou Kilns']'. *Dongnan wenhua*, no. 7 (2001): 71–73.

Qiu Long 邱隆. *Zhongguo gudai duliangheng tuji* 中國古代度量衡圖集 [Weights and Measures in China Through the Ages]. Beijing: Wenwu chubanshe, 1981.

Rastelli, Sabrina. 'The Concept of the Five Famous Wares of the Song Dynasty – A Modern Invention'. In *Songdai Wuda Mingyao Kexue Jishu Guoji Xueshu Taolunhui Lunwenji* 宋代五大名窑科学技术国际学术讨论会论文集 [Proceedings of International Symposium on Science and Technology of Five Great Wares of the Song Dynasty], edited by Shi Ningchang 史宁昌 and Miao Jianmin 苗建民, 460–466. Beijing: Kexue chubanshe, 2016.

Rawson, Jessica. *The British Museum Book of Chinese Art*. 2nd ed. London: British Museum Press, 2007.

Ren Shuanghe 任双合 and Yang Jianguo 杨建国. *Cizhouyao huapu* 磁州窑画谱 [Designs from Cizhou kilns]. Beijing: Wenhua yishu chubanshe, 2009.

Ren Yashan 任亚珊. 'Yuandai Zhang Honglüe Ji Furen Mu Qingli Baogao 元代张弘略及夫人墓清理报告 [Excavation Report of the Tomb of Zhang Honglüe and His Wife of the Yuan Dynasty]'. *Wenwu Chunqiu* 5 (2013): 28–41.

Ricci, Ronit. 'Islamic Literary Networks in South and Southeast Asia'. *Journal of Islamic Studies* 21, no. 1 (2010): 1–28.

Ricklefs, M. C. *A History of Modern Indonesia since c. 1200*. Stanford University Press, 2008.

Riello, Giorgio. *Cotton: The Fabric That Made the Modern World*. Cambridge University Press, 2013.

    'The Globalization of Cotton Textiles: Indian Cottons, Europe, and the Atlantic World, 1600–1850'. In *The Spinning World: A Global History of Cotton Textiles,*

1200–1850, edited by Giorgio Riello and Prasannan Parthasarathi, 261–287. Oxford University Press, 2009.

Robinson, David M., ed. *Culture, Courtiers, and Competition: The Ming Court (1368–1644)*. Cambridge, MA: Harvard University Asia Center, 2008.

Robinson, Kenneth R. 'Chosŏn Korea in the Ryūkoku "Kangnido": Dating the Oldest Extant Korean Map of the World (15th Century)'. *Imago Mundi* 59, no. 2 (2007): 177–192.

'Gavin Menzies, 1421, and the Ryūkoku Kangnido World Map'. *Ming Studies* 61 (2010): 56–70.

Rooney, Dawn. 'The Recessed Base (Hole-Bottom) Saucer: A Type of Chinese Export Ware'. *Arts of Asia* 12, no. 1 (1982): 114–118.

Rossabi, Morris. *A History of China*. Malden, MA: John Wiley and Sons, 2014.

Rougeulle, Axelle. 'Excavations at Sharmah, Ḥaḍramawt: The 2001 and 2002 Seasons'. *Proceedings of the Seminar for Arabian Studies* 33 (2003): 287–307.

Rougeulle, Axelle and Vincent Bernard, eds. *Sharma: un entrepôt de commerce médiéval sur la côte du Ḥaḍramawt (Yémen, ca 980–1180)*. Oxford: Archaeopress, 2015.

Sachsenmaier, Dominic. *Global Perspectives on Global History: Theories and Approaches in a Connected World*. Cambridge University Press, 2011.

Sakuma Shigeo 佐久間重男. *Keitokuchin Yōgyōshi Kenkyū* 景德鎮窯業史研究 [History of the Jingdezhen ceramics manufactures]. Tōkyō: Daiichi Shobō, 1999.

Schäfer, Dagmar. *The Crafting of the 10,000 Things: Knowledge and Technology in Seventeenth-Century China*. University of Chicago Press, 2011.

Schafer, Edward H. *The Golden Peaches of Samarkand: A Study of T'ang Exotics*. Berkeley: University of California Press, 1963.

Schneewind, Sarah, ed. *Long Live the Emperor!: Uses of the Ming Founder across Six Centuries of East Asian History*. Minneapolis, MN: Society for Ming Studies, 2008.

Scott, Rosemary E., ed. *The Porcelains of Jingdezhen*. London: Percival David Foundation of Chinese Art, 1993.

Sen, Tansen. 'Maritime Interactions between China and India: Coastal India and the Ascendancy of Chinese Maritime Power in the Indian Ocean'. *Journal of Central Eurasian Studies* 2 (2011): 41–82.

Shanghai Museum. *Splendors in Smalt: Art of Yuan Blue-and-White Porcelain* 幽蓝神采: 元代青花瓷器特集. Shanghai Museum, 2012.

Sharma, Piyush and Ricky Y. K. Chan. 'Counterfeit Proneness: Conceptualisation and Scale Development'. *Journal of Marketing Management* 27, no. 5–6 (2011): 602–626.

Shenzhen bowuguan 深圳博物馆. *Chanfeng yu ruyun: Song Yuan shidai de Jizhou yao ciqi* 禅风与儒韵: 宋元时代的吉州窑瓷器 [Jizhou ceramics from the Song and Yuan dynasties]. Beijing: Wenwu chubanshe, 2012.

Shi Runzhang 施闰章. *Juzhai zaji* 矩齋雜記. Congshu jicheng xu bian. Shanghai shudian, 1994.

Xueyutang wenji 學餘堂文集. Yingyin Wenyuange Siku quanshu. Taipei: Taiwan shangwu yinshuguan, 1983.

Shiba Yoshinobu. 'Sung Foreign Trade: Its Scope and Organization'. In *China among Equals: The Middle Kingdom and Its Neighbors, 10th–14th Centuries*, edited by Morris Rossabi, 89–115. Berkeley: University of California Press, 1983.

Shih Ching-fei 施靜菲. 'Jingdezhen Yuan Qinghua Qiyuan Zhi Bendi Yinsuo Kaocha 景德鎮元青花起源之本地因素考察 [Local Origins of the Beginnings of Jingdezhen Yuan Blue-and-White]'. *Zhejiang University Journal of Art and Archaeology* 1 (2014): 183–217.

———. 'Yunnan diqu qinghuaci qi de bianqian-jian tan qi yu jiangxi jingdezhen he yuenan qinghuaci de guanlian 雲南地區青花瓷器的變遷－兼談其與江西景德鎮和越南青花瓷的關連 [The Transformation of Blue-and-White Porcelain in Yunnan, with Consideration of the Relationship between the Blue-and-White Porcelains of Jingdezhen and Vietnam]'. *Taiwan National University Journal of Art History*, no. 25 (2008): 171–270+275.

Sims-Williams, Ursula. 'An Illustrated 14th Century Khamsah by Khvaju Kirmani'. *Asian and African Studies Blog* (blog), 1 August 2013. http://britishlibrary. typepad.co.uk/asian-and-african/2013/07/an-illustrated-14th-century-khamsah-by-khvaju-kirmani.html.

Sjostrand, Sten and Claire Barnes. 'The "Turiang": A Fourteenth-Century Chinese Shipwreck Upsetting Southeast Asian Ceramic History'. *Journal of the Malaysian Branch of the Royal Asiatic Society* 74, no. 1 (2001): 71–109.

Song Donglin 宋東林. 'Bei Song Jindai Jiaocang Ciqi Kaoshu 北宋金代窖藏瓷器考述 [Ceramics from Northern Song and Jin Hoards]'. *Journal of Gugong Studies* 1 (2012): 8–54.

Soucek, Priscilla. 'Ceramic Production as Exemplar of Yuan-Ilkhanid Relations'. *Res: Anthropology and Aesthetics* 35 (1999): 125–141.

Spallanzani, Marco. *Ceramiche alla corte dei Medici nel Cinquecento*. Modena: Panini, 1994.

Spiegel, Gabrielle M., ed. *Practicing History: New Directions in Historical Writing after the Linguistic Turn*. London: Routledge, 2005.

Spiess, Karl-Heinz. 'Asian Objects and Western European Court Culture in the Middle Ages'. In *Artistic and Cultural Exchanges between Europe and Asia, 1400–1900: Rethinking Markets, Workshops and Collections*, edited by Michael North, 9–28. Farnham: Ashgate, 2010.

Spriggs, A. I. 'Oriental Porcelain in Western Paintings, 1450–1700'. *Transactions of the Oriental Ceramic Society* 36 (1964–1966): 73–87.

Stargardt, Janice. 'Behind the Shadows: Archaeological Data on Two-Way Sea-Trade between Quanzhou and Satingpra, South Thailand, 10th-14th Century'. In *The Emporium of the World: Maritime Quanzhou, 1000–1400*, edited by Angela Schottenhammer, 309–393. Leiden: Brill, 2001.

Steinhardt, Nancy Shatzman. 'Review of Song Blue and White Porcelain on the Silk Road. By Adam T. Kessler'. *Journal of the Royal Asiatic Society (Third Series)* 25, no. 1 (2015): 184–187.

Strickland, D. H. 'Artists, Audience, and Ambivalence in Marco Polo's Divisament Dou Monde'. *Viator* 36 (2005): 493–530.

Styles, John. 'Embezzlement, Industry and the Law in England, 1500–1800'. In *Manufacture in Town and Country Before the Factory*, edited by Maxine Berg, Pat Hudson and Michael Sonenscher, 173–210. Cambridge University Press, 1983.

Sun, Xinmin. 'Recent Excavations at the Ru Kiln: Qingliangsi'. In *Song Ceramics: Art History, Archaeology and Technology*, edited by Stacey Pierson, translated by Benedetta Mottino, 209–219. Colloquies on Art & Archaeology in Asia 22. London: Percival David Foundation of Chinese Art, School of Oriental and African Studies, 2004.

'Shilun bei Song zaoqi de Yueyao mise ci 试论北宋早期的越窑秘色瓷 [Secret Colour Porcelain from the Yue Kilns from the Early Northern Song]'. *Jiangxi wenwu*, no. 4 (1991): 28–30.

'Songling Chutu de Dingyao Gongci Shixi 宋陵出土的定窑贡瓷试析 [Trial Division of Tribute Porcelain from the Ding Kilns Excavated from Song Imperial Graves]'. *Wenwu Chunqiu* 3 (1994): 47–51.

Tai, Yew Seng. 'Ming Gap and the Revival of Commercial Production of Blue and White Porcelain in China'. *Bulletin of the Indo-Pacific Prehistory Association* 31 (2011): 85–92.

Tam, Ka-chai. 'Favourable Institutional Circumstances for the Publication of Judicial Works in Late Ming China'. *Études Chinoises* 28 (2009): 51–71.

Tang Changpu 唐昌朴. 'Jiangxi Jizhou Yao Faxian Song Yuan Qinghua Ci 江西吉州窑发现宋元青花瓷'. *Wenwu*, no. 4 (1980): 4.

Tang, Hui (Claire). '"The Colours of Each Piece": Production and Consumption of Chinese Enamelled Porcelain, c.1728-c.1780'. PhD, University of Warwick, 2017.

Tang Ying 唐英. 'Tao ye tu bian ci 陶冶图编次'. In *Zhongguo taoci guji jicheng* 中国陶瓷古籍集成, edited by Xiong Liao 熊寥 and Xiong Wei 熊微, 299–306. 1743. Reprint, Shanghai wenhua chubanshe, 2006.

Tao Zongyi 陶宗儀 (fl. 1360–68). *Nancun chuogeng lu* 南村輟耕錄. Beijing: Zhonghua shuju, 1959.

Tichane, Robert. *Ching-Te-Chen: Views of a Porcelain City*. Painted Post, NY: New York State Institute for Glaze Research, 1983.

Titley, Norah M. *Persian Miniature Painting and its Influence on the Art of Turkey and India*. London: The British Library, 1983.

Tōkyō Kokuritsu Hakubutsukan. *Shin'an Kaitei Hikiage Bunbutsu = The Sunken Treasures off the Sinan Coast*. Nagoya: Chūnichi Shinbunsha, 1983.

Tōwakai 陶話会, ed. *Tōwakai sōji tenkan zufu* 陶話会宋瓷展観図譜 [Catalogue of the Exhibition of Song Stoneware of the Tokyo Ceramics Society]. Tōkyō: Ootsuka Kōgeisha, 1929.

Truong, Alain R. 'Decorated Porcelains of Dingzhou: White Ding Wares from the Collection of the National Palace Museum', 18 June 2014. www.alaintruong.com/archives/2014/06/18/30098378.html.

Tsing, Yuan. 'The Porcelain Industry and Ching-Te-Chen, 1550–1700'. *Ming Studies* 1978, no. 1 (1978): 45–54.

Tuấn, Hoàng Anh. 'Regionalising National History: Ancient and Medieval Vietnamese Maritime Trade in the East Asian Context'. *Medieval History Journal* 17, no. 1 (2014): 87–106.

Tuo tuo 托托, et al. *Song shi* 宋史 [Song History]. Beijing: Zhonghua shuju, 2011.

Turnbull, Stephen R. and Wayne Reynolds. *Fighting Ships of the Far East (1): China and Southeast Asia 202 BC–AD 1419*. Oxford: Osprey, 2002.

Valenstein, Suzanne G. *Handbook of Chinese Ceramics*. New York: Metropolitan Museum of Art, 2012.

Vallet, Éric. *L'Arabie marchande: état et commerce sous les sultans Rasūlides du Yémen (626–858/1229–1454)*. Paris: Publications de la Sorbonne, 2010.

Varela Santos, Alberto. *Portugal na porcelana da China: 500 andos de comércio (Portugal in Porcelain from China: 500 years of trade)*. Vol. 1. Lisboa: Artemágica, 2007.

Vivier, Brian Thomas. 'Chinese Foreign Trade, 960–1276'. PhD, Yale University, 2009.

Vogel, Hans Ulrich. *Marco Polo Was in China: New Evidence from Currencies, Salts and Revenues*. Leiden: Brill, 2012.

Volker, T. *Porcelain and the Dutch East India Company, as Recorded in the Dagh-Registers of Batavia Castle, Those of Hirado and Deshima and Other Contemporary Papers 1602–1682*. Leiden: Brill, 1954.

von Erdberg-Consten, Eleanor. 'The Manila Trade Pottery Seminar'. *Philippine Studies* 16, no. 3 (1968): 545–557.

von Glahn, Richard. *An Economic History of China: From Antiquity to the Nineteenth Century*. Cambridge University Press, 2016.

von Verschuer, Charlotte. *Le commerce entre le Japon, la Chine et la Corée à l'époque médiévale: VIIe-XVIe siècle*. Paris: Publications de la Sorbonne, 2014.

Waal, Edmund de. *The White Road: A Pilgrimage of Sorts*. London: Vintage, 2015.

Wagner, Donald B. *Ferrous Metallurgy*. Science and Civilisation in China, Vol. 5: Chemistry and Chemical Technology, Pt. XI. Cambridge University Press, 2008.

Walton, Linda. 'Family Fortunes in the Song-Yuan Transition: Academies and Chinese Elite Strategies for Success'. *T'oung Pao* 97, no. 1–3 (2011): 37–103.

Wang Bo 汪勃, Liu Tao 刘涛, Yin Zhihua 印志华 and Chi Jun 池军. 'Jiangsu Yangzhou Song dacheng beimen shuimen yizhi fajue jianbao 江苏扬州宋大城北门水门遗址发掘简报 [Excavation on the Water Valve Site at the Northern Gate of the Great Song City in Yangzhou, Jiangsu]'. *Kaogu*, no. 12 (2005): 24–40+97+100–101+103+2.

Wang Bu 王補 and Zeng Cancai 曾燦材, eds. *Minguo Luling xian zhi* 民國廬陵縣志. Nanjing: Jiangsu guji chubanshe, 1996.

Wang, Ching-Ling, 'Re-considering a Cizhou-Type Jar in the VVAK collection', *Aziatische Kunst* 45:1 (2015): 38–44.

Wang Dayuan 汪大淵. *Daoyi zhilüe jiaoshi* 島夷誌略校釋 [Annotated edition of the 'Report of the Island Barbarians']. Edited by Su Jiqing 蘇繼廎. Ming dyn. Reprint, Beijing: Zhonghua shuju, 1981.

Wang Jianzhong 王建中. *Cizhou yaoci jianding yu jianshang* 磁州窑瓷鉴定与鉴赏 [Appreciation of Cizhou wares]. Nanchang: Jiangxi meishu chubanshe, 2002.

Wang Ning 王宁. *Jizhou Yinghe yao zuopin ji* 吉州永和窑作品集 [A collection of Jizhou Ceramics from the Yonghe kiln]. Wuhan: Hubei meishu chubanshe, 2005.

Wang, Qingzheng and Chen Kelun. *A Dictionary of Chinese Ceramics*. Singapore: Sun Tree Publishing, 2002.

Wang Rui 王睿. 'Jizhou Yao Zhi Yonghe Yao Yu Linjiang Yao Chubu Bijiao 吉州窑之永和窑与临江窑初步比较 [Preliminary comparison between the Yonghe kilns at Jizhou and the Linjiang kilns]'. *Nanfang Wenwu*, no. 2 (2015): 150–152.

Wang, Xiaofeng 王晓峰, ed. *Jingdezhen: qiannian cidu* 景德镇：千年瓷都 [Jingdezhen: One Thousand Years of the Capital of Porcelain]. Nanchang: Jiangxi renmin chubanshe, 2015.

Wang Xiaomeng 王小蒙. 'Tang Yaozhou Yao Tai Heicai Ci de Gongyi Tedianji Qi Yuanyuan, Yingxiang 唐耀州窑素胎黑彩瓷的工艺特点及其渊源、影响 [Origin of the Technique of Porcelain with Black Drawings from the Yaozhou Kiln during the Tang Period and its Influence]'. *Kaogu Yu Wenwu* 3 (2013): 73–79.

'Yaozhou Yao Qingci de Meixue Linian Ji Fengge Bianqian 耀州窑青瓷的美学理念及风格变迁 [The Aesthetics and Stylistic Transformations of Green Porcelain from Yaozhou]'. *Sichuan Cultural Relics*, no. 5 (2009): 49–54.

Wang Xiaoying 王小迎 and Wang Rui 王睿. 'Jiangsu Yangzhou Nan Song Baoyoucheng xicheng menwai chutu taoci qi 江苏扬州南宋宝祐城西城门外出土陶瓷器 [Porcelain Unearthed Outside West Gate of Southern Song Baoyou City Site]'. *Journal of the National Museum of China* 146 (2015): 93–111.

Wang Xing 王兴. *Cizhou yao shihua* 磁州窑史话 [Stories of the Cizhou kilns]. Tianjin guji chubanshe, 2004.

Wang, Yunxia. 'Enforcing Import Restrictions of China's Cultural Objects: The Sino–US Memorandum of Understanding'. In *Enforcing International Cultural Heritage Law*, edited by Francesco Francioni and James Gordley, 240–255. Oxford University Press, 2013.

Wang, Yuquan. 'Some Salient Features of the Ming Labor Service System'. *Ming Studies*, no. 1 (1986): 1–44.

Wang Zongmu 王宗沐 and Lu Wan'gai 陸萬垓, eds. *(Wanli) Jiangxi sheng dazhi* 江西省大志. Nanjing tushuguan guben shanben congkan. 1597. Reprint, Beijing: Xianzhuang shuju, 2003.

Ward, Cheryl. 'Chinese Porcelain for the Ottoman Court: Sadana Island, Egypt'. In *Beneath the Seven Seas: Adventures with the Institute of Nautical Archaeology*, edited by George Fletcher Bass, 186–191. London: Thames & Hudson, 2005.

'The Sadana Island Shipwreck: An Eighteenth-Century AD Merchantman off the Red Sea Coast of Egypt'. *World Archaeology* 32, no. 3 (2001): 368–382.

Warf, Barney. *The Spatial Turn: Interdisciplinary Perspectives*. London: Routledge, 2014.

Watson, Oliver. 'Ceramics and Circulation'. In *A Companion to Islamic Art and Architecture*, 478–500. Hoboken, NJ: Wiley-Blackwell, 2017.

Watson, William. *The Arts of China 900–1620*. New Haven, CT: Yale University Press, 2000.

Watt, James. 'Notes on the Use of Cobalt in Later Chinese Ceramics'. *Ars Orientalis* 11 (1979): 63–85.

East Asian Lacquer: The Florence and Herbert Irving Collection. New York: Metropolitan Museum of Art, 1991.

Watt, James and Maxwell K. Hearn. *The World of Khubilai Khan: Chinese Art in the Yuan Dynasty*. New York: Metropolitan Museum of Art, 2010.

Way, Peter. 'Some Further Notes on the Percival David Ritual Vases and Their Inscriptions'. *The Percival David Ritual Vases* (blog), 16 February 2013. http://percivaldavidritualvases.blogspot.com/.

Welch, Patricia Bjaaland. *Chinese Art: A Guide to Motifs and Visual Imagery*. North Clarendon, VT: Tuttle, 2008.

Wen, R., C. S. Wang, Z. W. Mao, Y. Y. Huang and A. M. Pollard. 'The Chemical Composition of Blue Pigment on Chinese Blue-and-White Porcelain of the Yuan and Ming Dynasties (1271–1644)'. *Archaeometry* 49, no. 1 (2007): 101–115.

Weng Tianhu 翁天祐, Lü Weiying 吕渭英 and Weng Zhaotai 翁昭泰, eds. *Guangxu xuxiu Pucheng xianzhi* 光緒續修浦城縣志. Reprint of blockprint edition of 1900. Zhongguo difangzhi jicheng. Shanghai shudian, 2000.

Weststeijn, Thijs. 'Cultural Reflections on Porcelain in the Seventeenth-Century Netherlands'. In *Chinese and Japanese Porcelain for the Dutch Golden Age*, edited by Jan van Campen and Titus M. Eliëns, 213–229. Zwolle: Waanders, 2014.

Whitfield, Susan. *Life Along the Silk Road*. Berkeley: University of California Press, 2015.

Whitfield, Susan and Ursula Sims-Williams. *The Silk Road: Trade, Travel, War and Faith*. Chicago, IL: Serindia Publications, 2004.

Wilkinson, Endymion Porter. *Chinese History: A Manual*. Cambridge, MA: Harvard University Asia Center, 2000.

Wong, Winnie Won Yin. *Van Gogh on Demand: China and the Readymade*. University of Chicago Press, 2013.

Wood, Nigel. *Chinese Glazes: Their Origins, Chemistry and Re-Creation*. London: A. & C. Black, 2007.

Wood, Nigel and He Li. 'A Study of the Techniques Used to Make Laohudong Guan Ware in China in the Southern Song Dynasty'. *Archaeometry* 57, no. 4 (2015): 617–635.

Wood, Nigel and Sabrina Rastelli. 'Parallel Developments in Chinese Porcelain Technology in the 13th-14th Centuries AD'. In *Craft and Science: International Perspectives on Archaeological Ceramics*, edited by Marcos Martinón-Torres, 225–234. Doha: Bloomsbury Qatar Foundation, 2014.

Woolf, D. R. *A Global History of History*. Cambridge University Press, 2011.

Wu, Cheng'en. *The Journey to the West*. Translated by Anthony C. Yu. University of Chicago Press, 1977.

Wu Ke 武可. 'Liuzi yizhi chutu de Jizhou yao ciqi 柳孜遗址出土的吉州窑瓷器 [Jizhou ceramics excavated from Liuzi site]'. *Shoucang jie*, no. 12 (2008): 60–61.

Wu Rui 吴瑞, Wu Juan 吴隽, Deng Zequn 邓泽群, Li Jiazhi 李家治 and Guo Jingkun 郭景坤. 'Hutian Yao Chutu Heiyouci de Chandi Yanjiu 湖田窑出土黑釉瓷的产地研究 [Research on the Provenance of Black-Glazed Ceramics Excavated from the Hutian Kiln Site]'. *Zongguo Taoci* 41, no. 2 (2005): 77–81.

Wu Songdi 吴松弟. *Zhongguo yimin shi* 中国移民史. Vol. 4: Liao, Song, Jin, Yuan shiqi. Fuzhou: Fujian renmin chubanshe, 1997.

Wu Zimu 吴自牧. *Mengliang lu* 夢梁錄. Zhibu zuzhai congshu, 1814.

Xiang Kunpeng 项坤鹏. 'Songdai gongting yongci laiyuan shenxi 宋代宫廷用瓷来源探析 [Research on the Sources of Porcelain Used by the Court of the Song Dynasty]'. *Kaogu yu wenwu*, no. 01 (2015): 53–61.

Xiao Fabiao 肖发标. 'Bei Song Jingdezhen Yao de Gongci Wenti 北宋景德镇窑的贡瓷问题 [The Problem of Porcelain Tribute from Jingdezhen during the Northern Song]. *Zhongguo Gutaoci Yanjiu* 7 (2001): 253–262.

'Shilun Hutian Yao Chutu de Heyouci 试论湖田窑出土的黑釉瓷 [Black-glazed ceramics excavated from the Hutian kilns]'. *Shanghai Wen Bo Lun Cong*, no. 01 (2007): 40–44.

'Yicheng shanshui shihua, qiannian guzhen yaoli 一城山水诗画,千年古镇瑶里 [Yaoli: A City of Scenic Poems, a Town of Thousand Years]'. *China Cultural Heritage*, no. 03 (2014): 40–45+10.

Xie Min 謝旻 (fl. 18th c.), ed. *Jiangxi tong zhi* 江西通志. Yingyin Wenyuange Siku quanshu. 1732. Reprint, Taipei: Taiwan shangwu yinshuguan, 1983.

Xie Mingliang. *Dingyao baici tezhan tulu* 定窯白瓷特展圖錄 [Catalogue of the Special Exhibition of Ting Ware White Porcelain]. Taibei: Guoli gugong bowuguan, 1987.

Xiong Liao 熊寥 and Ma Xigui 馬希桂. *Gems of the Official Kilns* 官窯名瓷. Taibei: Yishu tushu gongsi, 1993.

Xiong Liao and Xiong Wei 熊微, eds. *Zhongguo taoci guji jicheng* 中国陶瓷古籍集成 [Anthology of Ancient Texts About China's Porcelain]. Shanghai wenhua chubanshe, 2006.

Xu Song 徐松 (1781–1848), ed. *Song Huiyao Jigao* 宋會要輯稿 [Draft of an Institutional History of the Song Dynasty], n.d.

Yan Chongnian 阎崇年. *Yu yao qian nian* 御窑千年 [A Thousand Years of Imperial Kilns]. Beijing: Sanlian, 2017.

Yang, Bin. *Between Winds and Clouds: The Making of Yunnan (Second Century BCE to Twentieth Century CE)*. New York: Columbia University Press, 2014.

Yang Houli 杨后礼. 'Jiangxi Yongxin Faxian Yuandai Jiaocang Ciqi 江西永新发现元代窖藏瓷器 [Porcelains Discovered in the Yuan Dynasty Hoard in Yongxin, Jiangxi]'. *Wenwu* 4 (1983): 47–49.

Yang Yumin 杨玉敏. 'Changzhou bowuguan cang Cizhou yao ciqi 常州博物馆藏磁州窑瓷器 [Cizhou Ceramics from the Changzhou Museum Collection]'. *Nanfang wenwu*, no. 01 (2001): 81–82+86.

Yi Gu 依谷. 'Jiangxi Gao'an Yuanci jiaocang faxian jishi 江西高安元瓷窖藏发现纪实 [The Discovery of a Yuan-Dynasty Hoard at Gao'an in Jiangxi]'. *Nanfang wenwu*, no. 1 (2002): 120–126.

Yip, Hon Ming. 'The Kuan-Ta-Min-Shao System and Ching-Te-Chen's Porcelain Industry'. In *Zhongguo Jinshi Shehui Wenhua Shi Lunwen Ji [Papers on Society and Culture of Early Modern China]*. Taipei: Institute of History and Philology, Academia Sinica, 1992.

Yokkaichi, Yasuhiro. 'Chinese and Muslim Diasporas and the Indian Ocean Trade Network under Mongol Hegemony'. In *The East Asian Mediterranean: Maritime Crossroads of Culture, Commerce and Human Migration*, edited by Angela Schottenhammer, 73–102. Wiesbaden: Harrassowitz, 2008.

Youn, Moo-byong. 'Recovery of Seabed Relics at Sinan and Its Results from the Viewpoint of Underwater Archaeology'. In *Shin'an Kaitei Hikiage Bunbutsu = The Sunken Treasures off the Sinan Coast*, edited by Tōkyō Kokuritsu Hakubutsukan, 81–83. Nagoya: Chūnichi Shinbunsha, 1983.

Yu Jiadong 余家栋. *Jiangxi Jizhou yao* 江西吉州窑 [The Jizhou kilns in Jiangxi]. Guangzhou: Lingnan meishu chubanshe, 2002.

Yu Rirong 余日蓉. 'Ming Jiajing 'Jiangxi tongzhi' banben kao 明嘉靖《江西通志》版本考 [Investigation of the editions of the Jiangxi provincial gazetteer of the Ming Jiajing period]'. *Jiangxi Social Sciences*, no. 12 (1998): 49–51.

Yun, Yong-i and Regina Krahl. *Korean Art from the Gompertz and Other Collections in the Fitzwilliam Museum: A Complete Catalogue*. Cambridge University Press, 2006.

Zhang Hui 张辉 and Gong Xicheng 宫希成. 'Sui Tang Dayunhe Tongjiqu (Bianhe) Tang Song Chenchuan Yu Yan'an Guwenhua Yicun 隋唐大运河通济渠（汴河）唐宋沉船与沿岸古文化遗存'. *Zhongguo lishi wenwu*, no. 6 (2010): 24–32.

Zhang, Ling. *The River, the Plain, and the State: An Environmental Drama in Northern Song China, 1048–1128*. Cambridge University Press, 2016.

Zhang Wenjiang 张文江, Li Yuyuan 李育远 and Yuan Shengwen 袁胜文. 'Jizhou yizhi jin jinian kaogu diaocha fajue de zhuyao shouhuo 吉州窑遗址近几年考古调查发掘的主要收获 [Archaeological Excavations of Jizhou Kiln Sites in Recent Years]'. *Zhongguo guojia bowuguan guankan*, no. 6 (2014): 13–41.

Zhang, Xiaokang, Haijiao Wang, Xiaomin Zhu, Yuewei Liu, Limin Wang, Qici Dai, Niane Cai, Tangchun Wu and Weihong Chen. 'Cohort Mortality Study in Three Ceramic Factories in Jingdezhen in China'. *Journal of Huazhong University of Science and Technology [Medical Sciences]* 28, no. 4 (2008): 386–390.

Zhao Bing. 'Apport de l'étude céramologique à la compréhension de la culture matérielle de la région de Jizhou au Jiangxi (Xe-XIVe siècles)'. *Études Chinoises* XXI, no. 1–2 (2002): 185–196.

'Chinese-Style Ceramics in East Africa from the 9th to 16th Century: A Case of Changing Value and Symbols in the Multi-Partner Global Trade'. *Afriques*.

Débats, Méthodes et Terrains d'histoire, no. 06 (2015). https://afriques.revues. org/1836.

'Érudition, expertise, technique et politique autour de la querelle de la datation du Taoji'. *Arts asiatiques*, no. 61 (2006): 143–164.

'Global Trade and Swahili Cosmopolitan Material Culture: Chinese-Style Ceramic Shards from Sanje Ya Kati and Songo Mnara (Kilwa, Tanzania)'. *Journal of World History* 23, no. 1 (2012): 41–85.

'Les imitations de porcelaines de Ding du Xe au XIVe siècle: le cas des officines de potiers de Jizhou au Jiangxi'. *Arts asiatiques* 56 (2001): 61–80.

Zhao Rugua 趙汝适 fl. 13th century. *Zhufanzhi* 諸蕃志. Siku quanshu. Taibei: Taiwan shangwu yinshuguan, 1983.

Zhao Zhiqian 趙之謙 (1829–1884), ed. *(Guangxu) Jiangxi Tongzhi* 江西通志. Zhongguo Fangzhi Ku. 1881. Reprint, Beijing Airusheng shuzihua jishu yanjiu zhongxin, 2009.

Zheng, Dekun. *Studies in Chinese Ceramics*. Hong Kong: The Chinese University Press, 1984.

Zhong Hua 钟华. 'Jingdezhen Liyang Mingdai ci yaozhi shidai kao–jian tan xingshuai yuanyin 景德镇丽阳明代瓷窑址时代考——兼谈兴衰原因 [Investigation of the dating of the Ming Liyang kiln site in Jingdezhen and the reasons for its rise and decline]'. *Nanfang wenwu*, no. 3 (2013): 77–82.

Zhou Bida 周必大. *Wenzhong ji* 文忠集. Yingyin Wenyuange Siku quanshu. Taipei: Taiwan shangwu yinshuguan, 1983.

Zhou, Daguan. *A Record of Cambodia: The Land and its People*. Translated by Peter Harris. Chiang Mai: Silkworm Books, 2007.

Zhou Guang 周廣, ed. *(Jiajing) Jiangxi tong zhi* 嘉靖江西通志. Zhongguo fangzhiku. Beijing Airusheng shuzihua jishu yanjiu zhongxin, 2009.

Zhou Hui 周煇 (1126-). *Qingbo zazhi* 清波雜志. Sibu congkan xubian. Shanghai: Shangwu yinshuguan, 1934.

Zhou Qufei 周去非. *Lingwai daida* 嶺外代答. Siku quanshu. Taibei: Taiwan shangwu yinshuguan, 1983.

Zhou Xingsi. *Ch'ien Tzu Wen. The Thousand Character Classic: A Chinese Primer*. Edited by Francis W. Paar. New York: F. Ungar Pub. Co., 1963.

Zhou Zhenhe and Kathy Lo. 'Migrations in Chinese History and Their Legacy on Chinese Dialects'. *Journal of Chinese Linguistics*, no. 3 (1991): 29–49.

Zhu Boqian 朱伯谦. 'Zhejiang Liangchu Taji Chutu Song Qinghuaci 浙江两处塔基出土宋青花瓷 [Song blue-and-white ceramics excavated from pagodas in Zhejiang]'. *Wenwu*, no. 4 (1980): 1–3.

Zhuang Wenbin 庄文彬. 'Sichuan Suining Jinyucun Nan Song Jiaocang 四川遂宁金鱼村南宋窖藏 [The Southern Song hoard of Jinyu village in Suining in Sichuan]'. *Wenwu*, no. 4 (1994): 4–28.

Zurndorfer, Harriet. 'Wanli China versus Hideyoshi's Japan: Rethinking China's Involvement in the Imjin Waeran'. In *The East Asian War, 1592–1598: International Relations, Violence and Memory*, edited by James Bryant Lewis, 197–235. London: Routledge, 2015.

Index

Note: Page numbers in **bold** refer to figures, and those in *italics* refer to maps.